Recreational Sport Management

Third Edition

Richard F. Mull, MS
Indiana University

Kathryn G. Bayless, MS
Indiana University

Craig M. Ross, ReD
Indiana University

Lynn M. Jamieson, ReD
Indiana University

Human Kinetics

Library of Congress Cataloging-in-Publication Data

Recreational sport management / Richard F. Mull . . . [et al.]. -- 3rd
  ed.
        p.   cm.
    Rev. ed. of: Recreational sports programming / Kathryn G. Bayless,
Richard F. Mull, Craig M. Ross. c1983
    Includes bibliographical references and index.
    ISBN 0-87322-808-1
    1. Recreational leadership.   2. Recreation--Management.   3. Sports-
    -Organization and administration.   I. Mull, Richard F.
II. Bayless, Kathryn G.   Recreational sports programming.
GV181.43.R43   1997
790' .06'9--dc20   96-44985
                                                         CIP

ISBN: 0-87322-808-1

Acquisitions Editor: Richard Frey, PhD; **Developmental Editors:** Rodd Whelpley and Kent Reel; **Assistant Editor:** Jennifer Stallard; **Editorial Assistant:** Jennifer Hemphill; **Copyeditor:** Danelle Eknes; **Proofreader;** Sarah Wiseman; **Indexer;** Joan Griffitts; **Graphic Designer:** Robert Reuther; **Graphic Artist:** Kathy Boudreau-Fuoss; **Photo Editor:** Boyd LaFoon; **Cover Designer:** Jack Davis; **Illustrators:** Craig Ronto, Jennifer Delmotte, and John Hatton; **Printer:** Braun-Brumfield

Printed in the United States of America   10 9 8 7 6 5 4 3

Human Kinetics
Web site: www.humankinetics.com

United States: Human Kinetics, P.O. Box 5076, Champaign, IL 61825-5076
800-747-4457
e-mail: humank@hkusa.com

Canada: Human Kinetics, 475 Devonshire Road, Unit 100, Windsor, ON N8Y 2L5
800-465-7301 (in Canada only)
e-mail: orders@hkcanada.com

Europe: Human Kinetics, Units C2/C3 Wira Business Park, West Park Ring Road
Leeds LS16 6EB, United Kingdom
+44 (0) 113 278 1708
e-mail: hk@hkeurope.com

Australia: Human Kinetics, 57A Price Avenue, Lower Mitcham, South Australia 5062
08 8277 1555
e-mail: liahka@senet.com.au

New Zealand: Human Kinetics, P.O. Box 105-231, Auckland Central
09-523-3462
e-mail: hkp@ihug.co.nz

CONTENTS

PREFACE

We designed *Recreational Sport Management* to help current and future leaders in recreational sport understand the concepts and applications of effective recreational sport programming and administration. We've built on the strengths of the previous two editions of this text to create a book you can use as an introductory text in college sport management, leisure studies, and recreation administration courses, and as a reference book for recreational sport professionals, regardless of recreational setting or management operation.

Over the past decade, important professional changes have developed in sport management and recreational sport. To help aspiring professionals keep pace with these changes, we have improved *Recreational Sport Management* in several ways. Part I, Foundations, lays the groundwork for understanding the history of today's recreational sport movement. Chapter 1, Identity, introduces the language of sport management, the evolutionary development of recreational sport, and the professional organizations that have shaped it. Chapter 2, Participant Development, provides an expanded treatment of client and spectator motivation, values clarification, and leadership.

In part II, Program Delivery Systems, we provide practical programming and methods of delivering quality recreational sport experiences in a variety of settings. Chapter 3, Fitness, which is new to this edition, emphasizes techniques of providing quality health-related fitness services in a variety of client settings. We have expanded traditional areas of instructional, informal, intramural, extramural, and club sport in chapters 4 through 7 to reflect changes in how these areas are currently offered and programmed.

There have been several changes in management theories, principles, and applications over the last decade. Mindful of these, we have expanded part III, Administrative Support Systems and Professionalization, by updating information in planning, evaluation, and control (chapter 8), personnel (chapter 9), finance, including funding sources and cost reduction (chapter 10), and managing facilities and equipment (chapter 11). Responding to current issues in the sport management field, we have added two new chapters: chapter 12, Risk Management, and chapter 13, Marketing, which underscore principles of client safety and service. The book concludes with chapter 14, Recreational Sport as a Profession. As an added feature, throughout the text we suggest computer applications for several programming and administrative functions. These highlight the usefulness of the computer in today's recreational sport environment.

Although there have been changes incorporated in this edition of *Recreational Sport Management*, many items have remained consistent from earlier editions. We've written the book from the programmer's point of view, providing information that will help initiate, maintain, and enhance recreational sport experiences for all people, those with special needs, in real settings. As it was when we wrote the first two editions, our number one desire is to help professionals experience success in recreational sport management endeavors. We hope this resource will contribute to the field's knowledge, growth, and development, and that relationships with recreational sport will positively affect professional and personal enhancement.

ACKNOWLEDGMENTS

We are grateful for the assistance and encouragement of many people without whom we could not have developed the third edition of this text. In particular, Jean Swartz efficiently and tirelessly completed the word processing of this edition. Wendy Smith provided hours of technical support for portions of the text. In addition, the Department of Recreation and Park Administration, through its chair Dr. Joel F. Meier, was an oasis of support and encouragement for this project.

Bruce Hronek, Professor in the Department of Recreation and Park Administration at Indiana University, contributed to the chapter on safety and risk management. Carol Kennedy, Assistant Director in the Division of Recreational Sports, helped develop the chapter on fitness. Their help was invaluable. In addition, contributors to the Shining Examples allowed us to share their successes in recreational sport management. Our thanks go to the following:

Jim Battersby, Lockheed Martin

Marlene Vass, Monroe County YMCA

Rich Robles, Henderson Parks and Recreation Department

Vern Stevens, Amelia Island Plantation

John Korphage, Foster City Parks and Recreation Department

Mick Renneisen, Bloomington Parks and Recreation

Ed Kelly, Amateur Athletic Union

University of Illinois

Indiana University

Alyce Slonaker, Ransburg Branch YMCA

Sally Meyer, Miami University of Ohio

Morgan Breedijk, Dallas Texins Association

Finally, we dedicate this book to recreational sport participants—both active players and spectators. It is for these people that all efforts suggested in the text are directed, and it is our hope that the recreational sport specialists serving these individuals will benefit from our experience and suggestions.

PART I

Foundations

Identity

Sport within our society reflects a multifaceted socioeconomic system. It also represents a tremendous diversity in participation—from a child's frolic, to unstructured play at home, to the dream fulfillment of winning a tournament championship, to a healthy lifestyle through sport participation.

The role of sport in the United States has been shaped by tradition, popularity, and potential for profit. This situation has resulted in prosperity and growth for some areas of sport, for example, recreational sport. You can see this potential by the demand for community sport, benefits to a participant's health and fitness, and the satisfaction of the participant who engages in a recreational sport lifestyle. This chapter presents the existing knowledge about recreational sport by considering the following questions:

- What is recreational sport?
- When does recreational sport occur?
- Why do people participate in recreational sport?
- How do people participate in recreational sport?
- Where is recreational sport offered?
- Who participates in recreational sport?
- How prevalent is recreational sport?

WHAT IS RECREATIONAL SPORT?

Traditionally, recreational sport has been described in many ways, including intramural sport, recreational programming, physical recreation, physical activity, or fitness programming. These terms, however, do not encompass or reflect what is tak-

ing place. In most settings, the content within a recreational sport program is similar, but the titles lack consistency and accuracy. The concepts of leisure, recreation, recreational sport programming, and sport management form the base of recreational sport management. So, we'll examine them closely.

Leisure

This is a concept that has many interpretations. The word leisure is derived from the Latin word *licere*, which means to be free, and is closely related to the French word *loisir*, to be permitted. The essence of leisure appears to be freedom as experienced in free time. Leisure is a time in an individual's life apart from earning a living or doing biological self-maintenance. Leisure, then, is a time span in which there is freedom of choice.

Recreation

Recreation is often defined as a diversion from work, a retooling of energy for work, or a positive and socially acceptable leisure activity. We support the view of recreation as a leisure experience in which the choices and expected outcomes of participation are left to the individual. The goal in recreational programming is to provide everyone with an opportunity to select from a variety of activities; then, to assist participants in gaining a positive experience as the outcome.

Recreational Sport Programming

Recreation is an encompassing term. For our purpose in identifying recreational sport, let's look at definitions for the major areas of recreation programming.

- **Social programming** fosters congenial, non-competitive participation in a common interest. It emphasizes human interaction and often takes the form of banquets, parties, dances, dining, or other social activities.
- **Cultural programming** provides opportunities for individuality, creativity, and self-expression in the following areas:
  - Art activities that focus on creating personally aesthetic objects. Examples are painting, woodwork, or macrame.
  - Dance activities such as folk, square, or ballet dancing that focus on rhythmic movement patterns.

- Drama activities like story telling or performing skits that result in theatrical expressions.
- Literary, mental, and linguistic activities focusing on mental challenge such as reading, working puzzles, or writing.
- Music activities involving vocal and instrumental expression.

• **Special events programming** is a catch-all area of activities providing a change of pace in a unique or nontraditional format. This category incorporates all types of recreational activities.

• **Sport programming** is an area of recreational programming in which practitioners provide sporting opportunities to participants.

Because this book is primarily about how best to provide sporting opportunity, let's explore the concepts of sport and sport programming in more detail. Although experts have made many attempts, no one has ever acceptably defined sport. Still, we define sport as a playing cooperative/competitive activity in the game form. This definition liberates sport from a traditional, restrictive mold that fails to recognize the diversity existing within the total sport process. Careful consideration of this idea involves breaking the definition into its major parts. The first part, *playing*, describes the expectation that evolves out of human action in sport. Playing is an encompassing word that represents the state of mind or feelings evolving from participation. We often describe these feelings as challenge, risk, and chance. We interpret the varying degrees of this state as fun or stress. Challenge incorporates the excitement of the contest and the struggle toward satisfaction. Risk is the element that stirs the mind toward failure and hazard. Chance represents the unpredictable or unknown element in sport. Play has been associated with sport in phrases such as playing cards, playing little league, or playing professional football.

Cooperative/competitive activity represents the manner or style of action in sport. The words cooperative and competitive reflect the behavior that occurs within any form of human interaction. Both are part of every sport experience, although one may predominate at a given time. By placing the words in two extremes on a horizontal continuum (figure 1.1), we can better understand their interrelationship in sport. The left side of the continuum represents harmony, coordination, and collaboration, and the right side represents rivalry, struggle,

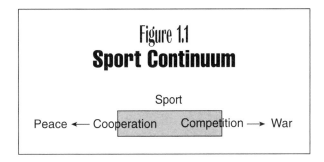

Figure 1.1
Sport Continuum

and conflict, with the extremes to either side being war or peace. The fact that cooperative and competitive behaviors blend within sport reflects the intensity that exists and accommodates different participant's interests and abilities.

The final part of the definition *in the game form* describes the design, structure, and format within which sport occurs. The game form, the structural component of sport, incorporates such characteristics as rules and regulations, strategies, and facilities and equipment. The rules and regulations of sport establish procedures for the cooperative or competitive activity and boundaries that control the action. Strategy represents the planning and judgment the participants exercise, which affect the outcome along with physical and mental abilities. Facilities and equipment are those structures and objects necessary for the sport to take place.

The game form is what separates sport from other cooperative/competitive activity, such as dance, music, art, and drama. We could consider these activities sport, in its broadest sense, if conducted in the game form. For example, auditions for musical or theatrical productions could incorporate characteristics of the game form, as do art contests designed to rank the artwork of contestants according to predetermined criteria. This interpretation is an extreme view of sport, and we mention it only to appreciate the recreational aspect of this approach to sport. It supports the concept that sport does not necessarily have to be physical, as in chess, euchre, and so forth.

To fully understand the impact of sport as a vital element of leisure, the leisure sport management model (figure 1.2) incorporates all the management and organizational areas of sport. We depict the model as a hierarchy of sport, showing at its base the widest range of participation (white area)—educational and recreational sport. Participation decreases in magnitude as one proceeds up the hierarchy to professional sport. At this apex, professional sport has fewer active, direct participants; however, there are more spectators (gray area). This

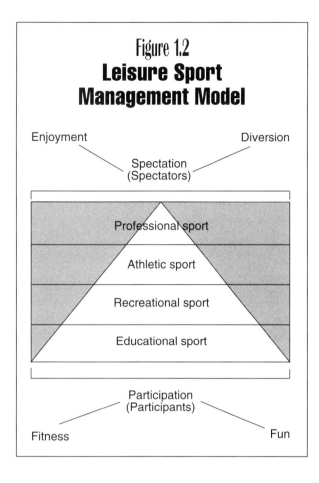

Figure 1.2
Leisure Sport Management Model

Enjoyment   Diversion

Spectation
(Spectators)

Professional sport

Athletic sport

Recreational sport

Educational sport

Participation
(Participants)

Fitness   Fun

• **Athletic sport** includes directing individuals in sport toward the margin of excellence in performance that we identify as winning. The participant receives specialized leadership, emphasizing excellence in performance. Athletic sport usually carries organizational sponsorship through two levels: junior varsity and varsity programming. Spectators of athletic and professional sport use the viewing as recreation.

• **Professional sport** includes marketing sport events with an emphasis on entertainment and a financial remuneration to highly skilled participants. Participation occurs between representatives of corporate sponsors. Spectator income is a major factor in professional sport because income affects the perpetuation or demise of the business. Professional sport is organized to employ the premier sport participants who will attract spectator and financial support. Spectators are considered program participants when they view the sport for their leisure.

All categories of this sport management model refer to playing, cooperative/competitive activity in the game form engaged in during leisure. The amount of direct involvement increases in intensity, skill level, and spectation of sport; however, the magnitude of direct participation decreases as the levels increase. The role of most participants shifts from playing sport to watching others play. Therefore, the focus of managerial concerns also shifts from programming for the participant to programming for the spectator and to marketing. The success of the management system is determined by the response of the targeted audiences.

Because the focus of this book is recreational sport, let's further identify its scope. The five program delivery dimensions in the recreational sport spectrum are instructional sport, informal sport, intramural sport, extramural sport, and club sport. Figure 1.3 illustrates this spectrum.

Instructional sport programs provide learning opportunities about sport skills, strategies, rules, and regulations to help participants improve performance. This often incorporates instruction to individuals or groups through lessons, clinics, and workshops. Usually there are three levels of instruction: beginner, intermediate, and advanced.

Informal sport involves a process of self-directed participation. An individualized approach to sport, this program area acknowledges the desire to participate in sport for fitness and fun, often with no predetermined goals except participation. The primary focus of informal sport requires minimal ad-

model shows the basis of sport involvement as direct participation (participant) and indirect participation (spectator). We can consider both types of involvement as engaging in sport during one's leisure.

The following descriptions should facilitate your understanding of sport application as shown in the leisure sport management model.

• **Educational sport** includes teaching sport skills, strategies, and knowledge to train students through academic courses. Both knowledge and performance are measured against a standard for credit through a formally prescribed course. Educational sport is applied in public and private educational systems, including preschool, kindergarten, elementary, junior high, high school, prep school, college, and university.

• **Recreational sport** includes programming sport activity for fitness and fun. It is a diverse area that incorporates five program divisions: instructional sport, informal sport, intramural sport, extramural sport, and club sport. Each division represents varying abilities and diverse interests in playing cooperative or competitive activity in the game form.

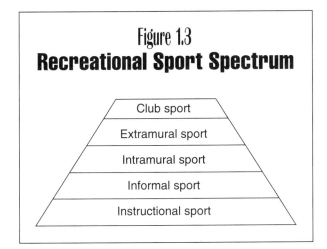

Figure 1.3
Recreational Sport Spectrum

Club sport
Extramural sport
Intramural sport
Informal sport
Instructional sport

ministration. Programming is making sport facilities and services available based on the individual's schedule, interests, and resources.

Intramural sport consists of structured contests, tournaments, leagues, or other events in which participation is limited to the setting where the recreational sport system is located. Only those individuals within the setting (school, business, community, military base, etc.) may participate. Eligibility restrictions usually are placed on participation. The participants themselves may mandate these restrictions through boards, committees, or councils. Most activities are structured into programs for males, females, and mixed participants, often considering ability levels.

Extramural sport is structured participation, usually between the winning teams in a setting. An extension of the intramural sport program, this programming area involves intramural champions; however, other systems for participation can be designed. Extramural sport can also incorporate sport extravaganzas, play days, or festivals that involve participation of representatives from many settings.

Club sport is undertaken by interest groups organized because of a common interest in a sport. Clubs vary in focus and programming because the membership manages the operation. For example, membership interests may focus on teaching, team sponsorship, socialization, or a combination of the three.

Sport Management

Sport management refers to the total process of structuring the business or organizational aspects of sport. In this text, management refers to processes that influence programming or delivering recreational sport.

Within the leisure sport management model, it is important to recognize the recreational sport spectrum, which breaks down into diverse program areas. These areas are instructional sport, informal sport, intramural sport, extramural sport, and club sport. All the program areas of recreational sport are participant driven. This means that the programmatic interests of the participant direct management efforts.

WHEN DOES RECREATIONAL SPORT OCCUR?

To describe when recreational sport occurs, we need to take another look into the concept of leisure. We can categorize leisure qualitatively or quantitatively. Qualitative concepts of leisure, exemplified by the early writings of Aristotle on the Greek upper class, perceive leisure as a way to express superior and spiritual activities of the mind and body. This school of thought subscribes to the theory that leisure is a state of being or state of mind in which people are free from any biological or work constraints. The mind focuses on contemplation and reflection, activities that were usually reserved for highly educated or upper class individuals. Because education is no longer restricted to an elite class and is available to the masses, we place less emphasis on leisure as a *state of being*.

A quantitative school of thought exists that views leisure as discretionary time, free time, or any time that the individual can choose how to use. We usually measure this time as days or hours of leisure. One functions in life within a time system where there are three blocks of time: personal care, work, and leisure. Personal care needs are eating, sleeping, or attending to individual maintenance and bodily functions. Work incorporates preparing for a vocation (training) and participating in gainful employment. Leisure is time not devoted to work or personal care functions. It is the time when recreational sport participation occurs.

Although we are interpreting leisure broadly, we can now take a more in-depth look at two leisure patterns pertinent to recreational sport participation. The first is the potential for negative use. People often do unhealthy or socially unacceptable things with their discretionary time, such as drinking excessively, using dangerous drugs, smoking, or driving recklessly. Excessive inactivity may also be a negative use of leisure. A person's value system and peer group are key factors that influence how he or she uses leisure time.

The positive use of leisure time is self-directed and may include social, cultural, or sport activities. Examples of positive leisure time activities include parties, dances, concerts, ball games, swimming, movies, reading, cards, touring, jogging, and other positive activities not related to work or personal care.

Public attitude toward leisure has undergone many changes, including a view of leisure as something to be earned after hard work, an opportunity improperly used by the masses, a luxury reserved for the privileged, or a legitimate pursuit by all segments of society. The leisure movement has had a tremendous economic impact on society. Current data indicate that leisure is the number one industry measured by consumer expenditures.

If leisure is discretionary or unobligated time, then the positive use of that time is recreation. As described, recreation incorporates several programming areas, one of which is sport.

WHY DO PEOPLE PARTICIPATE IN RECREATIONAL SPORT?

Why people involve themselves in recreational sport involves a theoretical explanation rather than a factual one. The recreational sport programmer, however, should understand why people participate in recreational sport in order to provide relevant programs. Further, recreational sport programmers should understand why their services are necessary. We will explore two categories in addressing *why*—personal and professional.

Personal (Avocation)

People participate in recreational sport during their leisure time for fun and fitness. However, enjoyable and satisfying participation for one person may not produce the same results for another person.

One popular motivation for participation is developing or maintaining fitness in mind and body. Research supports participation in sport as a contributor to well-being and life expectancy. Personal sport and fitness programs have acquired elevated social status and meaning as a result.

Other people are attracted to recreational sport participation because it affords opportunity for social interaction. Sport participation rarely occurs alone. It characteristically involves direct or indirect contact with others. The sport environment offers a means to relate to others; observe the effect of cooperative, competitive, and conflicting behaviors on social relationships; develop communication skills; and broaden one's viewpoint.

For others, sport participation is enjoyable because it affords a change of pace, physical exhilaration, goal attainment, ego gratification or release from tension. Regardless of the specific motivation, well-managed recreational sport systems are satisfying these and other desires.

Professional (Vocation)

Recreational sport is a specialization or field within recreation, business, or physical education. The specialist in recreational sport pursues three objectives that explain why the specialist is necessary: service, development, and relations.

Service

The primary purpose for the professional in recreational sport is to provide the highest quality program within the setting where he or she works. The programs and the quality of their application are a result of the commitment and philosophy of the setting. The service process encompasses sport delivery through a combination of activities, facilities, and personnel, with participant interest and satisfaction foremost in mind.

There are two reasons we provide recreational sport services. The first is encouragement of participation. The professional is motivated by knowing that the participant benefits from involvement. State or federal funds support programs to provide individuals with an equal opportunity to participate fully. Settings that observe this approach include educational, municipal, and military.

Second, we design and deliver services for profit. Fees are assessed for services rendered, and careful consideration is given to the marketing and quality of the service to sustain and expand participant involvement. These include YMCAs and YWCAs, resorts, bowling leagues, country clubs, and racquet clubs.

The two approaches are not mutually exclusive. Many settings benefit from a combination of tax support and service revenues. They are interested in providing a quality service and maximizing enjoyment and profit. Such combinations are becoming a standard practice rather than an exception. More recent studies and general understanding of why people participate in sport conclude that the main reason is to have fun.

Development

Involvement in sport holds developmental experiences for participants. These experiences develop social, mental, and physical awareness of self. The ability to guide participant experiences to be developmental adds value to the professional's role in society.

Social awareness results from interaction with others through sport. Discovering and understanding the consequences of cooperation, competition, and communication among people is critical to success in life and sport. Mental awareness is enhanced through sport because experiences can reveal an ability to control emotions, improve memory, interpret situations, and make appropriate adjustments. Physical awareness is often the most recognized value of sport. Through regular participation, we gain benefits to the cardiovascular, neurological, and muscular systems. A body that engages in regular exercise is a more sound body and one that functions more efficiently.

Relations

A quality delivery service of recreational sport, coupled with a developmental approach in programming, contributes to public relations. Benefits derived from sport participation often exceed those of other life experiences and, when properly designed, our programs contribute significantly to the appeal of a setting for inhabitants. Recreational sport programmers play a major role in shaping positive public relations through competent efforts.

HOW DO PEOPLE PARTICIPATE IN RECREATIONAL SPORT?

Describing how individuals participate in recreational sport is a complex area because values, standards, interest, and abilities are so varied. An individual's decision to participate in an activity involves interaction of internal and external motivations. Therefore, in reviewing how people participate in recreational sport, remember that there are varying degrees of involvement. For recreational sport, a decision regarding how to participate is an individual choice. The individual chooses when, where, and why, then sets goals on what he or she hopes to accomplish in personal satisfaction.

There are two classifications that we can use to demonstrate how people participate. One is *pas-sive* and represents the spectator aspect in sport. The other is *active* and represents participation in a sport.

Watching sport is part of the recreational sport domain. Anything an individual witnesses for enjoyment, on television or in person, qualifies as recreation. Spectation suggests watching athletic or professional sport, but it may include watching intramural sport, extramural sport, or club sport. People enjoy observing because they appreciate the skill of the participant, or because they may be a participant in that sport and identify with the athlete they are watching. As we've said, spectation, or passive participation, is important to athletic and professional sport. So the spectator, as a recreational participant, should be understood, appreciated, and provided for. The reasons motivating spectator behavior may be obscure, but spectators become involved in the sport mentally and emotionally. Helping people find a greater appreciation for sport as spectators is a worthwhile goal for the recreational sport programmer. Enhancing spectators' knowledge of a sport can increase their enjoyment.

Choosing and accomplishing active participation in sport is the next focal point. Recreational sport represents the sport segment with the greatest diversity of involvement. We don't consider any programming division described on pages 6 and 7 more important than another. A principle within recreation is the individual's choice of activity. We shouldn't judge an individual's interest or skill level in active participation. For some people, participation may entail little organization and commitment. Others may prefer activities involving extensive organization and commitment. Figure 1.4 indicates the range of involvement from which an individual may select. As we consider the spectra of sport, we can apply two forms of active participation: structured and self-directed.

Structured participation represents the instructional, intramural, extramural, and club sport program divisions, because each requires external leadership to facilitate participation. The informal sport participant requires little leadership, because the individual chooses when, where, and to what degree, and their activity is self-directed.

Another factor that may influence how a person chooses to participate is the individual's skill and performance levels. These levels may affect the satisfaction derived from participation. A sense of accomplishment following participation is important to most people. Individual performance depends on the participant's agility, strength, endurance, timing, and coordination, regardless of the

Figure 1.4
Degrees of Recreational Sport Participation

Informal	Formal
├── Organizational design ──┤	
Simple	Complex
├── Rules and regulations ──┤	
Low	High
├── Skill performance ──┤	
Minimum	Maximum
├── Physical exertion ──┤	
Relaxed	Intense
├── Mental concentration ──┤	
Low	High
├── Risk ──┤	
None	Numerous
├── Rule modification ──┤	
Low	High
├── Emphasis on winning ──┤	

programming area or specific sport. External factors also affect participation in sport and whether one becomes involved in a passive or active way. These factors include the following:

• **Geographic location and climate.** The availability of many recreational sport activities depends on terrain and climate. Skiing is more feasible in mountainous areas, and accessibility to water encourages aquatic sport activities.

• **Socialization.** Social environment influences how one chooses to participate in recreational sport. Parental and peer group attitudes toward sport have a tremendous impact on decision making, as do the participation patterns of family members and friends. People tend to reflect the participation patterns and attitudes of their families, peer groups, and other role models, especially through the adolescent years.

• **Experience.** Participation choices are shaped by previous experiences. If participation is pleasant and satisfying, it usually continues, but if it is unpleasant, it usually ceases. As programmers, we must design programs and experiences that will

have positive outcomes and encourage participants to try new activities.

• **Availability.** It is unlikely that people will engage in recreational sport pursuits unless opportunities are accessible. Program offerings should be diverse to accommodate different interests and abilities. Programmers should make services attractive to the consumer in terms of location, cost, and time.

WHERE IS RECREATIONAL SPORT OFFERED?

We can program recreational sport indoors or outdoors in many settings. Indoor sport ranges from bowling, martial arts, swimming, and racquetball to those that are traditionally outdoors but move indoors for year-round participation. Factors that influence the recreational sport programming of indoor facilities include cost of operation, construction, maintenance, and the interests of the participants. Outdoor programming emphasizes the traditional sports where participation occurs outside: football, tennis, swimming, rugby, soccer, golf, softball, and lacrosse, for example. A second consideration in outdoor programming emphasizes the environment. Many participants enjoy the interaction with natural elements, such as air, trees, water, grass, and terrain. We include sports such as white-water canoeing, hiking, fishing, skiing, hunting, mountain climbing, and spelunking in this interpretation.

Among the ways to provide recreational sport, the agency's philosophy and the nature of the program setting influence the approach you will take. Consequently, it is important to look into some settings where we can find recreational sport programs. *Settings* means both the administration and programming of recreation, a major portion of which is sport related. Figure 1.5 depicts settings where recreational sport can take place.

Let's examine the settings in figure 1.5:

• **City.** This setting consists of family units, employment structures, government, and school systems, all of which influence the lifestyle of people within the community. The city or municipal governmental structure provides funds, facilities, and leadership for recreation with a tax-based program that they may supplement with fees. The recreational sport programs in this setting are available to all residents.

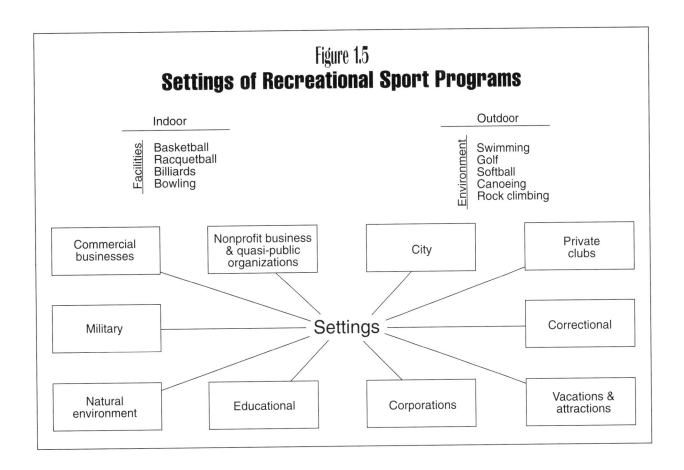

Figure 1.5
Settings of Recreational Sport Programs

- **Educational.** Among our education systems are public schools, private schools, and institutions of higher education. Each educational setting has goals that focus on student academic development. Sport, whether educational, recreational, or athletic, is considered part of the learning process within these settings.

- **Military.** The United States military is organized into four branches: Army, Navy, Air Force, and Marines. Because military personnel and families tend to stay within their settings, recreational programs become a major part of their daily life. Sport programming receives high priority as an avenue for positive use of leisure time.

- **Correctional.** This setting deals with people who have demonstrated socially unacceptable behavior and who need detention. When people are confined to this setting, the only benefit they may have is their recreational pursuits. Sport is popular and may be used in rehabilitative efforts through both structured and self-directed participation.

- **Private clubs.** Clubs provide a variety of recreational sport for their membership. Private clubs may limit their membership based on facility capacity or social status. An example is a coun-

try club that offers swimming, tennis, and golf, along with dining facilities for the pleasure of its members. Usually, the sport facilities are the primary attraction and, through dues and supplemental user fees, yield much of the income necessary for maintaining the operation.

- **Nonprofit business and quasi-public organizations.** Historically, organizations, such as YMCAs, YWCAs, YMHAs, YWHAs, Boys or Girls Clubs, and similar organizations, provided for community needs, such as short-term housing, social services, and youth development. As demand increased, additional facilities, such as gymnasiums, pools, and other facilities, were developed. These organizations have shifted focus to sport and fitness programming in many communities and are governed by a national organization.

- **Commercial businesses.** Because of the market demand for sport-specific enterprises, many commercial recreation entrepreneurs have established sole proprietorships, partnerships, and corporations in specific sport areas, such as handball, racquetball, squash, tennis, swimming, bowling, boating, and fishing. Profit is the chief motive in operating these businesses. Commercial recreational sport management has grown tremendously in the last 20 years.

- **Corporations.** Employee recreation opportunities exist in a majority of corporations. Employers offer these programs to stimulate employee health, morale, and productivity. Most programs emphasize fitness; extensive sport programs are offered on-site and through cooperation with community agencies.

- **Natural environment.** Public lands, such as forests, parks, and areas owned by local, regional, state, and federal governments, offer expansive settings for sport involvement in both informal and structured forms. Extensive facilities to accommodate skiing, boating, camping, hiking, swimming, and other sport interests are developed by the agency or through a commercial contractor.

- **Vacations and Attractions.** A variety of accommodations (lodging facilities such as hotels, motels, resorts, and cruise ships) offer extensive sport-theme special events and regular sport scheduling. Attractions such as theme parks offer many sport-oriented experiences, either on-site or nearby. Examples of sport offerings include aquatic sport leagues, clinics, theme weeks, tournaments, and classes.

WHO PARTICIPATES IN RECREATIONAL SPORT?

Recreational sport is intended for the enjoyment of all ages, with no limitations of shape, size, or skill level. Recent development of recreational sport programs for people with mental and/or physical disabilities has facilitated their inclusion into the mainstream of society. Currently, recreational sport constitutes an important part of day-to-day existence for many.

Table 1.1 provides an overview of the types of involvement in sport that are most common within specific age groups. The brief discussion that follows will elaborate on that table.

Children

The child, from newborn to age five, participates in activity centered in the home. Little participation in a cooperative or competitive activity in the game form occurs among children at this age. Activity is frolic with minimal structure.

As a preschool youngster has little organizational ability, almost everything he or she does requires limited physical and mental concentration. External leadership has little effect on actions that are exploratory and self-directed. Often parents and other adults influence early sport skill development, contributing to the child's performance ability later in life. Little emphasis is placed on winning and high achievement.

Youth

Between ages 6 and 12, many young people learn about the world of structured sport. Participation often revolves around the school or community in the form of *youth sport*. Youth sport has grown tremendously in the past two decades. It begins athletic sport careers for some, and for others it is simply recreation. This dichotomy involves conflicts in philosophy, but proper leadership may provide a healthy, meaningful, and balanced experience.

Leadership, a key to youth sport, teaches fundamental skills, strategies, rules, health, and well-being. In recent years, training programs for parents, coaches, and officials involved in youth sport have surfaced that have had a positive effect. Principal settings that sponsor programs include the YMCA, YWCA, YMHA, YWHA, Boys Club, Girls Club, schools, and community or municipal recreation departments.

Adolescents

The individual between the ages of 13 and 19 experiences a complex period of development leading to maturation. Involvement in sport may have a positive influence on this process. At this age, athletic sport receives its greatest emphasis, primarily in school settings. Unfortunately, recreational sport opportunities for the nonathlete barely exist. Adolescents unable to make an athletic team usually find themselves with few opportunities to participate in sport. These so-called nonathletes are discriminated against because of their limited mental and physical abilities or lack of interest in athletic sport.

We can find some programs for adolescents in other settings, primarily in the community or city recreation department or other service agencies. Unfortunately, the voluntary leadership support available to youth sport is not carried to the adolescent level. Emphasis on youth sport hampers the availability of facilities and resources for adolescent recreational sport. We hope to see more positive sport opportunities for adolescents in the future.

Adolescents not involved in structured sport may participate in other recreation activities on an individual, peer group, or family basis. Because

Table 1.1
Sport Participation by Age Groups

Participant group	Age	Instructional	Informal	Intramural	Extramural	Club	Athletic		Professional	
							Junior varsity	Varsity	Minor	Major
Children	Birth-5	X	X							
Youth	6-7	X	X	X						
	8-10	X	X	X	X	X	X	X		
	11-12	X	X	X	X	X	X	X		
Adolescents	13-14	X	X	X	X	X	X	X		
	15-17	X	X	X	X	X	X	X	X	
	18-19	X	X	X	X	X	X	X	X	X
Adults	20-30	X	X	X	X	X			X	X
	31-45	X	X	X	X	X				
	46-65	X	X	X	X	X				
Seniors	65-75	X	X	X						
	76+	X	X							

sport may not have a high priority for some, it is their responsibility to determine their own recreation needs and pursue them.

Adults

After 19 years of age, sport interests are well established. Other than those involved in an athletic or professional sport career, adults usually participate in recreational sport programming areas centered through where they live or work. Although dependent on the programmers' decision of what they can provide, adults have the most flexibility in choosing and evaluating their recreational sport experience. The degree of involvement is up to them. When the opportunity for involvement does not exist, they can influence its development. Alternatives, such as structured tournaments, self-directed activities, or club leadership positions, are all opportunities available to adults in most settings.

Seniors

One of the most rapidly growing areas in recreation is providing opportunities for participation by the elderly. More and more elderly people find enjoyment, satisfaction, and exercise through recreational sport participation. Their involvement depends on individual enthusiasm and physical and mental limitations. Although age may limit the degree of involvement, it does not prevent interest or enthusiasm for participation.

Retirees have more leisure time once they leave the work force. Recreational sport can now play a major part in their lifestyle and becomes an important outlet for many.

HOW PREVALENT IS RECREATIONAL SPORT?

Recreational sport participation in the United States is reaching unprecedented levels. Almost everyone finds some recreational sport expression, whether it be through personal fitness programs, organized sport competition, family sport outings, spectating, or playing video and other electronic sports.

A review of the evolution of recreational sport in the United States and other cultures has resulted in texts on sport history. Much documentation comes from teachers (the history of physical education) or coaches (the history of athletics).

Progression of Sport

The chief focus of this text is recreational sport. Origins of recreational sport are shown in figure 1.6. The existence of sport is depicted in the traditional school model triangle, which represents the physical education of all youth, intramurals as a competitive outlet for all, and athletics as sport participation for the highly skilled individuals.

Sport offerings have since expanded to a variety of settings within a community (we describe these later in the text). We refer to this as a community model, which takes into account management systems within schools, municipalities, and private entities that deal with all ages and levels of sport.

The recreational aspect of the community model is a particular focus in this text. You'll recognize that the final progression in figure 1.6 is the recreational sport spectrum (which serves as figure 1.3). This model emphasizes the player participant's direct involvement in sport during leisure regardless of setting (school or community). This model represents a contemporary view of recreational sport as a unique area of study that can stand alone as a specialization and management area within sport.

Status of Recreational Sport

Over time, sport interest has been influenced by the heritage of the people within each region. Historically, sport evolved from ritual, contests, and competition between differing groups. Presently, recreational sport is a major component of an individual's lifestyle, through either participation in or spectation of sport during leisure.

The following points show how recreational sport, globally and locally, supports learning about this exciting field:

- Recreational sport programs exist in hundreds of leisure settings.
- Over 40 countries offer a nationally sponsored *sport for all* concept to attract the recreational sport participant.
- Recreational sport, as a programming area in agencies or businesses, includes from 50 to 80 percent of recreational programming.
- A recent report on job prospects shows the employment of recreational specialists is fifth highest, and with sport as a dominant program, the job market is strong.

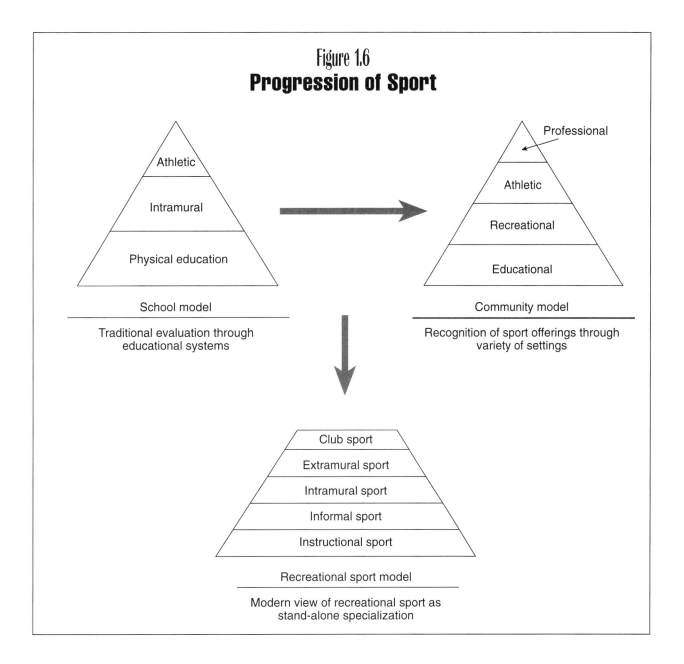

Figure 1.6
Progression of Sport

• The sporting goods industry has grown steadily in response to the demand for attire, equipment, and supplies by the recreational sport participant.

• Much prime and broadcast media attention focuses on the recreational sport participant.

• An increase in instructional and informational videos on recreational sport opportunities has been evident.

• Commercial sport enterprises use the recreational sport participant as a major market target as evidenced by P.L.A.Y. and Just Do It campaigns.

These points are a partial listing of the values of recreational sport as a field within a profession. The remainder of this text covers the foundations and management requirements in this field.

ADA Suggestions

In selected chapters, we will present suggestions to assist you in complying with the Americans With Disabilities Act (ADA). Recent legislation was passed in the United States that has had a positive impact on minorities and individuals with disabilities in practically all aspects of life. The ADA provides a comprehensive mandate that the 43 million disabled Americans not be discriminated against. Of concern to recreational sport programmers is that sport programs be available to all members of the community, regardless of gender, race, age, skill, or physical ability—in essence, sport for all.

Access to all recreational sport facilities and programs is a valuable right for people with or without disabilities. The ADA, signed into law by President Bush in 1990 and effective January 26, 1992, ensures that people with disabilities are afforded equal opportunities to participate in and benefit from recreational sport facilities and programs available to individuals without disabilities.

The ADA consists of five major titles or sections. *Title I* pertains to discrimination practices in employment. *Title II* addresses discrimination by local and state governments and agencies (e.g., parks and recreation departments, universities, community sponsored youth sport). *Title III* discusses discrimination in public accommodations or private agencies that are open to the public (e.g., health clubs, spas, gymnasiums, bowling alleys, golf courses, YMCAs). *Title IV* requires equal access for the disabled to telecommunications, and *Title V* involves miscellaneous aspects of accessibility. Although all the titles are important, *Titles I, II, and III* are specifically related to recreational sport management.

The ADA affects recreational sport departments as employers and as service providers. This legislation is an effective way to remove barriers and provide full participation, equal opportunities, and accessibility to facilities, goods, programs, services, and employment for *all* Americans. It requires that people with disabilities be provided accommodation and access to goods and services within places of public accommodation equal to or similar to those available to the general public.

It is important that as recreational sport programmers we keep in mind that ADA requirements are *minimum* guidelines that sometimes do not meet the needs of every participant in all facilities or settings. Whenever appropriate, the sport programmer should attempt to exceed these minimum suggestions.

There are two principles that we must consider when we plan recreational sport programs. First, all people, regardless of physical ability, have a right to participate in recreational sport programs and facilities. As participants in our programs, people with disabilities should be afforded the same privileges and opportunities as able-bodied participants.

Second, people with disabilities are human beings first and disabled second. They should be able to enjoy the value of the recreational sport experience as much as anyone else.

CONCLUSION

Actions recreational sport programmers take today will determine the direction of programs and the construction of facilities for the future. How well we provide services depends on our understanding of the foundation of recreational sport and on the impact current conditions have on the field.

The function of recreational sport as depicted in the leisure sport management model is to provide fun and fitness opportunities for the recreational sport participant. The traditional role of sport in an athletic, intramural, and physical education environment has given way to a broader community-based model.

The foundations of recreational sport include a full understanding of the scope of this field, from why people participate through the extent of sport involvement. Management of recreational sport is an important discipline that involves extensive understanding of programming design and direction.

DISCUSSION QUESTIONS

1. Diagram the leisure sport management model described in the chapter. Illustrate how involvement shifts from participant and spectator viewpoints.

2. Does the term *recreational sport* apply only to the collegiate setting?

3. List and describe the settings in which recreational sport can occur.

4. Explain the following: Sport is a broad spectrum of personal interpretation, with varying interest levels and degrees of involvement.

5. List and describe four benefits gained from recreational sport participation.

6. What role does competition play in recreational sport programming?

7. Define sport, instructional sport, informal sport, intramural sport, extramural sport, and club sport.

8. What does cooperative or competitive activity mean in terms of participating in recreational sport?

9. Describe your philosophy of leisure. Where are recreation and sport in your leisure philosophy?

10. What level of the leisure sport management model represents the broadest base for participation?

11. Identify the major areas of recreation programming.

12. Is being a spectator a part of the recreational sport experience?

13. Is there a difference between the leisure sport management model and the recreational sport spectrum? If so, explain your answer.

14. What obligation do we as professionals in recreational sport have to our colleagues and participants to standardize terminology we use in our profession, such as intramural sport, informal sport, club sport, etc.?

15. Is there a difference between the terms *sport management* and *sport programming*?

APPLICATION EXERCISE

A new municipal parks and recreation board has just been elected for your small community. The members on the new board do not have a background in sport and do not understand why recreational sport is important in a municipal parks and recreation program. In fact, rumor has it that they will eliminate all sport from the program. To save your program, and possibly your job as the coordinator of recreational sport, submit a position paper justifying the current recreational sport programs at your municipal parks department.

Your position paper should include answers to the questions what, why, where, when, who, and how as they pertain to recreational sport management. It is imperative that this paper be convincing; therefore, a personal statement emphasizing the need, rationale, and benefits of recreational sport to the community would be an asset in your defense before the board.

SUGGESTED READINGS

Athletic Footwear Association (AFA). 1990. *American youth and sports participation*. North Palm Beach, FL: Athletic Footwear Association.

Betts, J.R. 1974. *American sporting heritage, 1850-1950*. Reading, MA: Addison-Wesley.

Brown, S.C. 1990. Looking toward 2000. *National Intramural-Recreational Sports Association Journal* 14 (2): 32-34.

Dudenhoeffer, F.T. 1990. Genesis and evolution of the recreational sports profession. *National Intramural-Recreational Sports Association Journal* 14 (3): 12-13.

Geller, W.W. 1980. A selected bibliography of the influence of intramural sports on individual development. *National Intramural-Recreational Sports Association Journal* 5 (1): 24.

Honker, A. 1989. Who are we and where are we going? Campus recreation and the NIRSA's identity and direction. P. 7-24 in *Collected readings in recreational sports*. Corvallis, OR: National Intramural-Recreational Sports Association.

Jamieson, L., C. Ross, and J. Swartz. 1994. Research in recreational sports management: A content analysis approach. *National Intramural-Recreational Sports Association Journal* 19 (1): 12-14.

Kaufman, J.E. 1987. Enhancing the quality of life on campus. *National Intramural-Recreational Sports Association Journal* 11 (2): 3.

Matthews, D. 1985. The defense rests its case. *National Intramural-Recreational Sports Association Journal* 9 (3): 3-4.

Mull, R. 1986. Going beyond calling things by their right names. *National Intramural-Recreational Sports Association Journal* 10 (2): 3-4.

Mull, R. 1985. In support of calling things by their right names. *National Intramural-Recreational Sports Association Journal* 9 (2): 4-7.

Mull, R. 1982. Toward a philosophical basis. P. 253 in *Intramural-recreational sports: Its theory and practice*. Corvallis, OR: National Intramural-Recreational Sports Association.

Smith, S.R., and M.F. Carron. 1990. Comparison of competition and cooperation in intramural sport. *National Intramural-Recreational Sports Association Journal* 14 (2): 44-47.

Tanselli, L. 1991. A historical perspective on the development of the National Intramural-Recreational Sports Association national office. *National Intramural-Recreational Sports Association Journal* 15 (1): 50-56.

Zeigler, E.F. 1985. Guest editorial: Call things by their right names. *National Intramural-Recreational Sports Association Journal* 9 (2): 3.

CHAPTER 2

Participant Development

Chapter Objectives

After reading this chapter you will

- understand the theory that supports sport participant development,
- be able to identify and apply developmental characteristics of age groupings to the sport environment,
- understand differences in the way settings develop a sport participant, and
- understand the role of recognition in dealing with the participant.

Beyond managing program delivery tasks, recreational sport specialists should focus on the impact sport experience has on participants and volunteers. The tasks involved in program delivery are initially challenging, but they often become routine. A commitment to participant development adds meaning, direction, and continuity to the programmer's efforts. Procedural knowledge alone—how to set up tournaments, run a club, design and operate a facility, schedule personnel, or publicize a program—does not guarantee program quality. Such expertise does not contribute to development unless it's founded on insight into the characteristics and needs of participants. By understanding how program design and delivery satisfy needs, we can design systems to encourage a positive sport experience, develop leadership, and contribute to the growth and development of an individual.

In this context, growth refers to the physical and physiological changes that occur throughout life, and development refers to functional changes, such as language skills, emotional control, interpersonal skills, identity, competence, and autonomy. Although our knowledge of the nature and process of human development is incomplete, the following principles have received wide acceptance and may help the programmer understand participant development.

The first principle concerns life stages. A life stage is a time that establishes many developmental characteristics common among human beings. Human growth proceeds through successive life stages. It involves a progression from simpler to more complex activities, occurring with some continuity from stage to stage. As you face challenges, you draw on previous experiences and learning.

Even though a life stage is an arbitrary category and individuals progress from stage to stage at their own pace, it serves as a framework for program planning and operations (Miller and Prince 1977, 6-7).

The second principle involves developmental tasks of a particular life stage. Each life stage requires the acquisition of particular skills, attitudes, knowledge, or functions to meet challenges. Heredity, environment, and individual attributes determine the extent to which an individual succeeds in completing these tasks, although the tasks encountered within each stage are relatively uniform. For example, some developmental tasks associated with adolescence include achieving a balance between dependence and independence, learning a social role, accepting one's body, selecting and preparing for an occupation, developing a value system, and learning to give and receive affection (Miller and Prince 1977, 9-10).

Recreational sport programmers need this insight to design programs to fit a particular life stage and enhance its development. Using the college student as an example, Bryant and Bradley (1993) refer to some key developmental tasks college students experience, such as adapting, coping, and learning the new culture of a campus experience. The same circumstances may be true for new military personnel, new employees on the job, and new residents in a community.

PARTICIPANT CHARACTERISTICS

The notion of a developmental approach to recreational sport programming is not new. Since the beginning of organized physical education, recreation and intramural sport programs, practitioners, and educators have claimed that participation in sport contributes to emotional, social, mental, and physical development. These claims were based on theory, observation, and speculation, rather than research.

Since the 1960s, participant development has emerged as a major focus for physical education, recreation, and recreational sport practitioners. A major impetus has been the increased pressure on all sport programs to demonstrate accountability to taxpayers. Recession in the American economy necessitated cutbacks or elimination of those sport programs not making significant contributions to the goals of the setting or those unable to support themselves financially. In response, educators and practitioners sought to prove (through research) what contributions sport makes to physical, mental, personality, and social development. Although most inquiry has focused on interscholastic, intercollegiate, or professional sport, some studies apply to recreational sport.

With this in mind, let's form an understanding of participant characteristics. Table 2.1 (pp. 22-23) represents characteristics for established life stages—middle childhood or youth (6 to 12 years), adolescence (13 to 19 years), early adulthood (20 to 39 years), middle adulthood (40 to 65 years), and later adulthood (over 65). Each set of characteristics, describing the growth, development, and behavior of an average American, involve physical, mental, personality, and social parameters. Included within the characteristics are major developmental tasks associated with each life stage. Programmatic implications demonstrate how you can apply participant characteristics to program design and delivery. This material, although not conclusive, represents current knowledge regarding participant characteristics and the implications for programming based on recent research, a review of the literature, and professional experience.

You'll notice that table 2.1 omits information on the developmental characteristics of children from birth to age five and the implications of sport recreational programming for this group. Although some agencies sponsor programs for children (newborn to five years) in sports such as swimming, ice hockey, and gymnastics, the family provides their primary recreational sport involvement, emphasizing instruction and lead-up games. Because structured programs for children are not prevalent in sport literature, we will not include material on this life stage. The best advice for programmers is to follow guidelines established by the American Academy of Pediatrics, American Red Cross (aquatic programs), and similar developmental resources.

PROGRAMMATIC IMPLICATIONS FOR PARTICIPANT DEVELOPMENT

Table 2.1 provides a thumbnail sketch of the implications of designing and administering programs for participants across the life-stage continuum. Let's go into more detail so you can apply these principles to your recreational sport programs.

• **Age 6 to 12.** Sport programs for this age grouping parallel the teaching techniques used in school and the structure in traditional physical edu-

cation classes. The major emphasis is on skill development. There is one important difference—children have an opportunity to choose many sport experiences. They progress rapidly, if interested, and they drop out if bored. Often there is a need for parental guidance and leadership training for adult role models.

• **Age 13 to 19.** This age group needs greater opportunity for leadership development and self-direction, giving major attention to social development. They begin in a sport, they adapt, many become accomplished, and many drop out. The self-esteem factor of this age group may affect choices and adherence in sport. Participants may also be team leaders, organizers, and officers in sport organizations.

• **Age 20 to 39.** This age group is emerging in society. They have many things competing for their time. Sport represents an important outlet. Programmers may involve this age group in administrative experiences, such as team managers, volunteers, and officers, as well as players. People make real commitments to sport choices and invest greatly in time, energy, and money.

• **Age 40 to 65.** Some physical deterioration characteristics may appear, especially in those who have not maintained fitness. Programmers may accidentally stereotype this group as inactive, although strong sport involvement persists in many. This is a peak time for involvement, and long-term commitments often occur. Programs need to provide for renewed leisure pursuits and leadership opportunities.

• **Age 65 and up.** Health concerns increase because of aging, again more pronounced in those who have been sedentary. Programmers must be conscious of potential injury, but not fail to offer a variety of sports to this age group. There must be modifications as needed for those who desire participation.

PARTICIPANT DEVELOPMENT EXPERIENCES

There are two roles that a sport participant may have when choosing a sport: program participant or program leader.

Besides direct involvement in sport, the program participant gains experiences in many ways. He or she learns to handle winning and losing. This may be difficult at first, but gradually participants can

Table 2.1
Developmental Characteristics of The Five Age Groups

Age group	Physical	Mental	Personality	Social
Youth 6-12	44 to 62 in. 44 to 100 lb. Growth slow Muscles strong but immature Skeleton matures Heart grows at slow rate	Attention span lengthens Ability for reflective thinking improves Abstract thought developing Vocabulary developing Know right and wrong	Interactions with adults and peers serve as a base for self-concept Desire for achievement Preference for sex segregation Fears about personal safety decline Concern for competence	Comparisons of ideas, beliefs, may modify Internalize cultural rules Aware of others' intentions Developing own attitudes toward ethnic groups in relation to those of parents Social values vary Peer pressure significant Peer acceptance influences self-concept

Programming implications: Plan for skill development and creating a social environment for bonding sport interaction.

Age group	Physical	Mental	Personality	Social
Adolescence 13-19	Rapid growth, awkwardness Marked muscular growth Stocky appearance Lung capacity increases Onset of sexual maturity Sebaceous glands cause acne Vocal changes Improvement in strength, reaction, and coordination ability	Mental perspective in past, present, and future Use of symbols, system coordination, factors in problem solving Meaning of words in ideals and absolutes Inductive and deductive reasoning Can explain phenomena Think they are unique Industrious, sense of duty Meaning of life	Reexamine old values and experiment Stable self-concept Flex in general behavior What is right or moral, independent of expectations Possible premature acceptance of values in society Emotional independence	Peer group placement Social with both sexes Intimacy and norms Peer is testing ground Sharing of thoughts and feelings Compare values with popularity Look to adults for role models

Programming implications: Immense intensity of sport experiences and recognition of leadership development opportunities.

Stage	Physical	Intellectual	Self-concept	Social
Early adulthood 20-39	Full height 21 years. / Peak muscles 25 to 30 / Vision declines / Reaction time stable / Maximum physical potential / Setting vertebrae / Brain weight maximum / Aging not uniform	Intellectual skills stable / Ability for concepts declining gradually / Formal reasoning improves	Is more defined / Secure self-concept / Absorption in interests / Realistic perspective / Sex roles affect competence / Integration of self with roles within society	Open and honest / Less self-centered / Occupied with career, family, community involvement / Expand social relationships

Programming implications: Increased attention to programming sport for safety and time considerations. New learning experiences can occur, and greater responsibility, is assumed by the participants.

Stage	Physical	Intellectual	Self-concept	Social
Middle adulthood 40-65	Graying hair / Gain weight / Reaction time slows / Sensory function loss / Change in sensory functions / Moving function declines / Menopause occurs / Chronic illnesses prevalent	Brain physiology decreases / Peek productivity and creativity / Intelligence and cognitive skills	Stable self-concept / Renewed self-awareness / Psychological conflict / Focus on ego maturity	Peak time for involvement / Position of leadership pursued / Responsible for support of child and parents / Time for rest and interests once child leaves home / Become grandparents

Programming implications: Ongoing fitness needs apparent. Greater care in the physiological aspects of programming as chance of injury increases.

Stage	Physical	Intellectual	Self-concept	Social
Later adulthood Over 65	Risk of heart disease / Balance and coordination affected / Visual acuity declines / Hearing loss / Lost teeth / Internal organs less affected / Reduced motor performance	Short-term memory loss / Retain and improve verbal skills / Time required for memory recall	Self-concept based on internal thoughts / Women more passive / Men more active / Sense of competence / Sense of self-worth / Traditional sex roles may reverse	Influential in social interests / Many single women / Prefer to live independently / Time for married partner increases / Remarriage hindered by physical concerns / Impact of death of spouse

Programming implications: Greater education on the need for movement to prevent sedentary lifestyles.

gracefully handle success and loss. Second, program participants handle competition in many ways. Gaining experience in competitive situations is a valuable skill to transfer to life experiences at home and in the workplace. The control of aggression is a third developmental experience of the program participant. The ability to allow aggressive energy to focus on a sport in a positive way is an exceptional accomplishment. A final component of a program participant's experience is with design and direction of a sport experience. Thus sport experiences allow participants to gain knowledge about themselves. This knowledge may provide a basis for handling other life situations more effectively.

A program leader is a participant who volunteers for the additional duties of organizing teammates, sport experiences, or other participants. He or she is involved in learning and interpreting the sport program to others. There is greater exposure to rules and their interpretation. The program leader also enforces rules and standards of conduct. Finally, the program leader participates in leadership development and gains recognition for duties beyond that of a player.

Regardless of setting, programmers can develop sport programs that create learning experiences for the player participants and volunteer program leaders. Table 2.2 shows various sport settings and some differences in program participant development. An astute programmer will examine the purpose of the setting before undertaking program design and delivery. In each setting, it is possible to incorporate a development component that will encourage the following:

- Leadership skills
- Sport management skills applicable in other leisure pursuits
- Positive attitudes toward participation in sport

IMPACT OF PROGRAM DESIGN AND DELIVERY ON PARTICIPANT DEVELOPMENT

Program design and delivery factors that influence participant development are staff, program content, rules and regulations, governance, personnel, recognition, and evaluation. Because of the many variables (life stages, settings, and program divisions—informal, intramural, club), it is not possible to address each factor in detail. Rather, we indicate how these factors influence participant development.

Staff

Staff members have a positive impact on development when they understand the human growth process and can provide quality programs based on participant interests. However, knowledge and competence are not enough. Staff should develop positive relationships with participants by being accessible and possessing communication skills. Consequently, the recreational sport programmer should increase contact with participants by having an open door policy and providing leadership positions (team captain, unit manager, advisor, governing committee member, official, supervisor, or lifeguard) that include participants in the program operation.

Participants are encouraged to display acceptable behavior and explore their potential when staff members are competent role models. The programmer will assume several interrelated functions in this regard, including instructor, trainer, consultant, advisor, and evaluator. He or she should know the appropriate time for assuming each role.

Program

A common concern of recreational sport specialists is the need for suitable, well-balanced programs. The type and number of sport activities we provide are important. Because people have diverse interests and skill levels, programmers should provide variety in the sports, program types (informal, intramural, club) and skill classifications they offer.

Sports vary in the way they influence development. For example, table tennis offered as an intramural single elimination tournament provides different developmental opportunities than table tennis offered as a club sport. In addition, differences exist among and between team sport, dual sport, and individual sport.

The classification systems used within sport programs also affect development. Co-intramural sport participation may provide opportunities for males and females to appreciate differences and similarities in skills, interests, and limitations. Classification systems that allow variations in ability or intensity may contribute to autonomy, competence, and interpersonal relations skills. These systems structure opportunities to experience success

Table 2.2

Participant Development Considerations in Sport Management

Setting	Purpose	Participation	Personnel	Unique features	Types	Participant development tasks
Hotel	Sport is a supporting amenity	Employees and guests	Concierge, recreation specialists	Varied, facility-driven programs of limited duration	Instructional, informal, intramural	Information to hotel guests about self-directed activities
Military	Sport contributes to morale	Recruits, families, employees	GS personnel, UA personnel	Community-oriented services driven by logistics of base	Instructional, informal, club, athletic, professional, (intramural), (extramural)	Involvement of military in all activities, taking into account military priority
Corporate	Sport contributes to morale and productivity	Employees, families, associates	Human resources managers, recreation specialists	Limited by facility, profit motive, and philosophy of individual company	Instructional, informal, club, (intramural), (extramural)	Involvement of employees, taking into account work priority
Community	Sport contributes to quality of life of residents	Residents and nonresidents	Recreation specialists	Varied, competing services governed by politics, demand for services	Instructional, informal, club, athletic, professional, (intramural), (extramural)	Involvement of citizens in all activities, taking into account competing time variables
Education	Sport contributes to enhancement of academic experience and learning	Students, faculty, teachers, staff, community	Recreational sport specialists	Student development and athletic focus	Instructional, informal, intramural, extramural, athletic	Involvement of students as team managers, informational managers, officers, sport authorities
Correctional	Sport contributes to greater mental health	Inmates	Recreation officers	Limited by attitude and goal of incarceration	Informal and limited	Individual choice in trying circumstances

and gratification, outcomes that usually encourage continued participation.

Finally, the social interaction and challenge from sport participation, regardless of the sport, skill level, or program format, develop physical and mental abilities, emotional control, autonomy, self-esteem, interpersonal skills, integrity, identity, and health.

Rules and Regulations

Rules and regulations that facilitate equity and safety among participants contribute to development. When rules enhance the perception that one can achieve success, they encourage continued involvement. For example, most programs use eligibility statements to counter unfair distinctions between participants. One of the most common eligibility requirements in recreational sport programs restricts or eliminates the athletic or professional sport participant in a specific or related sport. This restriction, based on skill transfer research, indicates that domination by athletic and professional sport participants minimizes the chance for equitable participation by other players in recreational sport. A different approach to controlling unbalanced competition exists in some youth sport programs in which all members of a team are guaranteed an opportunity to participate, regardless of skill level. Each person has the chance to benefit in terms of self-esteem, acceptance, recognition, identity, emotional management, responsibility, interpersonal skills, and competence. Such rules recognize that development is contingent upon participation.

Rules and regulations provide explicit directions for behavior. When a rule is enforced, individuals learn to alter their thoughts and actions to comply with the rules, or they suffer the consequences.

Governance

When you invite players to sit on governance boards, committees, or councils, these bodies become vehicles for developing leadership capabilities. Membership in these groups permits frequent contact with staff and other role models. Involvement helps the player and leader develop decision-making skills; benefit from mistakes; interact with others; listen effectively; and consider the needs, concerns, and motives of others. As part of a governing body, participants learn responsibility, strengthen their identities, and develop consistency between their values and their behavior in decision-making situations.

Guidance, not domination, is key to objectivity in the governance process. The amount of responsibility granted participants making governance decisions depends on their age, experience, and maturity. Decisions made by a governing body should not be overruled without just cause. Otherwise, the value of the experience may be minimized.

Personnel

Other responsible positions within the recreational sport program that developmentally influence participants include team captain, unit manager, coach, committee member, club or committee officer, official, lifeguard, supervisor, and activity leader. Such roles contribute to autonomy, integrity, emotional control, competency, identity, and interpersonal skills.

The maturity required to assume one of these positions increases from team captain to coach, unit manager, official, supervisor, and governing committee. The programmer places people in positions commensurate with their abilities while allowing them room to develop.

Evaluation

The impact of program participation results in either satisfaction or dissatisfaction. The evaluation process provides opportunities for individuals to articulate their opinions and feelings about their program experiences. This gives the participant a sense of closure that allows for future sport choices.

Recognition

The public relations and recognition aspects of the program promote development by encouraging participation. Aspects that have particular impact are point systems, awards, and public relations personnel.

From a developmental standpoint, point systems have positive and negative aspects. They have a negative effect when people become discouraged and lose interest because a goal is unattainable. Point systems that regard achievement in participation and sporting behavior provide alternatives to winning as a prime objective.

Another form of recognition uses awards, which may be certificates, medallions, trophies, apparel, or other objects. They may discourage participation when directed exclusively to winners or best performers. By honoring accomplishments in leadership, sporting behavior, or service, awards

Shining Example

Ransburg Branch YMCA, Ransburg, Indiana

This full service YMCA provides family-oriented programs designed to develop the individual. According to its mission statement, this "Y" seeks to enhance the quality of life of people in the Greater Indianapolis Metropolitan area, particularly those who enroll as members and participate in the YMCA's Judeo-Christian values-oriented programs and services. This mission intends to use programs to develop, among other traits, self-confidence, responsibility, leadership, and optimum health.

Organization: The Ransburg Branch YMCA is operated on a volunteer leadership program through its branch Board of Managers. The Board is created by and responsible to the Metropolitan Board of Directors. It is responsible for the management of the branch including finances and programs, within approved goals.

Clientele: As many as 25,000 people.

Budget: $2.1 million annual operating budget.

Marketing: The Ransburg Branch YMCA target market is focused mainly on families. Following the family target market, the husband & wife category ranks 2nd. The following are ranked accordingly: senior citizens (3rd), adults and youth (4th) and children under 6 (5th).

Administrative Staff: The YMCA staff is divided into the following groups: 19 full-time staff, 200 part-time staff, 360 volunteers (Youth Sports Coaches, Parents of Preschoolers, Jr. High Leaders Club).

Program Detail: The Ransburg Branch YMCA currently oversees the following programs: Health & Fitness, Recreational Sports, Aquatics, Camping, Youth & Family Life, Youth Sports, and Parent-Child programs.

Facilities: The YMCA is located in a 55,000 sq. feet building that sits on 18 acres. It includes the following: 25 yard indoor pool, 50 meter outdoor pool, 2 gyms, 2 racquetball courts, indoor running track, 2 outdoor basketball courts, 1 baseball field, 1 multi-purpose field, free weights room, CYBEX room, 4 multi-purpose rooms, 3 classrooms, and a baby-sitting room.

encourage participation. You can treat the program or administrative participants like staff in recognizing their accomplishments.

Finally, you may incorporate the public relations and recognition tasks into a volunteer leadership position to offer opportunity for development. Participants can improve their sense of purpose by experiencing practical vocational situations, promote self-reliance by completing specified tasks on their own, and feel competent by practicing art, journalism, photography, telecommunications, and marketing skills.

RECOGNITION IN PARTICIPANT DEVELOPMENT

Recognition is a social expression for acknowledging accomplishment. In today's competitive society we reinforce those who aspire to succeed. We condition people from childhood to expect recognition when they meet their goals. As an example, consider the preschooler who receives a treat for accurately reciting the ABCs, or the first grader who gets money from Mom and Dad for a report card filled with As.

Consequently, we perceive recognition as a way to bolster self-esteem. Although we satisfy physiological (food and shelter), safety (security), and social needs (acceptance and affiliation) daily, we experience only sporadic ego gratification. Although this need provides a rationale for including recognition within recreational sport, it remains a controversial aspect of programming.

Exceptional performance and achievement in sport are customarily recognized through a tangible award. Historically, problems have arisen within athletic sport concerning this aspect of recognition. Whenever one agency gave awards to participants, another agency would attempt to outdo it. This rivalry continued until the cost of awards became prohibitive, and the trophies became more important than the desire to participate.

The shift in focus from enjoyment to accomplishment and victory has been gradual. Part of the responsibility for this change rested with programmers who recruited the best athletes to a program, regardless of consequences. Another factor was a lack of understanding about the effect awards have on participant attitudes.

The controversy over recognition has carried into recreational sport. Although recognition remains associated with athletic achievement and supremacy, the programmer can broaden its scope by acknowledging the efforts of participants, employees, and volunteers. Recognizing those who excel or reach a goal maintains interest, but an overemphasis on outcome discourages it. Honoring only the few who are capable of top performances conveys an attitude that anything short of excellence is unworthy of recognition. Limited opportunities for recognition foster apathy, resentment, and low self-esteem. When the system acknowledges involvement, improvement, and contribution, it encourages participation, reinforces program control, promotes goodwill, and aids participant development.

Participant development reinforces desirable behavior and serves as a learning opportunity for participants, employees, and volunteers.

The recognition system must acknowledge individual accomplishments to motivate learning and involvement. When guidelines for recognition are realistic and fair, individuals know what is required.

Types of Recognition

The methods available for bestowing recognition include awards, point systems, and personalized approach. When selecting types of recognition, consider the needs and characteristics of your clientele. For example, age is a factor. Recognition is not as significant to most children as it is to an older participant who places a social value on it.

Personal Approach

An effective form of recognition to offer to all participants, employees, and volunteers is the personal approach. The traditional recognition system acknowledges performance outcome and neglects performance output. For example, the softball player who hits three long fly balls that fall short of a home run gets little recognition. Although the performance (batting stance, swing, eye contact, follow-through) is excellent, the outcome is insufficient to merit recognition. A recognition system must consider effort. A simple handshake, smile, and thank-you may be all the reinforcement people need. These gestures require little effort but still promote goodwill. Intangible reinforcement that recognizes individual effort may do more to motivate individuals than tangible awards.

Awards

Many agencies use awards as the primary component of their recognition system because they cater to participants desiring evidence of individual merit. Many professionals in the field oppose their use, contending that tangible incentives should not be the basis of participation. Table 2.3 summarizes the advantages and disadvantages of awards.

The nature and value of an award should correspond to the accomplishment it represents. An award can be a meaningful memento or symbol of accomplishment, regardless of its monetary value. However, when the cost and attention associated with an award is out of proportion to the significance of the performance, individuals may develop unrealistic expectations toward participation. Once you give awards indiscriminately, they lose their value.

Many objects are used as awards within the recreational sport program. The most common are trophies, medals, medallions, plaques, clothing, certificates, ribbons, and accessories.

- **Trophies** may be awarded on a permanent or rotating basis, depending on the budget and philosophy of the setting.
- **Medals** are ideal for individual and meet events and may be used as platters, paperweights, wall hangings, or decorations on clothing. As with trophies, they permit the use of interchangeable sport figures. A color code usually indicates first place (gold), second place (silver), and third place (bronze).
- **Medallions** are similar to medals. Medallions are machine engraved and may include a custom design, such as the agency's logo or a sport motif. Depending on weight, a medallion may be suitable as part of a dish, paperweight, keychain, or charm.

- **Plaques** are ideal awards because of their durability and potential for engraving. Multiple plates are also available for adding names to permanent plaques.
- **T-shirts** are popular, especially among youth and young adults. The T-shirt may serve as a walking advertisement of the agency and event. Disadvantages include the expense of distributing them to many people, the space required to maintain stock in various sizes, and the expense and time required to handle special orders.
- **Certificates** represent the most simple and economical award because you can design them in advance and print them in bulk. Certificates customarily include the agency's name and logo, a blank line for the recipient's name, the purpose of the award, and a blank line for the signature of the program director.
- **Ribbons** of various sizes and colors are available in large quantities and you can purchase them before the sport program. Custommade ribbons often include the agency's name, event, and location. Traditional colors, representing place of finish are blue (first place), red (second place), and white (third place).
- **Rosettes** provide a more expensive and classier look than ribbons because of their ruffled perimeter.
- **Gift certificates** redeemable for items at a pro shop, sporting goods store, or a local merchant are another form of award. These awards do not supply identification with the agency or specific accomplishment.

Table 2.3 **Giving Awards**	
Advantages	**Disadvantages**
1. Recognizes achievement in a tangible way.	1. Emphasizes the award rather than inherent values of sport participation.
2. Serves as incentive for participation.	2. Involves more expense.
3. Provides an excellent public relations tool.	3. Stresses winning, promoting increased intensity of competition.
4. Fosters esprit de corps.	4. Recognizes a few highly skilled individuals or teams rather than a majority of participants.
5. Represents a way to recognize accomplishments in all program divisions—informal, intramural, and club sport.	5. Represents artificial incentives.

- **Desk items** are formal awards often given for adult program recognition: paperweights, calendars, pen and pencil sets, desk sets, ashtrays, envelope openers, name plates, mugs, and clocks.
- **Apparel and accessories** include jackets, blazers, sweaters, jerseys, sun visors, caps, cuff links, tie clasps, belt buckles, charm bracelets, pendants, blankets, patches, lapel pins, emblems, keychains, and team pictures. Each requires a system for maintaining an accurate inventory and adequate stock.

Point Systems

Point systems have had a traditional association with intramural sport programs on college campuses, but you also can use them for employee organizations, military bases, and other organizations with a consistent and accessible clientele. The point system may not be appropriate for community recreation or organizations with dispersed personnel. However, agencies are finding applications for them in programming areas such as fitness, club, and informal sport. The purpose of a point system is to stimulate interest and maintain participation by awarding points to individuals or teams that participate in designated sport activities. You may allocate additional points for

achievement. At the conclusion of an event, you can use the point tally in two ways: charting individual improvements in performance or ranking all the participants for comparison. Point systems, like awards, have their advantages and disadvantages (see table 2.4).

Point systems differ because of diverse program offerings and philosophy. Here are some suggestions to consider when designing a point system:

- Encourage involvement by many people. Take into account differences in age, ability, and interests to develop a suitable classification system.
- Encourage participation in diverse activities to enhance participant development.
- Establish realistic standards of accomplishment and communicate them to all potential participants.
- Maintain a simple point distribution process for easy interpretation and recording. Use a small point spread when allocating points to maintain involvement by as many people as possible over a long time.
- Recognize and allocate points based on participation and effort in addition to achievement and winning.

Table 2.4
Using Point Systems

Advantages	Disadvantages
1. Encourages participation.	1. Represents an artificial incentive system for participation.
2. Stimulates interest in an event that continues for an extended time.	2. Encourages forced participation just to receive points for the team or group.
3. Reorganizes both participation and performance.	3. Eliminates some activities because they cannot be quantified to fit into a point system.
4. Increases attendance.	4. Discourages participation if the focus is too much on excellence rather than participation.
5. Provides a standard system for determining recognition.	5. Discourages participation if the classification system for involvement is not equitable.
6. Encourages individuals to participate in a range of activities they might otherwise have hesitated to participate in.	6. Necessitates record keeping that is time consuming and a burden for office staff.
7. Stimulates goal-directed behavior, which motivates individuals to strive for improvement.	7. Encourages possible unsporting or unethical conduct to earn more points.
8. Fosters camaraderie.	8. Creates unnecessary pressure to excel.
9. Provides a way for individuals to measure their ability or achievement with past performance or the performance of others.	

- Don't allocate more points for activities requiring specialized skills.
- Recognize components of desirable behavior as well as performance.
- Maintain up-to-date records and communicate results regularly.

In addition to these suggestions, operational factors to consider when developing a point system include purpose, classification system, and point distribution.

- **Purpose.** The programmer must determine the purpose for the point system. Will you use the system to encourage participation, maintain interest, reward achievement, reinforce behavior, or serve as criteria for an awards system? Are you designing it for one event or for several events throughout a specified time span? Will you use the point system for individuals or groups? Without a clear explanation of its purpose, a point system is ineffective.
- **Classification.** To assign equitable point values, group similar events and activities together when possible. You could base classifications on the following:
  - Sport area—team sport, individual sport, dual sport, meet sport, club sport, and fitness
  - Skill level—advanced, intermediate, novice, and other
  - Special focus—major sports, minor sports, special events, and specific goals
  - Extent of involvement—number of teams, number of individuals, number of games or matches, length and type of tournament (round-robin, single elimination, challenge)
  - Degree of difficulty—physical skill, knowledge, endurance, and conditioning
  - Demographic background—age, sex, height, weight, size, and unit of participation

After choosing your classifications, keep the point distribution equitable in terms of performance standards. Although some events receive emphasis because of the higher point distribution assigned to them, the programmer should reassure the participants that all recreational sport activities receive equal treatment in programming considerations.

- **Point value designation.** The distribution of points should be simple. Keep the sum of the point scale as low as possible, even though participants enjoy accumulating a large point total. The lower the amount, the easier the computation of points and record keeping. Distribute points on a descending high-to-low order, giving the most points top placement. If you design the system to encourage participation, give points to all individuals and teams that enter. However, monitor those who enter events only for accumulating entry points without intending to participate. Failure to attend a scheduled activity is unacceptable, and the programmer should do whatever is necessary to discourage such behavior. If you design the point system to recognize performance, award bonus or advancement points for winning a contest or surpassing a designated goal. The following sections describe two methods of point distribution.

CRITERIA FOR RECOGNITION

You need criteria for recognition before you select the recipients. When you use formal recognition presentations, the criteria should follow an established policy in the agency's administrative manual. When possible, develop uniform criteria regardless of sport program area. Examples of recognition criteria to use with different target groups follow.

Recreational Sport Employee

Outstanding work performance

Reliability

Communication skills (written and oral)

Conflict resolution skills

Volunteer service

Successful employment evaluations

Customer service skills

Recreational Sport Volunteer

Ability to promote participation

Enthusiasm

Contributions

Cooperation

Dependability

Competency

Attendance

Recreational Sport Participant

Degree of participation in team sport, lifetime sport, meet events, club sport

Above average sport skill, demonstrated by success in the sport

Positive attitude for sporting behavior, citizenship, fair play, and honesty

Leadership contributions to group or team

Effort to improve group or team morale

Compliance with established rules and regulations

Ability to promote participation and sporting behavior

After defining the award criteria, choose a panel of judges to select the deserving recipients. Conduct the judging process professionally to preserve credibility.

Recognition Presentations

Recognition presentations usually follow an activity or occur later with a formal presentation, reception, or banquet. Proponents of the first approach contend that the excitement level is at its highest immediately following an event and recognition received then is more significant to the recipient. On the other hand, recognition for individual outstanding achievement, unusual service, and other significant awards are appropriate for special ceremonies distinct from an activity. Although the thrill of an achievement may have waned, the opportunity for the recipient to relive the experience with teammates, relatives, peers, and other participants in the program is a rewarding one. Examples of such ceremonies include a seasonal or year-end party, recognition banquet, an annual sport dinner, and a reception.

Regardless of when or how you give recognition, plan your presentations carefully. Make certain that the presenter is knowledgeable about the purpose of the recognition. Whenever possible, select someone who has a positive rapport with the recipient or someone who witnessed the event for which the recognition is being given. Keep the presentation brief. Recipients and audiences have little patience for long speeches or delays in the ceremonies.

Formal ceremonies, receptions, or banquets require time and effort to assure that they will run smoothly. Approach these events from the same perspective as sport programs in terms of the ef-fort needed to plan, conduct, and evaluate them. It makes little sense to develop a sound recognition concept only to have the presentation fail.

ADA Suggestions

Participant development opportunities are important to provide for all individuals regardless of interests and abilities. Recreational sport programs and facilities are places where every individual can become a fully functioning member of the community. In fact, we can now extend all the benefits of the recreational sport experience to any person with a disability. In enacting the ADA in 1990, Congress maintained the broadly defined term of *disability* used in the Rehabilitation Act of 1973. Under the ADA, three categories of individuals with disabilities are protected:

Individuals who *have* a physical or mental impairment that substantially limits one or more major life activities; individuals that have a *record* of a physical or mental impairment that substantially limited one or more of the individual's major life activities; and individuals who are *regarded as having* such an impairment, whether they have the impairment or not (Department of Justice 1993, 9).

If an individual meets one of these criteria, he or she is considered an individual with a disability and is protected under the Americans With Disabilities Act. For the purposes of the ADA, a *major life activity* includes caring for oneself, speaking, hearing, seeing, breathing, learning, or working.

In many instances, if people's (participant or staff) attitudes are negative, they can be a greater obstacle in implementing the ADA than the steepest path or sharpest turn. Negative attitudes about people with disabilities exist for many reasons. These negative attitudes, which can result in discriminatory practices, are usually from lack of exposure and education about people with disabilities. It is our professional responsibility to turn these negative attitudes into positive ones by being proactive in programming by making rule modifications and facility renovations to participation This can have a positive impact on all Americans.

CONCLUSION

Sport is a mini-society because it holds opportunities for individual growth that parallel those found outside the sport environment. Benefits occur from active participation in sport and exercise, through rules and regulations, due process, peer discipline, winning and losing, and competition. The recreational sport programmer has an opportunity and a responsibility to enhance the quality of life for people of all ages, interests, and abilities. A commitment to participant development is central to attaining this goal. A major factor in program design and delivery is recognition of the participant. This enhances the enjoyment and satisfaction of participating in recreational sport.

DISCUSSION QUESTIONS

1. How would you implement a participant development system in your recreational sport program on a daily basis?

2. What is the difference between the terms *human growth* and *development*, and why are these concepts important to recreational sport programmers?

3. How can recreational sport programmers influence participant development in their sport programs?

4. What is a *life stage*? In general, how do human growth and development progress at each stage?

5. At what age and life stage do we first understand rules and regulations?

6. How might we justify a recreational sport program as an important aspect of life on a military base?

7. What type of experience exposes the adolescent to the effects of competitive and cooperative behavior on group goals, objectives, and morale?

8. What life stage in the developmental group process is essential in making the individual search for his or her identity?

9. Explain how the governance process in an intramural sport program could lead to participant development.

10. What do we mean by the phrase *recreational sport is really a minisociety*? Do you agree that we should refer to recreational sport with this phrase?

11. What are the similarities and differences between *program participant* and *program leader* as they relate to participant development in a recreational sport environment?

12. Is the developmental approach to recreational sport programming a new concept? Explain.

13. What is the key word or concept in maintaining objectivity in the governance process?

14. How can recreational sport personnel (full-time and part-time) have a developmental impact on participants?

15. What are some advantages and disadvantages to participant development in recreational sport as described in the chapter?

APPLICATION EXERCISE

You have been analyzing your recreational sport program to determine whether its offerings are diverse enough in appeal and opportunity for participants to find a suitable, enjoyable activity. Briefly explain why a broad spectrum of sport activities are desirable when considered from a

a) physiological standpoint (e.g., safety, learning skills),

b) sociological standpoint (e.g., acceptance, meeting new people), and

c) psychological standpoint (e.g., challenge, emotional control).

REFERENCES

Bryant, J., and J. Bradley. 1993. Enhancing academic productivity, student development and employment potential. *National Intramural-Recreational Sports Association Journal* 17 (3): 42-44.

Department of Justice. 1993. *The Americans With Disabilities Act*: *Title III technical assistance manual*. Washington, DC: Bureau of National Affairs.

Miller, T.K., and J.S. Prince. 1977. *The future of student affairs*. San Francisco: Jossey-Bass.

SUGGESTED READINGS

Broughton, J.C., and D. Griffin. 1994. Collegiate intramurals, where do they go from here? *National Intramural-Recreational Sports Association Journal* 18 (1): 10-11.

Chesnutt, J.T., P.J. Nadeau, and W. Taylor. 1985. *An analysis of nonparticipation in campus recreational sports activities*. Paper presented at the 1985 National Intramural-Recreational Sports Association Conference, Columbus, OH.

Kaufman, J.E. 1987. Enhancing the quality of life on campus. *National Intramural-Recreational Sports Association Journal* 11 (2): 3.

Milton, P.R. 1992. Relating student development theory to women's recreational sports participation. *National Intramural-Recreational Sports Association Journal* 17 (1): 3-4, 6-7.

Smith, L.G. 1993. Developmental theories and models for today's changing student populations. *National Intramural-Recreational Sports Association Journal* 17 (3): 20-23.

Snodgrass, M.L., and C.E. Tinsley. 1990. Recreation and wellness: Identifying motivations for participation in recreational sports. *National Intramural-Recreational Sports Association Journal* 15 (1): 34-38.

Todaro, E. 1993. The impact of recreational sports on student development: A theoretical model. *National Intramural-Recreational Sports Association Journal* 17 (3): 23-26.

Todaro, E. 1993. Introduction to participant development. *National Intramural-Recreational Sports Association Journal* 17 (3): 14-15.

PART II

Program Delivery Systems

CHAPTER 3

Fitness

Chapter Objectives

After reading this chapter you will

- understand the role of fitness as it relates to wellness,
- identify participant fitness as a goal in recreational sport programming,
- identify components of total fitness in recreational sport, and
- understand the direct and indirect programming methods recreational sport managers use to deliver fitness programming.

The demand for fitness sessions, increased purchases of home fitness machines, larger attendance in fitness classes, and more participation in recreational sport programs demonstrate that more people are valuing fitness. In fact, when asked why they participate in a recreational sport program, people are most likely to answer "to have fun" or "to get fit." Many of those who list having fun as their reason for participating in a recreational sport program also believe they are reaping health rewards by doing so.

This chapter discusses the fitness initiative in the United States and touches on how good fitness relates to good health. Next, it discusses components of fitness. A grounding in the health and performance components of fitness provides a foundation for understanding and programming fitness. Finally, we addresses two methods of fitness program delivery: indirect and direct.

FITNESS AND EXERCISE INITIATIVE

Establishing citizen fitness is an important goal for nations around the world. More than 30 countries are part of the *Sport for All* concept that documents efforts of nations to create and support fitness programs nationally. These initiatives yield impressive results as mass sport events, competitive walking and running campaigns, physical fitness demonstration days, individual fitness incentives and awards, and support for many sport and fitness opportunities for the public.

In America, the Office of Disease Prevention and Health Promotion's focus has shifted from reducing sickness to preventing disease and pro-

moting better health. Research findings agree that inactivity, high stress, and poor nutrition are risk factors that can bring on illness and shorten life expectancy, whereas healthy behaviors can improve longevity and the quality of life (Blair, Kohl, and Gordon 1992). As part of the effort to create a national focus on health, the U.S. Department of Health and Human Services published *Healthy People 2000: National Health Promotion and Diseases Prevention Objectives*. This document sets public health goals for Americans that will alleviate risk factors and promote healthy behaviors. Among the goals for the year 2000 are the following:

- Increase to at least 30 percent the proportion of people age 6 and older who engage regularly, preferably daily, in light to moderate physical activity (less than 50 percent $\dot{V}O_2$max) for at least 30 minutes per day.
- Increase to at least 20 percent the proportion of people age 18 and older, and to at least 75 percent the proportion of children and adolescents age 6 through 17, who engage in vigorous physical activity (greater than 50 percent $\dot{V}O_2$max) that promotes the development and maintenance of cardiorespiratory fitness three or more days per week for 20 or more minutes per occasion.

As you can see, these goals and many others like them reflect the consensus that activity among all ages needs to increase to improve health and fitness. In his book, *Fitness and sports medicine: A health-related approach*, David Nieman (1995) refers to the status of these activity levels, specifically stating the following:

- Few Americans exercise enough.
- Women and the elderly exercise less.
- People with higher income exercise more.
- The exercise boom has plateaued. (P. 9-12)

Achieving the initiatives for a healthier America begins with increasing fitness offerings in kindergarten through 12th grade physical education programs, college and university recreational sport, work site physical activity, and public agency and commercial fitness programs. Although the school system provides a large portion of fitness education, our mission as programmers is to recognize that, regardless of the setting, recreational sport program goals underscore the need to improve healthy behaviors through participation in physical activity.

Recreational sport programs can provide opportunity for physical fitness experiences. Involvement in physical activity leads to participation in a spectrum of sport programs. This progressive involvement counteracts a sedentary lifestyle and stimulates participation in sport and fitness programs that can improve physical fitness.

Through recreational sport, we can improve our health and help ward off those illnesses that result from poor fitness. Fitness as a recreational sport program goal is best described by the reasons corporations have designed sport and fitness programs for the workplace:

- Lower insurance premiums and health-related claims
- Improve morale and productivity
- Ensure health awareness and education
- Improve recruitment of quality employees

According to the National Employee Services and Recreation Association, corporations and organizations develop sport programs around the goal of fitness. Fitness is also the goal in military sport programs, in therapeutic recreation settings, and in most settings where recreational sport opportunities are available. Newly constructed YMCAs and similar organizations attest that fitness is a major goal of most recreational sport organizations.

COMPONENTS OF FITNESS

Sport managers must incorporate fitness and health basics into the programming goals. In order for you to incorporate fitness goals into a recreational sport program, you must understand the components needed to achieve total fitness. These involve the physical and mental health associated with good nutrition, exercise, positive health practices, and an optimistic outlook on life. With this in mind, let's examine the physical aspect of fitness, then discuss how sport and exercise programming can contribute to physical fitness.

Physical Aspect of Fitness

Table 3.1 divides the measurable elements of physical fitness into two groups (performance components and health components) and provides a list of sport programming options that support the development of each group.

Health Components of Fitness

Health-related components of physical fitness contribute to well-being by reducing the risk of degenerative diseases, increasing work efficiency, and improving the quality of life. These components include cardiovascular and muscular endurance, strength, flexibility, and body composition:

- **Cardiorespiratory endurance** refers to the capacity of the heart, lungs, and blood vessels to function efficiently during vigorous muscular activity over time. Unless the heart, circulatory, and respiratory systems function efficiently, insufficient oxygen supply impairs activity.

- **Muscular endurance** is the capacity of a muscle group to apply and sustain force over time. Muscle endurance helps maintain good posture, resist fatigue, and prevent injuries.

- **Muscular strength** refers to the maximum force a muscle or muscle group can exert against resistance. In athletes, strength has been a traditional symbol of fitness for many years. Although developing and maintaining muscular strength leads to an attractive physique, its major fitness benefits are protecting the joints and preventing injury during participation.

- **Flexibility** refers to the capability of the joints to enjoy a full range of movement. When the joints are not exercised often enough through a full range of motion, the surrounding connective tissues can't retain their normal length and flexibility. Lower back pain and postural misalignment are problems associated with inflexibility. Limited range of motion in a joint decreases the functional capabilities of the muscles around that joint. A reduced range of motion often involves compensation from the proper mechanical principles of a movement, lowering the performance level and possibly resulting in injury.

- **Body composition** has also received recognition as an important component of fitness. Most people use total body weight as the indicator of health, rather than the relationship between fat and lean body mass. Because muscle is denser than fat, body weight is a deceptive measure. Although concern with weight is understandable, it is the ratio of body fat to weight that reflects a healthy body. Meeting the recommended percentage of lean body fat will improve performance and decrease problems associated with obesity, such as hypertension,

Table 3.1
Measurable Elements of Physical Fitness and Sport Programming Options

Performance-related components of fitness	Health-related components of fitness
1. Agility	1. Cardiovascular endurance
2. Power	2. Muscular endurance
3. Coordination	3. Muscular strength
4. Speed	4. Flexibility
5. Reaction time	5. Body composition
6. Balance	

Performance-related fitness	Both	Health-related fitness
Archery	Basketball	Aerobic dance
Badminton	Handball	Backpacking
Baseball	Ice skating	Bicycling
Bowling	Racqetball	Calisthenics
Downhill Skiing	Roller skating	Cross-country skiing
Fencing	Squash	Rope jumping
Football		Rowing
Golf		Running
Soccer		Snowshoeing
Table tennis		Stair climbing
Tennis		Swimming
Volleyball		Walking
		Weight lifting

Adapted from Caspersen, C.J., Powell, K.E., Christenson, G.M. Physical Activity, Exercise, and Physical Fitness: Definitions and Distinctions for Health-Related Research. Public Health Rep 100:126-131, 1985.

diabetes mellitus, gall bladder disease, degenerative arthritis, digestive diseases, respiratory infections, kidney disease, and posture dysfunction.

Performance Components of Fitness

Performance components are the skills important for enjoyable participation in recreational sport activities. These components involve agility, power, coordination, speed, reaction time, and balance:

• **Agility** refers to an ability to change the direction of the body or body parts rapidly. This involves speed, accuracy, and control in making quick starts and stops; rapid changes of direction; and efficient footwork. Influenced by heredity, agility improves through practice, training, and instruction involving reaction time, strength, and coordination of the large muscle groups.

• **Power** is defined as the ability to transfer energy into a fast rate of speed. Participants capable of combining strength with movement speed are considered powerful. Power is exhibited in activities such as shot putting, rowing, pitching, and punting.

• **Coordination** is the integration of muscular movements necessary to execute a task smoothly. Heredity tends to affect coordination. Although it is possible to improve coordination through practice, progress is often specific to the task, so the programmer should offer a range of recreational sport activities.

• **Speed** is the rate at which a person moves his or her body or body parts from one point to another. Speed of movement is exemplified in running, boxing, swimming, skating, fencing, and lacrosse.

• **Reaction time** is time required to initiate a response to a stimulus. Individuals who have quick reaction times make fast starts in football, swimming, or running events; react quickly to a moving baseball or basketball; and move rapidly to dodge or defend against attacks in fencing or martial arts.

• **Balance** involves an ability to maintain body position. Static balance is the ability to maintain equilibrium while in a standing position. Dynamic balance is the ability to maintain equilibrium while moving or performing some task. Three major principles affecting balance are the following:

- • **Center of gravity**—the lower the center of gravity, the greater the balance and stability.

- • **Base of support**—the larger the base of support, the greater the balance and stability.

- • **Relationship between center of gravity and base of support**—the closer the center of gravity is to the center of the base of support, the greater the balance and stability.

Sport and Exercise Contributions to Fitness

To maximize the benefits from health and performance-related fitness, we should help individuals learn which sport and exercise activities contribute to each aspect of physical fitness.

Table 3.2 demonstrates health benefits of sport and other activities. Each sport is rated according to its contribution to health-related fitness components.

Benefits to health from sport participation depend on the frequency, intensity, and duration of participation. The ratings in table 3.2 require that the sport be performed regularly. Determining the relationship of sport or exercise to health-related fitness requires an understanding of the following:

- • **Fitness training zone.** Identify a range of participation from the minimum necessary to improve fitness to a maximum amount, beyond which activity may be counterproductive. This continuum constitutes the fitness training zone.

- • **Overload principle.** To improve an aspect of health-related fitness, engage in more than normal (overload) participation.

- • **Threshold of training.** Identify the minimum amount of participation that will improve each aspect of health-related fitness.

Just as there are sports and exercises that contribute to health benefits, table 3.3 demonstrates which aspects of performance-related fitness various sports require. We have based the ratings on

recreational participation. A *Poor* rating means no skill is needed, *Fair* means little skill is needed, *Good* means some skill is needed, and *Excellent* means much skill is required for that sport.

Physical fitness requires regular exercise. The recreational sport programmer contributes to participant fitness by promoting exercise opportunities, rather than leaving participation to chance. Sport and exercise are the primary techniques of fitness programming. Exercise, as a fitness activity, involves vigorous or continuous physical activity. You can exercise without participating in a sport, for example, riding a stationary bike. Most people engage in an exercise program to attain a specific fitness outcome. Sport, on the other hand, encompasses a broad category of nonwork activity that may or may not involve exercise. Those who engage in sport may do so for fun and socialization, with little regard for fitness.

Because of differences in participant preferences and fitness benefits from sport activity, an informal sport program should provide a variety of activities. Programmers should make facilities, equipment, and playing partners accessible. Otherwise, any inconvenience involved in making these arrangements becomes a deterrent to participation.

Fitness programs emphasizing the health-related components of fitness must recognize that results are affected by the type, frequency, and duration of the workout. Calisthenics and weight training contribute very little to cardiorespiratory endurance and require supplemental activity to stimulate the heart and lungs. A sound exercise program offers variety. Because people vary in fitness level, body structure, motivation, and fitness needs, an individual approach to assessment and exercise may be more beneficial than a group approach.

FITNESS DELIVERY

Today, people of all ages, body types, and sport preferences are demonstrating interest in an active, healthy lifestyle. An awareness of the benefits of regular exercise and sport activity does not guarantee participation. People need encouragement and facility convenience to make time available for regular involvement.

If fitness improvements are going to take place, programmers need to counter the sedentary patterns perpetuated by the rise of technology. We must program exercise and sport into current lifestyles and encourage participation as a lifetime pursuit.

Table 3.2
Health-Related Benefits of Sports and Other Activities

Sport or Activity	Develops Cardiovascular Endurance	Develops Strength	Develops Muscular Endurance	Develops Flexibility	Helps Control Fatness	Lifetime Sport or Activity
Archery	Poor	Fair	Poor	Poor	Poor	x
Backpacking	Good	Good	Excellent	Fair	Good	x
Badminton	Good	Poor	Fair	Fair	Good	x
Baseball	Poor	Poor	Poor	Poor	Fair	
Basketball	Excellent	Poor	Fair	Poor	Good	
Bowling	Poor	Poor	Poor	Poor	Poor	x
Canoeing	Fair	Poor	Fair	Poor	Fair	x
Dance, ballet	Good	Good	Good	Excellent	Fair	
Dance, disco	Good	Poor	Good	Fair	Good	x
Dance, modern	Good	Fair	Good	Excellent	Good	
Dance, social	Fair	Poor	Fair	Poor	Fair	x
Fencing	Fair	Fair	Good	Fair	Fair	
Football	Fair	Good	Fair	Poor	Fair	
Golf (walking)	Fair	Poor	Poor	Fair	Fair	x
Gymnastics	Fair	Excellent	Excellent	Excellent	Fair	
Handball	Good	Poor	Good	Poor	Good	x
Hiking	Good	Fair	Excellent	Fair	Good	x
Horseback riding	Poor	Poor	Poor	Poor	Poor	x
Judo	Poor	Fair	Fair	Fair	Poor	x
Karate	Poor	Fair	Fair	Fair	Poor	x
Mountain climbing	Good	Good	Good	Poor	Fair	x
Pool; billiards	Poor	Poor	Poor	Poor	Poor	x
Racquetball; paddleball	Good	Poor	Good	Poor	Good	x
Rowing, crew	Excellent	Fair	Excellent	Poor	Excellent	
Sailing	Poor	Poor	Poor	Poor	Poor	x
Skating, ice	Good	Poor	Good	Poor	Fair	x
Skating, roller	Fair	Poor	Fair	Poor	Fair	x
Skiing, cross-country	Excellent	Fair	Good	Poor	Excellent	x
Skiing, downhill	Poor	Fair	Fair	Poor	Poor	x
Soccer	Excellent	Fair	Good	Fair	Good	
Softball (fast)	Poor	Poor	Poor	Poor	Fair	
Softball (slow)	Poor	Poor	Poor	Poor	Fair	x
Surfing	Fair	Poor	Good	Fair	Fair	
Table tennis	Poor	Poor	Poor	Poor	Poor	x
Tennis	Fair	Poor	Fair	Poor	Fair	x
Volleyball	Fair	Fair	Poor	Poor	Poor	x
Waterskiing	Fair	Fair	Fair	Poor	Poor	

From *Fitness for Life* by Charles B. Corbin and Ruth Lindsey. Copyright © 1979 Scott, Foresman and Company, p. 169. Reprinted by permission.

Table 3.3
Performance-Related Benefits of Sports and Other Activities

Activity	Balance	Coordination	Reaction time	Agility	Power	Speed
Archery	Good	Excellent	Poor	Poor	Poor	Poor
Backpacking	Fair	Fair	Poor	Fair	Fair	Poor
Badminton	Fair	Excellent	Good	Good	Fair	Good
Baseball	Good	Excellent	Excellent	Good	Excellent	Good
Basketball	Good	Excellent	Excellent	Excellent	Excellent	Good
Bicycling	Excellent	Fair	Fair	Poor	Poor	Fair
Bowling	Good	Excellent	Poor	Fair	Fair	Fair
Canoeing	Good	Good	Fair	Poor	Good	Poor
Circuit training	Fair	Fair	Poor	Fair	Good	Fair
Dance, aerobic	Fair	Good	Fair	Good	Poor	Poor
Dance, ballet	Excellent	Excellent	Fair	Excellent	Good	Poor
Dance, disco	Fair	Good	Fair	Excellent	Poor	Fair
Dance, modern	Excellent	Excellent	Fair	Excellent	Good	Poor
Dance, social	Fair	Good	Fair	Good	Poor	Fair
Fencing	Good	Excellent	Excellent	Good	Good	Excellent
Fitness; calisthenics	Fair	Fair	Poor	Fair	Fair	Poor
Football	Good	Good	Excellent	Excellent	Excellent	Excellent
Golf (walking)	Fair	Excellent	Poor	Fair	Good	Poor
Gymnastics	Excellent	Excellent	Good	Excellent	Excellent	Fair
Handball	Fair	Excellent	Good	Good	Good	Good
Hiking	Fair	Fair	Poor	Fair	Fair	Poor
Horseback riding	Good	Good	Fair	Good	Poor	Poor
Interval training	Fair	Fair	Poor	Poor	Poor	Fair
Jogging	Fair	Fair	Poor	Poor	Poor	Poor
Judo	Good	Excellent	Excellent	Excellent	Excellent	Excellent
Karate	Good	Excellent	Excellent	Excellent	Excellent	Excellent
Mountain climbing	Excellent	Excellent	Fair	Good	Good	Poor
Pool; billiards	Fair	Good	Poor	Fair	Fair	Poor
Racquetball; paddleball	Fair	Excellent	Good	Good	Fair	Good
Rope jumping	Fair	Good	Fair	Good	Fair	Poor
Rowing, crew	Fair	Excellent	Poor	Good	Excellent	Fair
Sailing	Good	Good	Good	Good	Fair	Poor
Skating, ice	Excellent	Good	Fair	Good	Fair	Good
Skating, roller	Excellent	Good	Poor	Good	Fair	Good
Skiing, cross-country	Fair	Excellent	Poor	Good	Excellent	Fair
Skiing, downhill	Excellent	Excellent	Good	Excellent	Good	Poor
Soccer	Fair	Excellent	Good	Excellent	Good	Good
Softball (fast)	Fair	Excellent	Excellent	Good	Good	Good
Softball (slow)	Fair	Excellent	Good	Fair	Good	Good
Surfing	Excellent	Excellent	Good	Excellent	Good	Poor
Swimming (laps)	Fair	Good	Poor	Good	Fair	Poor
Table tennis	Fair	Good	Good	Fair	Fair	Fair
Tennis	Fair	Excellent	Good	Good	Good	Good
Volleyball	Fair	Excellent	Good	Good	Fair	Fair
Walking	Fair	Fair	Poor	Poor	Poor	Poor
Waterskiing	Good	Good	Poor	Good	Fair	Poor
Weight training	Fair	Fair	Poor	Poor	Fair	Poor

From *Fitness for Life* by Charles B. Corbin and Ruth Lindsey. Copyright © 1979 Scott, Foresman and Company, p. 129. Reprinted by permission.

Shining Example

The Body Shop, University of Illinois at Urbana-Champaign

The University of Illinois at Urbana-Champaign's McKinley Health Center offers a fitness program known as "The Body Shop Stations." This program is geared towards university students who are interested in wellness and fitness. They are asked to complete five specific worksheets focused on flexibility, body composition, muscular strength, aerobic capacity, and nutrition. After completing the five specific worksheets and tasks, they are asked to take a nutrition quiz and then return their packet to "The Body Shop." The body shop staff will have the student complete an evaluation form and then the student is eligible for a free campus recreation fitness program pass. This program is designed to assess the students current fitness levels and knowledge and then ultimately get them interested in a fitness program.

Organization: The Body Shop is an organization offered for students at the University of Illinois at Urbana-Champaign. The program, which is also run by students, is designed to access students' fitness levels and knowledge and to get the students interested in fitness programs.

Clientele: The clients of The Body Shop are made up of the following: students, faculty, and staff of the University of Illinois at Urbana-Champaign.

Budget: As this program is predominately run by students, the Body Shop's budget is estimated to be between $500 and $600. This money is used for the following supplies: grip strength, tape measures, calculators, 8-inch benches, boom box, and goniometer.

Marketing: Since this program is required for HPER majors at the University of Illinois at Urbana-Champaign, marketing is not that important. However, what little marketing is done is through residence assistants, Greek peer advisors, and brochures.

Staff: The Body Shop is a volunteer-based program which is made up of 3 full-time staff and 6 part-time staff (undergraduate students).

Program Detail: The Body Shop focuses on 5 different areas: flexibility, body composition, muscular strength, aerobic capacity and nutrition. The Body Shop then evaluates students based on the different areas and if the student is eligible, he/she receives a free campus recreation fitness program pass.

Facilities: Since the Body Shop is portable, it's the only facility operated.

Table 3.4
Fitness Delivery Systems

Indirect fitness programming	Direct fitness programming
• Instructional	• Testing
• Informal	• Monitoring
• Intramural and extramural	• Assessment
• Club	

As table 3.4 shows, you can offer fitness programming to participants indirectly, through instructional, informal, intramural, extramural, and club programming, and directly, through exercise consultation. Neither approach is more important than the other, but they are different in application and purpose.

Indirect delivery represents a recreation and leisure studies application and places the role of fitness as a benefit of the recreational sport experience, not as a goal for staff to monitor. In this process, the participant is motivated by fun, socialization, and the outcome of participation. The individual seeks the benefits of the recreational sport experiences, and the programmers provide these.

Direct delivery represents a physical education and kinesiology application that influences fitness through direct supervision. Here, trained and certified fitness specialists apply the fitness techniques of testing, exercise consultation, and monitoring and supervise the participant.

You can deliver fitness directly, through testing and assessment, and indirectly, from participation in program areas. The more influence you have on the person's fitness level, the greater responsibility you have in teaching and leadership. It is not the recreational sport manager's concern to provide direct fitness prescription for all involvement in recreational sport. To understand the differences, the remainder of this chapter will discuss two areas of fitness delivery. First we'll examine the indirect fitness delivery systems. Then we'll look at fitness testing as it relates to direct programmatic issues.

Indirect Delivery Systems

Here we present the delivery of specific fitness formats within the recreational sport spectrum and the participant programming involved. In this portion of program delivery, people with a background in recreational sport management develop programs to meet the goals of fun and fitness. In these programmatic areas, you may hire a fitness specialist to deliver classes requiring more specialization, such as aerobic or weight-training classes. Managing these program areas still rests, however, with the recreational sport specialist. The specific programmatic areas are instructional, informal, intramural, extramural, and club.

Instructional Sport and Fitness

In situations where resources limit providing fitness testing or special activity and event programs, a program may be limited to educational functions. Common approaches that you can take to educate participants include clinics and workshops, lecture series, media presentations, and establishing a fitness planning center. The shining example on page 44 describes an assessment program to develop fitness awareness.

Clinics and workshops are helpful when information is too difficult or lengthy to explain in printed materials, when the information requires demonstration, when it will receive better attention if you can answer questions on the spot, and when the participant needs to try an activity.

Orientation workshops can focus on equipment use, exercise sessions, and the role of weight-room consultants. You can schedule these as needed or set them up and promote them regularly. The time for these events ranges from one hour to two days.

In contrast, a lecture series is not designed for participant interaction, other than a question and answer period. A speaker simply addresses an audience on a fitness or health topic. The format may offer different views on the same topic, involve several speakers, involve one speaker on many related topics, or provide an in-depth view of a topic over several sessions. You can schedule events successively on the same day, during a weekend, or over a number of weeks. Generally this format should not exceed one and one-half hours per topic. Fitness-related topics are wide ranging as shown by table 3.5.

In instances where knowledgeable, credible, and effective speakers are unavailable, use films and slide or tape presentations. This is an expensive approach when rental fees are involved, but most professional audiovisual pieces are effective attention getters. Always preview your material for appropriateness and accuracy before use. Pamphlets and brochures address a variety of topics, and you can obtain them through local, state, or national health organizations or medical and professional

---

Table 3.5
Fitness-Related Topics for Lectures, Workshops, and Clinics

Aging and exercise

Alcohol, drugs, smoking, and exercise

Body awareness

Cardiovascular system

Cardiac rehabilitation

Clothing and footwear

Conditioning
  Specificity
  Overload
  Frequency, intensity, duration
  Warm-up
  Cool-down

Exercise
  Intensity
  Duration
  Frequency
  Target heart rate
  Exercise prescription
  Medical screening

Flexibility
  Ballistic stretch
  Static stretch
  Stretch reflex
  Specificity

Heart disease

Injury prevention
  Blisters
  Muscle soreness
  Runner's knee
  Achilles tendonitis
  Shinsplints
  Stress fractures
  Stone bruises
  Dehydration
  Heat stroke
  Heat exhaustion

Nutrition
  Adequate diet
  Fats
  Carbohydrates
  Protein
  Minerals
  Vitamins
  Fiber
  Water
  Cholesterol
  Triglyceride level
  Salt
  Sugar
  Fast foods
  Food preparation

Posture and body mechanics

Pregnancy

Relaxation

Risk factors
  Age, sex, family history
  High blood pressure
  Diet
  Cigarette smoking
  Heart disease
  Stress
  Glucose intolerance
  Inactivity

Sport
  Endurance
  Muscular strength
  Flexibility
  Agility
  Coordination
  Reaction time
  Balance
  Power

Strength development
  Isometric
  Isotonic
  Isokinetic

Stress management
  Alarm, resistance, exhaustive stages
  Body responses to stress
  Stress-related problems
  Role of exercise

Test for fitness
  Cardiovascular
  Muscle strength
  Muscle endurance
  Flexibility
  Body composition
  Balance
  Agility
  Power
  Reaction time
  Speed
  Coordination

Training programs
  Continuous exercise
  Internal training
  Circuit training
  Strength training
  Mode of training

Weight control
  Overweight, underweight, or obese
  Calorie needs
  Exercise
  Diet and nutrition

---

associations, often free of charge. However, distribution of printed materials alone precludes an opportunity to rectify misconceptions, emphasize important points, and secure feedback.

A newsletter is a useful communication medium for a specific readership. It may include announcements, fitness and safety tips, articles, a fitness hot line for questions and answers, surveys, program reminders, recommended reading lists, and addresses for obtaining outside materials. TV and radio are also valuable tools for increasing fitness awareness. Success requires familiarity with avail-

able options and wisdom in selecting qualified spokespersons. The main types of public service broadcasts include full-length specials, panel discussions, interviews, and shorter segments, such as news stories, announcements, and editorials. Some stations program regular spots for fitness tips. Because competition for public service air time is intense, effective preparation and presentation are essential for obtaining continued access.

Posting attractive and informative materials about fitness and related topics on bulletin boards is underestimated as an effective mechanism to promote awareness. Such materials are inexpensive and reusable. Most public and private buildings and sport facilities have bulletin boards or display cases, so your sole expense may be for materials and artwork. Change your materials frequently (every two to four weeks) to maintain viewer interest.

A fitness consultation center can help participants assess their knowledge and interests regarding sport and fitness and familiarize them with existing opportunities. A center serves as an assessment, planning, and referral system, and clearing house for those interested in discovering their current fitness level, modifying detrimental habits, and deciding future sport and fitness endeavors.

Also included in instructional sport are fitness classes guided by a qualified instructor. These may take place in a fitness room, in a pool, outside, at home, and so forth. The main point is that these programs offer the structure of a class and the guidance of a trained leader to create a safe and effective workout environment. The instructional portion of the class is learning how to monitor intensity, specific routines, the phases of a workout, and what to expect with each portion of the class.

The instructional sport area features personal training, which involves one-on-one instruction. This is a growing area of interest. Personal trainers create an instructional class of one and are good about getting people started on exercise. As this guidance increases the self-reliance of an individual to engage in fitness and sport programming, personal trainers are less essential.

Informal Sport and Fitness

In all recreational sport, the most popular form of participation is informal sport. All agencies that recognize this form of participation can enhance their reputation by providing well-managed, self-directed sport opportunity. This unstructured, casual, and general supervision process allows individuals to participate in their own style. In the commercial industry, via tennis clubs, racquet clubs, weight-lifting clubs, and so forth, a person who wants to exercise, when they want and how they want, joins through a membership or enters as a participant. To work out according to a schedule you want increases involvement and makes this industry a success. In this case, marketing the fitness benefit creates and maintains participation. The noncommercial settings, such as colleges, public agencies, universities, and military bases are subsidized by state or federal funds and have fitness as one of many program goals.

Sport brings about exercise in many settings. You can sponsor informal sport to enhance fitness for those who choose to participate. Sometimes in these settings, resources for structured sport activity or even fitness activity programs are limited. You can encourage people to participate through self-directed sport, based on their needs and interests. Recreational sport programmers aid in this process by promoting information on facility hours and equipment available and by maintaining personal fitness profile cards on participants and providing incentive for their continued involvement. The cost for informal sport is low, yet it creates a self-directed opportunity for many people.

Keep in mind that a self-directed program does not involve setting up specific activities or events, but helps people understand the advantages and disadvantages of their current sport and exercise patterns and provides incentives for fitness improvement. Fitness testing helps participants maintain a record of their results and monitor their progress. Provide a log for those interested in monitoring how their participation contributes to fitness. Form 3.1 is a typical page from a fitness log.

To further motivate participation, use an award points system based on the intensity and duration of sport or exercise. The aerobics point system developed by Cooper is based on research that indicates this form of exercise is the most beneficial to cardiovascular conditioning. It suggests that keeping records of personal progress is a great motivational tool. An example of such a chart is provided in form 3.2.

An additional motivation technique is to recognize those who achieve their goal. In addition to certificates and trophies, other effective incentives are to recognize participants in the newspaper, establish 25-, 50-, 100-mile clubs with presentations of T-shirts or other clothing items, give discount coupons for sporting goods stores, implement the Presidential Physical Fitness Award and Sports Programs, or give discount prices for enrollment in other sport programs.

A fitness trail often stimulates people to participate regularly in self-directed exercise by providing a fun activity alone or with others. Such trails vary in cost, depending on the number of stations, materials used in construction, and the expense of purchasing or clearing land for its installation. Most trails have low construction and maintenance costs compared to those for other sport facilities. A resource guide describing fitness trail options and marketing information is available through the National Parks and Recreation Association.

DAILY FITNESS LOG

Date _____

Sleep _____

Weight _____

Aerobic workout _____

Total aerobic time or mileage _____

Training area _____

Anaerobic workout _____

Training area _____

CALORIE CONSUMPTION

Breakfast _____

Lunch _____

Dinner _____

Total _____

Physical attitude _____

Mental attitude _____

Personal comments & observations _____

Form 3.1   Sample daily fitness log.

WEEKLY PROGRESS CHART

Date	Activity	Distance	Duration	Points	Total

Form 3.2   Sample weekly progress chart.

The informal sport approach to fitness programming used to appeal mostly to people who are highly motivated, self-disciplined, or already engaged in regular physical activity. People today are more pressed for time, yet are attracted to the informal sport programming area because they want to enhance their fitness level.

Intramural and Extramural Sport and Fitness

Structuring fitness into a tournament system represents a marketing approach to foster fitness ideals. The media has familiarized people with the idea that the sport industry, whether it is recreational, athletic, or professional, has created population awareness to enhance participation in a sport. The next step past informal and instructional sport programming would be an ongoing, self-directed learning process to meet participant's fitness needs.

Sometimes individuals condition themselves, using sound fitness knowledge, to enhance their tournament performance. The leadership efforts that allow for this interest, through sound planning, organizing, and eventually conducting such events, contribute to the participant's success and satisfaction. Often, fitness level can influence the satisfaction of meeting a goal in the tournament or contest, where the fitness capacity can be personally reviewed or even judged. Fitness may not be the primary motivation in intramural sport, but it can be part of the process to facilitate satisfaction, even in a losing situation.

Some examples of programming using fitness principles include the following structured events specific to fitness:

• **Distance and fun runs or walks**.   Runs and walks have become popular across the country, particularly in communities where the parks and recreation department, YMCA, or YWCA sponsor them. Flexibility in distance, eligibility, and number of entries receiving recognition furthers participation. Guidelines on race organization are available from the National Jogging Association.

• **Jog and walk day**.   These events involve as many people as possible in jogging or walking set distances. Provide group recognition by keeping track of the number of people representing organizations (Lions Club, sorority, squadron, industry) and individual recognition by determining the greatest distance a participant accumulated in a specified time. Both races and jog or walk days can include presentations and demonstrations concerning proper running, jogging, and walking techniques; injury prevention; and proper clothing and footwear.

• **Marathons**.   Marathons involve continuous physical activity over a specified time, rewarding those who continue the longest or accumulate the greatest distance or time. Interest may focus on individual or group activities in dancing, skating, cycling, swimming, jumping rope, running, tennis, basketball, racquetball, and so forth. Although marathons attract spectators and media, few participate because of the strenuous demands on the body.

• **Presidential Physical Fitness Award Program**.   To be eligible for this program, participants must be between 10 and 17 years of age. They must have scored at or above the 85th percentile for the respective age group on all six items of the AAHPERD Youth Fitness Test. Winners of the award receive a certificate suitable for framing and an emblem to wear on sweaters, jackets, or blazers.

• **Self-challenge**.   Here an individual enters a fitness program directly supervised by qualified personnel. All health-related information is gathered and recorded. The individual then works toward the primary objective—to improve on all the data by setting goals. As the participant meets these goals, he or she establishes other goals, challenging each fitness level and hoping for improvement. This is a simple self-challenging intramural effort that many people enjoy.

• **Data comparison**.   Participants who are sensitive about their fitness can keep track of their exercise pattern, recording strength, repetitions, length of engagement, and possibly number of workouts per week. As they log these, they may compare the data with another participant. In that process, each becomes challenged by the other person's progress. Comparisons become motivational, competition is established, and, in time, one may be more successful than another.

Although the fitness movement does not use intramural sport, structured tournaments, or contests to deliver its principles, you can program these options occasionally to foster fitness interest and participation. Depending on the event, you may require specialized leadership. You should consider this in planning any intramural sport activity that emphasizes fitness.

Club Sport and Fitness

With fitness being as popular as it is, interest groups have formed that bring people together to participate in a sport and to demonstrate fitness benefits. A programmer can influence this enthusiasm through a voluntary leadership system and organizational methods. You can hold meetings to involve these individuals as leaders of sport contests, assistants for fitness assessment programs, helpers for fitness awareness weeks or any event that fosters fitness. Sometimes the depth and extent of the fitness require specialized leadership: qualified people to do the work properly.

Recreational sport clubs come together because of their desire to be fit and well. Fitness is the core component of the interest group. They are motivated by its ideals; they socialize around its principles; they interact and enjoy one another's company because of their fitness commitment. Some examples of these clubs include weight-lifting clubs, walking clubs, and cycling clubs.

In a majority of clubs, their bylaws, mission statements, or purposes have fitness as a primary goal. Club systems are voluntary, requiring club leadership, not the technical supervision that the fitness industry provides, but there is no doubt that club programs endorse fitness.

Direct Fitness

Someone with a background and certification in fitness should direct delivery of fitness programs (that is, supervision of fitness assessment, prescription, and evaluation). Because recreational sport programmers often manage direct fitness programs, they may become involved with direct delivery methods, particularly fitness testing.

When you do testing, you must first decide the purpose of the results. Testing provides a physician, program coordinator, or exercise leader with sufficient information to plan appropriate participant activity. Test results help a participant assess current fitness levels and monitor changes over time. In any case, encourage participants to have a physical examination before starting any sport or exercise program.

We recommend a medical screening and fitness evaluation before prescribing individual fitness programs for a non-apparently healthy population. If participants do not pass, they must see a medical provider. The procedure may include a complete medical history, physical exam, and a resting and exercise ECG (electrocardiogram) before evaluation. Some flexibility exists in these requirements, depending on the participants' age, health, family history, and present fitness level. The American College of Sports Medicine (ACSM) has provided a useful guideline. Table 3.6 shows the ACSM's prerequisite screening before exercise.

If a person is under 40 and considered a low risk for coronary heart disease, the screening and testing requirements may be less stringent. A simple assessment recommended by the American College of Sports Medicine is shown in form 3.3. Settings that do not offer individualized exercise programs may require medical screening and fitness evaluation before sport and exercise participation if they have access to qualified personnel and equipment through a local hospital, physician, or a college medical, health, or exercise physiology program.

When resources are limited, a fitness program may focus on self-directed participation, dispensing with medical screening and fitness evaluations. Examples of representative tests used to assess health-related fitness follow. This section groups the options sequentially, from basic and inexpensive to more complex, technical, and expensive.

Testing Levels

We conduct fitness testing to assist a recreational sport participant with specific programmatic directions, such as which instructional, informal, intramural, extramural, and club programs will meet fitness goals. We'll examine three levels of fitness testing and describe what staffing is required.

Level 1

This inexpensive basic test involves the following:

- Aerobic capacity, measured by a 12-minute field test or step test
- Body composition, waist to hip ratio, using a tape measure
- Flexibility, evaluating trunk extension and flexion through the sit and reach method
- Muscular strength, using a hand grip dynamometer
- Muscular endurance, using one-minute push-up and bent-leg sit-up tests.

Personnel

Level 1 testing requires knowledgeable personnel who understand when to refer a participant to a physician to make blood pressure readings. Testing staff should know the purposes and procedures for using resting heart rate, dynamometer, waist to hip measurement, and flexibility testing.

Table 3.6
ACSM Guidelines for One-On-One Consultation Referral

ACSM recommendations for medical examination and exercise testing before participation

	Apparently healthy[1]		Increased risk[2]		Known disease[3]
	Younger	Older	No symptoms	Symptoms	
Moderate exercise[5]	No[6]	No	No	Yes[7]	Yes
Vigorous exercise[8]	No	Yes	Yes	Yes	Yes

[1]See the Initial Risk Stratification Table that follows for definitions of "apparently healthy," "increased risk," and "known disease."

[2]See the Coronary Artery Disease Risk Factors Table that follows.

[3]Persons with known cardiac, pulmonary, or metabolic disease.

[4]Younger implies $\leq$ 40 years for men, $\leq$ 50 years for women.

[5]Moderate exercise is defined by an intensity of 40% to 60% VO_2max. If intensity is uncertain, moderate exercise may alternately be defined as an intensity well within the individual's current capacity, one which can comfortably be sustained for a prolonged time—that is, 60 minutes—which has a gradual initiation and progression and is generally noncompetitive.

[6]A "No" response means that an item is deemed "not necessary." The "No" response does not mean that the item should not be done.

[7]A "Yes" response means that an item is recommended. For physician supervision, this suggests that a physician is in close proximity and readily available should there be an emergent need.

[8]Vigorous exercise is defined by an exercise intensity >60% VO_2max. If intensity is uncertain, vigorous exercise may alternately be defined as exercise intense enough to represent a substantial cardiorespiratory challenge or if it results in fatigue within 20 minutes.

Initial Risk Stratification

1. Apparently healthy	Individuals who are asymptomatic and apparently healthy with no more than one major coronary risk factor. (See the Coronary Artery Disease Risk Factors Table that follows.)
2. Increased risk	Individuals who have signs or symptoms suggestive of possible cardiopulmonary or metabolic disease or two or more major coronary risk factors. (See the Coronary Artery Disease Risk Factors Table that follows.)
3. Known disease	Individuals with known cardiac, pulmonary, or metabolic disease.

Coronary Artery Disease Risk Factors

Positive risk factors   **Defining criteria**

1. Age	Men > 45 years; women > 55 or premature menopause without estrogen replacement therapy
2. Family history	MI or sudden death before 55 years of age in father or other male first-degree relative, or before 65 years of age in mother or other female first-degree relative
3. Current cigarette smoking	
4. Hypertension	Blood pressure $\geq$ 140/90 mm HG, confirmed by measurements on at least two occasions, or antihypertensive medication
5. Hypercholesterolemia	Total serum cholesterol > 200 mg/dL (5.2 mmol/L) (if lipoprotein profile is unavailable) or HDL < 35 mg/dL (0.9 mmol/L)
6. Diabetes mellitus	Persons with insulin dependent diabetes mellitus (NIDDM) who are > 35 years of age should be classified as patients with disease
7. Sedentary lifestyle or physical inactivity	Persons comprising the least active 25% of the population, as defined by the combination of sedentary jobs involving sitting for a large part of the day and no regular exercise or active recreational pursuits

Negative risk factor   **Comments**

1. High serum HDL cholesterol	>60 mg/dL (1.6 mmol/L)

Reference: *ACSM Guidelines for Exercise Testing and Prescription* (1995). Williams & Wilkins, Baltimore, MD, 5th edition.

Physical Activity Readiness
Questionnaire—PAR-Q
(revised 1994)

PAR-Q & YOU

Regular physical activity is fun and healthy, and increasingly more people are starting to become more active every day. Being more active is very safe for most people. However, some people should check with their doctor before they start becoming much more physically active.

If you are planning to become much more physically active than you are now, start by answering the seven questions in the box below. If you are between the ages of 15 and 69, the PAR-Q will tell you if you should check with your doctor before you start. If you are over 69 years of age, and you are not used to being very active, check with your doctor.

Common sense is your best guide when you answer these questions. Please read the questions carefully and answer each one honestly: check YES or NO.

YES NO

❑ ❑ 1. Has your doctor ever said that you have a heart condition *and* that you should only do physical activity recommended by a doctor?

❑ ❑ 2. Do you feel pain in your chest when you do physical activity?

❑ ❑ 3. In the past month, have you had chest pain when you were not doing physical activity?

❑ ❑ 4. Do you lose your balance because of dizziness or do you ever lose consciousness?

❑ ❑ 5. Do you have a bone or joint problem that could be made worse by a change in your physical activity?

❑ ❑ 6. Is your doctor currently prescribing drugs (for example, water pills) for your blood pressure or heart condition?

❑ ❑ 7. Do you known of *any other reason* why you should not do physical activity?

If you answered

YES to one or more questions

Talk with your doctor by phone or in person BEFORE you start becoming much more physically active or BEFORE you have a fitness appraisal. Tell your doctor about the PAR-Q and to which questions you answered YES.

- You may be able to do any activity you want—as long as you start slowly and build up gradually. Or, you may need to restrict your activities to those which are safe for you. Talk with your doctor about the kinds of activities you wish to participate in and follow his/her advice.
- Find out which community programs are safe and helpful for you.

NO to all questions

If you answered NO honestly to *all* PAR-Q questions, you can be reasonably sure that you can:

- start becoming much more physically active—begin slowly and build up gradually. This is the safest and easiest way to go.
- take part in a fitness appraisal—this is an excellent way to determine your basic fitness so that you can plan the best way for you to live actively.

DELAY BECOMING MUCH MORE ACTIVE:

- if you are not feeling well because of a temporary illness such as a cold or a fever—wait until you feel better; or
- if you are or may be pregnant—talk to your doctor before you start becoming more active.

Please note: If your health changes so that you then answer YES to any of the above questions, tell your fitness or health professional. Ask whether you should change your physical activity plan.

Form 3.3   Canadian Society for Exercise Physiology's PAR-Q & You physical activity readiness questionnaire.

Comments

This system does not require certified or licensed personnel or an exercise physiologist present on the testing staff, although ideally, we recommend having professional staff certified by ACSM. Staff should not issue opinions about test results or make recommendations on the type of exercise program a person should pursue based on results unless they are trained. The participant may compare results with accepted norms and standard scores and keep an ongoing chart for recording them.

Level 2

Another test you can perform outside a laboratory measures the following:

- Blood pressure readings using a stethoscope and blood pressure cuff.
- Heart rate and blood pressure readings, with sub-maximal bicycle ergometer testing to indicate cardiorespiratory fitness
- Body composition, using skinfold calipers and girth, height, and weight measurements
- Flexibility, using goniometer measurements on the normal range of motion, in degrees, for various joints
- Muscular strength, using a series of one-repetition maximal exercises using weights
- Muscular endurance, using exercises such as bent-knee sit-ups and dips on the parallel bars

Personnel

Once testing involves more extensive equipment and skills, you will need additional monitoring skills. Certain tests require the ability to determine resting heart rate and heart rate recovery from exercise. Staff must know how to administer these tests and detect when they should stop a test. Most programs require a medical check-up and clearance before administering the sub-maximal bicycle ergometer test. Testing staff should know the purpose of exercise testing and the procedure for measuring results.

Comments

Testing staff need to be certified, licensed, or hold a degree in kinesiology with an emphasis in exercise physiology. We also suggest requiring health history and a medical clearance for participants who engage in this or any similar testing format.

Level 3

This test requires specialized equipment and laboratory work to determine the following:

- Cardiorespiratory function, using a resting and stress ECG on a motorized treadmill, and pulmonary function, using computer analysis
- Body fat composition, using a water immersion tank
- Joint flexibility, involving mechanical means for measuring joint extension, flexion, or rotation
- Muscular strength and endurance, using barbells or specially adapted weight-training machines

Personnel

This procedure requires trained medical personnel, exercise physiologists, or someone with a degree from an accredited college or university in fitness or sports medicine. We recommend that a physician oversee the ECG testing.

Comments

This approach provides the most expensive and comprehensive test of fitness, requiring a high degree of expertise.

ADA Suggestions

One goal of the ADA legislation is to provide equal participation by individuals with disabilities in the mainstream of society which includes recreation and sports. According to the ADA, principles of mainstreaming include the following:

- Individuals with disabilities must be integrated to the maximum extent appropriate.
- Separate programs are permitted as necessary to ensure equal opportunity. A separate program must be appropriate to the individual.
- Individuals with disabilities cannot be excluded from the regular program or required to accept special services or benefits. (Title III Technical Assistance Manual, 15)

For example, an individual in a wheelchair who would like to participate in a fitness program should have the same opportunity to enroll and participate as any other participant would.

CONCLUSION

The role of fitness in recreational sport takes on two directions—indirect fitness attainment through programming and direct fitness programming through assessment and classes for follow-through on this assessment. The former is the concern of a recreational sport manager, and the latter requires attention to developing programs with a fitness specialist. Fitness is recognized in a recreational sport environment as one of the goals of participation, along with enjoyment and diversion.

Fitness from a wellness perspective involves more than physical fitness; however, the purpose of this chapter was to emphasize physical fitness attainment. Fitness delivery occurs through programming recreational sport and through the recommendation resulting from fitness testing.

With the *Healthy People 2000* goals and the guidelines from the American College of Sports Medicine, recreational sport programs can meet an individual's fitness goals, provide fun through sport and leisure, and enhance quality of life for participants.

Fitness/Wellness Software

As the fitness boom accelerates, it is quite evident that computer technology has even spread into the weight rooms that were once considered dungeons. Fitness software is becoming more and more sophisticated with customized programs for practically every aspect of fitness conditioning and assessment. This approach to fitness has outdated the traditional "3 sets of 10" mentality.

Fitness machines and management techniques are becoming more sophisticated, but so are fitness participants. As participants get more involved and accustomed to computer advances in everyday living, they are also expecting the same in their fitness workouts. These new expectations require recreational sport professionals to keep pace with technology.

Fitness/wellness software programs have been designed to assist fitness professionals as they help participants achieve personal fitness goals, maintain maximum efficiency, and become aware of safety concerns. Most programs have been developed and tested by top fitness professionals to address the needs of people who desire general fitness conditioning.

There are basically three types of fitness/wellness software: nutrition programs; personal/home training and workout systems; and comprehensive health and fitness systems. *Nutrition programs* generally include modules for health risk assessments, weight management, meal planners, and exercise prescriptions. *Personal/home training and workout systems* are applications that give users interesting, effective, and continually varying workouts. These systems focus on safety and the importance of performing the most appropriate exercises in the proper sequence. These programs have been specifically designed for those who prefer to exercise privately in their homes or for those who have limited equipment and time.

Comprehensive health and fitness systems usually provide fitness assessment profiles, health risk assessments, and exercise prescriptions. *Fitness assessment profiles* usually include pre-exercise questionnaires to help identify those people who should obtain medical approval before proceeding with the assessment profile, updating their medical history, and taking part in various fitness tests for muscular strength, flexibility, body composition, and cardiovascular fitness.

Health risk assessments generally analyze a person's health history and current lifestyle. Factors such as percentage body fat, cholesterol level, tobacco use, and alcohol consumption are examined and assessed in order to estimate the participant's risk of early illness or death. Health risk assessments use a combination of education, motivation, and peer support to help individuals adopt and maintain healthier personal habits. Software programs, using data from national institutes—such as the CDC, the National Cancer Institute, and the American Heart Association—produce wellness scores with specific recommendations.

Exercise prescription modules monitor a person's profile for the most recent percentage body fat, strength, flexibility, and cardiovascular data. Profile component scores are then highlighted with suggested exercise prescription recommendations for improvement. The prescriptions allow participants to choose areas which they would like to improve upon by committing to a weekly workout schedule. The following is a sample exercise prescription printout from *RJL Systems, Inc.,* which includes weight loss recommendations, exercise prescriptions, and cardiac risk evaluation results.

Samuel J. Thompson
123-45-6789

male, 34 years   August 11,
                                                                     1:02 am

Height : 70.0 in.	Weight : 190.0 lbs.
Resistance : 457 ohms	Activity Level : Moderate
Reactance : 52 ohms	Resting Heart Rate : 61 Beats/Min.
Body Water : 57%, 107.4 lbs.	Optimal Body Water : 55 to 65 %
Body Lean : 77%, 146.8 lbs.	Optimal Body Lean : 81 to 87 %
Body Fat : 23%, 43.2 lbs.	Optimal Body Fat : 13 to 19 %
Lean/Fat Ratio : 3.4 to 1	Ideal Lean/Fat Ratio : 4.3 or higher
Body Mass Index : 27.3 kg/cm²	Rest. Energy Expend. : 2083 calories

Weight Loss Recommendations

Starting Weight : 190.0 lbs.	Target Weight Range : 173 - 181 lbs.
Fat Weight : 43.2 lbs.	Target Fat Weight : 27 lbs.
Lean Weight : 146.8 lbs.	Target Lean Weight : 151 lbs.
Weight to Lose : 9 - 17 lbs.	Rate of Loss : 1.0 lbs./wk
Weeks to Reach Target : 13 weeks	Calories/Day : 2292

Exercise Prescription

Exercise Type : Aerobics	Aerobic Heart Rate Low : 136
Days/week : 3	Aerobic Heart Rate High : 161
Minutes/Session : 30	

Cardiac Risk Evaluation Results
    A. (4) 2 relatives with heart disease after 60 years of age.
    B. (2) Never had heart disease.
    C. (5) 1 relative with diabetes.
    D. (3) Quit smoking within one year or now smokes 1-10 per day.
    E. (3) Sometimes calm with frequent impatience.

Blood Cholesterol : 178 mg %	Systolic B/P : 135 mm hg
Blood Glucose : 156 mg %	Diastolic B/P : 78 mm hg
HDL : 89 mg %	Triglycerides : 112 mg %
LDL : N/A	

    Risk Category : borderline
    Change of CHD within 8 years is less than 1%

Comments:
    Follow the recommended diet and exercise plan.
    Next appointment is on Nov. 27 at 10 am.

_____

___ Exercise Prescription

___ Dietary Prescription   By: _____

Reimbursement : [ ] 93720   [ ] 93721   ICD-9-CM: _____

Fitness/wellness software programs can certainly be a valuable tool in assisting professionals in providing a quality program by offering the following benefits:

- If participants obtain results in actual printouts and see their progress, they will be motivated to continue using your facility and program.

- You can help participants meet their goals by providing them with personalized caloric, nutrition, and exercise programs.
- Conducting mini-test promotions will promote your facility or program and attract new members. For example, one week you could focus on stress assessment, the next week you could focus on blood pressure, and the next week you could focus on body composition, and so on.
- Conduct group evaluations, which are ideal for contests and wellness programs. Single tests are excellent for testing large groups of people at different special events and for marketing your program.

While several software packages offer a low-cost alternative to an educated fitness instructor, there is no substitute for a well trained fitness professional. However, proper software can be a way of providing support to professionals in making decisions about a participant's fitness program. If used properly, computers can be a means to providing an overall cost-effective and efficient fitness program. Computers can also be tremendous motivational tools because they are able to create and maintain participants' awareness of the benefits of fitness and wellness activities.

RJL Systems, Inc., Mt. Clemens, MI, 800-528-4513

Other fitness/wellness software products: HealthCheck Fitness and Nutrition Software, Advanced Software Design Group, HealthFirst, MicroFit, and the Family Health Tracker.

DISCUSSION QUESTIONS

1. Describe the major components of fitness.

2. Do you believe fitness is a separate programming component or an element of each programming area (informal sport, intramural sport, etc.)?

3. Why do you think corporations have designed sport and fitness programs?

4. Describe five performance components of physical fitness.

5. Explain the relationship of sport or exercise to health-related fitness.

6. You can deliver fitness programming to participants in two primary ways. Describe these two delivery methods and give specific examples that you could use in each method.

7. Compare and contrast the different levels of fitness testing. Which level would you use for your facility and why?

8. What are the major differences between self-directed and staff-directed fitness programs?

9. Describe the advantages and disadvantages of self-directed fitness programs.

10. List five special events that could enhance fitness activity programming.

11. Describe several topics that could be discussed in fitness lectures, workshops, and clinics.

APPLICATION EXERCISE

You are the sport coordinator for a municipal parks and recreation department and you are interested in starting a fitness program. There has been a demand for this program for some time, primarily from women participants. What considerations should you make when selecting a fitness leader? What fitness activities would you consider implementing? What concerns would you anticipate from your participants? How would you attract men to the program? Use examples to support your responses.

REFERENCES

American College of Sports Medicine (ACSM). 1995. *ACSM Guidelines for Exercise Testing and Prescription.* 5th ed. Baltimore: Williams & Wilkins.

The Americans With Disabilities Act—Title III technical assistance manual: Covering public accommodations and commercial facilities. Washington, DC: United States Government Printing Office.

Blair, S., H. Kohl, and N. Gordon. 1992. Physical activity and health: A lifestyle approach. *Medicine, Exercise, Nutrition and Health* 1 (1): 54.

Nieman, D. 1995. *Fitness and sports medicine: A health-related approach*. Palo Alto, CA: Bull.

SUGGESTED READINGS

American Academy of Pediatrics. 1992. HIV and sports: American academy of pediatrics policy statement. *Physician and Sportsmedicine* 20 (5): 189-191.

Anderson, V.J. 1990. The future of fitness in recreational sports. *National Intramural-Recreational Sports Association Journal* 14 (2): 23-25.

Bell, J.A., and T.C. Doege. 1987. Athletes' use and abuse of drugs. *Physician and Sportsmedicine* 15 (3): 99-102.

Cosley, A. 1993. Fitness programming for the well elderly: Some practical pointers. *Journal of Physical Education, Recreation, and Dance* 64 (4): 58-68.

Dewlen, R. 1990. Self-concept changes in physically disabled men following physical fitness training. P. 232-248 in *Management strategies in recreational sports*. Corvallis, OR: National Intramural-Recreational Sports Association.

Felker, K., and T. O'Mara. 1989. Developing a comprehensive wellness program. *National Intramural-Recreational Sports Association Journal* 13 (2): 51-53.

Fuller, J.R., and M.J. LaFountain. 1987. Performance-enhancing drugs in sport: A different form of drug abuse. *Adolescence* 22 (88): 969-976.

Goldberg, B. 1989. Injury patterns in youth sports. *Physician and Sportsmedicine* 17 (3): 174-176.

Hamel, R. 1992. AIDS: Assessing the risk among athletes. *Physician and Sportsmedicine* 20 (2): 129-140.

Highstreet, V.D., and K.K. Scheele. 1989. Century fitness club, UNL. P. 97-99 in *Collected readings in recreational sports*. Corvallis, OR: National Intramural-Recreational Sports Association.

Merberg, B. 1990. Pre-screening for fitness evaluation: Health and risk management considerations. P. 118-124 in *Management strategies in recreational sports*. Corvallis, OR: National Intramural-Recreational Sports Association.

Pealo, W. 1992. Leisure and active lifestyles: Moving into the twenty-first century. *Journal of Physical Education, Recreation, and Dance* 63 (8): 26-28.

Pemberton, C., and P. McSwegin. 1993. Sedentary living: A health hazard. *Journal of Physical Education, Recreation, and Dance* 64 (5): 27-32.

Railey, J., and P. Tschauner. 1993. *Managing physical education, fitness, and sports programs*. 2d ed. Mountainview, CA: Mayfield.

Rudolph, R. 1989. Management of surfing injuries: A plastic surgeon's viewpoint. *Physician and Sportsmedicine* 17 (3): 110-116.

Samples, P. 1989. Alcoholism in athletes: New directions for treatment. *Physician and Sportsmedicine* 17 (4): 192-194.

Snodgrass, M., and C. Finsteg. 1990. Recreation and wellness: Identifying motivations for participation in recreational sports. *Journal of Physical Education, Recreation, and Dance* 15 (1): 34-38.

Staber, K., and C. Causey. 1992. Fitness administration for the recreational sports director. *National Intramural-Recreational Sports Association Journal* 17 (1): 4949-50, 52, 55-56.

Tropp, R., S. Gambino, and T.E. Gwiazdowski. 1990. Development of a low-cost fitness program for college-age adults. *National Intramural-Recreational Sports Association Journal* 15 (1): 30.

Work, J.A. 1991. Are java junkies poor sports? *Physician and Sportsmedicine* 19 (1): 82-84.

CHAPTER 4

Instructional Sport

Chapter Objectives

After reading this chapter you will

- understand the nature and value of instructional sport within a recreational setting,
- be able to identify the process for recruiting and selecting qualified personnel in instructional sport, and
- be able to identify the process of instruction essential to quality sport learning.

A logical step toward sport participation is learning about it. Instructional sport is the area within recreational sport programming that provides knowledge and skill to participants. Fundamentally, instructional sport begins in the home. Family members provide the opportunity to develop sport knowledge, skills, and lifetime participation patterns.

The most important occurrence in instructional sport during the 20th century has been its development in communities, military bases, churches, private clubs, YMCAs, YWCAs, Boys and Girls Clubs, commercial and industrial settings, resorts, and country clubs. As interest in recreational sport participation has increased, instructional sport programs expanded to these noneducational settings to supplement existing programs. A quality instructional sport program serves as a natural springboard to ongoing participation in recreational sport. Recreational sport programmers need to recognize this important relationship and know how to develop and deliver instructional sport programs.

FOUR SYSTEMS OF INSTRUCTION

All sport participation, whether recreational, athletic, or professional, has its roots in some type of instruction. The manner in which you deliver instructional sport is influenced not only by participant needs but also by its purpose and the systems through which it is offered. There are four systems that provide ways to learn about sport. They are educational, recreational, athletic, and professional. For comparison, an overview of each follows.

Educational

The educational approach to learning sport relies on the formal academic process. This is the way sport is delivered within elementary schools, preparatory and secondary schools, colleges, and universities. Within these formal educational settings, sport is taught under the same premise as other traditional subjects, such as history, math, and English. These formal programs are called *courses* and have a trained and certified teacher in charge. There are usually many students in the course, with varied backgrounds. The teacher chooses the content of the course, based on the growth and development patterns of the students, their ages, and capabilities. Various skill levels are taught based on progress in ability. The teacher sets the guidelines for delivering the material and measuring the students' progress in skills and knowledge.

Recreational

Delivering instructional sport in nonschool settings evolved as people outside the schools wanted recreational outlets through sport. This approach to instructional sport is present in private clubs, YMCAs and YWCAs, Boys and Girls Clubs, military bases, municipal centers, churches, and industrial and commercial recreational facilities. Instructional sport in these settings is more informal than in educational settings and includes fun and participation in the sport as focuses. Although learning about a sport is important, emphasis is also on enjoying the learning experience and gaining satisfaction from improving your knowledge and skills.

These instructional sport programs are referred to as *lessons*, *sessions*, *clinics*, or *workshops*. The length of these sessions can vary from one to two hours per week for participants taking private lessons, to full sessions of six to eight weeks with a large group. You can combine men and women or make clinics gender specific, and you can involve a variety of age levels. Instructional sport programs are conducted at local sport sites, such as gymnasiums, fields, or courts, and usually happen when people are most available.

Athletic

The thrust of the athletic approach to instructional sport is influencing the *margin of excellence* in ability for the participants. Often, participants associated with a school varsity sport team, an industrial sport team, a club sport team, or an Amateur Athletic Union (AAU) team pursue this margin of excellence. It is also pursued by those who challenge themselves to succeed athletically, such as someone who wishes to complete a marathon or a bicycle trip.

Within the context of these systems, the athlete is taught to gain as much skill and knowledge as possible. Performance is crucial because success is often measured by records of wins and losses or other standards of performance. Because success is such a crucial part of the athletic approach, all schools, club sport teams, and AAU teams use specialized instructors or coaches. These coaches are the decision makers about delivery and instruction methods. Thus, most of the success or failure comes from the coaches' abilities as instructors.

Emphasis is placed on the individual for personal performance as well as team performance. Only a select number of participants, usually the best performers, become involved in an athletic instructional program. Instructors influence all aspects of mental and physical training to create the optimum personal and team conditions that will ensure success.

Professional

The professional approach to learning sport is the final system we will discuss and probably the most visible. Whether it is football, baseball, hockey, basketball, tennis, or soccer, almost every major city in the U.S. supports professional sport. In this situation, the bottom line is to influence the margin of excellence of the athletes through instruction so they gain enough success to generate a profit. These organizations are run as corporations, with owners, presidents, and executive board members making the decisions. Individuals involved in this approach often pay coaches and athletes large amounts of money for their involvement. Instruction for its own sake receives less emphasis because professional athletes already know how to perform. Most practice time is devoted to maintaining and refining skill levels.

Coaches of professional systems are often former professional athletes. There are also professional athletes who are employed as instructors, especially in individual sports like tennis, golf, bowling, and so forth. These individuals are *teaching professionals* who instruct sport for a profit, most often at a golf course, racquetball club, tennis club, martial arts studio, yacht club, country club, or resort. These teaching professionals are usually certified by the governing bodies of their respective sport. As in the recreational approach, you can give lessons to one person at a time or to a large group. These individual instructors play a major role in generating income that is fundamental to the success of the business operations.

SELECTING INSTRUCTORS

The inclusion of instructional sport within the total recreational sport operation means considering several factors: interests of the target population, funding, availability of facilities and equipment, and the ability of instructional personnel. Of these, selecting qualified personnel is critical because the instructor makes direct contact with the participant and is primarily responsible for designing a meaningful learning experience.

The recreational sport programmer is usually not responsible for doing the instruction but is involved in hiring and supervising the instructors. Because instructional sport occurs within the recreational environment, the standards of instruction may vary and the programmer must be selective in finding an individual who meets certain standards. This allows flexibility on selection, but you still must have predetermined criteria and expectations.

An absence of guidelines for personnel selection opens the door for criticism and suggests that the programmer has an unprofessional attitude. However, a lack of criteria does not necessarily stem from indifference, but more from inexperience in hiring and supervising instructional sport personnel. Therefore, the purpose of this section is to address this concern by exploring how to select the instructor within the context of a recreational setting.

Training and Background

Two main avenues exist for finding instructors. The first avenue is soliciting individuals with formal training in instructional sport. The second is soliciting personnel who have an informal background.

The person with formal training typically carries certification that verifies training and experience in a sport. In many instances, certification also specifies a ranking, which indicates the person's level of expertise. The certification process is customarily handled by national sport associations or similar organizations recognized as a sport's governing body. Establishing contact with these organizations is one way of identifying local people to contact about becoming instructors.

Another formal certification process is governed by the education system through physical education teacher preparation programs. Individuals completing degree programs are usually certified for specific age groups and often focus on one or two sports. These individuals are highly qualified in the academic approach to sport. In this instance, you can direct personnel recruitment strategies toward college and university campus placement offices and conferences. Sometimes the cost for securing instructors with formal preparation is an obstacle. However, the goal should always be to select the most qualified instructor you can afford.

Often, the recreational sport programmer deals with potential instructors from an informal preparation process. Although they carry no formal credentials, they may have considerable knowledge, skill, and experience from investing many hours in learning a sport. People in this category may not pursue instructional sport as a career but prefer concentrating on one or two sports and becoming involved as the time and opportunity permit. Their sport interest may not have a national organization or certification program through which they can pursue formal training.

Also, some people with informal preparation come from athletic or professional sport and lack certification from a national organization. The absence of such credentials means that the recreational sport programmer has to decide whether personality and experience make the person a good instructor for a sport. It may be that the person has had enough practice and study time in a sport to parallel the requirements of any certification program. They may also carry a reputation that reflects positively on their ability to be an instructor. Reliance on this avenue for personnel, although not acceptable by some standards, is better than nothing. If used, the programmer must assume greater responsibility in the design and control of the instructional sport program until the ability of the person can be fully ascertained.

Planning

In the early stages of instructor recruitment, use systematic planning to ensure that you anticipate the position requirements and find the best staff. Determine the number of instructors you need. This will depend on the number of programs you will offer and potential income and expense involved. Also, compare advantages and disadvantages of using one full-time instructor to teach many lessons with using a few part-time instructors to meet the needs. Plan the program based on the ideal schedule. Then, cut back as the instructor resource pool develops, and restructure to best meet the interest.

Another planning consideration is to choose the criteria for the abilities of each instructor. A recreational sport programmer could face a dilemma if

instructors from an athletic or professional background have excellent sport skills and complete understanding of their sport strategies, but can't deliver the sport knowledge to participants, especially beginners. On the other hand, instructors from informal backgrounds may have exceptional skill, but not the needed technical knowledge about instructional methods and techniques. When deciding these standards, focus first on the knowledge and skill, then on ability to instruct. An instructor can always be taught how to properly instruct.

Announcement

The next step is to develop a job description, including what the instructor's position will require. You can design it as an announcement because the information describes the duties and responsibilities you will expect the instructor to meet. The announcement content will vary depending on which form of solicitation you use. Once you do this, the next consideration is to decide how to solicit applicants. You could share these announcements through school newspapers, campus activity fairs, word of mouth, employment offices, physical education departments, national organizations, civil service, club sport members, and radio. Which of these outlets works best will depend on your experience and the sport to be taught. Also, you could seek advice or see what other agencies have done. Other resources or options include classified ads, display ads, information packets, and flyers.

Application

No matter how people learn about an instructional opportunity, you should make them aware of the requirement for application. Things you could require include completed application, letter of interest, telephone call of interest, letters of reference, results from skill and knowledge tests, academic transcript, copy of certification, and resume. If there are minimum requirements for the applicant, you should present them through the announcement. This saves time, both for the applicants, in case they do not qualify, and for you, the programmer, from reviewing applicants who will not be hired. Some points to consider for minimum requirements include time of experience, certification levels, number of letters of recommendation, high school or college degree, and types of experience. You can determine most of these considerations ahead of time with staff or advisory committee members involved with the instructional sport programming.

Shining Example

City of Foster City Parks and Recreation Department, Foster City, CA

The city of Foster City Parks and Recreation Department is a municipal recreation agency. There are 29,000 residents of Foster City, of which approximately 1,000 participate in the sports program per quarter. The recreation department offers a variety of youth sports programs such as tennis, ice skating, basketball, karate, and soccer. The adult sports opportunities consist of softball, volleyball, scuba, ice skating, golf, tennis, and more. Foster City Parks and Recreation utilizes schools, the local mall (ice skating), and city apartment complexes to offer their large variety of programs. Their agency collaborates with other organizations throughout the city to meet the needs of the residents of Foster City.

Organization: The City of Foster City Parks & Recreation Department is a municipal recreation facility.

Clientele: Of the 29,000 residents of Foster City, approximately 1,000 participate in the sports programs each quarter.

Budget: The sports budget is $14,987 per year.

Marketing: The City of Foster City Parks & Recreation Department distributes a quarterly Leisure Update. This brochure is mailed to every home in Foster City. Pertinent flyers are sent to targeted audiences as well.

Staff: The administrative staff includes full-time Recreation Supervisors, part-time Scorekeepers, and part-time Referees. They also have contracts with instructors and umpires.

Program Detail: The Adult Softball League consists of seven leagues that run from Sunday through Friday evenings. Our Adult Volleyball League runs with two leagues that play on Wednesday evenings. In addition to this, they also offer various sports classes during afternoons and evenings.

Facilities: The facilities that the City of Foster City Parks & Recreation Department operate include: one adult softball field with lights, use of two school gymnasiums, and the Recreation Center's multi-purpose room. The City also owns and maintains Sea Cloud Park which is used by volunteer run youth sports programs. This park houses seven baseball fields, eight soccer fields, a maintenance yard, restrooms, and a refreshment stand.

ASSESSING CREDENTIALS

Screening applicants can be time consuming. Whether it be done by individuals or by a committee, it should be taken seriously because instructors play a major role in the success of a program. Set aside uninterrupted time when reviewing applicants. Take notes, especially if there are a large number of applicants. You might create a checklist of factors important for the position (see form 4.1, for example). This can become a rating system for each applicant.

After you have gathered the application and background on all potential instructors, conduct a careful review of credentials. The ability to judge appropriateness of credentials and other attributes of the applicants is essential to make the best selection. Gather the basic information on each candidate from the application forms. We suggest the following areas for additional consideration in evaluating potential instructors. Each area pertains to applicants with either formal or informal preparation.

Knowledge and Skill

Ascertain what and how much the person knows about a sport in terms of rules, regulations, strategy, facilities, equipment, and skill development. Also, take into account how much a person knows about instruction methods, techniques, and aids. Inquire about qualifications for working with different skill levels and ages. In essence, ask questions that reveal the extent of knowledge about how to deliver the sport. Later in this chapter, we discuss the instructional process and sport content to

---

PROGRAMMER'S SCREENING ASSESSMENT
Tennis Instructors

Candidate's name _____   Date _____   Time _____

CATEGORY	POINTS		CATEGORY	POINTS	
Position held			Tournament experience		
Head pro	12		High school	4	
Assistant pro	10		Sanctioned	6	
Staff pro	6	_____	State	9	
Certification			Regional	12	_____
USPTA	12		Facility worked at		
USPTR	12	_____	Indoor	10	
Coaching			Outdoor	10	
Juniors	6		Outdoor lighted	5	
High school	8		Hard court	5	
College	10		Hard true or clay	5	_____
Pro	12		Tournament scheduling	9	_____
Travel team	8	_____	Eligibility	7	_____
Instructing			Computer knowledge	8	_____
Children	5		Customer service	8	_____
Juniors	8		Promotions	8	_____
Adults	12		Public relations	8	_____
Handicapped	12	_____	Professional development	8	_____
Level			Recommendation letters	10	_____
Beginner	5				
Intermediate	8				
Advanced	10	_____			
Played as				Total	_____
Junior	3				
High school	7				
College	10				
Pro	12	_____	Name _____		

Form 4.1   Sample form for screening applicants for a tennis instructor's position.

help the programmer design questions to critique an individual's knowledge and skill base for instructional sport.

Willingness

The first indication that you should not start an instructional sport program is when you have to plead to obtain instructors. Some sports are so popular that it is easy to secure instructors, and the less common sports may mean a sparse resource pool from which to draw. In either case, the programmer should not resort to begging for instructors. This lack of willingness to offer services on a paid or volunteer basis can easily result in a morale problem that damages the quality of the instructional sport effort.

Volunteers should have a high interest and motivation because, by nature, volunteering stems from a desire to serve. Paid personnel may or may not be as motivated or willing as the volunteer, but expect them to maintain their interest because they are being paid. In practice, there is no sure way to determine whether the volunteer or paid position will be the best approach in terms of willingness. It is an individual matter to assess through interaction with candidates. One thing is sure: knowledge and skill are useless unless the instructor is willing and self-motivated.

Reputation

Experience handling personnel interviews or reviewing credentials does not guarantee the ability to accurately judge character or behavior patterns. Unless you give thorough attention to this assessment area, you may select a person based on a good interview, only to find later that the individual is less capable or qualified than he or she appeared. This risk is minimized by carefully evaluating the reputation of an applicant as an individual and instructor.

Information about reputation is most commonly obtained through references provided by the applicant. Whenever possible, confirm these references and cross-check them with additional sources provided by the applicant or an individual on the applicant's list.

Experience

An individual's background can provide insight to what an instructor can do. Critique experience by looking at age, maturity, and time involved with the sport. You can quantify some of this informa-

tion by years, months, weeks, or hours. Additional areas of experience to consider include lecture or speaking ability and involvement with particular age groups or skill levels.

This area can be hard to handle for a potential instructor who is seeking a first chance at instructional sport. In this case, concentrate on the other areas and don't automatically disregard these applicants, unless the nature of the responsibility requires previous experience. Check thoroughly into an applicant who lists a lot of experience to determine if there is some history of difficulty in holding a position.

Enthusiasm

To some extent, you can judge enthusiasm by learning about the candidate's previous experience. For a candidate to have boundless energy is not necessarily a good sign. Rather, commitment for working with sport participants goes a long way. The idea that the candidate has a special interest for asserting the learning process is a good sign. Enthusiasm for the sport and teaching can often compensate for a less than desirable environment or second-hand equipment. It can help withstand the redundancy of instructing the same routine, which is necessary in sport skill development. Instructional sport often involves long, tedious hours and sometimes the enthusiasm of the instructor makes all the difference in participant satisfaction. So, assessing the instructor's interest, spirit, and excitement for the sport can be critical.

PREDELIVERY CONSIDERATIONS

This discussion views the factors involved in preparing for instructional sport before its on-site delivery. Familiarity with these factors will help the programmer with supervisory duties and improve the quality of instructional sport programs. The factors for predelivery consideration are planning, orientation, site review, participant assessment, format development, and content.

Planning

An instructor needs to plan each phase of the program and the content of each lesson. Identify general and specific topics that you can prepare as outlines for the participants. The instructor should polish presentations to eliminate an off-the-cuff instruction method. Sound planning is essential in anticipating problems and identifying alternative strategies for unexpected situations. Planning is the primary way to ensure that the instructional process meets the desired objectives.

Orientation

Organize an opportunity for the instructor and potential participants to meet in an orientation session before starting an instructional sport program. During an orientation meeting, review the topics and goals of the program. Highlight participants' expected benefits, and discuss procedural matters, such as fees, attendance, safety, lockers, dressing facilities, showers, and equipment.

An orientation session provides an opportunity for participants to ask questions about the program. By handling their questions in advance, you can avoid misunderstandings. The instructor uses the meeting to learn about concerns and personalities of the participants, and, accordingly, can alter how to teach the lesson. Use an orientation meeting to motivate, reassure, enlighten, and challenge participants to become involved.

On-Site Review

The environment you use for an instructional session can affect how well participants learn and their attitude toward the program. Therefore, inspect the location and double-check its availability before the scheduled start for a program. At the site, verify that it is free from noise and distractions. Check the size to make sure it can hold the number of participants scheduled. Also, if relevant, consider seating capacity, equipment availability, parking, concessions, and showers.

When reviewing the environment for problems, consider it from the point of view of the participant. Many participants in limited space will perceive a situation differently than a group with adequate space. The size of the group in relation to the available space and equipment influences instruction method and delivery. Another aspect of the environment that influences the method is whether the instruction will be indoors or outdoors. When instruction is outdoors, minimize distractions and plan for weather conditions. Similarly, unpredictable situations at indoor sites can always happen, so plan to adjust accordingly.

The Participant

Focus attention on individual capabilities and needs when you design and implement any instructional sport program. Homogeneous grouping of individuals by age, sex, skill level, and ability is common within instructional sport, but you should organize it only after reviewing current participants, not as a standard practice. Allow for exceptions. What works for one individual or group may not work for others. Consider similarities and differences, age and maturity, interests, socioeconomic background, and learning readiness before finishing instruction plans.

Format

In addition to identifying the action plan and content areas within the instructional sport program, you need to develop the format and content for each session. In the individual lessons consider attendance, announcements, warm-up or lead-up activities, skill or knowledge information, demonstrations, active participation or practice, reminders, questions, and dismissal. The time allotted for each topic will vary, depending on participant characteristics, skill level, and instructor effectiveness. Generally, plan more active participation and synthesis of knowledge and skill at the beginning lessons.

Using instruction methods that make learning easier are important, not only for effectiveness as an instructor, but also to encourage continued participation. There are many formats you can use to instruct a particular sport, and we hope those presented here are helpful.

Content

Content is the information and skill instruction that makes up a lesson. Because each sport is unique, the lesson content for different sports can be varied and complex. Factors such as number of participants; motivation; purpose of the sport; individual, dual, or team sport; skill requirements; fitness level; age and maturity; and participant readiness to learn affect content for the instructional process. With so much to consider, content planning for each lesson is critical.

Two issues to consider when you develop content are the participants' mental and physical characteristics and safety. Some participants learn more easily than others. Some participants are more coordinated, flexible, faster, have better timing, have better judgment, and have a wider range of motor skills than others. The safety issue involves keeping the participants injury free and protected at all times. Every participant has to be kept within his or her physiological limits. Site temperature, exhaustion levels, and the state of protective equipment and facilities are all variables that affect participants' safety.

Emphasize safety precautions with instructors of high-risk sports, such as wrestling, rugby, football, archery, mountain climbing, shooting sports, and gymnastics. Instructors of high-risk sport can become inattentive to risk factors due to inexperience with injuries. It is difficult to see the potential for injury or an accident when it has never happened. The only way to keep instructors of high-risk sport aware of safety is to remind them of their duties in this area.

Although you can include a variety of information in instructional content, the general categories of content are history, rules and regulations, skill and performance, facilities, equipment, strategy, and special factors, such as officiating, that affect the control of the sport.

During instructional sport programs, participants spend most time on basic sport knowledge and drills. However, as their ability improves, they should spend more time on rules and regulations, strategy, and officiating. The main idea to consider when you design content is the knowledge and ability of participants—more specifically, whether they are beginners, intermediates, or advanced in their sport.

METHODS FOR DELIVERY

Instructional methods for sport purposes vary from instructor to instructor, depending on abilities and experience. They can also vary from setting to setting, depending on how the application of the instructional process is perceived. The programmer in recreational sport needs to know these methods to assist instructors or monitor their performance. The methods we will discuss are lectures, discussion, demonstration, part and whole, drills, and game and play experience.

Lecture

Of all instruction methods, the lecture is the most basic. Lectures can be problem centered, argumentative, or knowledge based. Perhaps the biggest advantage of the lecture method is that you can present a large amount of information to many people at once.

However, problems do exist. The lecture method is impractical when skill acquisition is required because most learning takes place with active two-way communication. Lecturing on sport information, such as history, rules, regulations, strategies,

and skill is useful, but learning sport skills requires practice.

Discussion

The discussion method is participant centered and good for problem-solving experiences. It creates feedback and understanding of a participant's view of where they are. The discussion method is best in small groups and allows everyone to pool their ideas. This method is used most often in seminars, clinics, workshops, debates, case studies, and role playing situations. The discussion method has a place in instructional sport sessions, but should be limited to special topical situations. Use this method within the context of the educational and recreational approaches to instructional sport.

Demonstration

Unlike the previous instruction methods, demonstration provides a visual image of the skill performed. There are two ways you can use this method. The first is choosing an individual from the group to perform the skill so the instructor can offer information to help the observer be aware of his or her own performance. In the event that there is no suitable group member, the instructor can perform the demonstration. The second option is to bring in an expert to demonstrate the skills of a sport. Well-known athletes who have devoted years to developing their skills and who demonstrate enthusiasm for sharing their competence are excellent choices for demonstrators. Have this person demonstrate for one or two lessons; this can go a long way toward helping a participant appreciate good sport. The use of a demonstration can require preparation and coordination. Repeat the demonstration several times so the participant gains the most benefit.

Part and Whole

A popular way to present sport in a learning situation is through the part and whole method. In this method, the skills necessary for participation are broken down into parts and, later, brought together as a whole.

Learning the performance of most sport is complicated and difficult, especially for beginners. So, when the instructor teaches a component and builds on it in a meaningful progression, learning can take place faster and with more satisfaction. The way instructors break down a sport into parts is a function of the instructor's background and knowledge. A programmer needs to watch for the instructor's ability in delivering this method. Different instructors may have unique ways to present the parts of a sport.

There are thousands of examples that we could give to demonstrate how to break down sport skills. This method allows for the less difficult element of sport performance to be taught first, leading to the more difficult skills. Using this progression results in greater participant satisfaction and understanding.

Drills

The instructional sport process must lead to active participation to maintain interest, use what has been learned, and improve skills. Drills enable any number of participants to simultaneously practice specific aspects of a sport. Depending on what sport skill is being learned, the practice drills can be individual, partner, or group. The instructor has the option to participate in the drill or to rove from one person to another, critiquing the performance individually. One type of drill is called a mimic drill. This drill involves using the instructor as the role model for demonstrating a skill. Then, participants copy the performance of the role model until they attain competency for that skill.

Design drills so the learning is progressive, moving from the simple to complex. Usually, the instructor scans the performance of the entire group, also focusing on individual strengths and weaknesses. In this way, some one-on-one instruction takes place and the instructor can analyze and correct performance. Continual encouragement during drills is needed from the instructor.

You can also organize drills by stations. In this effort, certain sport skills are practiced at different areas of the facility, usually with selected equipment and group leaders. At each station, the participant repeatedly performs the skill as a self-analysis, although the instructor also comments on strengths and weaknesses. At the completion of the practice session, a signal for rotation occurs. The participant moves to another station to practice another skill. This type of drill enables large groups of participants to be active simultaneously and be involved with several skills within a sport.

Game and Playing Experience

A game simulation of the sport, or a portion of the sport, requires the participant to use acquired skills and knowledge. It is best to employ this method when the participants have learned the fundamentals of the sport. Without some ability, the participants will not be able to get involved or play the game with enjoyment. This, in turn, may result in frustration and discouragement from further participation.

When the instructor introduces game situations, they should be within the ability of the participants, yet challenging enough to demonstrate new areas. Game situations require that participants draw on their knowledge of the sport and formulate strategies for playing. Throughout the use of this method, the instructor is responsible for observing the performance of participants as if it were a drill. This permits opportunity for recognizing individual weaknesses for practice and correction in the future.

PARTICIPANT MOTIVATION

Throughout the instructional sport process, give attention to maintaining the participant's commitment and interest. The ability to properly motivate participants requires knowledge about the subject, as well as refined teaching skills. Some participants come to the instructional sport program highly motivated to learn; others come motivated but lose their motivation after a while; and others come with some degree of anxiety or reluctance. In each instance, the instructor must be able to detect the level of motivation and develop or maintain a positive involvement and eagerness to learn. Successful application of motivational techniques should make learning easier and add to participant satisfaction. Therefore, we present selected aspects of motivation to provoke thought about applying motivational techniques in the learning process.

The Motivating Instructor

Perhaps the most important factor in motivating participants in instructional sport is the instructor's delivery style and personality. When the instructor believes in the benefits of participation in a sport, it is conveyed through his or her personality to the participants. Participants can easily notice an instructor's friendliness, attentiveness, and genuine interest in what he or she is doing. Similarly, an unenthusiastic personality can discourage participants. As a programmer, make every attempt to gauge an instructor's personality during the interview process. Although you should not rely on personality as a substitute for knowledge about the sport or how to instruct, it is an important ingredient that adds to participant enjoyment.

Recreation Registration Software

Recreation registration software programs were developed to assist with program registration for recreational sport activities. The software enables recreational sports programmers to disseminate information more effectively and efficiently to participants, instructors, facility managers, registration clerks, and other office staff members. Most commercial application packages are fully integrated with other recreation modules and offer complete menu-driven and easy-to-use programs that are adaptable to a wide variety of recreational sports agencies.

Automated recreation registration software streamline the process of registering individuals and/or groups for all types of recreational sports programs, classes, aquatics, trips, seminars, and memberships—regardless of the setting.

A computerized registration system should include the following features or modules:

1. Program brochure/catalog generator
   - Allows formatting and previewing of various program catalog styles on-screen and actually produces copy for program brochure/catalog, including the activity description, dates, times, facility location, fees, instructor, etc.

2. Mass mailing list management
   - Produces mailing labels of all current and past enrollees for follow-up post card or other correspondence.

3. Activity/class management
   - Tracks activity/class enrollment totals.
   - Handles waiting lists and roster changes. Supports lottery enrollments and enrollment transfers.
   - Tracks any activity/class prerequisite requirements, insurance forms, age limitations, equipment/supplies, etc. for each activity/class.
   - Automatically displays open and closed activities/classes.
   - Allows for pre-registration as well as mail-in, phone-in, and walk-in registrations.
   - Provides "carry-over" of activity information from season to season, which eliminates the need to re-enter similar information.
   - Provides an enrollment history for each participant.
   - Places subsequent enrollments on a prioritized waiting list when an activity is closed. Calculates second-choice activities for any participants placed on a waiting list.

4. Membership management
   - Manages membership entries and sales totals.
   - Tracks enrollments for particular individuals or families.
   - Develops financial and membership reports.

5. Facility reservation system
   - Performs facility searches by user-defined criteria.
   - Processes activity/class facility requests.
   - Checks the availability of desired facility with activity/class usage demands and automatically reserves facility.
   - Prints facility site calendar and daily reservations.

6. Instructor management
   - Calculates multiple pay rates based on hourly, percentage, or flat fee rates for multiple instructors assigned to any given activity. Calculates total hours of instruction provided by each instructor.
   - Tracks personnel information such as job descriptions, performance appraisals, etc.
   - Prints teaching assignments.
   - Produces instructor contracts or agreements.
   - Allows unlimited number of teaching assignments per instructor.
   - Maintains enough flexibility to have multiple instructors assigned to teach any given activity.
7. Reports
   - Prints registration receipts for participants.
   - Prints activity/class rosters.
8. Fiscal management
   - Handles refunds, activity/class transfers, etc.
   - Produces end-of-the-day and/or end-of-the-period financial reports.
   - Calculates income, expense, and net revenue reports.
   - Performs basic cost analysis functions.
   - Allows for cancellations with full or partial refund processing.
   - Tracks balances of individual membership dues and automatically updates the remaining amount due and the date due.

Computerized recreation registration systems are a tremendous tool for recreational sport programmers. An effective system will consolidate several functions of the manual registration process into one streamlined automated process. This system will enable you to maintain accurate and detailed information on all of your recreation programs and instructors, thus creating an effective information and communication network. An automated registration system will enhance and improve the service that your department is

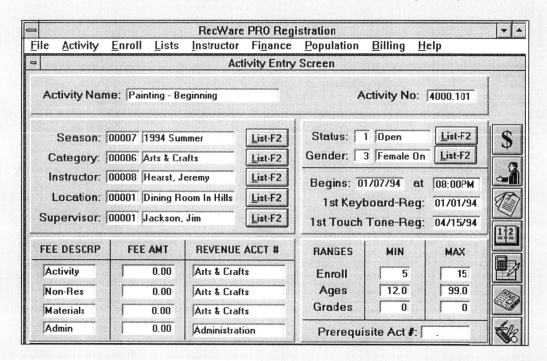

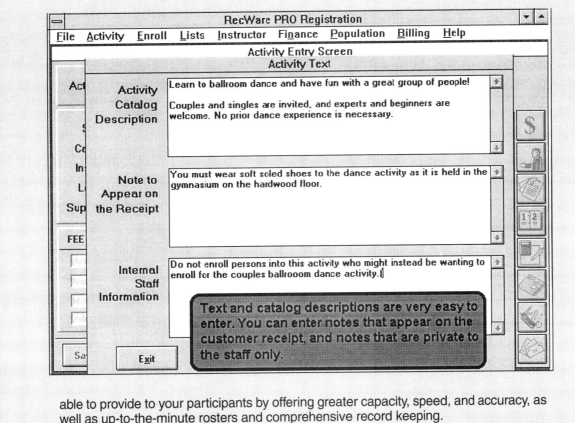

able to provide to your participants by offering greater capacity, speed, and accuracy, as well as up-to-the-minute rosters and comprehensive record keeping.

An example of a registration program, *RecWare PRO* by Sierra Digital, is presented in the screens on pages 70-71.

In the Activity Entry Screens that are shown, the user can easily add text, catalog descriptions, and other notes that can appear on the participants' receipts. The user also has the flexibility of adding private notes to the recreational sports staff.

RecWare PRO, Sierra Digital, 937 Enterprise Drive, Sacramento, CA, 95825, 916-925-9096

Other recreation registration software products: RecWare, Escom Software, and A.E. Klawitter.

Sport as Motivator

The selection of sports for the instructional sport program, if you do it based on expressed needs and interest, serves as a motivational technique in itself. It may seem like a common sense approach to take, yet programmers sometimes rely on their own opinions of what interests and needs are instead of assessing them within the population. The major rationale for using a needs assessment is to identify what sport activities to consider for implementation within the instructional sport program. You can obtain additional information, such as skill level, time spans, and days that participants prefer. Once you determine specific needs and interests of participants, you can select appropriate instructional programs.

Motivational Benefits

Individuals pursue sport involvement for many reasons. Some may seek an opportunity for social contacts or a change of pace; others want to improve their sport performance or their personal fitness. Because the reasons for involvement are varied and participants may not know the benefits they could gain, you should review these at some point. Many times, it is helpful to indicate potential benefits as part of the publicity for the program. In this way, individuals are exposed to information that might persuade them to sign up. Once individuals have become involved, offer a more in-depth focus on the potential benefits. When individuals feel that their commitment will result in a satisfying experience, they are more motivated to learn.

Two principal areas of interest that motivate participation in sport are enjoyment and fitness. Many individuals are interested in sport because they feel it will be an enjoyable experience. This expectation may be based on experience, speculation, or observation of others who are participating. On the other hand, some people are deterred from participating when they have negative experiences or are exposed to negative attitudes regarding participation. Therefore, take necessary precautions when structuring the program to minimize obstacles to enjoyment.

The other possible benefit of sport participation is fitness. Not all sports can contribute to developing fitness. However, with proper planning, the instructional sport program can maximize contributions to fitness. Share information about supplemental activities that enhance fitness, and point out the misconceptions associated with the sport and its potential fitness benefits. A renewed public interest in fitness offers motivation when you incorporate it into instructional sport participation.

Motivation From Recognition and Reinforcement

Inherent within instructional sport is the need to provide participants with feedback on their performance. As individuals develop their knowledge and skills, they require a frame of reference to measure progress and correct mistakes. The manner in which you provide this feedback can be motivating or discouraging.

People are motivated by receiving positive reinforcement for their efforts. Usually, you should provide reinforcement for accomplishments before comments regarding weaknesses or mistakes. This approach helps to establish rapport with participants and conveys the idea that the instructor is interested in their development, as opposed to embarrassing or ridiculing them. Base all statements that are positive reinforcement on actual progress and effort, not contrived statements. False, ingenuine statements are transparent and ruin the credibility of the program. In addition, don't use reinforcement and recognition in place of correction. The purpose for instructional sport is to guide individuals through their learning and skill development. You can only do this by correcting mistakes. Quality instructors provide encouragement and focus on the positive, even when correcting mistakes.

Incentives and Motivation

There may be occasions when the instructor can use incentives to encourage participants. This refers to an out-of-the ordinary approach to designing or influencing participant learning. Incentive techniques within instructional sport can provide novelty and stimulate interest. The type of incentives used are not standardized but are the product of the instructor's imagination. Incentives within instructional sport can include prizes for the best performance of the day, a point system to accumulate a running score for achievements, ladder tournaments to rank participants, and novelty drills and games to break the monotony. Carefully select these incentives so that they have an effect but do not become the focus of the participants' development.

INSTRUCTIONAL AIDS

Instructional aids are devices an instructor can use to communicate sport information. They include tape recorders, motion and slide pictures, overhead projectors, videotape machines, handouts, and specialized equipment. These aids are not a substitute for instruction. However, they can supplement the process and make learning more interesting for the instructor and the participants. Instructional aids are excellent devices to stimulate participants to learn faster and more completely. All instructional sport personnel need to be familiar with aids that can help deliver sport information. We present general instructional aids to provide a background for the recreational sport programmer. Consider these aids in detail based on the instructional situation:

• **Bulletin boards.** Bulletin boards can aid instructors and participants. Select a high visibility location where the sport is taught.. Place the messages, and the boards themselves, at the average eye level so all people can easily see them. Use diagrams, drawings, graphs, charts, still pictures, or pictures in sequence to transmit information. There are also permanent boards (chalk boards, flannel boards, and magnetic boards) that you can write on or use as a bulletin board. Information boards are an aid often overlooked by sport instructors, but they merit consideration, especially when instructors have some creativity.

• **Recorders.** There are several recorders you can use for instructional sport: record players, cassette players, compact disc players, and reel-to-reel players. One way a recorder can help in sport learning is documenting a presentation for review when participants are unable to attend a session. You can use records and tapes, commercially produced or developed by the instructor, for other types of instructional sport content. When you use drills for a sport, you can play the tape with the verbal information while the instructor moves around the room supervising skill performance. Music may be an asset in some learning situations. Several commercial companies have produced instructional sport recordings. They have developed products to enhance participation in almost every recreational sport. An awareness of these options in instructional aids, especially with few qualified instructors, presents a viable avenue for instructional sport programming.

• **Videotapes.**   In recent years, the videotape machine has made a valuable contribution to the instructional process. There are many commercially available videos that will instruct sport and fitness skills. An instructor with a video camera can provide participants with immediate feedback from tape, which allows participants to observe their strengths and weaknesses. Self-analysis is helpful at all skill levels. Using videotape machinery for instruction enhances learning and serves as a tangible form of motivation.

• **Handouts.**   A handout is any material given to the participant to study; it can provide a reminder for what was taught. Here are some forms of information that you can print on handouts: rules and regulations, sport facilities diagrams, skill performance tips, strategy information, safety information, content not covered during lessons, lists of books and articles, and lists of radio or TV programs to enhance interest.

• **Special equipment.**   Because sport is popular and so many people want to learn sport skills, much specialized equipment, in the forms of devices and gimmicks, has been developed and put on the market. The purpose of these devices is usually to help a person improve some specific sport skill. Examples of such equipment are rubber molded grips for tennis and golf, stroke developers for tennis, putting mats for golf, air shields to punch for karate, automatic ball pitchers, tennis ball machines, and blindfolds for practice dribbling a basketball. This specialized equipment can help participants gain skill when they otherwise might not improve.

EVALUATION

In order for instructional sport to have a positive, ongoing effect, feedback on the effort is essential. Evaluation informs staff whether the program is being delivered and received properly. It can provide the instructors feedback on how the participants perceived them.

A variety of evaluation styles can be developed. Some of the most common are checklists, multiple choice questions, rankings, short essays, or computerized forms that can provide in-depth analysis. Some areas you can consider evaluating include the following:

- Active participation opportunities
- Demonstrations
- Lectures
- Facilities
- Equipment
- Instructor
  - Communication skills
  - Knowledge
  - Interest in subject
  - Performance
  - Rapport
  - Respect
  - Session organization
- Group control or discipline
- Safety

You can expand each of these areas, depending on the instructor, the sport, the age of the participants, and the degree of administrative involvement. We highly recommend that you do some type of evaluation, because, too often, this final step is avoided.

You can choose from three styles for evaluating: instructor evaluation, group evaluation, and programmer evaluation. The instructor evaluation is a self-assessment process. This may not be the best way to gain feedback; however, it is reasonable when an instructor is highly sensitive about being evaluated or when you have limited time to do any other form of evaluation. Using a self-assessment evaluation influences an instructor to think about his or her effort and how the participants may have perceived their experience.

The group evaluation is the most common technique for assessing participant opinion. Here, an instructor distributes a questionnaire that covers

---

PROGRAM AND INSTRUCTOR'S EVALUATION FORM

Instructor's name _____ Date _____

Sport _____ Number in session _____

Respond to each statement in terms of your agreement or disagreement. One (1) represents strongly agree and five (5) represents strongly disagree.

1. The session always starts on time.	1	2	3	4	5
2. The sessions are well organized.	1	2	3	4	5
3. The instructor is well prepared.	1	2	3	4	5
4. Overall, I would rate my learning experience as outstanding.	1	2	3	4	5
5. The instructor explains information well.	1	2	3	4	5
6. The instructor is enthusiastic.	1	2	3	4	5
7. The instructor demonstrates skill well.	1	2	3	4	5
8. The instructor is knowledgeable about the sport.	1	2	3	4	5
9. The instructor is always neat in appearance.	1	2	3	4	5
10. The instructor has a positive attitude for the sport.	1	2	3	4	5
11. The instructor communicates well verbally.	1	2	3	4	5
12. The progression of skill was easy to follow.	1	2	3	4	5
13. The environment was safe at all times.	1	2	3	4	5
14. The instructor was patient.	1	2	3	4	5
15. Skill diagnosis and correction were always helpful.	1	2	3	4	5

Comments _____

_____

_____

_____

_____

(Optional) Evaluator's name _____

Form 4.2 Group evaluation form.

the effectiveness of what they experienced. This is the most objective form of evaluation, providing feedback that represents a fair assessment. Form 4.2 is an example of a useful group evaluation form.

The recreational sport programmer is part of instructional sport programs, and they usually have predetermined objectives that they share with the instructor. From these objectives, the programmer would develop an assessment form (such as form 4.3), make observations, take notes, and possibly interview participants to obtain the feedback. The programmer may or may not share these findings with the instructor; however, we recommend that you do, so the instructor perceives the evaluation process properly and can make the necessary adjustments.

You should use multiple evaluation forms to improve any ongoing instructional sport program. Failure to evaluate outcomes is often counterproductive, especially when instructors are hard to come by. Good instructors need to and can handle being evaluated.

CONCLUSION

There have been tremendous interest and developments in recent years for people to enhance their

---

PROGRAMMER'S TENNIS INSTRUCTOR ASSESSMENT

Instructor's name _____   Date _____   Time _____

Client(s) name _____   Lesson level _____

Circle number that represents assessment, 1 being Very Poor and 7 Excellent.

Comments

Stroke knowledge	1	2	3	4	5	6	7	_____
Forehand	1	2	3	4	5	6	7	_____
Backhand	1	2	3	4	5	6	7	_____
Serve	1	2	3	4	5	6	7	_____
Volley	1	2	3	4	5	6	7	_____
Lob	1	2	3	4	5	6	7	_____
Overhead	1	2	3	4	5	6	7	_____
Drop shot	1	2	3	4	5	6	7	_____

Specialty shots

_____	1	2	3	4	5	6	7	_____
_____	1	2	3	4	5	6	7	_____

Demonstration	1	2	3	4	5	6	7	_____
Diagnosis and correction	1	2	3	4	5	6	7	_____
Progression	1	2	3	4	5	6	7	_____
Patience	1	2	3	4	5	6	7	_____
Enthusiasm	1	2	3	4	5	6	7	_____
Voice tone	1	2	3	4	5	6	7	_____
Appearance	1	2	3	4	5	6	7	_____
Attitude	1	2	3	4	5	6	7	_____
Safety	1	2	3	4	5	6	7	_____
Summary	1	2	3	4	5	6	7	_____

Evaluator _____   Date _____

Form 4.3   Programmer's assessment form for a tennis instructor.

sport performance through instruction. With proper marketing, an instructional sport program can provide a valuable service as well as generate additional income for many recreational settings.

Critical to any successful instructional sport program, as well as providing the participant with a satisfactory experience, is the ability of an instructor. This begins with understanding the different instructional systems so that the varied interest in sport can be understood and appropriately serviced. Also, the actual instructor selection process and its many details with assessing candidates is key to finding the best qualified person.

It does not end with finding the instructor. A recreational sport programmer has ongoing responsibilities to be sure that the different delivery considerations are applied to the participant's advantage. Also, the method of delivery has to be decided on and applied along with an ability to recognize and encourage the different motivational techniques that enhance the learning experience. Finally, any instructional program must be sensitive to the impact and level of satisfaction the participant gains, and an evaluation should be conducted to gain that insight.

To understand and properly apply an effective instructional sport program requires a recreational sport manager with special interest in this area. Nothing can be more rewarding than making a difference in sport participation because of a well-delivered lesson or clinic in sport instruction.

DISCUSSION QUESTIONS

1. Describe the four current types of instructional sport systems.

2. Explain the procedure and criteria for recruiting instructors.

3. How would a recreational sport programmer assess the credentials of an applicant for an instructional sport instructor position?

4. Discuss the predelivery considerations necessary before teaching the class.

5. Describe several instructional aids available to the instructor.

6. Why does instructional sport have the broadest base of all recreational sport programming participation?

7. In deciding to offer an instructional sport program, what programming factors must you consider?

8. What certifications or qualifications would be important for a tennis instructor to possess?

9. To be an effective instructor, must the individual be highly skilled in that particular sport? Explain your answer.

10. When developing the content for lesson plans, what factors are important to keep in mind?

11. Maintaining interest and motivation is sometimes difficult, particularly in instructional sport programs. From an instructor's standpoint, how might you maintain a participant's interest in the program?

12. Discuss the evaluation forms and styles available to assess teaching effectiveness.

13. What type of evaluation is most common for assessing participant opinion?

14. What sports tend to be included in an adult instructional sport program? What sports in a youth program?

15. From a financial cost-analysis standpoint, how effective are instructional sport programs?

APPLICATION EXERCISE

Develop a proposal for a new instructional sport program in your setting of choice. In your proposal include the following: definition of instructional sport, purpose, need for the program, implementation timeline, projected sport offerings, fees for each sport, and recruitment strategies for hiring instructors.

SUGGESTED READINGS

Leonida, M. 1986. Planning strategies for a non-credit instruction program. *National Intramural-Recreational Sports Association Journal* 10 (2): 38-48.

Meyers, D.P. 1991. Instructor employment: Independent contractor or employee?. *National Intramural-Recreational Sports Association Journal* 15 (3): 24.

Murphy, C. 1983. *Teaching kids to play.* New York: Leisure Press.

Rapp, N.L. 1991. Instructional programs in campus recreation. *National Intramural-Recreational Sports Association Journal* 15 (3): 15-16.

Spitzer, T. 1986. Non-credit recreational instruction—Safe aerobic dance classes. *National Intramural-Recreational Sports Association Journal* 10 (2): 42-43.

Stewart, M.J., and R. Clark. 1989. Health promotion activities through campus recreation. P. 71-87 in *Collected readings in recreational sports.* Corvallis, OR: National Intramural-Recreational Sports Association.

Strohmeyer, B. 1986. Present trends in non-credit activity classes. *National Intramural-Recreational Sports Association Journal* 10 (2): 31-37.

CHAPTER 5

Informal Sport

Chapter Objectives

After reading this chapter you will

- understand the purpose and nature of informal sport,
- recognize the unique characteristics of informal sport, and
- be able to identify operational requirements for a sound informal sport program.

Although some seek an avenue for leisure enjoyment in structured programs, others prefer facilities without imposed design or direction. Informal sport is self-directed participation in cooperative/competitive play activity in the game form which utilizes indoor and outdoor sport facilities that are not scheduled for short-term events or ongoing structured programs.

Informal sport, in the broadest context, encompasses traditional and nontraditional activities and settings. A backyard volleyball game, a card game, skiing, an evening bike ride, roller skating at a roller rink, target shooting, wind surfing, an early-bird swim, basketball with friends—all these are examples of informal sport. Participants determine the type of sport and facility site for participation, as well as the length of their involvement.

Informal sport could be regarded as a precursor to the more structured areas of instructional, intramural, extramural, club, athletic, and professional sport. Consider intramural team members who meet at the gymnasium to play a pick-up basketball game, the beginning tennis player who practices strokes with a friend before a lesson, the karate club member who finds an open spot in the gym to practice moves, the varsity football player who runs track to improve endurance, or the Olympic athlete hopeful who uses a weight room to work out for power-lifting competition. Each needs access to a facility free from structured events and ongoing programs.

Informal sport has not received recognition as a program area requiring planning to meet an important need. Its identity has developed through renewed interest in personal fitness and increasing public enthusiasm for recreational sport participation. The current growth of commercial and private sport facilities demonstrates the popularity of self-directed sport activity. Informal sport now involves the largest number of participants within a recreational sport program.

Whenever sport facilities exist, whether commercial, military, correctional, industrial, community, or educational, an informal sport program is possible. This program area requires as much planning as structured sport programs to allow adequate time and space for the participant who prefers self-directed sport activity.

PARTICIPATION FACTORS

When delivering an informal sport program, a programmer should concentrate on factors that facilitate participation. Our highest programming priority is creating a positive, satisfying experience—an elusive goal because the quality of the experience is a matter of personal interpretation. Although program design for attaining this goal varies from setting to setting, some participation factors have universal relevance.

Membership Services

Regardless of the less structured design of the informal sport program, participants are members of a specific programming group and an overall program. Often a positive experience in an informal sport leads to more structured involvement in other phases. Therefore, incentives to participation can include some spontaneous structured events, recognition, and fun to encourage a sense of camaraderie among participants.

Facility Availability

A quality informal sport program recognizes the diversity in participant interest and abilities by providing an adequate number and variety of sport facilities for potential users. You can initiate this process by analyzing the participants and promote it by using the setting's philosophy toward facility use. For instance, a commercial skiing developer would carefully scrutinize terrain, weather, transportation, economy, and participant interest before committing resources to constructing and operating a ski lodge. The primary goal would be to provide a quality service at a profit. In a military setting, facilities reflect two objectives: training and fitness of military personnel and recreational opportunities for their families. Constructing supplemental facilities or access to community facilities enhances opportunities for informal sport.

Informal sport facilities should serve all age groups. When possible, locate them close to residential areas to facilitate accessibility for children, the disabled, the elderly, and others with transportation problems. Schedule facility availability to coincide with the free time of various target groups. Examine design problems that pose obstacles for people with disabilities and recommend the necessary renovations. Recent legislation on accessibility requires that facilities be available for all participants with disabilities.

Seasonal Factors

Many recreational sport activities—basketball, racquetball, waterskiing, soccer, snowmobiling, softball, snow skiing, tennis, volleyball, hunting, and so forth—are associated with a season or time of the year. Anticipate increased participation in sports that are in season and keep facilities available as much as possible. Sometimes fees are adjusted so they are higher during peak season than in nonprime time. Also, maintenance requirements and supervision can change based on the season and use levels. Programmers should be sensitive to the changing season and how it influences resources and responsibilities.

Scheduling

Because informal sport participation involves convenience, facility scheduling is critical. Scheduling should take into account such factors as participant age, the time required for participation, the needs of other programs using the same facilities, budget constraints, and the popularity of a sport. An effective communication plan should inform participants about the location of all facilities and the times they are available. In addition to a printed schedule for mass distribution, a daily notice posted at each facility site, communicating temporary changes, is necessary.

One of the most difficult problems in facility scheduling for informal sport is balancing use. Consistency is difficult to achieve because structured programs often affect the time available for informal sport use. Although scheduling specific percentages of time, protecting that time for informal sport use, has not been common, this policy could become more popular with increasing demand for this type of sport participation.

Other techniques for facility use include short-term reservations and specified times for groups, such as children, women, club, senior citizens, youth sport practice, faculty, and so forth. Monitor all scheduled use to ensure that it does not become so structured it compromises opportunities for self-directed use.

Conveniences

People interested in using a facility for informal sport are attracted to conveniences that add to the enjoyment of their recreational experience. Availability of equipment is a bonus to the individual interested in trying a new sport. Others who own equipment often do not have a convenient way to transport or store it, and a way to do so creates satisfaction.

Another convenience promoting participation is the availability of locker and shower rooms. The size of the area, number of showers, and such amenities as sauna and steam rooms can go a long way. Most participants appreciate the convenience of storing their sport clothing and equipment at the site and the luxury of showering after a workout. When participants live close to the facilities, as in a college, military, or correctional setting, some of these services are unnecessary.

Additional conveniences attracting participants to facilities for informal sport include adequate parking, restrooms, seating, food and vending services, pro shops, lounge areas, video game area, conditioning area, concessions, shelters, telephones, water fountains, and proper lighting.

Cleanliness

Clean and attractive facilities for participants have a positive influence on the user's image of any program. Although a facility may not be extensive or modern, participants appreciate well-maintained and attractive space. If resources are unavailable to fund major facility repairs and renovations, attention to such details as picking up trash, maintaining attractive bulletin boards and outdoor signs, cleaning restrooms, sweeping and mopping floors, keeping lights functional, replacing broken or bent basketball rims, using nets without rips, keeping water fountains clean and unobstructed, and mowing the grass preserves participant confidence in the integrity of your program.

Personnel

Even the most attractive, well-maintained, and complete recreational sport facility may not attain the greatest use or provide maximum participant enjoyment if the supervising personnel do not act appropriately. Informal sport personnel should not only be congenial, helpful, and knowledgeable about the facility's uses, but also capable of controlling safety hazards, facility misuse, and disciplinary problems. Personnel must employ effective communication and conflict resolution skills with maturity and tact.

Another factor affecting participation is the reliability of information provided to participants. It is vital that all personnel be current on schedules, policies, and procedures and communicate the correct information to avoid inconveniencing participants.

Cost

Charging fees, which characterizes commercial sport operations, has begun affecting the informal sport program. Commercial sport facilities that provide racquetball, ice skating, tennis, swimming, skiing, bowling, and so forth, rely on individuals pursuing their sport opportunities and paying a fee to participate. Noncommercial settings dependent on local, state, or federal funding to support facility operations are experiencing cutbacks and have turned to using fees to offset operating costs for informal sport. Such revenue, if positive, can expand services and facilities, and enhance informal sport opportunities.

The cost for informal sport facility use can affect how much it is used. Fees that are common to informal sport programming follow.

- **Annual user or membership fees.** This fee creates the opportunity to have access as a recognized member. It can provide unlimited access to sport facilities for informal use. There may be instances, particularly in commercial or club settings, where an additional user fee is charged for a specific activity. For example, most racquetball clubs charge an annual fee for membership plus a daily fee or reservation fee for court time.
- **Daily user fees.** These fees are charged for unlimited facility use during a given day. Examples include a greens fee, a swimming pool daily pass, a snow ski lift ticket, ice rink admission, and a tennis court reservations. The daily user fee can accommodate guests or serve as a back-up for people who cannot provide the proper identification to show they are members.
- **Reservation fees.** These fees are for access to specific space for a specific time. The user has a starting time and an ending time. You can control use with reservation or walk-in arrangements and with fee adjustments to encourage use during less popular times.
- **Rental fees.** These are payments guaranteeing exclusive use of a facility or equipment.

The user may enjoy all the advantages of use as long as property is not destroyed, damaged, or lost. A rental fee is usually applied when informal sport facilities or equipment are available, during low use times of the day, week, or month.

- **License and permit fees.** These are charges for the right to participate in government-monitored activities such as hunting or fishing. During these sports, the participant usually is involved informally with few restrictions except to follow the written laws.

POLICIES AND PROCEDURES

As an administrator, you must design formal policies and procedures for all programs you direct—informal programs are no exception. Policy statements outline the conditions for participation, and procedures direct the manner in which these policies are enforced. The objective is to explain the ground rules for informal sport participation. The policy and procedural statements for an informal program often take the form of a participants' manual. Pages 80-81 provide you with tips on how to create a participants' manual.

Creating an Informal Sport Participant Manual

A manual for your informal sport program is an excellent means to help employees and participants understand the program and follow its policies and procedures. Your distinctive informal sport program will be more inviting and more effectively delivered if you put it in writing. We suggest you design the manual to cover the topics listed in the outline below. In fact, you can easily convert the following outline to the table of contents for your manual.

I. Introduction

II. Informal sport advisory council

III. List of facilities

IV. Schedule of availability

V. User policies

    A. Eligibility

You can produce the manual simply using your word processor, copy machine, and stapler. Or, if time, talent, and budget allow, you can have the manual professionally designed and printed. Regardless of the document's cosmetic attributes, make sure you distribute this useful tool to all your participants and on-site staff.

Eligibility

Eligibility statements specify who is permitted to use the sport facilities, most often in terms of individual or group eligibility: student, faculty, staff, alumni; public employee, executive; noncommissioned officer; inmate, guard; resident, nonresident; and member, guest. Group eligibility statements may specify age levels (children, teens, adults, senior citizens), social or civic groups (Lions Club, Girl Scouts, Boy Scouts), living units (dormitory, fraternity, sorority, married housing), or affiliation with the agency or setting (residents, nonresidents; university, public; members, guests).

Settings may prohibit certain categories of individuals from facility access, or they may restrict access to specific days, times, or activities: a private swimming club may limit guest pool use to certain hours during the week; a university may prohibit nonaffiliates from facility access; a military base may confine the dependents of active duty personnel to facility access during the evenings and weekends; a corporation may designate in an industrial plant special hours for executive staff access to a weight room.

Eligibility statements describe the intended user of a program. As eligibility requirements become more stringent, you need a monitoring system to discourage ineligible participation. Developing eligibility statements involves the following considerations:

- What kinds of people are we serving?
- What can our facilities handle?
- Are there certain facilities or times when we must restrict use?
- What personnel are available or necessary to monitor facility use?
- What financial resources are available to support monitoring and control systems?
- What effect will eligibility statements have on public relations?
- Are there any legal considerations that affect eligibility?
- How will participants prove they are legitimate users of the facility site?

Fees and Charges

Charging fees requires developing a sound collection and security system. It may involve an identification system that enables the user to verify payment for facility use. Determine procedures for fee collection and identification systems well in advance. Are adjusted fees available for low-income participants? Can fees be prorated? Are credit cards or money orders acceptable? Are charge accounts available? Is there a penalty for bad checks or delinquent accounts?

Facility Reservations

The priorities for facility use largely determine the amount of time available for informal sport. Once you finalize these priorities in policy form, participants will know how to reserve facilities for informal sport participation.

The most prevalent reservation technique used within informal sport is the court or field reservation. You need this technique to accommodate a large number of participants, and it is useful for handball, racquetball, squash, tennis, basketball, and softball facilities. Most common reservation policies make several of the following stipulations:

- Reservations may be made in person or by computer.
- One in-person reservation will be accepted, then one phone-in reservation.
- A valid identification card or user pass is required to make a reservation.
- Only one reservation per day is permitted.
- Reservations may be made only for same-day use.
- Reservations may be made several days in advance.
- Cancellations must be made in person with proper identification.
- Cancellations must be made 24 hours in advance or a no-show penalty will be imposed.
- Persons absent 10 minutes past the reserved playing time forfeit all rights to the facility.

Programs that prohibit phone-in reservations or cancellations either have no way to verify user eligibility, require a user fee, or rely on the phone for other uses. Programs that accept phone-ins check eligibility at the facility when they collect fees. The major advantage of accepting phone calls is to accommodate participants having legitimate scheduling conflicts. A disadvantage regarding phone-in cancellations is the potential for tampering with reservations.

Although variations exist, reservations reflect demand, use patterns of participants, and staff availability. Publicize your reservation policy in writing and include information on eligibility, reservation procedures, court availability, and fee requirements. You should also post a reservation chart (form 5.1) so users can see what times are available.

Sport Facility Use Policies

These policies present information for all eligible facility users, regardless of their sport interest. Because participation is self-directed, participants must understand these policies in the interest of their safety and enjoyment.

Accident Prevention and Reporting

The risk of injury and accident is a concern of all informal sport programmers. To protect participants and personnel and minimize the potential for legal action stemming from injury, develop a comprehensive plan for accident prevention, first aid, and reporting. Focus your efforts on facility and equipment inspection, hazard control, risk management, staff training, accident prevention,

emergency medical procedures, and participant awareness.

Policies for informal sport facility use must convey information to participants regarding safety awareness and procedures for handling accident situations. Printed statements, supported by notices at activity sites and staff supervision, help ensure proper facility use and participant behavior. All policy and procedure statements should describe how and where to obtain assistance at the facility site for an accident or injury.

Participants must be aware of their responsibility to provide the necessary information for accident reports. Accurate and complete forms are essential for hazard and injury analysis, insurance claims, and possible legal action. Accident reporting begins at the scene as soon as it is possible to communicate with the victim. Unnecessary delays may result in incomplete or inaccurate information.

Finally, policy statements should inform participants whether the facility carries insurance to cover injuries sustained at the site. If the facility requires outside insurance or a medical examination before participation, the informal sport staff may bear responsibility for ensuring participant compliance.

Emergency Procedures

Risks apart from the potential for accidents merit our attention. A fire, tornado, electrical failure, chemical leak, avalanche, explosion, or bomb threat necessitate an emergency plan, despite the unlikelihood of their occurrence. Such a plan includes provisions for training personnel and informing the public of emergency procedures. Post specific evacuation plans, procedures, and safety codes prominently at facility sites. In an emergency, informal sport staff should be ready to take charge.

Children

The presence of children and young adults often requires specific policies governing their participation. This group lacks the maturity, safety consciousness, and awareness of other participants. Rules to structure informal sport participation by children and young adults include the following:

- Require that children be directly supervised by a parent or adult.
- Provide supervision for children.
- Designate times for children to use facilities.
- Require parents or guardians to sign statements acknowledging potential risks of youth activities and their awareness of user policies and procedures.

HANDBALL-RACQUETBALL-SQUASH COURT RESERVATIONS

Day _____   Date _____

	4:00 p.m.	5:00 p.m.	6:00 p.m.	7:00 p.m.	8:00 p.m.	9:00 p.m.	10:00 p.m.
Court 1							
Court 2							
Court 3							
Court 4							
Court 5							
Court 6							
Court 7							
Court 8							
Court 9							
Court 10							
Court 11							
Court 12							

Note. A valid ID must be shown when making reservations. Only one court time per day, per ID will be allowed.

Form 5.1   Informal sport reservation form.

Although these strategies cannot eliminate problems or the potential of an injury, they represent our best effort to minimize risk for all informal sport participants.

Participant Conduct

One of the most demanding responsibilities in informal sport is observing, controlling, and reporting participant conduct and facility use. Pay regular attention to this to maintain staff awareness. Policies in this area are to encourage appropriate participant conduct and include the following:

- Where to dispose of litter
- Where smoking is permitted
- Where food and beverages can be purchased and consumed
- Where spitting receptacles and fountains are located
- Recommended or required clothing and footwear
- Restrictions about pets (mandated by some states)
- Expectations for fair play, positive social interaction, and proper conflict resolution behavior
- Procedures for lost and found items

Individual Facility Policies

Most settings establish policies specific to each facility. The key to public acceptance of policy statements is justifying their existence, enforcing them consistently, and being sensitive to public relations. If personnel are brash and aggressive in policy interpretation or enforcement, they provoke negative participant reaction.

Participant acceptance of facility use policy requires their involvement in the decision-making process. The programmer can accomplish this through informal conversations or more structured channels, such as survey feedback, evaluation sessions, and advisory councils.

Governance

An outgrowth of facility policies is a process called governance, which you should design to deal fairly with difficulties that arise. Personnel need preparation to handle situations involving participant abuse to facilities, employees, and others. Each occurrence requires documentation for objective review and possible disciplinary action. When a problem arises, determine whether current program practices contributed to it. We suggest these guidelines to minimize problems:

- Provide attractive, well-lit, and well-maintained facilities.

- Facilitate participant access to facilities and services by minimizing red tape.
- Use committed, conscientious, and diplomatic personnel.
- Replace or repair vandalized equipment.
- Provide adequate supervisory or security personnel for monitoring participation and identifying maintenance needs.
- Enforce policies consistently.

Effective governance involves keeping participants and staff informed about conduct expectations, including the consequences of policy violation and the procedure for resolving problems. In practice, policy statements need written administrative approval before implementation. Otherwise, the programmer may be thrust into an embarrassing situation if his or her decision is overruled or disregarded. To ensure fair and thorough governance, we recommend that you use the following principles.

- Record the situation as soon as possible.
- Obtain statements from the party involved, employees, and witnesses.
- Conduct an investigation and review the facts with all involved parties.
- Establish a ruling based on severity of the incident and precedent.
- Provide an appeals process.

OPERATIONS

Operations include everything that influences delivering and receiving informal sport programming. With the casual, self-directed, and low-leadership requirement, this program area has a unique influence and control. A good rule, especially pertaining to personnel, is to think of three functions: safety, security, and public relations. Safety means having complete attention and sensitivity toward creating and maintaining an environment that protects against injury. Take every precaution to protect the participant. Security deals with creating a sense of comfort with the participant. Such things as access, control, communication, cleanliness, and convenience all contribute to one's comfort zone. The public relations element results from doing everything in the best interest of the participant. Informal sport is naturally popular, and providing operational tasks effectively contributes to image and prestige. The programmer must anticipate

problems in these areas, have procedures for reporting problems and plans to resolve them, and maintain records for references.

In the process of influencing safety, security, and public relations, you need to review some direct areas of responsibility. A sound understanding and appreciation for these areas can go a long way to fulfill the programmer's responsibilities.

Personnel Considerations

Informal sport activities typically require the services of door checkers, cashiers, equipment room and locker room attendants, supervisors, lifeguards, facility managers, and custodians. The programmer should determine what jobs are necessary for program delivery and proper supervision of facilities and participants, taking care that job descriptions specify the tasks you expect personnel to perform. Even though a written description explains performance expectations, use an oral presentation and discussion to specify responsibilities common to all jobs and the tasks peculiar to each job.

An effective tool to inform personnel is an employee manual. This manual discusses job descriptions, program philosophy, organizational structure, employment application and payroll procedures, benefits, performance expectations, dress code, reasons for termination, liability concerns, financial accountability, grievance procedures, program policies, and facility maps.

Due to the minimal involvement by personnel in informal sport, interaction with participants is sporadic and tasks often become routine and unchallenging. To avoid apathy, inconsistent job performance, and resentment that may result, we suggest that a programmer do the following:

- Develop a regular system for monitoring performance and conducting evaluations.
- Keep work shifts short, especially for less desirable tasks.
- Know the personalities of your staff and match them up with the demands of the job.
- Use a sequential pay rate scale that increases with the demands of each job type.
- Develop a job classification system that provides upward mobility.
- Seek recommendations from personnel for improving job conditions.
- Take disciplinary action as warranted.
- Recognize and reward quality job performance.

Shining Example

Lockheed Martin Employees' Recreation Association, Sunnyvale, CA

The Lockheed Martin Employees' Recreation Association, (LMERA), is a non-profit industrial recreation program. LMERA is managed by staff who's function is to set-up, coordinate, and conduct social, education, recreational, and athletic activities for the employees of Lockheed Martin Missiles and Space Company, Inc., (LMMSC). The LMERA provides recreation, sports, and fitness services to employees, retirees, and families. The sports complex includes two lighted softball fields, a regulation soccer field, two sand volleyball courts, locker and shower facilities, and a picnic area. Special employee sporting events include coed soccer, softball, 3 on 3 and 5 on 5 Basketball, Sand Doubles Volleyball, and Grass Volleyball. In addition, the LMERA provides a Fitness Center which includes a fully equipped weight room, aerobics studio, basketball court, and shower facilities. LMERA's mission is to improve morale, instill company loyalty, and emphasize healthy lifestyles for their employees and families.

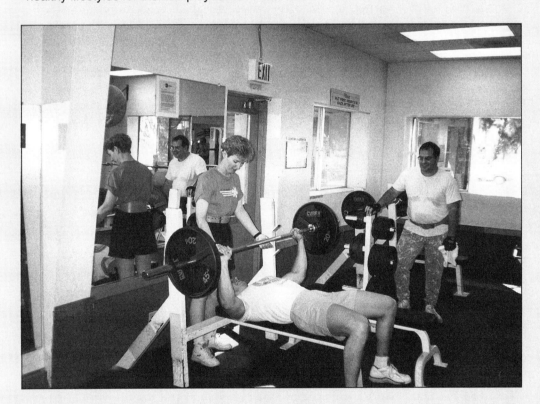

Organization: Employee Services and Recreation Association

Clientele: The association services employees, dependents, spouses, and retirees as well as outside rental groups. The sports program serves 32,000 clients on an annual basis. Clients tend to be male (70 percent in the 24-45 age group).

Budget: The association operates on a $500,000 budget generated from revenues. The Company provides buildings, land, utilities, and maintenance costs worth approximately $150,000 annually.

Marketing: At the association, marketing is aimed at employees, families and retirees through increased use of electronic mail, inserts in company newspaper, flyers, bulletin boards, and by word of mouth through 150 LMERA Representatives.

Staff: The current staffing includes six full-time Lockheed Martin employees, two full-time contract employees, and seven part-time contract employees for a total of 15 employees. An elected board of Directors (11) serves in an advisory function. The company provides assistance from Legal, Insurance, Finance, Facilities, Procurement, and Executive Staff to act as facilitators and advisors to the board.

Program Detail: LMERA currently operates over 70 different programs including sports, fitness, clubs, retirees, children's programs, family programs, golf and golf instructions, discount merchandise, discount tickets, photo developing, walking club, recreation vehicle storage, field rentals, room rentals, line dancing, travel programs, dry cleaning, cellular phone sales, flower sales, fitness evaluations, pickelball, softball, volleyball, basketball, and sports car club.

Facilities:

- **Building 160** - Store and merchandise area – Auditorium, Photo Club, Ham Radio Club, Recreation Vehicle Storage Administration, Discounts for Amusement Parks, Lodging, Camp areas, and Travel and Retiree Programs.

- **Building 161** - LMERA Fitness Center - Full fitness program. Aerobic classes, golf program, Achievers Club, Fitness and Wellness Special Events.

- **Building 162** - Multipurpose facility - Ceramics, lapidary rooms, video and computer clubs, hosts bridge and chess tournaments, Employee Assistance Program Drop In Center. Converted gun range hosts Blood Banks and large company activities. Many clubs meet at this facility.

- **Building 164** - Sports Complex - Two night-lighted athletic fields, sand volleyball, picnic and BBQ facilities, Field House with lockers and showers, 1/3 mile track with parcourse. Field House includes concession stand.

Recreation Vehicle Storage - Three lots totaling 8.5 acres provide storage to over 800 employees and retirees.

All informal sport personnel should understand that you expect them to project a positive, capable image in appearance, attitude, and actions—regardless of the pressures of the job.

Reporting Considerations

The programmer has the responsibility for recognizing, reporting, and reviewing operational concerns within the informal sport environment. You can facilitate this by a communication network, including on-site supervisors and participants who are familiar with the reporting process.

One of the primary reasons for establishing a reporting system using personnel and participants is the impossibility of having professional staff at each facility site during all hours of operation. Using volunteers, employees, or participants already on-site increases the likelihood that important items will be reported, because everyone has a stake in making improvements and can add new perspectives to situations in which staff may have blind spots.

Although we discuss the principal areas of reporting in the personnel chapter, those that have particular relevance for the informal sport program are facility usage reports and financial summary reports.

Facility Usage Reports

Profit and nonprofit informal sport programs can obtain useful information through facility usage reports. Regular monitoring reveals user trends in terms of increased or decreased participation, popularity of facilities and activities, and peak or low times for use. Further analysis specifies the type or age group of user—male, female, youth, senior citizen, student, resident, officer, or executive.

Facility usage reports (as in form 5.2) aid planning and evaluating informal sport participation. Data can suggest a demand for additional facilities, a change in the number of supervisors needed for certain facilities, alternatives for the number of hours a facility is available, strategies for improving use of certain facilities, and cost-efficient methods of operating them.

Financial Summaries

Financial transactions require keeping records to satisfy legal requirements, safeguard assets, and

TENNIS COURT FACILITY USAGE REPORT

Day _____   Date _____

Time	South battery	North battery	Waiting to play	Total	Initial
12:15 p.m.					
12:45 p.m.					
1:15 p.m.					
1:45 p.m.					
2:15 p.m.					
2:45 p.m.					
3:15 p.m.					
3:45 p.m.					
4:15 p.m.					
4:45 p.m.					
5:15 p.m.					
5:45 p.m.					
6:15 p.m.					
6:45 p.m.					
7:15 p.m.					
7:45 p.m.					
8:15 p.m.					
8:45 p.m.					
9:15 p.m.					
9:45 p.m.					
Total					

Count everyone using and waiting to use the facility for informal tennis. Do not count spectators, classes, intramurals, club sport, athletics, or reserved time.

Supervisor taking count should add the row total and then initial it.

After final count, supervisors should add the columns.

Form 5.2   Informal sport facility usage report.

control operations. Transactions that commonly involve informal sport personnel include sale of membership and user passes, season passes, equipment rentals, concession sales, clothing or equipment sales, and locker and towel rentals.

Although we cover accounting procedures in detail in chapter 10, here we offer guidelines for transactions that informal sport facility personnel handle:

- Provide each person responsible for cash with a separate and fixed change fund and a safe depository.
- When cashiers use the same cash drawer, have the incoming replacement verify the amount left before shift exchange. Record discrepancies and include the signature of each party.
- Use written receipts for all income.
- Keep a daily record of revenue and deposits.
- Regularly compare sales to an inventory or merchandise.

ADA Suggestions

The ADA legislation mandates that measures be taken to provide equal access for individuals with disabilities to those areas where goods and services are available to the general public. In our recreational sport facilities this would include adjusting a literature rack displaying sport entry forms,

Facility Reservation Software

For a computerized sports facility reservation system to be successful, many items need to be identified. Each agency has diverse needs and constraints, different sports facilities, and varying levels of staff and financial support. All of these factors must be taken into consideration before a reservation system can be effectively computerized. The goals of any facility reservation system should be identified to maximize the use of available sports facilities and to provide all staff with instant access to accurate information regarding site availability.

Specifically, the following features of a facility reservation program may be important to you as a recreational sports programmer:

- Automatically assigns a unique reservation confirmation number.
- Allows reactivation of canceled reservations.
- Tracks deposit transactions.
- Allows overbooking of a site by a certain percentage factor by season or by month.
- Calculates the estimated total facility charge for advanced reservations.
- Allows for additions, changes, cancellations, report printing, and reactivation. Duplicates user information from one reservation to another.
- Accommodates special requests and comments for each reservation.
- Prints billing information by site and user.
- Tracks complaint/problem maintenance for each site and tracks preventative maintenance performed by each site's supervisors and users.

Reservation modules should also have the ability to display screens that perform the following functions:

- Display sites available for booking during any range of dates.
- Display a particular site.
- Display user groups by summary or by details.
- Block/unblock a site by user group.
- Show all reservations assigned to a particular site.
- Show all sites assigned to a specific reservation.
- Display total sites reserved versus total sites available for any date.
- Display the total number of sites reserved by user type per day.
- Display all facilities reserved for a specific date and time.
- Forecast facility availability reports.

Finally, many recreational sport programmers who reserve facilities are often called upon to provide program counseling to inexperienced individuals who are using their facilities. Examples of counseling range from recommending how to conduct sports events to how to schedule tournaments. An effective computerized facility reservation system should provide ways to monitor facility counseling sessions and checklists. This will not only protect you legally, but will also allow users to have safe and enjoyable experiences at your sports facility and will encourage them to return in the future.

The following are several screens from R.I.C. Corporation's *ConCentRICS for Windows* facility reservation program. This is a very comprehensive program that will meet the many needs of recreational sports programmers.

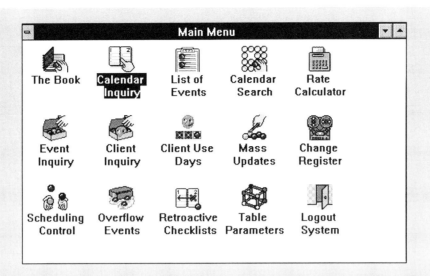

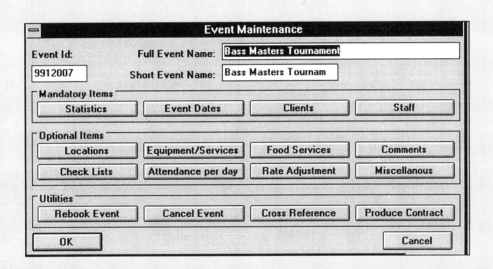

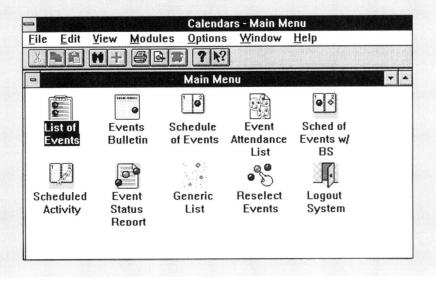

ConCentRICS for Windows, R.I.C. Corporation, 6215 Constitution Drive, Fort Wayne, IN 46804, 770-944-8730
Other facility reservation software products: RecTrac!, RecWare, HTE-Programmed for Success, Overtime Software, Escom Software, and A.E. Klawitter.

rearranging weight-resistance machines to allow wheelchair access, providing braille signs on the swimming pool deck, widening a door to a racquetball court, and providing visual emergency alarms in the field house.

CONCLUSION

Unlike structured sport programs, the informal sport program emphasizes facility management and supervision more than activity design and supervision. Although the informal sport participant determines the activity and format for involvement, he or she depends on the programmer for access to facilities and services. When we consider the variety of participant interests that require facility access, the programmer faces a major challenge to provide sufficient and diverse facilities to meet these interests.

The programmer has a further responsibility for making the facilities and participation opportunities as attractive as possible. A quality informal sport program involves more than constructing enough facilities and making them available for self-directed use. It entails establishing effective operating policies, providing capable supervision, responding to participant feedback, and maintaining facilities properly to increase their usefulness.

DISCUSSION QUESTIONS

1. We define informal sport as "self-directed participation in cooperative or competitive play activity in the game form." Cite five examples of informal sport.

2. Describe several operational factors pertaining to informal sport programming.

3. One of the more difficult problems in informal sport programming is balancing facility scheduling and use. Explain the techniques that could assist with this problem.

4. Explain typical informal sport user policies and procedures.

5. Describe the types of information that informal sport programmers can obtain through facility usage reports.

6. A suggested informal sport participant's policy manual would include what items?

7. Name three participation factors for informal sport.

8. What do we mean by conveniences in informal sport programming?

9. Explain common facility reservation policies in informal sport.

10. What are typical examples of participant misconduct in informal sport?

11. Cite guidelines or examples that would encourage appropriate participant conduct.

12. Financial transactions and record keeping associated with informal sport programs would commonly include what types of transactions?

13. Informal sport programs are often given low priority in facility scheduling. Why? What can the programmer do to correct this?

14. Do you think a governance system should exist in an informal sport program? Explain.

15. Can you have structure in an informal sport program? Explain.

APPLICATION EXERCISE

In developing a summer facility use plan for a recreational sport complex, you notice that two user groups have requested the same facility at the same time and date. One group is a youth flag football camp, which involves approximately 500 participants per week for an eight-week period. The other group is an adult softball program, which involves approximately 400 participants per week for a nine-week period. How would you resolve this potential conflict fairly? What factors would you have to consider? What facility reservation policies would you develop to avoid this conflict in the future?

SUGGESTED READINGS

Gaskins, D.A. 1993. Order on the court: Effective participant management in informal sports. *National Intramural-Recreational Sports Association Journal* 17 (3): 10, 12-13.

Lamke, G. 1985. Facility supervision: A vital function in overall facility management. *National Intramural-Recreational Sports Association Journal* 9 (3): 42-46.

Meagher, J. 1990. 43 steps to a successful facility. *Athletic Business* 14 (8): 41-43.

Scheele, K., and T. Hernbloom. 1990. Campus recreation supervisors—A comparison. *National Intramural-Recreational Sports Association Journal* 14 (2): 38-43.

Intramural and Extramural Sport

Chapter Objectives

After reading this chapter you will

- be able to identify the operational factors of a successful intramural or extramural tournament,
- understand how to organize intramural and extramural sport events, including team, dual, individual, and meet sport, and
- know the organizational requirements of extramural sport.

Historically, intramural sport has been the term for collegiate recreational sport. By 1975, the popularity of informal sport programs, club sport, extramural sport, and other programming areas required an expansion in terminology. Thus, the term *recreational sport* surfaced, with intramural sport just one of its programming areas. The intramural principles originally documented by Dr. Elmer Mitchell are relatively unchanged. This new term, recreational sport, represents the diverse recreational interests of participants and relates to both theory and practice.

Another interpretation of intramural sport, outside of the collegiate setting, occurred at the turn of the 20th century. Municipal and community recreation departments, churches, elementary and secondary schools, industries, and private clubs offered a variety of sport events. Although programs within these settings have not been traditionally termed *intramural sport,* they meet the definition as presented.

The word "intramural" is a combination of the Latin words *intra* meaning "within" and *muralis* meaning "wall." When used as an adjective with the term sport, it refers to sport events for members confined within the walls or jurisdiction of a setting. Intramural sport represents structured sport participation, which requires design and leadership for its provision. The term intramural sport may be used in any recreational sport setting, for example, a sport program sponsored by a community parks and recreation department, Boys Club, Girls Club, YMCA, or YWCA. Youth sport is more appropriately termed youth intramural sport.

Extramural sport is an extension of the intramural sport program. Participants, usually champions of intramural programs, compete outside of the setting against champions from other institutions. Extramural events include sport days, play days, or other structured events conducted without a season-long schedule, league competition, or championship.

A high-quality intramural or extramural sport program encourages maximum participation in voluntary and wholesome sport activities for all. Equal opportunities in sport should be available to all interested individuals regardless of age, sex, race, religion, creed, employment, or economic status. The motto *Sport for Everyone* represents the philosophy of intramural and extramural sport. It provides a natural outlet for competition and challenge.

PROGRAM OF EVENTS

Developing a program of events is an important ingredient in intramural and extramural sport programs. Although many activities are possible, the successful program reflects those best suited to most participants. It is better to offer a few well-selected activities than several poorly administered ones. The following principles may aid in developing program offerings:

- **Needs, interests, and preferences of participants.** Develop the program content with participant input. When conducting interest surveys, ask questions that determine what people do now, what they would like added or changed, what skills they possess, and what activity they would participate in if it were offered. A good start would be to offer traditional events that have wide appeal based on programs offered by similar agencies elsewhere. The programmer may begin to modify the content as new input indicates.

- **Balance of offerings.** Individuals have different sport interests and skill levels. Consequently, the programmer should offer a balance of individual, dual, and team sport; nontraditional events, special events, and meets; indoor and outdoor sport; competitive and casual emphasis; strenuous and less strenuous events; and the number of events offered during a season, session, or term.

- **Flexibility.** Remain open-minded in selecting events to meet the demands of the participants. What is appropriate one year changes the next. Factors affecting program selection include the following:

  - Age
  - Number of events
  - Gender

- Time factors
- Skill levels
- Climate and season
- Levels of competition
- Budgetary limitations
- Physical capacity
- Area and facility availability
- Safety
- Equipment restraints
- Number of participants
- Leadership and supervisors

These factors may not apply to every sport setting. Institutions have unique restrictions or limitations. The effective programmer seeks to offer well-conducted events serving the majority of clientele.

Types of Events

You can classify events in the sport program in various ways. Among them are the following:

- **Individual sports**, such as swimming, golf, bowling, and archery, allow the individual to participate alone.
- **Dual sports**, such as table tennis, racquetball, badminton, or handball, require at least one opponent.
- **Group sports**, such as relays, allow various size groups to participate.
- **Team sports**, such as flag football, basketball, or soccer, require a specified number of players who play as a unit or organized team.
- **Meets** are organized competitions that include separate events and are usually completed within a specified time, ranging from several hours to several days. Swimming, track and field, and wrestling are examples of meets.
- **Special events** consist of nontraditional events, not usually practiced by the participant. Special events are excellent ways to promote positive public relations.
- **Cointramural sports**, applicable to many sport events, offer a balanced programming area that emphasizes fun, team spirit, and social interaction with members of both sexes.

Units of Participation

Units of participation are the select groupings that categorize participants for intramural or extramural play. These units are essential for a well-balanced program. Make every effort to develop reasonable units that will foster enthusiasm and maintain tradition in a wholesome competitive atmosphere. Suggestions for assigning units of participation include age groups, housing units, organizations, facilities, precincts, residential zones, and work shifts. Regardless of the setting, participation units should be equitable in size for a system to function effectively.

PROGRAM POLICIES AND REGULATIONS

The program policies and regulations of the intramural and extramural sport programs should be clearly stated and available to all participants before the sport event. Some programmers have found it helpful to prepare these statements as written handouts as *guides to participation*. Whenever possible, discuss the most pertinent information with participants, perhaps at a participants' or team captains' meeting before play. As a program administrator you should consider policies covering eligibility, protests, disciplinary action, forfeits, postponement and rescheduling, and preparticipation medical clearance. In the next few pages, we'll discuss how to develop policies and regulations for each of these areas.

Eligibility

Develop and enforce eligibility rules for intramural and extramural sport to ensure fair competition and eliminate controversy. Theoretically, all should be able to participate in the program. Realistically, you must establish regulations governing individual and organizational eligibility. Pages 96-98 serve as a guide to eligibility policy making.

Eligibility Policy Guidelines

As a recreational sport programmer, you want to provide all participants with good competition and a fair opportunity to win. The outline below provides an example of commonly accepted eligibility requirements.

I. Individual eligibility

   A. An individual may play for only one team per sport or contest. The team first represented should be the sole team for which a person may play for the remainder of the sport or contest.

   B. Declare any player using an assumed name ineligible. The team involved should forfeit any contest in which the individual played under the assumed name.

   C. Only individuals living, working, or attending a specified unit of participation should be allowed to play for that unit. Examples of this eligibility requirement are employment for a company or industry, regular attendance at a church, or union membership.

II. Skill level eligibility

   A. Professional eligibility

      1. Any person established as a professional in any sport should be ineligible in that intramural sport or its counterpart.

      2. Definition of a professional is any person recognized by a national governing body, such as the USLTA, PGA, NCAA, or a professional meber of the NFL, CFL, NBA, major or minor league baseball, NASL, or other professional or semiprofessional organization.

   B. Intercollegiate athletic eligibility

      1. A person who has won a collegiate letter or award (i.e., trophy, plaque, jewelry, certificate, jacket) in a sport should not be eligible to compete in that sport or its counterpart for a three-year period.

      2. Only one varsity letter winner is eligible to compete for a team in their sport or its related counterpart.

      3. A person who has received an athletic scholarship or is a member of an intercollegiate athletic team, but did not receive a collegiate letter or award, should not be allowed to compete in that sport for one year following competition.

      (a) A person is considered a member of a collegiate team if they have practiced three weeks before the first regularly scheduled athletic contest.

      (b) Athletic coaches are considered members of their teams and are, therefore, restricted from participation.

      (c) If an individual practices with a collegiate team for one year and does not letter, but is dropped from the team the following year, three weeks before the first regularly scheduled athletic contest, he or she should be ineligible to compete in that sport and its counterpart in the intrmural sport program during that year.

   C. Club sport eligibility

      Club sport members may participate in their specific or related sport. Allow one past or present club sport member to compete per team during a game to prevent domination by the club. A club sport member is any individual who registers, pays dues, or practices with the club within three weeks of the first game or match of the club season. At the end of one year a past club member should return to a regular status for that specific or related sport.

   D. Related sport

      The following is a list of sports and their counterparts that refers to professional, intercollegiate athletics, and club sport eligibility:

Professional, Athletic, Club Sport	Related Intramural Sport
Badminton	Badminton
Baseball	Softball
Basketball	Basketball, free throw, super shoot, one-on-one
Billiards	Billiards
Bowling	Bowling
Cross country	Cross country, track, jogging
Diving	Diving
Field events	Field events
Football	Flag football, touch football

Professional, Athletic, Club Sport	Related Intramural Sport
Frisbee	Frisbee
Golf	Golf, miniature golf
Handball	Handball
Judo	Judo
Racquetball	Racquetball
Soccer	Soccer
Softball	Softball, baseball
Swimming	Swimming, water polo
Table tennis	Table tennis
Track (running event)	Track, cross country, jogging
Volleyball	Volleyball, cageball, walleyball
Water polo	Water polo, swimming
Weight lifting	Weight lifting
Wrestling	Wrestling

III. Organizational eligibility

A. Individuals belonging to one or more teams should declare membership with only one team before the event. Individuals who change teams during the event should have the option of completing the specific schedule with their original team if they have participated in an event before moving.

B. Before participation, list team participants on the official entry form or score sheet in the sport office.

C. Only affiliated members are eligible to compete for an organization.

Others may participate in any open division in the program.

Protests

Inevitably, there will be times when participants feel an official has made a mistake, someone has used an ineligible player, or some situation has occurred that seems unfair and prompts a verbal protest. In anticipation of protests, the sport programmer should have a procedure for receiving, documenting, and reviewing them.

Accept protests, but do not encourage them whenever someone feels a wrong has been committed. Regardless of the ruling that results, the programmer can review the program and personnel objectively to reveal their strengths and improve on their weaknesses. A protest process brings the programmer into direct contact with participants and provides an opportunity to establish better understanding with them.

Protests may be made when an ineligible player has participated or improper interpretation or enforcement of the rules has occurred. Protests about a sport official's judgment call are usually not accepted. In some situations, protests arise from judgment calls as a way to take a break in the action. This permits the participants to let off steam by writing out a grievance instead of directing emotion toward an official. Although the programmer generally does not accept a protest on a judgment call, a review of the protest and discussion with participants may reveal a need to work more closely with officials on their mechanics or some other aspect of performance.

Any team or individual protesting the eligibility of an opposing player should provide evidence that the player is ineligible. Such evidence may consist of the following:

- Written and signed testimony of a witness.
- Days, dates, and times validating illegal participation.
- Pictures, rosters, and so forth, that depict ineligibility. Usually this evidence must be filed by a deadline designated by the sport staff.

If the protest does not involve eligibility, it should occur on the field of play and be noted by the sport officials or supervisors on duty. The protesting team should make sure that the officials or supervisors note the time of the contest, score, and particulars of the play in question before resuming play. The aggrieved party can accomplish this by filing a protest form (see form 6.1). If the protest (other than eligibility) is sustained, replay the contest from the point of protest.

All protests should be verified in writing by the participant and submitted to the sport staff in a timely fashion. In many intramural and extramural programs, each protest must be accompanied by a *protest sincerity fee*. This fee is returned to the protesting team if the protest is sustained. Otherwise, the department retains it. Such a fee discourages many unwarranted protests.

When you receive an initial written protest and documentation of evidence from the participant, the staff should further investigate the complaint. After reviewing all materials, an appropriate staff member should make a decision. Staff should always have the authority to investigate an alleged

---

PROTEST FORM

Sport _____   Date _____

• **TEAMS INVOLVED**

Protesting:

Team A _____   Team B _____

Team captain _____   Team captain _____

Phone _____   Phone _____

Time-outs remaining _____   Time-outs remaining _____

Score _____   Score _____

• **DETAILS**

Period _____ (Volleyball) Game _____ (Softball) Inning _____

Time remaining _____

Team in possession _____ (Softball) At bat _____

Explanation of protest and what occurred

_____

_____

_____

_____

_____

How and where is ball to be put into play? _____

_____

Protesting team captain _____

(Signature)

• **OFFICIALS**

Referee _____   Phone _____

Umpire _____   Phone _____

Officials' comments _____

_____

_____

Supervisor _____   Phone _____

Form 6.1   Intramural sport protest form.

violation of policy without a formal protest by a participant.

If the staff member makes an *invalid protest* ruling, the participant should have the right to appeal the decision to an appeals or governing board. This board serves as ruling body for all intramural or extramural sport programs. In making their final decisions, the board should be governed by the same rules and regulations adopted by the program. To reach its decision, the board may request any staff, sport official, supervisor, witness, or representative from the teams involved to attend a meeting or hearing. All decisions rendered by this board should be final and not subject to appeal.

Disciplinary Action

People participating in sport may encounter disappointments or frustrations that they are unable to control. Unless the programmer has an objective and consistent procedure for dealing with negative behavior and personnel who can implement this procedure, problems will continue. Other participants may lose interest in the program, and the programmer may encounter problems securing officials. The effective control of negative behavior is a major factor in the enjoyment of participants and personnel.

If an individual or spectator acts in an unsporting manner during intramural or extramural competition, the game official has authority to take action, as necessary, to keep control of the game. Depending on the severity of the incident, an official may take the following action according to his or her judgment: give a warning, eject from the game, eject from the area, or suspend the game.

Game officials should report all incidents to the intramural supervisor and document them for use by the staff in investigating the incident. Incidents that indicate unsporting conduct (using an ineligible player; theft or damage to facilities or equipment; physical or verbal abuse toward officials, supervisors, players, or spectators) should be investigated by the staff. The staff should question the individuals or teams involved and require a written statement of the incident on the day following the incident. Obtain written statements from the officials and supervisors on duty, in addition to a disciplinary action form. At the conclusion of the investigation, the staff may rule on the individuals and teams involved. Penalties could include suspension from a game, games, or season; temporary or permanent probation; or suspension from the sport program for a given time. Only action relating to the intramural or extramural sport program is suggested. However, refer any serious incident to the appropriate law enforcement office.

Forfeits

Forfeits have a detrimental effect on the intramural and extramural sport programs and are frustrating to those individuals or teams who were ready to play and no opponent appeared. To minimize forfeits the programmer should schedule events at the most convenient times for participants, communicate schedules to participants early, categorize participants by skill level or age, and remind participants of their scheduled event.

All contests should be played on the scheduled date and hour. A team not ready to play within a specified period, usually five minutes after the scheduled time, is charged with a forfeit, subject to the discretion of officials, supervisor, or staff. Games lost by forfeit are not rescheduled for any reason.

If a team leaves before the forfeit is noted by an official or supervisor, charge both teams with a forfeit. The team that is present at a forfeit must have a full complement of players required for that sport or both teams are given a forfeit.

If one team is short the required number of players, the other team captain or manager should have the option to agree to play the game if provided for by the rules of that sport. It would then become a legal game and could not be protested on the grounds that an illegal team was fielded.

If both teams and the staff agree to play the game after the scheduled starting time has elapsed, no protest based on the game starting time is considered. Policies and procedures to discourage a forfeit include the following:

- One forfeit results in the elimination of an individual or team from playoff competition in that sport.
- Two forfeits results in the elimination of an individual or team from all further competition in that sport.
- The individual or team may be assessed a forfeit fee.
- A forfeit means reduction of a certain number of league or tournament points if a point system is in effect.
- Allow a team to play with reduced number of players if its opponent agrees and there are no safety concerns.

Regardless of forfeit procedures and policies adopted, communication plays a vital role. Improve communication by posting the game schedule for 24-hour accessibility and using forfeit letters to inform teams. Notify the forfeiting individual or team and the opponent immediately with a phone call or forfeit letter. Figures 6.1 and 6.2 are examples of effective forfeit letters. They are short, restate the forfeit rules and policies, and encourage the participant to take action in case a clerical error has occurred.

This personal approach might eliminate future occurrences and will indicate to the participants the concern of the staff in providing the best possible program.

Postponement and Rescheduling

All sport events should be played at the scheduled time unless major problems occur that affect most participants. Inform teams to have enough players on their roster in case several of their members have conflicts with other activities.

Figure 6.1
First Forfeit Letter

Dear _Mr. Smith,_

According to our records, your _flag football_ team, _Smith's Team_, has forfeited one of its regular season games. The rules governing intramural play state that any team forfeiting one game during regular season play will be disqualified from postseason play, and a team forfeiting two regular season games will lose all entry points and be dropped from further competition.

Forfeits are disruptive to our program and frustrating to those teams ready to play who receive the forfeit. Therefore, please make every effort to play the remaining games on your regular season schedule.

If you think your team will not be able to play your remaining games or if our records are in error, please contact us as soon as possible so we can make the necessary arrangements.

Figure 6.2
Second Forfeit Letter

Dear _Mr. Smith,_

According to our records, your _flag football_ team, _Smith's Team_, has forfeited two of its regular season games. The rules governing intramural play state that any team forfeiting two games during regular season play will lose all entry points and be dropped from further competition.

If our records are in error, please contact us as soon as possible so we can make the necessary arrangements.

Sincerely,

If rescheduling is necessary, postpone a scheduled contest only with the consent of the opposing participants and the staff. Present a reschedule request form (form 6.2), providing all pertinent information, to the staff at least 24 hours before the originally scheduled contest so all participants and game officials can be notified of the cancellation.

Postponements may occur because of poor playing conditions due to inclement weather. In this case, the intramural staff should notify all affected participants if possible. One method of notification gaining popularity by both sport agencies and participants is using 24-hour recorded telephone messages. The obvious advantage to this system is that it affords up-to-date game schedules and postponement or rescheduling information _after_ regular office hours, which is when most intramural and extramural programs are conducted.

If a participant has not received notification of postponement due to inclement weather before the scheduled contest, it is his or her responsibility to be present for the game or contact the sport office for a ruling. Always reschedule any games postponed by the staff; don't cancel them.

Preparticipation Medical Clearance

Urge all participants to obtain a physical examination before participating in the intramural and extramural sport program. Because most programs are voluntary, participants are responsible for knowing their physiological limitations before the competition and are accountable for their involvement in the program.

In situations with participants who are minors, have parents or guardians sign a statement indicating approval for their participation. If medical examinations are required before participation, the programmer may need to keep a copy of the exam on file to verify it has been conducted.

RESCHEDULE REQUEST

Directions

1. All games will be played at the scheduled time unless *major* problems are present. Teams should anticipate having a player (or players) not available for a game (or games) because of conflicts with other activities and have an ample number of players on their team roster.

2. If rescheduling is necessary, a scheduled contest may be postponed only with the consent of both teams' captains and the intramural staff.

3. This form must be completed and signed by both team captains and returned to the Recreational Sport Office by 5:00 p.m. the day before the contest.

Team initiating request _____

Reason for rescheduling _____

The team of _____ and _____ agree to reschedule
                 (Team name)   *(Team name)*

their _____ game originally scheduled for _____, _____, at _____,
         (Sport)   *(Day)*   *(Date)*   *(Time)*

on _____, to a time to be decided by the intramural sport staff.
        (Field or court)

_____   _____   _____
    (Team)   *(Team captain or manager)*   *(Phone)*

_____   _____   _____
    (Team)   *(Team captain or manager)*   *(Phone)*

- **FOR OFFICE USE ONLY**

League # _____

The above game has been *rescheduled* to

_____, _____ at _____ on _____
 (Day)   *(Date)*   *(Time)*   *(Field or court)*

Form 6.2   Reschedule request form.

DESIGNING TOURNAMENTS

There are several designs you can use in tournament competition. To determine the most appropriate tournament plan, consider the following six factors before implementation:

1. Objectives of the tournament
   - Determine a winner quickly.
   - Provide maximum participation.
   - Encourage social interaction.
   - Determine a true champion.
   - Emphasize the element of competition.
   - Motivate participants for a long time.
   - Increase sport skills.
   - Provide an equal number of matches per entry.
   - Rank all entries according to ability.

2. Characteristics of the participants
   - Age level—child, youth, adolescent, adult, or senior
   - Sex—men, women, or co-intramural groups
   - Playing ability—beginner, intermediate, or advanced
   - Interest—participant interest level for the sport
   - Attention span—short (youth) or long (adult)
   - Intensity of competition—competitive or informal

3. Facility, equipment, and personnel
   - Policy for facility reservation
   - Number of available facilities
   - Availability of fields or courts
   - Condition of facility and costs of preparing facility

- Accessibility to locker room facilities
- Provisions for equipment rental and checkout
- Adequate number of sport officials and supervisors
- Funding for personnel

4. Time parameters
   - Length of time available to complete tournament
   - Dates, days, and hours available
   - Provisions for inclement weather, rescheduled games, and championship play-offs

5. Type of event
   - Individual sport
   - Dual sport
   - Group sport
   - Team sport
   - Meet
   - Special event
   - Co-intramural

6. Other factors
   - Budget restrictions
   - Coaches' qualifications
   - Administrative personnel requirements
   - Medical supervision
   - Publicity and promotion
   - Efficient maintenance staff
   - Program control
   - Governance procedures
   - Spectator (crowd) control

All tournaments have advantages and disadvantages; each serves different objectives. In the following pages we'll present six methods of designing tournaments:

    I. Round-robin tournaments
    II. Single-elimination tournaments
    III. Double-elimination tournaments
    IV. Consolation tournaments
    V. Challenge tournaments (with variations)
    VI. Meets

Each has its own schematic, advantages, disadvantages, applicable formulas, and programmatic procedures.

I. Round-Robin Tournaments

The round-robin tournament (see figure 6.3) provides maximum participation because each entry plays against each other entry an equal number of times. The winner of the round-robin tournament is usually determined on a won-loss percentage.

The advantages of round-robin tournaments include the following:

- They are the most popular tournament format.
- They are easily organized and administered.
- They allow complete prescheduling of entries into leagues.
- Participants know opponents and game times in advance.
- Emphasis is on maximum participation for an extended time.
- Each entry competes against each other on a scheduled basis, regardless of won-loss record.
- A single round-robin produces the true champion.
- You can rank entries at the end of the tournament.
- They are effective for outdoor sport programming when weather is a concern, because postponed games can be replayed later in the tournament.
- Participants easily understand them.
- It is not necessary for rounds to be played consecutively, although it is preferred.
- Participants can get acquainted because of the extended season.

The disadvantages of round-robin tournaments include the following:

- They are the most time consuming of all tournaments.
- They require a lot of facility utilization.
- Many forfeits may occur toward last rounds when an entry realizes there is no chance of winning league championship.
- With more than eight entries, participant interest is hard to maintain.
- If you divide a large number of entries into smaller leagues, several winners result with no true champion. You must use an elimination tournament to determine the winner or have co-champions.
- It is possible for a league to end in a tie, which would require extra contests to decide a winner.
- They do not provide an instant winner.

Figure 6.3
Round-Robin Tournament Schematic

Teams entered	Rounds							Total games per team
	1	2	3	4	5	6	7	
	Bye-7	Bye-6	Bye-5	Bye-4	Bye-3	Bye-2	Bye-1	
	1-6	7-5	6-4	5-3	4-2	3-1	2-7	
7	2-5	1-4	7-3	6-2	5-1	4-7	3-6	6
	3-4	2-3	1-2	7-1	6-7	5-6	4-5	

Formulas for Round-Robin Tournaments

With N = total number of entries, you can use the following formulas:

Formulas

Example if N = 7

A. Number of games per league $\dfrac{N(N-1)}{2}$

$\dfrac{7(7-1)}{2} = \dfrac{42}{2} = 21$ games

B. Number of games per entry $N-1$

$7-1 = 6$ games

C. Number of rounds

Even number of entries $N-1$

Odd number of entries N

$7 = 7$ rounds

D. Number of games per round

Even number of entries $\dfrac{N}{2}$

Odd number of entries $\dfrac{(N-1)}{2}$

$\dfrac{7-1}{2} = \dfrac{6}{2} = 3$ games per round

E. Determining percentages

Games won / games played = .000

$\dfrac{5}{6} = .833$

Note: Ties should count as a half game won and a half game lost.

F. Number of games behind

$\dfrac{(W_a - W_b) + (L_b - L_a)}{2}$

W = Number of wins

L = Number of losses

a = First place entry

b = Specific entry in question

Standings

	Won	Loss
Al	6	0
Jeff	4	2
Rob	2	4
Lee	0	6

Number of games Rob is behind?

$\dfrac{(6-2) + (4-0)}{2} = \dfrac{4+4}{2} = 4$

Round-Robin Procedures

The first step in scheduling the round-robin tournament is to develop a master calendar that indicates playing dates, times, and facilities available for the tournament. Exclude days or hours in which no games will be played (i.e., religious holidays or conflicts).

Once you have prepared the calendar, construct pairings for the tournament by arranging all entries, by either name or assigned number, into two vertical columns. List them consecutively down the first column and continue up to the second. When an odd number of entries are scheduled, place a *bye* in the fixed upper left position. This means that the entry scheduled against the bye is *standing by* and has no game in that round. An example follows:

7 Entries	8 Entries
Bye - 7	1 - 8
1 - 6	2 - 7
2 - 5	3 - 6
3 - 4	4 - 5

To obtain pairings for subsequent rounds, rotate the names or numbers *counterclockwise* around the participant located in the upper left position of the column.

Round 1	Round 2	Round 3	Round 4
Bye - 7	Bye - 6	Bye - 5	Bye - 4
1 - 6	7 - 5	6 - 4	5 - 3
2 - 5	1 - 4	7 - 3	6 - 2
3 - 4	2 - 3	1 - 2	7 - 1

Round 5	Round 6	Round 7
Bye - 3	Bye - 2	Bye - 1
4 - 2	3 - 1	2 - 7
5 - 1	4 - 7	3 - 6
6 - 7	5 - 6	4 - 5

Record Keeping for Round-Robin Tournaments

A simple form you can use to notify participants of the tournament progression is shown in figure 6.4.

List all entries in the league at both the top and left sides of the chart. At the end of a contest, record the date and score in the appropriate boxes. Read the chart horizontally with the score of the horizontal team recorded first. Read the examples in figure 6.4 as follows:

- All-Stars defeated Heroes by the score of 1-0 (forfeit) on November 8.
- Rejects lost to Sluggers by the score of 2-12 on November 1.
- "F" represents a forfeit.

Write wins and losses in different colors for distinction. Once all rounds have been completed, determine the league champion. If two or more entries have an identical won-loss record at the end of the tournament, you may choose from several methods to determine the winner:

- Play a single-elimination play-off between the entries that tied.
- Declare the winner of the contest in which the tied entries played during league play the tournament champion.
- Allow tie to stand and award co-champions.
- Use a point differential system in which the points each entry allowed opponents are subtracted from the entry's total points scored. The entry with the largest total is the champion.

Round-Robin Tournament Programming Tips

The following are suggestions for programming round-robin tournaments:

- The most desired number of entries per league ranges from four to eight. Divide a larger number of entries into several smaller leagues.
- If several entries have similar time conflicts, group these entries together for easier scheduling.
- Try to schedule each entry to play at least once a week.
- Designate several open dates for rescheduling.
- Double-check all work!

A variation to the traditional round-robin tournament is the Lombard tournament. In this round-robin format the entire tournament is completed in several hours. The entries play in an abbreviated time frame that is a fraction of the regular game. For example, if the regulation time for volleyball was 40 minutes and eight teams entered, there would be eight 5-minute games. At the conclusion of 40 minutes, record each entry's scores, and the entry with the largest total is the winner.

Figure 6.4
League Record-Keeping Chart

Sport _____ *Softball* _____ League _____ *Church* _____ Division _____ *Men* _____

Name of team	All-Stars	Sluggers	Rejects	Batboys	Heroes
All-Stars					Nov 8 1-0 W ⬜F
Sluggers			Nov 1 12-2 W		
Rejects		Nov 1 2-12 L			
Batboys					
Heroes	Nov 8 0-1 L ⬜F				

The Lombard tournament usually works best when there are 6 to 12 entries and you use two or three courts at once.

Round-Robin Tournament Scheduling Procedures

After selecting the appropriate tournament design, the programmer can proceed with the tournament scheduling. The first step is to develop a master tournament calendar, illustrating when you will conduct the tournament. After assigning days and dates, the programmer designates times that will not be played for various reasons (i.e., holidays, team captains' meetings, other sport conflicts). If you will assign specific dates for practice, include these too. Because postponements are inevitable, it is wise to allocate extra playing dates for rescheduling, league tiebreakers, and play-offs. Figure 6.5 is an example of a master tournament calendar.

After creating the tournament calendar, develop a facility schedule (form 6.3), indicating one week of playing times for each court or field. The example in form 6.3 indicates there are 36 game openings per day, or 144 game openings in one playing week of four days. In other words, 288 teams could participate in one game each during the first week of the tournament. Using this type of schedule helps the programmer determine the maximum number of entries that the tournament could accommodate.

Once you have received entries, sort them into appropriate participation units. For example, an initial step is to place all men, women, and co-intramural entries into separate groups. Then you can further divide each group into smaller subunits, such as advanced, intermediate, and novice classes. Continue this process until you have separated all entries into small units, placing entries with special scheduling requests together as much as possible. Now that you have sorted the entries, you can assign them into leagues (round-robin) or place them on elimination brackets.

The task of league assignment plays a major role in the success of a tournament. The programmer must have a thorough knowledge of the requirements of each sport event, the availability of facilities, and the interest level of the participants. If, for example, 28 teams signed up for a basketball tournament, but you only wanted 5-team round-robin leagues, how would you create the leagues?

- Five 5-team leagues plus one 3-team league
- Three 6-team leagues plus two 5-team leagues
- Four 5-team leagues plus two 4-team leagues

The programmer should base the solution on the number of available facilities and their operating hours, the maximum time required for each event, and the days participants have conflicts. You must use creative planning when you develop the league

Figure 6.5
Master Tournament Calendar

Month _____ *May* _____

Sunday	Monday	Tuesday	Wednesday	Thursday	Friday	Saturday
1	2	3	4	5	6 No games	7 No games
8	9	10	11	12 Religious holiday; No games 5:00-8:00 p.m.	13 No games	14 No games
15	16	17	18	19	20 No games	21 No games
22	23	24	25	26	27 No games	28 No games
29 Hold for rescheduling	30 Hold for rescheduling	31 No games; Team captain's meeting for play-offs				

structure. Maintain equal playing opportunities for all entries as much as possible.

After forming the leagues, attach each league's entries to a scheduling worksheet (see the appendix at the end of this chapter for scheduling worksheets). On the cover of the worksheet, complete the league number, division, names of the entries, and any special scheduling request. Once you have completed this task for all leagues and entries, construct a master schedule.

The process of scheduling each league's round-robin contests is simple if schedulers display care and accuracy. As one scheduler reads aloud the first league number and two corresponding team numbers, a recorder transcribes these figures on a master schedule and responds aloud with the date, time, and field or court assignment for that contest. In the example shown in figure 6.6, at 5:00 p.m. on court 1, teams 1 and 2 from league 1 will play. At 6:00 p.m. on court 2, teams 3 and 4 from league 2 will play.

This process continues until you have scheduled all entries and contests. Whenever possible, sched-

ule all leagues on the same day and times throughout the tournament. Also, when scheduling several units, such as men's, women's, and co-intramural, develop special codes for each or use different colored pencils.

With the completion of the rough draft league schedules, check and double-check all work for accuracy. A single error in this step may cause mass confusion for the scheduler. Once organized, type the schedules, duplicate, and distribute them to the participants.

An alternative to this process of tournament scheduling is instant scheduling. Instant scheduling is a method in which team captains or participants have scheduling responsibilities. After following a specified entry procedure, the participants schedule themselves into a league. League scheduling forms, with playing days and game times, are posted on a bulletin board, usually outside the sport office. Individuals look for openings in leagues where they can play. Once a suitable league is found, the individual writes in his or her name or the team name and copies down the playing

FACILITY SCHEDULE

| Month | Date | Day |

Time/field	A	B	C	D	E	F
5:00						
6:00						
7:00						
8:00						
9:00						
10:00						

| Month | Date | Day |

Time/field	A	B	C	D	E	F
5:00						
6:00						
7:00						
8:00						
9:00						
10:00						

| Month | Date | Day |

Time/field	A	B	C	D	E	F
5:00						
6:00						
7:00						
8:00						
9:00						
10:00						

| Month | Date | Day |

Time/field	A	B	C	D	E	F
5:00						
6:00						
7:00						
8:00						
9:00						
10:00						

Form 6.3   Facility schedule.

date, time, and facility location. Thus, the individual has a copy of the league schedule.

Maas (1979) suggests several advantages and disadvantages of using instant scheduling. Advantages of this system include the following:

- Responsibility for scheduling shifts from the intramural programmer to the team captain or participant.
- Participants may select from a variety of available times, and their schedule will be consistent from week to week for the entire season.

- Participants select alternate playing times if the preferred time is not available.
- The system encourages entries well before the deadline.
- You do not need to contact participants again until play-offs, unless there is a schedule change.
- Intramural programming time is reduced substantially and scheduling is finished on the deadline date except for late entries.
- Schedules do not need to be typed and copied for the participants.

Figure 6.6
Master Tournament Schedule

	Court 1	Court 2
5:00 p.m.	League 1 1-2	League 2 1-2
6:00 p.m.	League 1 3-4	League 2 3-4

Figure 6.7
Single-elimination Tournament Schematic

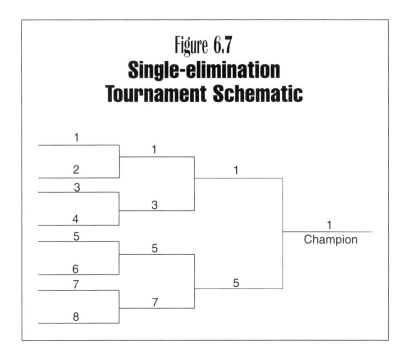

The disadvantages of instant scheduling include the following:

- You need to predict the breakdown of leagues in each classification, or be flexible about changing league designations if an imbalance occurs.
- You need a physical setting (hallway, large room, bulletin board space) to conduct the process with large numbers of people.
- There may be problems initiating this process until participants are familiar with the procedure.

Instant scheduling provides a unique concept for the sport programmer in tournament scheduling.

Although this method may not be applicable for all sport settings, the programmer should consider it as an option.

II. Single-elimination Tournaments

A single-elimination tournament is well known and simple to design (see figure 6.7). All entries compete in the first round, but only the winners of each round compete in the subsequent rounds, with the winner of the final contest becoming the champion. Often there is a drawing for position placement with the best entries being *seeded* to provide better competition as the tournament progresses toward the finals. Also, byes are awarded in the first round if the number of entries is not equal to a power of two.

The advantages of single-elimination tournaments include the following:

- The participants understand them easily.
- They are the simplest tournament to conduct.
- They are useful in determining a champion for preliminary tournaments, such as a round-robin.
- They determine the champion in the shortest time compared with other tournaments.
- They can be conducted with limited facilities.
- They can accommodate a large number of entries.
- They are interesting for spectators.
- They are the most appropriate format for a one-day event.
- They are economical to conduct.

The disadvantages of single-elimination tournaments include the following:

- They involve minimum participation.
- They place maximum emphasis on winning.
- The champion may not represent the best team or player. This also applies to the second place finisher because entries in the other half of the bracket may be better.
- They do not allow for an *off-day*.
- Competition may become too intense because the entry must win every contest or face elimination.
- Outdoor sport programs, with their potential for weather-related postponements, cause scheduling problems because contests must be played sequentially.
- They provide the least flexibility for the participant.

Formulas for Single-elimination Tournaments

With N = total number of entries, you can use the following formulas:

Formulas		*Example if N = 13*
A. Number of tournament games	$N - 1$	$13 - 1 = 12$ games
B. Power of 2—number of times 2 has to be multiplied to equal or exceed the number of entries		
	$2 \times 2 = 4$ or (2^2)	
	$2 \times 2 \times 2 = 8$ or (2^3)	
	$2 \times 2 \times 2 \times 2 = 16$ or (2^4)	16
	$2 \times 2 \times 2 \times 2 \times 2 = 32$ or (2^5)	
C. Number of byes	(power of 2) $- N$	$16 - 13 = 3$ byes
D. Number of rounds—the power to which 2 must be raised		(2^4) or 4 rounds
E. Number of first-round games	$N - $ (next lower power of 2)	$13 - (8) = 5$ games
	or	
	$\dfrac{N - \text{byes}}{2}$	$\dfrac{13 - (3)}{2} = \dfrac{10}{2} = 5$ games

The design of a single-elimination tournament depends on the number of entries. You cannot complete a tournament schedule or bracket arrangement until you have accepted all entries.

Procedures for Single-elimination Tournaments

The following process is a guide for developing a single-elimination draw:

1. Check and recheck that you have correctly spelled all names on the entry form and that units of participation, divisions, and affiliations are correct. Misspelling or overlooking entries is inexcusable.

2. Select the appropriate sized draw sheet (4, 8, 16, 32, 64, etc.).

3. Determine the seeds. The purpose of seeding is to separate the stronger entries so they will not compete against each other until the later rounds; do this by distributing strength throughout the draw. Although there is no requirement to have seedings, they ensure a fairer tournament when the superior players meet in the final rounds. The rule for the number of seeds is no more than one seed for each four entries. Place the top seed, chosen by ability, previous performance, and ranking, in the top of the upper bracket and the second seed at the bottom of the lower bracket (see figure 6.8).

To check the draw placement of seeds, those at the extreme of each bracket should equal a consistent number when totaled. For example, in a 32-entry draw, place seeds so the eight quarters of the bracket equal 17 (1 + 16, 9 + 8, 5 + 12, 13 + 4, 3 + 14, 11 + 6, 7 + 10, 15 + 2).

An alternative method is to place the first seeded entry on the top line of the upper bracket and the second on the bottom line of the lower bracket. Place the third seed at the bottom of the upper bracket, the fourth at the top of the lower bracket, and so on (see figure 6.9).

In this method, don't attempt to equalize the upper or lower brackets. If the seeding procedures ranked entries according to ability, it would be advantageous to require the first seed to play a weaker opponent (i.e., fourth seed instead of third seed).

4. Determine the number of byes. When the number of entries is not an exact power of two (2, 4, 8, 16, 32, 64, etc.), the first round should have byes to avoid an uneven number of contestants remaining in the final round. **All byes must be played in the first round.** The number of byes should ensure the number of contestants to be equal to a power of two (full brackets) in the second round.

5. Place the byes. Distribute all byes evenly between the upper and lower brackets. Grant seeded entries byes in order of their ranking. First seed receives first bye, second seed receives second bye, and so on. In other words, the placement of byes should complement the placement of seeded entries.

6. Number the games. The numbering of games should progress by round in sequential order. If you are using several bracket sheets simultaneously, number all games in the first round on each sheet first, before proceeding to the second round. Place game numbers where the winner's name will appear. Figure 6.10 illustrates the placement of game numbers and the even distribution of byes.

List the date, time, and location of the game on the bracket sheet. An alternative to placing the game information on the bracket sheet is to attach an additional sheet that contains only this information.

Single-elimination Tournament Programming Tips

The following are suggestions for programming single-elimination tournaments:

- Indicate the appropriate round on the bracket sheet for scheduling purposes. Remember, complete round one before progressing to round two.

- Rather than indicating bye games, you could have *implied byes* or blank spaces replace the first round bye and only second round games appear. For example, see figure 6.11.

- The placement of byes starts at the extremes and moves toward the center.

- When the number of entries is only a few over the number on a draw sheet (power of 2), for example 17, it is less confusing to add one game to a 16-entry draw than it is to have several byes listed on a 32-entry draw. To accomplish this, start at the center of the bracket and create two-line pairings until you have as many lines as there are entries.

- Determine position assignments on the bracket sheet at random, by known ability (seeding), or in the order the entries were received.

III. Double-elimination Tournaments

The double-elimination tournament (see figure 6.12), also known as the *two loss and out* tourna-

Figure 6.8
Seed Placement for Single-elimination Tournaments

Figure 6.9
Alternative Seed Placement for Single-elimination Tournaments

16-team seed	8-team seed	4-team seed	2-team seed

No. 1 seed

No. 1 seed

No. 1 seed

No. 1 seed

No. 9 seed

No. 13 seed

No. 5 seed

No. 5 seed

No. 7 seed

No. 7 seed

No. 12 seed

No. 13 seed

No. 3 seed

No. 3 seed

No. 3 seed

No. 4 seed

No. 4 seed

No. 4 seed

No. 12 seed

No. 16 seed

No. 8 seed

No. 8 seed

No. 6 seed

No. 6 seed

No. 14 seed

No. 10 seed

No. 2 seed

No. 2 seed

No. 2 seed

No. 2 seed

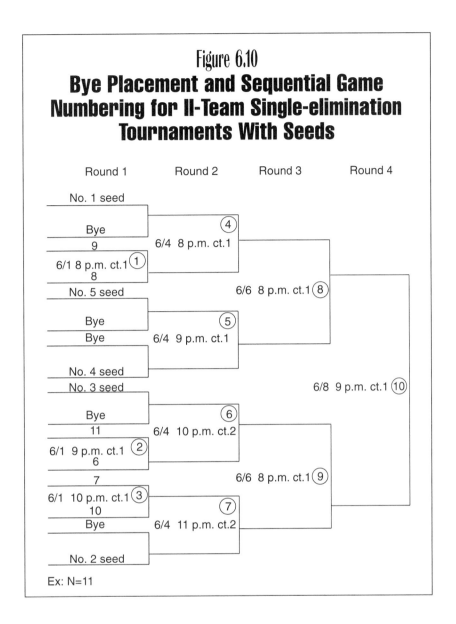

Figure 6.10
Bye Placement and Sequential Game Numbering for 11-Team Single-elimination Tournaments With Seeds

Ex: N=11

ment, is an adaptation of the single-elimination with consolation format. No contestant is eliminated until two losses occur. An entry that loses in the championship or winners' bracket is scheduled to play other losers in a losers' bracket or second elimination tournament. Play continues until there is a winner of both the championship bracket and the losers' bracket. These two winners are matched to determine an overall winner. If the champion of the losers' bracket defeats the champion of the winners' bracket, an additional contest is required because both have only one loss.

The advantages of double-elimination tournaments include the following:

• One of the fairest types of tournaments because each entry must be defeated twice

before being eliminated from the tournament.

• Provides at least twice as much participation as the single-elimination tournament.

• Holds participant interest for a longer time than the single-elimination or consolation tournament.

• Affords entry who has had an off day, been upset, or received a poor pairing a chance to win the losers' bracket and play for the championship.

In addition to those disadvantages associated with a single-elimination tournament, double-elimination tournaments have the following problems:

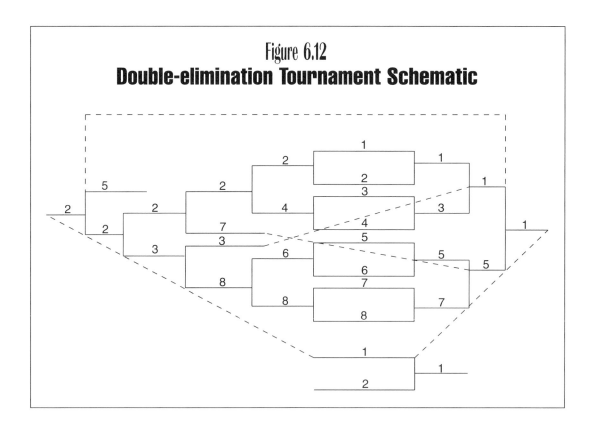

Figure 6.11
Implied Bye Schematic

Round 1   Round 2   Round 3   Round 4

John

Al

Jeff

Lee

Alex

Mark

Figure 6.12
Double-elimination Tournament Schematic

- They are complicated to show graphically because the loser rounds keep adding new contestants as teams lose in the winners' rounds.

- They are confusing to participants who have difficulty understanding the tournament format.

- They are more time consuming than a single-elimination tournament.

Formulas for Double-elimination Tournaments

With N = total number of entries, you can use the following formulas:

Formulas

A. Number of games   Minimum = 2N – 2

                               Maximum = 2N – 1

Example if N = 13

$2(13) – 2 = 26 – 2 = 24$ minimum games

$2(13) – 1 = 26 – 1 = 25$ maximum games

Note: The maximum number of games occurs when the champion of the losers' bracket defeats the champion of the winners' bracket, thus creating an extra game.

B. Number of rounds—twice the power to which 2 must be raised to equal or exceed the number of entries, plus an additional round if an extra contest is required.

$= 2(2^4)$

$= 2(4)$

$= 8$ rounds

Procedures for Double-elimination Tournaments

The procedures of a single-elimination tournament apply to the winners' bracket of the double-elimination tournament. However, entries into the losers' bracket are more involved. Arrange byes so you don't give a second bye to an entry that has already had a bye. Give special attention to *crossing* losers from the top and bottom halves of the winners' bracket. This prevents pairing entries who played each other in the winners' bracket from playing each other a second time in the losers' bracket until the latest possible opportunity. You can achieve this crossing by using either of the following two scheduling methods.

1. Back-to-back. As we saw in the previous schematic, the winners' and the losers' brackets are arranged side-by-side, with the winners progressing to the right and the losers following the broken lines to the left. This ensures that the earliest two previous opponents meet would be late in the losers' bracket.

2. Over-under. This method arranges the losers' bracket under the winners' bracket and eliminates the broken lines. An example of this bracket may be seen in figure 6.13. The method requires that each pairing of the winners' bracket include the words "Loser to ____" followed by a letter of the alphabet. In the losers' bracket, the line of the pairings is indicated by a consecutive listing of respective letters. This method is the simplest for participants, spectators, and tournament directors to read and understand. Regardless of the method you choose, the results of the brackets are the same.

Semidouble-elimination—A Double-elimination Tournament Variation

A variation to the double-elimination format is the semidouble-elimination tournament. An example of this bracket is in figure 6.14.

This tournament is similar to the double-elimination in that all first-round losers and those entries scheduled a first-round bye, but lost in the second round, are placed in the losers' bracket. However, from this point on in the tournament both the winners' and the losers' brackets continue on a straight single-elimination basis with the winners of each bracket playing for the championship. In other words, each entry is guaranteed a minimum of two contests but not necessarily two losses.

Double-elimination Tournament Programming Tips

The following are suggestions for programming double-elimination tournaments:

- After the first round in the losers' brackets, each additional round in this bracket must have two contests.
- Number contests consecutively, as well as possible, depending on the facility limitation and playing times.
- List the times, playing locations, and game numbers of each contest on the bracket. This lessens the possibility of a participant losing any additional sheets of information.
- In numbering the contests, make sure an entry is never scheduled to play two games in succession.

IV. Consolation Tournaments

These elimination tournaments are superior to the single-elimination tournament in that they permit each entry to participate in at least two contests. This tournament produces two winners: the champion of the elimination bracket and the winner of the consolation bracket.

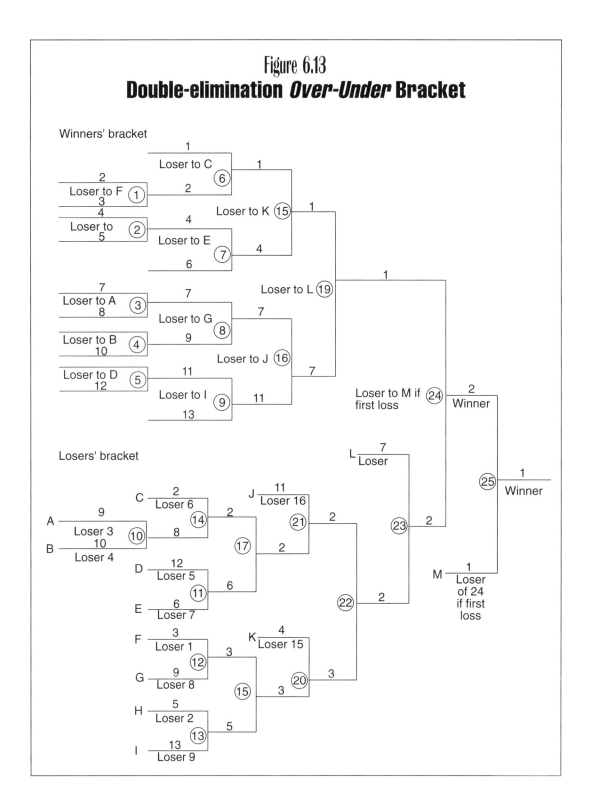

Figure 6.13
Double-elimination *Over-Under* Bracket

There are two types of consolation tournaments: Type A and Type B (see figure 6.15). In Type A, or a *simple consolation*, all losers in the first round (or those who lose in the second round after drawing a bye in the first) play another single-elimination tournament. The winner of the second single-elimination tournament is the consolation winner.

Type B consolation elimination tournaments, or *second place consolation*, provide an opportunity for any loser, regardless of the round in which the loss occurred, to win the consolation championship.

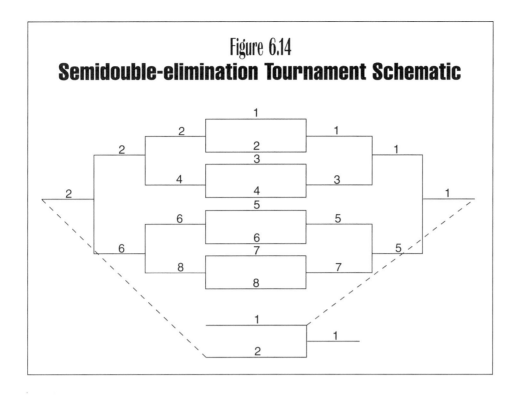

Figure 6.14
Semidouble-elimination Tournament Schematic

This is similar to double-elimination tournaments, except the winner of the consolation tournament is the third place finisher and does not play the winners' bracket champion.

The advantages of consolation tournaments include the following:

- Each entry is guaranteed at least two contests.
- More participation is provided than in straight single-elimination.

The disadvantages of consolation tournaments include the following:

- Interest is sometimes lost if there is no chance for winning the championship.
- Forfeits are higher than in single-elimination tournaments.

Procedures for Consolation Tournaments

The rules that apply to the single-elimination tournament also apply to a consolation tournament.

V. Challenge Tournaments

Challenge tournaments, or ongoing tournaments, emphasize participation rather than winning. Contestants issue and accept challenge matches from each other with the ultimate goal of winning all challenges and advancing to the top of the tournament structure. However, all contestants continue to play regardless of the outcome of the challenge. This type of tournament is used primarily with individual and dual sport but can be used in team sport as well. Commercial recreational institutions often use challenge tournaments, and they have proven to be an excellent tournament design for individuals with busy and fluctuating schedules.

The advantages of challenge tournaments include the following:

- They are easily organized and programmed.
- They need minimum supervision.
- They emphasize maximum participation.
- Winning is not a requirement for continued participation.
- They don't eliminate a participant.
- They encourage participants to choose opponents and engage in social interaction.
- They afford opportunity for social interaction.
- Won-loss records need not be maintained.
- Participants play at their convenience.
- They are useful for ranking participants.
- Each contest is self-programmed.
- No formal scheduling is required.

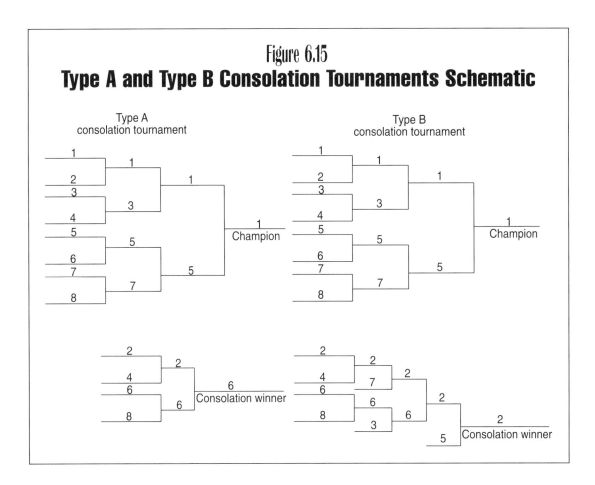

Figure 6.15
Type A and Type B Consolation Tournaments Schematic

All ages and skill levels may be involved.

- Participation is informal.
- Tournaments may be ended at any time by the programmer.
- Formulas are not required for this tournament.

The disadvantages of challenge tournaments include the following:

- Participants must contact each other to arrange date and time for match. Communication can become a problem.
- They lack challenge for some participants.
- They are suited for a small number of entries.
- They could appear complicated to participants.
- They often need external awards or motivational incentives to continue interest and participation.
- They need limited security, pertaining to operating the actual challenge board.

Procedures for Challenge Tournaments

A challenge tournament begins by transferring from the entry form all names and telephone numbers to cards, circular discs, or other suitable material that permits removal into slots or hanging on hooks. Once you have completed this process, there are several methods you can use to position or rank the players on the tournament board. These methods involve the following:

- Order in which participants entered or registered.
- Random draw.
- Ranking according to ability. (If you use this method, place the top player at the bottom of the tournament structure.)
- Rankings derived from other tournaments.

Once you determine placement, conduct the tournament using a series of challenges issued by the participants. The objective is to advance to the top of the structure and remain there. Movement to the top is gained by issuing a challenge to an individual on a higher level, defeating that individual and changing positions.

In conducting a challenge tournament, establish rules and regulations before the competition and inform the participants. Although these rules may vary according to the design of the tournament, the following seven principles apply:

1. Specific sport rules—use sanctioned rules governing play with any local intramural modification.

2. Challenge rules

   a) Participants initiate their own challenges.

   b) All challenges must be accepted and played within or at an agreed upon time (usually three to five days).

   c) Challenge options for participants include the following: only those one level above, those one or two levels above, anyone in the tournament (not recommended), or someone at their own level and win before challenging a level above.

   d) If the challenger wins, the individuals exchange positions in the tournament. If the challenger is defeated, both individuals remain in their original position. However, the loser usually may not rechallenge the winner until a designated time passes or until he or she has played at least one other match.

   e) It is the winner's responsibility to update the tournament board.

   f) Challenges may not be refused and should be met in the order that they were issued.

   g) If a challenge has been accepted and one of the contestants fails to appear, declare a forfeit and exchange positions.

3. Keep the position of each entry up-to-date so challenges can be arranged at any time.

4. Add late entries to the lowest level.

5. Establish a minimum and maximum number of contests that may be played during any given period.

6. Announce a definite date for completing the tournament before the start of play in fairness to all participants.

7. The ranking of all players at the conclusion of the tournament determines the winner.

Challenge Tournament Programming Variations

Challenge tournaments can follow any number of schemes. Let's examine nine of the most popular challenge tournament formats.

Ladder Tournament

This is probably the most popular format of a challenge tournament.

Sport _____   Ending date _____

Rules and regulations

Contact list

John
Mark
Bill
Jack
Dan
Lee
Tom
Al

In the ladder tournament, list the entries' names on horizontal rung and place them in a vertical column, usually with the best player at the bottom. As in climbing a ladder, use the rungs to advance players from one position to another according to challenge procedures previously outlined. The winner of the tournament is that individual at the top rung of the ladder when play is stopped.

If you receive a large number of entries, group the entries into several smaller tournaments that provide for both horizontal and vertical movement. At the end of the tournament, each ladder winner may participate in a play-off to determine the champion.

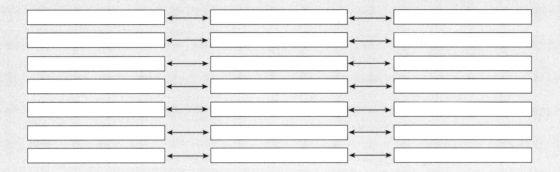

Pyramid Tournament

The pyramid design provides more participation and permits greater freedom to challenge than the ladder format.

Arrange the names in rows, with one at the top, two in the second row, and so on, with the number of rows depending on the number of entries. This design allows an infinite number of entries by adding another base level to the pyramid. However, you should determine a realistic number based on the time available to complete the tournament and to allow the base level entry the opportunity to reach the top.

King or Crown Tournament

As in the ladder tournament, several smaller tournaments may be appropriate. This variation of the pyramid tournament is suitable when large numbers of entries are competing. Group entries into three smaller pyramids at different levels. After an individual has reached the top of the lower units, he or she may challenge horizontally into a higher unit, then vertically again to advance to the crown or first position.

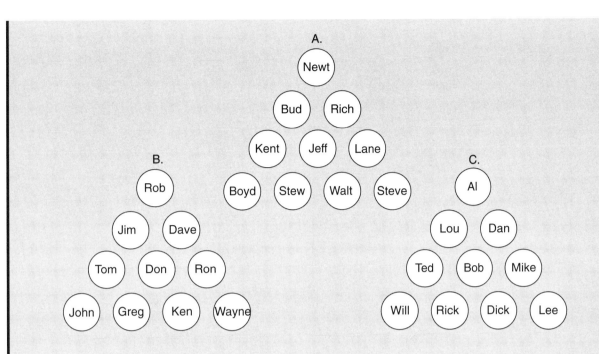

Funnel Tournament

The funnel tournament design is a combination of the ladder and the pyramid tournaments. In the example, the top seven positions are played as a ladder tournament, and the bottom positions follow rules similar to a pyramid tournament. Place additional entries on the bottom row of the pyramid section. This tournament provides for a large number of entries as well as a ranking of the top seven individuals.

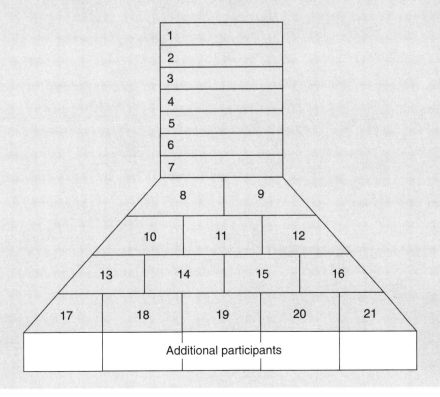

Spiderweb Tournament

This hexagonal tournament design affords greater opportunity for participation and involvement than traditional ladder or pyramid methods.

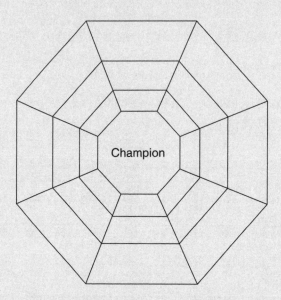

Although you conduct this format like the pyramid tournament, its main disadvantage is that the number one or middle position is constantly being challenged by six players. To reduce this number of direct challengers to the middle position, require challengers to defeat an individual or individuals on their level before issuing a challenge.

Round-the-Clock Tournament

This design is similar to the face of a clock. Assign all entries an hour number represented on the clock. The object of the tournament is for a player to advance completely around the clock, challenging no more than two players (hours) ahead, and returning first to his or her original starting position. Variations could require two or three revolutions of the clock face or, if there are many entries, several clocks with the winners of each clock playing in an elimination tournament to determine the champion.

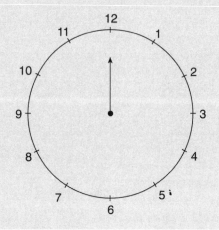

Bump Board Tournament

Rather than participating against each other, the contestants in this tournament participate against records, posted on a result board, previously achieved in that sport. The contestant who breaks one of the posted records is placed in that respective position with the others being bumped one position lower.

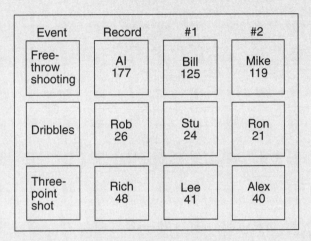

Event	Record	#1	#2
Free-throw shooting	Al 177	Bill 125	Mike 119
Dribbles	Rob 26	Stu 24	Ron 21
Three-point shot	Rich 48	Lee 41	Alex 40

Progressive Bridge Tournament

This challenge tournament is a self-operating tournament that works like bridge or other card sports. It works best for sports that have three or more playing facilities (courts, fields) located close together (i.e., tennis, badminton, or volleyball).

Establish a number one or head court before participation, with the contestants placed according to traditional challenge rule procedures for the first match. Following this initial match, the winner moves over one court toward the head court. The losers remain on the court where they lost, except the loser on the head court, who moves all the way over to the last court to begin the long battle again. It is best to time the matches so all players are ready to change at the same time. This type of challenge tournament is useful when supervision is minimal and motivation is needed to maintain the participant interest.

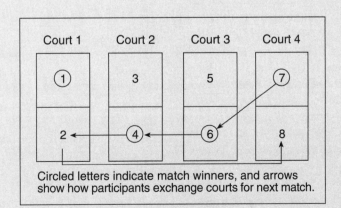

Circled letters indicate match winners, and arrows show how participants exchange courts for next match.

Tombstone Tournament

The tombstone or *marker* tournament involves a cumulative score or long-term goal established before the tournament for all contestants to strive for. You may list these goals in terms of time, total points, and distance.

In this example of basketball free-throw shooting, you could establish a goal of 100 successful free throws, with a limit of 25 free-throw attempts per day for five days. The first contestant to record 100 free throws (Mike) is the winner.

Basketball Free Throw										
	Day 1		Day 2		Day 3		Day 4		Day 5	
Entries	Daily results	Accum total	Daily results	Accum total	Daily results	Accum total	Daily results	Accum total	Daily results	Accum total
John	20/25	20	17/25	37	19/25	56	20/25	76	20/25	96
Sally	18/25	18	20/25	38	20/25	58	21/25	79	20/25	99
Mike	23/25	23	20/25	43	21/25	64	20/25	84	21/25	105
Sue	18/25	18	19/25	37	20/25	57	18/25	75	20/25	95

Challenge Tournament Programming Tips

The following are suggestions for programming challenge tournaments:

- You can construct a challenge board from wood, cardboard, peg board, or similar sturdy material. Arrange small nails or eye hooks to suit the design of the tournament, with wood tongue depressors (ladder) or circular price tags or discs (pyramid, crown) to record the participant's name and telephone number. Instead of using nails or eye hooks, you can use three-by-five-inch card holders. You can insert the participants' name cards in the card holder and move them as players change places in the tournament.
- If several skill levels are evident, it is advisable to set up two challenge tournaments— one for beginners and another for more skilled players.
- You can give awards for top position, player with the most wins, player who issued the largest number of challenges, regardless of the outcome.
- A message board, located adjacent to the challenge board, serves as an excellent communication device.

- Placing entries on the challenge board in the order they were received encourages players to register as quickly as possible.

VI. Meets

The intramural or extramural sport meet is an organized competition in which individuals participate in separate events conducted in several sessions, usually lasting one to four days. A meet can take on different characteristics, such as a championship representing months of training, a season-long program, or an informal play day. Meets lend themselves to a variety of sport settings (i.e., military, educational, and community), in which you need only minor modifications for the setting.

There are two types of participation in a meet event: individual and team. A contestant who enters an event with no team affiliation participates as an individual. In team participation, teams have an equal number of participants who win points for placing in specific events. The team accumulating the most points is the meet champion.

The following are common meets that you can use in a recreational sport program:

Meets with several events

- Track and field
- Swimming and diving
- Wrestling
- Gymnastics
- Ice skating
- Skiing
- Play day
- Martial arts
- Triathlon

Meets with one event

- Cross country
- Golf
- Surfing

Develop meet sport programming to suit the interests, population, and resources of the setting. We will discuss the major programming areas common to all meets, accompanied by a detailed application using a track and field meet as an example. In this way, the programmer can sense the detail within meet sport programming. Meet programming occurs in a more concentrated time span than other program designs, such as round-robin, ladder, or single-elimination tournaments.

Meet Organization

Before organizing the meet, the programmer should review every facet of the event, from personnel to vehicle parking. This process is a valuable aid in programming and alleviates many potential problems. Probably 80 percent of the programmer's efforts take place before the meet begins. Once you have selected the type of meet, determine the program of events. Factors that influence this selection include the following:

- **Age of the participants.** For young children, fun events are more suitable than strength or endurance events. Relays and unusual events using game skills are popular with the younger age group.

- **Physical capabilities of the participants.** Events such as the discus, hammer throw, or javelin throw would not be appropriate for a community meet because of the unique physical skills required.

- **Level of competition.** A highly competitive meet with official sanction may require prior approval from an appropriate governing body.

- **Class groupings.** If you use several groupings, each class should compete at intervals, so no participant must compete in consecutive events.

- **Time factors.** Determine the time required to complete each event by estimating the approximate number of entries. If you can decide on these variables in advance, it is possible to determine the total number and the order of events. Conduct as many events simultaneously as possible. The design and nature of meets could result in undue fatigue and stress if a participant must remain at the site for several hours before participating in an event. Consequently, the programmer must carefully schedule the meet events to avoid delays or back-to-back participations, each of which could pose a threat to safe, enjoyable participation.

- **Facilities and equipment.** Proper facilities, suitable for the events and big enough to accommodate the number of participants, are essential to a successful meet. Carefully prepare all facilities for each event. For example, in a track and field meet, properly mark running lanes and the start and finish lines; be sure the jumping and vaulting pits are in good condition and the locations for the field events are clearly designated before the meet. Quality signs should indicate locations for meet activities and stations for the participants and meet personnel. Providing spectator and participant seating is important if you anticipate a large crowd. It is customary to distribute a map of the indoor or outdoor facility, which indicates where participants are to report for registration, an outline of the course (if applicable), spectator seating, or other pertinent information.

Conducting a Meet

Once you have chosen the program of events and the meet location, distribute a meet entry form (see form 6.4) and a participant information announcement two or three weeks before the meet. The entry format should provide the following information:

- Date and place of the meet
- Entry fee
- Eligibility restrictions

TRACK AND FIELD MEET ENTRY FORM

Sport	Men's and women's track and field
Entry deadline	Thursday, March 7, 1996, 4:00 p.m.
Entry fee	$5.00 per team (See minimum numbers under eligibility.) $1.00 per individual
Competition	Individuals are limited to three events, including the relays. No more than two field events may be entered by an individual. No team may enter more than two individuals per event. An organization may only enter one team per relay.
Eligibility	To be eligible for team competition and points at the divisional level or the all-meet championship, a team must be comprised of the following: Minimum number A—six members B—six members C—five members D—six members
Mandatory meeting	Intramural sport office, room 119, 7:00 p.m., Wednesday, March 6.
Dates & places	Tuesday, March 12, 7:00 p.m. Divisional track preliminaries Men's and women's Wednesday, March 13, 7:00 p.m. Divisional field finals Men's and women's The one-mile and two-mile events will be run on this day. Thursday, March 14, 7:00 p.m. Final track events Men's and women's
Further information	335-8359 or 335-2371

• ENTRY FORM

❑ Team entries only   ❑ Individual entries only

Team _____   Individual _____

Manager _____   Address _____

Address _____   Phone number _____

Phone number _____

Program   **Division**

❑ Men   ❑ A

❑ Women   ❑ B

                                      ❑ C

                                      ❑ D

• ELIGIBILITY STATEMENT

This certifies that I know and understand the intramural sport eligibility rules and have completely checked the eligibility of all participants listed on the reverse side. If there is any discrepancy, I will assume full responsibility. I understand that failure to comply with these rules will result in disciplinary action as outlined in the Guidelines to Participation.

_____   _____
Individual/manager signature   *Date*

Form 6.4   Track and field entry form.

- Required meeting dates and places for participants
- Entry deadline
- Brief rules governing the specific events
- List of events
- Roster of team members

The participant information sheet may cover the following items:

- Participant entrance to the facility
- Reporting time
- Location of registration table
- Location of locker rooms
- Schedule and order of events
- Brief explanation concerning the rules and regulations for each event
- Scoring method
- Eligibility rules
- Equipment policies
- Parking information

After accepting entries, place individual names on a heat result form that you will use during and after each event (see form 6.5).

Meet Personnel

The success of any meet depends on the quality of the meet personnel and their leadership ability. Each person should be familiar with the rules that govern their events, be responsible for their specific functions, and be able to anticipate problems.

The number and type of officials or employees depend on the type of meet, the level of involvement, and the events on the program. In general, you need the following personnel to conduct a successful meet:

- **Meet committee** is responsible for supervising the meet, including the following:
  - Forming heats
  - Determining number of contestants
  - Deciding on the order of events
  - Ruling on appeals
  - Suspending meet because of weather, poor facility conditions, and so forth
- **Meet coordinator** monitors the organization and implementation of the meet and supervises personnel. If there is no meet committee, the meet director usually assumes all administrative and organizational duties.
- **Referee** is in charge of activities during the meet, assigning officials to specific duties, and explaining their responsibilities.
- **Starter** controls the start of each event.
- **Clerk of the course** is responsible for recording the name and number of each contestant and assigning them to proper heat and starting positions. The clerk is also responsible for giving instructions about rules for each event.
- **Others** include clerical staff, judges, scorer, announcer, marshals, timers, inspectors, press stewards, runners, and supervisors.

Once you have identified and instructed meet personnel about their responsibilities, you can start the

---

MEET SPORT OFFICIAL HEAT RESULT FORM

Event _____   Division _____   Heat _____

Lane	Place	Division points	Final points
_____	_____	_____	_____
_____	_____	_____	_____
_____	_____	_____	_____
_____	_____	_____	_____
_____	_____	_____	_____
_____	_____	_____	_____

Form 6.5   Heat result form.

meet. At a designated time before the meet, all contestants in the first event must report to the clerk of the course. The clerk verifies each entry and informs them of the heat and lane assignments. At this time, complete an event card for each participant (see form 6.6)

While the first event is being conducted, the announcer informs contestants of the second event so they can receive their assignments and the event can follow immediately. Conducting a meet in this fashion reduces the time between events. Allow participants to warm up in a designated area before starting their event. Assign appropriate personnel or attendants to set up and remove equipment, such as hurdles, barriers, mats, standards, or other equipment as soon as possible. Arrange for the press steward or runner to record the results of each event promptly for the participant and the meet announcer.

Scoring a Meet

There are two types of scoring systems. The first type is *event scoring*. Assign each event in the meet a scoring system to indicate the points awarded for overall placement. For example, for the long jump of a track and field meet, you can base the scoring system on the 12 best places within each division, as shown in figure 6.16.

The second type of scoring is *divisional scoring* in which points are assigned for performance during preliminary and final events.

After the final event, the meet committee or coordinator should make sure that the following details have been attended to:

- All score sheets have been collected.
- Tabulations of results have been made official.

EVENT CARD

Men _____   Women _____

Division   A   B   C   D

Track event   60-m hurdles   100-m dash   Mile run   400-m dash   800-m run

                    200-m dash   800-m relay   Mile relay   2-mile relay

Name(s) _____

Name(s) _____

Team name _____

Timer #1 _____   Official time _____

Timer #2 _____   Place _____

Heat _____   Lane _____   Race _____

Recorded by _____

Form 6.6   Meet event card.

Figure 6.16
Scoring System for a Track and Field Meet

Place	1	2	3	4	5	6	7	8	9	10	11	12
Points	15	12	10	9	8	7	6	5	4	3	2	1

- Proper awards have been distributed.
- Press releases announcing winners and other items of interest have been prepared.
- All equipment and supplies have been collected and returned.
- Facility has been cleaned and equipment placed in original place.

Meet Programming Tips

Meet programs encompass a variety of events according to the nature and age groupings of the participants. The possibilities for arranging and conducting a meet are limitless and depend primarily on the setting or environment. The sport programmer should ensure that every meet, regardless of its type, contributes to the enjoyment of the participants and spectators. Proper preliminary planning, competent meet personnel, suitable facility site, and necessary equipment ensure a successfully conducted meet.

EXTRAMURAL SPORT

Although extramural sport is similar to the intramural sport program regarding programming policies or procedures, the extramural program is distinctive in many ways. Extramural sport may be defined as an extension or outgrowth of the intramural program. Intramural champions from various institutions compete against each other to determine an extramural champion. You can conduct participation in extramurals either informally, emphasizing a fun and social interaction, or formally, a highly organized event that stresses winning and recognizes individual champions.

The extramural sport concept has tremendous potential for providing visibility for the host institution and recognition for the participants. Traditionally, extramural sport programming has received minimal attention within the total recreational sport operation. Major reasons are the time, resources, and planning required to host participants from outside the setting and the resources required to send participants to extramural sport events. In essence, programmers discourage extramural sport events when participation by the few who are highly skilled is more expensive than events that provide opportunities for many individuals with varying skill levels. Although this principle is a good guideline, the programmer should explore alternative sources of funding, perhaps through donations or commer-

cial sponsorship, to provide for extramural sport. A quality extramural sport event may be valuable for generating public awareness about recreational sport and facilitate positive relations with other settings.

Scheduling and Organizing Extramural Sport Events

Schedule the extramural sport event as far in advance as possible to obtain housing accommodations suitable for the number of participants expected. When reviewing facility availability, make plans to schedule facility times before the tournament for practice.

Investigate any conflicting events scheduled in the proposed time to prevent problems. Once you have secured preliminary approval of dates, times, and facilities, begin developing entry forms and invitations to distribute one or two months before the established date. Develop an effective publicity campaign to secure participant and spectator interest in the event.

The host institution, with assistance from participating institutions, should be responsible for coordinating all pertinent details of the extramural sport event. These would include the following:

- Specific events to be held
- Number of participants allowed per team
- Eligibility rules
- Modified rules of the sport, if applicable
- Type of participation
- Number of institutions invited
- Housing accommodations, transportation, and hospitality
- Liability insurance
- Personnel requirements
- Finance and budgeting
- Equipment needs
- Registration procedure
- Recognition
- Promotion and publicity

Because extramural sport is an extension of the intramural sport program, the specifics on tournament scheduling, seeding, bye placement, officiating, and facilities supervision are the same as those in intramural sport programming.

Letters of Invitation and Entry Forms

The invitations and entry forms should include all pertinent information. Because you will usually handle communication by mail or telephone, it is important that this literature be as complete as possible. The common items to include follow:

- Type of event and specific activities to be conducted
- Date, time, place, and duration of the event
- Eligibility requirements
- Expected entry fee and other costs
- Approximate costs for housing accommodations, including travel distance to the sport facility
- Insurance coverage, if applicable
- Travel information concerning planes, trains, buses, and route directions for those driving
- Facilities for event and practice
- Appropriate clothing or personal sport equipment and supplies needed for each event
- Entry deadline date and the return address

In addition to an entry form, request the name and phone number for the agency's event coordinator and a signed affidavit verifying participant eligibility.

Follow-Up Letter

After an agency accepts the invitation to attend the extramural event and forwards the completed entry form, send a follow-up letter. This correspondence provides more specific information and any new points of information, such as the following:

- Registration time and location
- Tentative schedule of activities
- Appropriate attire for social events
- Parking arrangements and costs
- Restaurant information, including approximate prices
- City and facility map

Financing Extramural Events

Organize a finance committee to handle the business transactions involving the expenses and income of the event. Examples of the types of financial transactions requiring attention follow:

<u>Expenses</u>

Office supplies, mailing expenses

Duplicating

Facility rental

Equipment and supplies

Maintenance

Personnel—supervisors and officials

Insurance

Awards

Publicity

Hospitality functions, including banquet

<u>Income</u>

Entry fees for team or participants

Sponsors' contributions

Donations

Gate receipts

Business advertising in program

Concessions

Generally, participants attend an extramural event at their expense, unless a sponsor has provided some financial support.

Extramural Event Officials

The number of officials will vary from sport to sport, but the customary number you use for an intramural event should suffice. The host institution is generally responsible for securing officials; however, it is not unusual for each institution to provide one or more qualified officials.

Facilities and Equipment for Extramural Events

Official regulation facilities should be available for the event. Make special arrangements at the facility site for a registration table or tent, locker rooms, shower facilities, rest rooms, concession stand, lounge area for officials, and spectator seating. You may need equipment, such as a scorer's table, standards, timing devices, or public address systems, before the event.

Extramural Rules and Regulations

Whenever you organize an extramural sport event, establish the rules and regulations early, and communicate them to potential participants when you send invitations and entry forms.

When the event being offered is an outgrowth of intramural sport tournaments, pay special attention to rules and regulations to see if participating teams or individuals will need to learn any modifications. Unless differences are communicated early, participants will not have time to adapt to different rules and regulations. Such a situation places pressure on participants and officials, results in possible disciplinary problems, makes the tournament less than fair, and reflects negatively on the host agency.

Travel and Liability for Extramural Events

If a host agency or an agency sending a representative is providing travel funding, the programmer should know of any liability associated with this assistance. For example, if participants have access to a vehicle through an agency, what precautions do you need to take about insurance, adult supervision, and counseling for proper use? The host agency should also carefully review liability concerns stemming from facility and equipment use and the handling of injuries.

Recognition and Extramurals

Design recognition and awards to highlight achievement. Extramural awards can be similar to those distributed at an intramural event. Although the focus of an extramural sport should be on participation, the events lend themselves to a recognition ceremony at the end of participation. This type of ceremony may recognize tournament finalists and other performances, such as sporting behavior, the most participants representing an agency, most valuable players from each agency, an all-star team, and so forth. Finally, the ceremony can recognize people responsible for organizing the event or contributing to its provision.

PERSONNEL CONSIDERATIONS

Leadership, paid or volunteer, is an important factor determining the success of a sport program. The term leadership suggests a range of responsibilities within the sport program. Among them are four distinct leadership levels: func-

tional, supervisory, administrative, and executive or policy-making. Discussion in this chapter will focus on functional leadership: the employees and volunteers that deal directly with the participants in an intramural or extramural event.

Leadership implies that an individual has job duties and responsibilities involving authority to influence participants' habits or attitudes. A person achieves this authority in two ways. First, the person is placed in a leadership position and given thorough training about details of the job. Second, the leader demonstrates competence on the job to gain the respect, trust, and admiration of the participant. The two most important leaders in the intramural or extramural sport program are sport officials and sport supervisors.

Officials

Officiating is one of the most difficult leadership positions in sport. Some consider it a thankless task, and others feel it is a personal challenge that results in the satisfaction of being responsible for participants abiding by the sport rules. A good official extends his or her influence on the participants without being noticed. To this extent, officiating is an art. A good official should possess the following characteristics:

- **Quick reaction time.** An official must make split-second decisions. The tempo of most games allows little time to make a decision.

- **Confidence.** An official can portray confidence in such ways as speaking in a strong, firm voice, making positive motions in announcing decisions, or blowing a sharp and loud whistle.

- **Emotional control.** By using poise, calm, and control, a good official will have a relaxing effect on participants and spectators.

- **Consistency.** One of the finest attributes of a good official, consistency ensures that calls or decisions will be the same regardless of participants or circumstances.

- **Integrity.** An official should be honest at all times.

- **Knowledge of the rules.** An official must understand the rules of the game, the mechanics of the job duties, and the human relation aspects of officiating before refereeing sport at any level.

Officials' Checklist

This checklist, developed by Richard Schafer (1977, 20), illustrates several points in officiating.

☐ **Be competitive.** The players give maximum effort; so should you. Tell yourself, "I'm not going to let this game get away from me; I am better than that." You are hired to make the calls that control the game. Make them!

☐ **Have your head on right.** Don't think your striped shirt grants you immunity from having to take a little criticism. It's part of officiating. Plan on it. Successful officials know how much to take. Ask one when you get the chance.

☐ **Don't be a tough guy.** If a coach or team captain is on your back but not enough to warrant a penalty, then stay away from him or her. This is especially true during time-outs. Standing near an unhappy coach, just to *show him*, will only lead to further tensions. Some officials develop irritating characteristics. Don't be one of them.

☐ **Get into the flow of the game.** Each game is different. Good officials can feel this difference. Concentrate on the reactions of the players. Take note if the tempo of the game changes. A ragged game calls for a different style of officiating than a smooth one.

☐ **Don't bark.** If you don't like to be shouted at, don't shout at someone else. Be firm but with a normal relaxed voice. This technique will do wonders in helping you to reduce the pressure. Shouting indicates a loss of control—not only of yourself, but also of the game.

☐ **Show confidence.** Cockiness has no place in officiating. You want to inspire confidence. Your presence should command respect from the participants. As in any walk of life, appearance, manner, and voice determine how you are accepted. Try to present the proper image.

☐ **Forget the fans.** As a group, fans usually exhibit three characteristics: ignorance of the rules, highly emotional partisanship, and delight in antagonizing the officials. Accepting this fact will help you ignore the fans, unless they interrupt the game or stand in the way of you doing your job.

☐ **Answer reasonable questions.** Treat coaches and players in a courteous way. If they ask you reasonably, answer them in a polite way. If they get your ear by saying, "Hey, ref. I want to ask you something," then start telling you off, interrupt and remind them of the reason for the discussion. Be firm, but relaxed.

☐ **Choose your words wisely.** Don't obviously threaten a coach or player. This will only put them on the defensive, and you will have placed yourself on the spot. If you feel a situation is serious enough to warrant a threat, then it is serious enough to penalize without invoking a threat. Obviously some things you say will be a form of threat, but using the proper words can make it subtle.

☐ **Stay cool.** Your purpose is to establish a calm environment for the game. Fans, coaches, and players easily spot nervous or edgy officials. Avidly chewing gum, pacing, or displaying a range of emotions before or during a game will make you seem vulnerable to the pressure.

Recruiting Officials

Recruiting competent sport officials may be a taxing, yet satisfying experience. Finding individuals for leadership positions requires the agency to know how many sport officials it needs and to have a job description explaining position requirements.

Distribute and post position announcements pertaining to the openings. Ads placed in local newspapers can attract new officials to the sport program. Another good practice is to have an applicant complete an *Official's information card* (form 6.7) indicating sports desired, daily availability, and

---

OFFICIAL'S INFORMATION CARD

Date _____

Name _____
        (Last)   (First)   (Middle)

Address _____

Phone _____ Registered official _____ Yes _____ No

• SPORTS DESIRED

Men	**Women**	**Co-intramural**
_____ Basketball	_____ Basketball	_____ Basketball
_____ Flag football	_____ Cageball	_____ Inner tube
_____ Soccer	_____ Flag football	_____ Water polo
_____ Softball	_____ Kickball	_____ Softball
_____ Volleyball	_____ Inner tube	_____ Volleyball
_____ Water polo	_____ Water polo	
	_____ Volleyball	

• AVAILABILITY

Monday	**Tuesday**	**Wednesday**	**Thursday**	**Sunday**
____ 5-8 p.m.	____ 5-8 p.m.	____ 5-8 p.m.	____ 5-8 p.m.	____ 1-4 p.m.
____ 8-11 p.m.	____ 8-11 p.m.	____ 8-11 p.m.	____ 8-11 p.m.	____ 4-7 p.m.
____ Either	____ Either	____ Either	____ Either	____ 7-10 p.m.
				____ Any

Approximate number of hours per week desired _____

Form 6.7   Official's information card.

the number of hours desired per week. These cards provide a quick reference source once the season begins.

In-Service Training for Officials

After recruitment, the selected applicants should attend an in-service training program to familiarize them with policies, procedures, and rules relevant to their job description.

Hold several meetings with the new officials, beginning with an orientation meeting. At this meeting, discuss the agency's goals, philosophy, benefits, job conduct, uniforms, safety, scheduling, and other information pertaining to the job. This is also an ideal time for the employee to complete any necessary payroll or personnel forms.

Hold a second meeting to review rule interpretation, mechanics, and positioning, using slides, films, or other audiovisual aids. This meeting is vital to the success of the program because it ensures that all officials are familiar with specific interpretations and enforce them consistently during games.

After a rule interpretation meeting, provide an on-the-field or court practical clinic in which the potential sport official officiates a practice game, working on floor, hand, and verbal mechanics. Experienced or senior officials as instructors can provide leadership and a means for strengthening the relationship between new and veteran officials.

Following these meetings, give all officials written and practical knowledge tests developed either by the intramural staff or by a state or national officials' association. Require passing scores on proficiency and knowledge tests before scheduling; provide individual counseling for those scoring below the minimum.

After the tournament or season has begun, schedule periodic in-service sessions for the officials. The purpose of these sessions is to strengthen skills, build on what the official has learned through experience, and review persistent problems in rule interpretation if they are occurring.

Whatever method you use, in-service training is necessary to ensure a sound, quality officiating program. More agencies are deciding not to conduct these training sessions because of staff time and budget limitations. However, the dividends in reinforcement, morale, and positive public relations are more valuable than the cost. When thought of as an investment, in-service training is a worthwhile practice.

Scheduling Officials

Methods of assigning officials vary among institutional settings. Several methods, such as contract scheduling, weekly scheduling, and so forth, we discuss in the personnel chapter. Whatever method you choose, you need a carefully developed assignment plan.

Once you complete this master schedule, you can attach a daily list of scheduled officials (see form 6.8) to the sport supervisor's clipboard, indicating assigned course and shifts at the facility site. Later you can transfer the officials' names and hours worked from this form to a master payroll form.

Sport Official Evaluation

Evaluating officials is a difficult task that occurs continually throughout the season. Consider evaluations with a positive attitude to achieve maximum job performance. When officials and administrators look on the evaluation process as an aid instead of a threat to employment, the quality of the program is enhanced. Presenting positive solutions and helpful suggestions rather than reprimands and criticisms is important.

A popular evaluation method in intramural sport is a written evaluation form. Form 6.9 illustrates one example of a grouped officials' evaluation form. This form may be adapted for individual evaluations in order to ensure confidentiality.

Fellow officials, sport supervisors, participants, or teams may complete evaluations. It is a good practice to employ quality, experienced officials as daily evaluators to provide leadership. Whatever evaluation method you choose, the official should have the opportunity for positive feedback and an opportunity to examine the report.

Sport Supervisors

Although the characteristics of a competent sport official also apply to sport supervisors, they need several additional qualifications. First, require all supervisors to obtain sport emergency training,

---

VOLLEYBALL OFFICIALS' SCHEDULE

Supervisor _____ Day _____

Sport _____ Date _____

Location _____

	Court 1	**Court 2**	**Court 3**	**Court 4**
6:00 p.m. to 8:00 p.m.	Ref. *Smith* In ___ Out ___	Ref. *Murphy* In ___ Out ___	Ref. *Hudson* In ___ Out ___	Ref. *Finn* In ___ Out ___
	Ump. *Jones* In ___ Out ___	Ump. *Long* In ___ Out ___	Ump. *Howell* In ___ Out ___	Ump. *Cline* In ___ Out ___
	Court 5	**Court 6**	**Court 7**	**Court 8**
	Ref. *Burk* In ___ Out ___	Ref. *Johnson* In ___ Out ___	Ref. *Frye* In ___ Out ___	Ref. *Boyd* In ___ Out ___
	Ump. *Roberts* In ___ Out ___	Ump. *Moore* In ___ Out ___	Ump. *Evans* In ___ Out ___	Ump. *Baker* In ___ Out ___

Form 6.8   Daily officials' schedule.

BASKETBALL OFFICIALS' EVALUATION

Date _____

Evaluator _____

Check appropriate rating
7 = excellent   6 = very good   5 = good
4 = average   3 = fair   2 = poor   1 = bad

Officials' names	Smith	Jones	Miller	Johnson
I. Attitude				
Enthusiasm	7 6 5 4 3 2 1	7 6 5 4 3 2 1	7 6 5 4 3 2 1	7 6 5 4 3 2 1
Hustles	7 6 5 4 3 2 1	7 6 5 4 3 2 1	7 6 5 4 3 2 1	7 6 5 4 3 2 1
II. Rapport with participants				
Courteous	7 6 5 4 3 2 1	7 6 5 4 3 2 1	7 6 5 4 3 2 1	7 6 5 4 3 2 1
Takes criticism	7 6 5 4 3 2 1	7 6 5 4 3 2 1	7 6 5 4 3 2 1	7 6 5 4 3 2 1
Self-control	7 6 5 4 3 2 1	7 6 5 4 3 2 1	7 6 5 4 3 2 1	7 6 5 4 3 2 1
III. Mechanics				
Position as lead official	7 6 5 4 3 2 1	7 6 5 4 3 2 1	7 6 5 4 3 2 1	7 6 5 4 3 2 1
Position as trail official	7 6 5 4 3 2 1	7 6 5 4 3 2 1	7 6 5 4 3 2 1	7 6 5 4 3 2 1
Jump ball administration	7 6 5 4 3 2 1	7 6 5 4 3 2 1	7 6 5 4 3 2 1	7 6 5 4 3 2 1
Free-throw administration	7 6 5 4 3 2 1	7 6 5 4 3 2 1	7 6 5 4 3 2 1	7 6 5 4 3 2 1
Throw-in administration	7 6 5 4 3 2 1	7 6 5 4 3 2 1	7 6 5 4 3 2 1	7 6 5 4 3 2 1
Call and report fouls	7 6 5 4 3 2 1	7 6 5 4 3 2 1	7 6 5 4 3 2 1	7 6 5 4 3 2 1
Switching at dead balls	7 6 5 4 3 2 1	7 6 5 4 3 2 1	7 6 5 4 3 2 1	7 6 5 4 3 2 1
Use of signals	7 6 5 4 3 2 1	7 6 5 4 3 2 1	7 6 5 4 3 2 1	7 6 5 4 3 2 1
Whistle	7 6 5 4 3 2 1	7 6 5 4 3 2 1	7 6 5 4 3 2 1	7 6 5 4 3 2 1
Eye contact w/ partner	7 6 5 4 3 2 1	7 6 5 4 3 2 1	7 6 5 4 3 2 1	7 6 5 4 3 2 1
IV. Consistency				
Calls both ways	7 6 5 4 3 2 1	7 6 5 4 3 2 1	7 6 5 4 3 2 1	7 6 5 4 3 2 1
No hesitation in calls	7 6 5 4 3 2 1	7 6 5 4 3 2 1	7 6 5 4 3 2 1	7 6 5 4 3 2 1
Total				
V. Comments				

Form 6.9   Officials' evaluation form.

encompassing first aid skills. This training may be conducted by the intramural sport office or by an appropriate health agency. First aid training allows the supervisor to provide immediate first aid care to an individual who has been injured or suddenly taken ill while participating in the sport program. It does not allow a supervisor to practice medicine, but it provides the knowledge and skills to handle life threatening situations. In addition to their sport emergency training, supervisors are responsible for accident reporting. The risk management chapter discusses safety and accident reporting procedures.

Along with proper safety training, a supervisor should have experience as a sport official. This allows the supervisor to provide advice pertaining to interpretations and protests, as well as to have a better appreciation of the difficulties in officiating. Because a sport supervisor is an extension of the office and the person in authority at the activity site, a thorough understanding of office policies, procedures, and rules of the game is also essential. Supervisors must be alert, anticipate hazards that may be dangerous to the players, officials, or spectators, and eliminate them before

Shining Example

Amateur Athletic Union of the United States, Inc.
c/o Walt Disney World Resort,
P.O. Box 10000, Lake Buena Vista, FL 32830-1000

The Amateur Athletic Union of the United States, Inc. (AAU) is the largest not-for-profit volunteer-driven multiple sport amateur athletic organization in the United States. AAU has a partnership with Walt Disney World Resort, and its National Headquarters are located in Lake Buena Vista, Florida. The AAU registers 300,000 members annually with ninety-five percent of the membership being under 18 years of age. The AAU sponsors both young and adult sporting opportunities. Along with the sports programs, the AAU also sponsors the AAU Junior Olympic Games, the AAU James E. Sullivan Memorial Award, the President's Challenge Youth Physical Fitness Award Program, and the Presidential Sports Award.

Organization: The mission of this not-for-profit AAU is to offer a lifelong progression of amateur sports programs for persons of all ages, races, and creeds; to enhance the physical, mental, and moral development of amateur athletes; and to promote good sportsmanship, good citizenship, and safety.

Clientele: The AAU registers 300,000 members annually. Ninety to ninety-five percent of the membership is 18 years old or younger. The male-to-female ratio of the total registrations is 60 percent male and 40 percent female.

Budget: The overall operating budget for 1996 is $5.4 million.

Marketing: The AAU target market is focused on youth age 6-19. The AAU uses Radio and Television PSAs, the USA Today Amateur Sports page, numerous brochures, press releases, and volunteer word of mouth.

Administrative Staff: The AAU is divided into the five following departments (The number of staff for each department is listed in parentheses): Sports Operations (10), Administrative Services (2), Association Services (6), External Relations (7), and Finance (3). The AAU is run by five elected volunteer officers, with assistance from a 20-person volunteer board of directors.

Program Detail: The AAU sponsors both youth (32) and adult (15) sporting opportunities. Along with the sports programs, the AAU also sponsors the AAU Junior Olympic Games, the AAU James E. Sullivan Memorial Award, the AAU/Milky Way Brand High School All-American Awards, the President's Challenge Youth Physical Fitness Award Program, and the Presidential Sports Award.

Facilities: The AAU currently has plans of opening a sports complex in 1997 which will host some 25 AAU events. The multi-million dollar facility will provide enormous potential for the AAU Junior Olympic games.

play begins. More specific job responsibilities follow.

Sport Supervisor's Pregame Responsibilities

Before any event the supervisor on duty must do the following:

- Check that needed sport equipment and supplies are present and in good condition.
- Determine whether all sport officials have signed in on the appropriate work-time form.
- See that the games are started on time, observing the forfeit time rule.
- Verify the team's roster on the official score sheet.

Sport Supervisor's Game Responsibilities

The sport supervisor is responsible for all games and situations on the field or court. The supervisor should be alert for disputes, protests, or other problems and should prevent them before they occur. Circulating from field to field or court to court, he or she can determine whether all games are progressing properly. The supervisor should attach game rules to a clipboard to refer to in case of a dispute.

A sport supervisor handles questions of eligibility. If a participant is ineligible, the supervisor should insist that he or she not participate. Report any problem to the sport office.

In case of unfavorable weather after the games have begun, play should not continue if it becomes too dangerous. Supervisors must exhibit good judgment in these cases.

Supervisors are also responsible for improving the quality of officiating and working with the officials to develop proficiency whenever possible.

In rating the officials, use an evaluation form accurately.

Supervisors should prevent the misuse of any sport facility. If participants are misusing a facility, the supervisor should inform them of the proper use. If they fail to comply with the supervisor's instruction, request law enforcement assistance.

If a protest occurs while the supervisor is on duty, complete a *Protest Form* on the field or court and return it to the sport office.

Sport Supervisor's Postgame Responsibilities

The supervisor makes sure each official signs the completed game score sheet. If there are numerous games, the supervisor should circulate and collect score sheets after *each* game is completed.

Report all cases of unsporting conduct by a team or individual to the proper authority. Submit a written report to the sport office to document such behavior.

Complete sign-out forms when equipment is checked out and file forms properly. Supervisors should also complete a *Maintenance Repair Form* when reporting facilities needing repair. Without the help of the supervisors in this area, maintenance problems will increase.

ADA Suggestions

The ADA is a civil rights law, not a building code or construction law. Even so, the ADA is the first civil rights law that has directly affected the building and construction industry. Unlike traditional building codes, there are no ADA inspectors to review compliance with suggested guidelines. Thus, facility design and modifications are always subject to challenge or a civil lawsuit.

It is important for recreational sport programmers to remember that the ADA re-quirements are minimum guidelines and do not meet the needs of every participant in all facilities and programs. Whenever appropriate, attempt to exceed minimum guidelines. The goal should be to follow not only the letter of the law but also the spirit of the law.

Sports Scheduling Software

The greatest computer need expressed by recreational sport programmers most likely pertains to sport scheduling software, which includes league and tournament scheduling programs. There are a number of scheduling software programs currently on the market that range in price from $89 to $3,000. The wide range of prices reflects the diversity and complexity of the features available in software packages.

Computerized sport scheduling programs are not suited for every sport program. Realistically, computerized scheduling is best designed for tournaments of 50 teams/individuals or more. For tournaments of less than 50, the recreational sport programmer would probably be wise to manually schedule the tournament.

When considering the purchase of a sport scheduling software program, a number of key features should be considered:

- **Team Capacity**—What are the upper limits in terms of the number of teams, leagues, divisions, and facility sites that can be handled by the program?

- **League Formation**—Is there flexibility in the program's selection of teams and the creation of leagues and divisions? That is, do you have the option of using either an automatic random selection by the computer or a selection based on a set of staff-defined criteria?

- **Scheduling Conflicts**—Can the program identify scheduling overlaps and re-schedule game dates due to team conflicts, weather cancellations, and other programming concerns?

- **Scheduling Formats**—Does the program appropriately seed teams when scheduling various tournament formats, such as round robin, double round robin, single-elimination, double-elimination, meets, and various challenge tournament formats?

- **Master Schedule**—Can the program create master schedule reports that can be viewed in advance—either on-screen or on a printed report—for a particular date, facility, league, or team?

- **Team Schedules**—Does program scheduling include on-screen viewing, hard copy or disk file creation, editing capability, and rotating home and visitor assignments?

- **Reports**—The design and actual printouts of reports and team schedules are the most important components of the scheduling program. Game times, to alleviate the participants' confusion, should be printed in standard A.M./P.M. format rather than military time, and dates should include the day of the week. Facility sites should be represented by the name of the facility rather than a code. Printing individual game score sheets, including eligible players, is also very beneficial. Facility schedules/reports are useful when managing sports tournaments if they are arranged by specific sites, by court/field, or by a range of dates, times, divisions, or leagues.

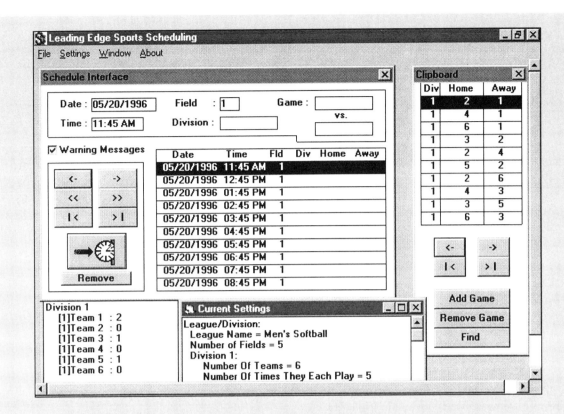

- **Team Rosters**—Will the program list teams and rosters by sport, division, and league? Will the program generate an alphabetical phone and address list of team captains for use in a mail merge?
- **Standings**—Can the program generate league standings with win-loss records and "games behind" calculations?

This page shows an example of a screen from *Leading Edge Sports Scheduling* by MarketShare Development that illustrates the Schedule Editor, which allows you to edit and fine-tune your schedule game by game.

An effective computerized sport scheduling system can save many hours of routine yet tedious work and can eliminate the human mistakes that are an inevitable aspect of sport scheduling.

Leading Edge Sports Scheduling, MarketShare Development, 160 N. Sweetwater Road, Lithia Springs, GA, 30057, 404-944-8730

Other sport scheduling software products: A.E. Klawitter, EZ Score Promotions, Intramural Participation System, Overtime Software, RecWare, and Vermont Systems.

CONCLUSION

The sport programmer plays a significant role in the success of the intramural and extramural sport program at an operational level. A sound philosophy is a prerequisite for effective programming. The programmer should have abilities in human relations, decision making, and conflict resolution and know rules and regulations, tournament scheduling methods, and policies and procedures

of the program. Above all, the programmer must have a genuine interest in recreational sport, specifically, intramural sport.

Each institutional setting has its unique programming approach. Consider the material in this chapter as tools for programming. It is up to the programmer to apply these principles to daily situations.

Intramural and extramural sport are rewarding phases of recreational sport for the programmer and the participant. Both disciplines, with their diversity of sport events, offer wholesome competition and cooperation regardless of the skill and interest level of the participant.

DISCUSSION QUESTIONS

1. Describe criteria to consider when selecting sport events for intramural and extramural sport programs.

2. What is your philosophy of eligibility for intramural sport participation regarding varsity and professional athletes?

3. Describe techniques that reduce forfeits, game rescheduling, and protest.

4. What is your opinion of having a policy that requires medical examinations for all participants before participation?

5. What are the advantages and disadvantages of establishing a co-intramural program? Include rule modifications, eligibility, safety, equipment, and other issues.

6. Should a woman be allowed to play on a men's team in an all-men's league or vice versa? What liability concerns should you consider? What equity concerns?

7. Under what conditions would you use round-robin, single-elimination, double-elimination, and challenge tournaments?

8. Explain the procedures you would use in determining the number and placement of byes and seeds in single-elimination tournaments. What is an *implied bye*?

9. What is a challenge tournament? Briefly explain the advantages and disadvantages of this kind of tournament.

10. Diagram a pyramid tournament for a tennis tournament with 11 individuals.

11. List the programming details of an extramural sport event (i.e., eligibility rules, housing, liability, finance, etc.).

12. How does instant scheduling differ from regular tournament scheduling?

13. Describe the programming problems of sport events, such as swimming and track-and-field competitions, that involve meet organization.

14. What is the role of the intramural sport official in interpreting game rules? What is the role of the intramural supervisor?

15. The philosophy of recreational sport should include striving for fun, fair, and honest competition. How can intramural sport officials contribute to this philosophy?

APPLICATION EXERCISE

You are in charge of programming a tennis tournament for a YMCA. The YMCA operates three indoor tennis courts that you may use a maximum of six hours a day on Saturday and Sunday. You are allowing one hour for each match scheduled. Twenty-nine participants have entered the tournament, and all will play in the same division.

a) Draw the single-elimination bracket for these entrants.

b) Seed the top four players by indicating their positions with the numbers 1, 2, 3, and 4. Indicate the position of the others with *Xs*.

c) Position byes appropriately.

d) Schedule matches so each player has at least one hour of rest between matches.

e) Determine how much money you will spend for officials if you provide one official per court per match until the semifinals, and provide two linesmen plus the official for the semifinal and final matches. All officials and linesmen will be paid $10.00 per game.

REFERENCES

Maas, G. 1979. Instant scheduling for intramural sports. Paper presented at the Big Ten Recreational Sports Directors' Conference, Chicago, December, 1 979.

Schafer, R.C. 1977. Thinking right. *Referee*. (Jan-Feb): 20.

SUGGESTED READINGS

Brown, E., S. Smith, and T. Bartley. 1989. Expanding all-campus play-off opportunities without quality deterioration. *National Intramural-Recreational Sports Association Journal* 14 (1): 14-15.

Burwell, P., and S. Yeagle. 1990. Developing potential: The extramural sport clubs conference. P. 207-213 n *Management strategies in recreational sports*. Corvallis, OR: National Intramural-Recreational Sports Association.

Byl, J. 1990. Formalizing a ladder tournament: Revisiting Rokosz proposal. *National Intramural-Recreational Sports Association Journal* 15 (1): 41.

Gaskins, D.A. 1994. Can Jennifer come out and play? *National Intramural-Recreational Sports Association Journal* 18 (3): 12-14.

Gaskins, D.A., and T.B. McCollum. 1990. Energizing officiating programs through extramural sports. *National Intramural-Recreational Sports Association Journal* 15 (1): 16.

Goodwin, J., and D. Flatt. 1990. Improve intramural programs through officiating. *National Intramural-Recreational Sports Association Journal* 14 (3): 46-47.

Haderlie, B., and C. Ross. 1993. Computerized sports league scheduling: Is it right for you? *Employee Services Management—A Journal of Employee Recreation, Health and Education* (March): 12-15.

Hall, D. 1990. Encouraging good sportsmanship: A behavior modification tool approved by East Carolina University intramural participants. *National Intramural-Recreational Sports Association Journal* 15 (1): 8.

Ross, C., and T. Vaughn. 1995. Recruitment and retention of quality intramural sports officials. *National Intramural-Recreational Sports Association Journal* 19 (3): 17-22.

Ross, C., and S. Wolter. 1995. On Schedule. *Athletic Business*. (April): 47-52.

Ross, C., S. Wolter, and C. Handel. 1994. Computers in sport scheduling: Features of available software. *Employee Services Management—A Journal of Employee Recreation, Health and Education* (October): 6-14.

Wade, G. 1991. The intramural sports officiating dilemma: Is self-officiating a viable solution?. *National Intramural-Recreational Sports Association Journal* 15 (3): 45.

Chapter 6 Appendix

One of the most difficult aspects of tournament scheduling is providing accurate and consistent schedules and brackets. This appendix provides selected round-robin schedule forms and sample-elimination bracket forms that you can use when you conduct tournaments. If the number of entries in your tournament matches the number of entries these bracket forms accommodate, you may copy and use these forms as needed. If you have more (or fewer) entries, use these forms as guides for customizing your brackets.

Sport		League		Division

Team	Team	Date	Time	Ct/Field
1 vs 4				
2 vs 3				
1 vs 3				
4 vs 2				
1 vs 2				
3 vs 4				

Team	Won	Lost
1.		
2.		
3.		
4.		

Form 6A.1   Four-entry round-robin league worksheet.

Sport _____

League _____

Division _____

	Team	Won	Lost
1.	_____	_____	_____
2.	_____	_____	_____
3.	_____	_____	_____
4.	_____	_____	_____
5.	_____	_____	_____

Team Team	Date	Time	Ct/Field
1 vs 4			
2 vs 3			
5 vs 3			
1 vs 2			
4 vs 2			
5 vs 1			
3 vs 1			
4 vs 5			
2 vs 5			
3 vs 4			

Form 6A.2   Five-entry round-robin league worksheet.

Sport _____

League _____

Division _____

	Team	Won	Lost
1.	_____	_____	_____
2.	_____	_____	_____
3.	_____	_____	_____
4.	_____	_____	_____
5.	_____	_____	_____
6.	_____	_____	_____

Team Team	Date	Time	Ct/Field
1 vs 6			
2 vs 5			
3 vs 4			
1 vs 5			
6 vs 4			
2 vs 3			
1 vs 4			
5 vs 3			
6 vs 2			
1 vs 3			
4 vs 2			
5 vs 6			
1 vs 2			
3 vs 6			
4 vs 5			

Form 6A.3   Six-entry round-robin league worksheet.

Sport _____

League _____

Division _____

Team	Won	Lost
1. _____	_____	_____
2. _____	_____	_____
3. _____	_____	_____
4. _____	_____	_____
5. _____	_____	_____
6. _____	_____	_____
7. _____	_____	_____

Team Team	Date	Time	Ct/Field
1 vs 6			
2 vs 5			
3 vs 4			
7 vs 5			
1 vs 4			
2 vs 3			
6 vs 4			
7 vs 3			
1 vs 2			
5 vs 3			
6 vs 2			
7 vs 1			
4 vs 2			
5 vs 1			
6 vs 7			
3 vs 1			
4 vs 7			
5 vs 6			
2 vs 7			
3 vs 6			
4 vs 5			

Form 6A.4   Seven-entry round-robin league worksheet.

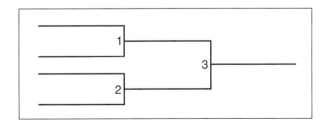

Form 6A.5   Four-entry single-elimination bracket.

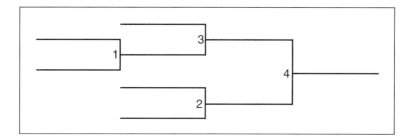

Form 6A.6   Five-entry single-elimination bracket.

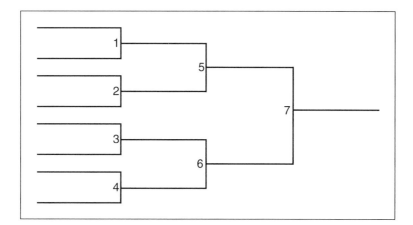

Form 6A.7   Eight-entry single-elimination bracket.

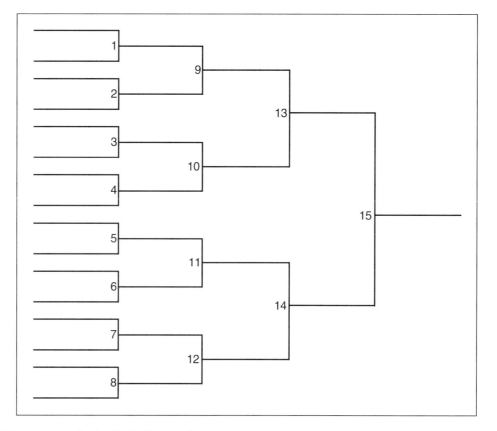

Form 6A.8   Sixteen-entry single-elimination bracket.

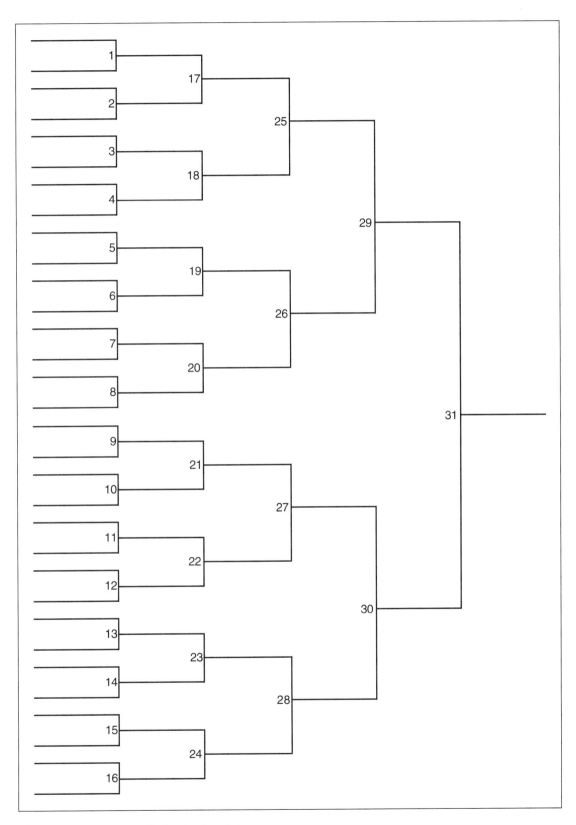

Form 6A.9   Thirty-two-entry single-elimination bracket.

CHAPTER 7

Club Sport

Chapter Objectives

After reading this chapter you will

- be able to differentiate the three purposes of club sport,
- understand financial and administrative patterns in club sport, and
- identify club sport governance.

Club sport participation is a major program area within recreational sport. It involves groups that organize because of a common interest in a sport. Self-administration and self-regulation are characteristics common to all clubs, whether they revolve around bridge, chess, sailing, hot-air ballooning, track, rugby, or spelunking. Those who desire club sport membership seek regular participation under a more coherent design than informal, intramural, or extramural programs offer.

Historically, you can trace club sport in America to the strong community club sport tradition that still exists in Europe. European clubs provide the main source of sport participation and instruction for all ages, interest, and skill levels. Clubs are self-governed by volunteer, elected, or paid personnel. Members customarily participate with or compete against those representing other communities.

Club systems in the United States vary depending on their setting. For example, clubs in municipal settings are organized by age group. Clubs in military settings parallel athletic sport by sponsoring the most skilled participants to compete against those from other military bases. Clubs in a commercial setting may incorporate more than one sport. They are privately owned and operate for profit through membership fees and charges for space use. Clubs within a correctional setting operate on one site with restricted or no opportunity for travel. Clubs in an educational setting are at colleges and high schools on a limited basis. Perhaps the biggest reason for the diverse approach to club sport in America is that all sport programs were developed independently through educational or municipal settings.

Club sport organizations determine their own activities, leadership, and internal operating policies. Self-determination, unity, and common interest are the most appealing aspects of club sport for potential members. Such characteristics distinguish club sport from informal, intramural, and extra-mural sport. Additional factors associated with club sport programs include an ability to provide sport participation unavailable elsewhere, an opportunity to engage in the sport of one's choice, service to special interest groups, and extramural opportunities distinct from those offered in the intramural sport programs.

CLUB SYSTEMS

As club members pursue their sport interests, specific emphasis emerges, including tournament participation, socialization, instruction and skill development, or a combination of the three. Factors that influence how the club evolves include traditions of the sport, interests and abilities of the members, capabilities of the leadership, availability of facilities and equipment, financial support, and the proximity of opponents. The following descriptions of each major club type may help identify their characteristics.

Athletic Club System

Clubs interested in scheduling and hosting tournaments, leagues, or structured events operate like athletic or professional sport teams. Club members tend to be goal oriented and enjoy the rivalry and competition of structured tournaments. Consequently, clubs hold regular practice sessions, often hire a coach, and maintain an organized tournament schedule. Sometimes, clubs hold tryouts to select a traveling team or individual to compete against others having a similar skill level. In some instances, club-sponsored teams or members participate in structured events through the NCAA, NAIA, AAU, ACU-I, and Olympics. To maintain a recreational sport philosophy, however, membership should not be denied if the participant does not have the interest or ability to play at a high skill level.

The biggest difference between clubs that focus on tournaments and athletic sport is the degree of administrative support and complexity of the regulations governing their operations. Clubs bear the responsibility for generating and managing their finances, developing leadership, and determining guidelines and activities. If these functions were being performed for the club, it would more closely resemble an athletic sport approach. In community youth sport programs, such as soccer, traveling teams are often selected, coached, and financially supported to participate in scheduled tournaments. Similarly, commercial racquetball clubs may sponsor individual members to participate in tournaments on behalf of the club.

Although enthusiasm and resolve for high-skill performance should be encouraged, this may lead to participation by too few club members. Because involvement in scheduled activity requires many fund-raising mechanisms to handle the costs of entry fees, uniforms, equipment, travel and lodging, officials' and judges' fees, and so on, each club member should help choose how the club resources meet such expenses.

Instructional Club System

Another popular type of club concentrates on instruction, knowledge, and skill development. Although some teaching takes place among the membership in every club, learning is not left to chance or dealt with in a haphazard way. Instructional clubs hire or recruit qualified personnel to structure lessons or clinics at practice sessions appropriate for the interests and abilities of their membership. Some clubs will design testing situations and in-house tournaments so the members can see what they have learned and where they need improvement. Other avenues for displaying newly acquired or polished skills include demonstrations, clinics, and extramural participation.

An instructional club may meet its financial needs through membership fees, lesson charges, and fines. The biggest expenses arise from instructors' wages and equipment purchases. If a club wants to support members or a team in tournaments or rent a facility, they may have to mount fund-raising efforts.

Social Club System

In social club settings, participants seek membership to meet others who enjoy the same sport. The major interest shared by members is a specific sport, but participation becomes more a means for socializing than learning, skill development, fitness, or tournament play. Enjoyment arises more from rapport and camaraderie among members than from performance or competition. The fun of participation may diminish if too much structure and competitive rivalry are present, although some clubs maintain regular intramural tournaments for their members to encourage social interaction. Other social club activities include sponsoring clinics, giving demonstrations, or tournaments. Members of socially oriented clubs commonly provide their own equipment and support their activities through membership dues.

CLUB SPORT PROGRAM CONSIDERATIONS

For a club sport organization to continue operating, it must maintain its resources. Changes in membership levels, interest, funding, facility availability, and leadership will influence its longevity. Consequently, an external support system may reinforce the club's internal leadership, helping provide continuity, organization, and programming assistance.

External administration for the club sport program should be centralized under one board, department, unit, or agency. (Where applicable, the administration should be housed with the other recreational sport programming areas.) A central approach maintains continuity, standardizes operational procedures, establishes equitable access to resources, allows an assessment of needs, and permits an evaluation of the total club program. Although external leadership support is not always vital to the continuation of a club sport, it may make valuable contributions to the stability and quality of club sport operations.

The degree to which external administration and program services exist depends on the philosophy of the institution, agency, or board assuming administrative responsibility, as well as the potential of the setting for providing program resources. When the higher administrative levels decide the extent of support, they communicate this to the club sport programming staff as policy or procedure. The club sport programming staff and the administrator of the recreational sport program should seek an opportunity to influence these decisions.

While examining the type of program leadership and services to offer, consider possible legal restraints. At a minimum, a staff member should investigate the legal aspects of working with clubs within a particular setting and serve as a resource person to solve problems for the club sport program. Examples of additional services that can be provided to clubs include partial or total support for finances, instructional or coaching personnel, equipment, facilities, travel, office space, storage space, telephone access, clerical assistance, and publicity.

Because the program services provided to clubs vary, there are no established models dictating how to program a club sport. Two philosophical approaches to club programming exist: conservative, or formal; and liberal, or informal. The major principle of the conservative approach is that club members have little or no discretion in determining operational procedure. Characteristics of this approach include the following:

- Clubs receive financial support from the institution or agency having administrative responsibility.
- Club schedules and activities must receive administrative approval.
- Club travel must be approved. Properly insured vehicles must be used for travel, and approved supervisors must accompany the club.
- Clubs must have an approved advisor or coach (may be a paid position).
- Clubs must maintain a formal document, for example, a constitution or guidelines.
- Club members must have insurance coverage and a medical examination.
- Club financial transactions and purchases must be approved by a person within the administrative structure or a program staff person.
- Medical or athletic training supervision may be provided at club events.

Common characteristics of the liberal approach include the following:

- Club members control operations, such as funding, travel, scheduling, and purchasing.
- Clubs receive minimal or no external assistance in funding, equipment, facilities scheduling, office use, or medical supervision.
- Club members are responsible for their own insurance coverage and for knowing their own physiological limitations.

Agencies that provide partial or complete funding and adequate staff supervision usually select the conservative approach. The liberal approach is most frequently used when funding and staffing are limited or unavailable. The greater the financial dependence on an agency, the greater the external leadership involvement in the club.

Quality club sport programs may flourish under either approach. The liberal approach relies heavily on volunteer leadership and voluntary assumption of risk, and is more limited in the program services it can offer. When selecting a programming approach, make a firm decision to go in one direction or the other. Those who combine approaches may find themselves faced with legal liability because of indecisive or inconsistent administrative decision making.

Organizational Structure of Club Sport

After considering the program approach, establish the specific organizational structures within which the club will operate. These structures usually exist at two levels—external and internal.

External Structure

Developing a sound external organizational structure involves documenting the policies that influence club operations, identifying supervisors and coordinators for the club sports, and specifying the services available to clubs. The latter function includes the procedures necessary to provide access to services.

Most club sport programs operating under a conservative administration have one supervisor who enforces operational policy; advises club leadership and employees; serves as a liaison between the clubs and administrative personnel, shareholders, or groups within the setting; supervises services provided; handles disciplinary problems; maintains documentation; and works to meet the clubs' needs. When the need exists and resources permit, additional full- or part-time personnel may be involved on a paid or volunteer basis.

A number of club sport programs use a club sport council, federation, or board to shape and implement operational policy. Composed of a representative from each club, the council and its executive officers play an active role in policy development, club leadership, and club governance (usually in conjunction with a liberal administrative approach). Alternatively, the council may advise the programming personnel in charge of club sport (a conservative approach).

Regardless of the involvement of the council leadership and governance functions, the format allows for systematic input from each club. It keeps programming personnel aware of club needs, develops a sense of unity, provides representative input for decision making or operational procedures, facilitates the acceptance of policy, and serves as a forum for problem solving.

Internal Structure

Most clubs elect officers because they recognize the need for leadership. They know certain tasks must be accomplished for the club to function. Under a conservative approach to club sport programming, clubs must maintain elected officers. To an extent, the club sport staff dictates and supervises election procedures. This requirement reflects a desire to structure stability and establish an avenue for accountability to the club sport staff. The positions most likely to exist within a club include a president, vice-president, secretary, and treasurer. The responsibilities of the officers include the following:

- Convene regular club meetings for communication and business purposes.
- Be familiar with an approved code of parliamentary procedure.
- Monitor compliance with club operational policies.
- Maintain necessary records.
- Recruit new members.
- Initiate financial transactions.
- Prepare budget requests and annual reports.
- Serve as the liaison to the external administrative structure for the club sport program.
- Know agency policies and procedures affecting clubs.
- Know legal parameters affecting club operations.
- Know safety precautions and accident reporting procedures.

Specific duties for each club officer include the following:

President

- Organize and conduct all club meetings.
- Appoint necessary chairpersons and committees.
- Serve as an ex-officio member of all committees.
- Coordinate and schedule all club activities.
- Supervise election procedures.
- Maintain contact with club officers and committee members.
- Call for oral and written reports as necessary.
- Represent the club to the agency or setting.

Vice-President

- Assume duties of the president in his or her absence.

- Oversee club equipment and purchase requests.
- Oversee all club committees.
- Assist president as required.

Secretary

- Notify members of meetings.
- Record minutes of all meetings.
- Handle all club correspondence.
- Maintain club membership roster.
- Maintain club records and files.
- Prepare club annual report for approval.

Treasurer

- Maintain accurate and up-to-date club financial records, salary schedules, and payroll.
- Prepare purchase requests for approval.
- Collect membership dues.
- Prepare club budget request and annual financial report.
- Pay all club bills.
- Report club financial status to general membership on request.

Other possible leadership positions in clubs include the following:

- **Club advisor**—serves as a resource person to approve club activities and to advise club members
- **Safety officer**—responsible for checking equipment and facilities for hazardous conditions and handling accident situations
- **Coach**—responsible for scheduling and coaching practice sessions and contests
- **Instructor**—responsible for designing structured learning experiences for club sport members
- **Publicity manager**—responsible for initiating and implementing all publicity for the club

Each club member should play a significant role in the success of the club. Without membership involvement, a club often grows stale, despite the enthusiasm of its officers. Each club member should attend meetings and participate in decision making; help shape the club constitution, bylaws, membership requirements, and dues structure; have a say in selecting club officers; and uphold club and agency policies.

Each club should develop written information on operations. This information aids continuity for a club when leadership and members change. It reflects the evolution of the club. A conservative program approach may require development of a constitution and bylaws. Once a document has been prepared, it is a common practice that the club sport staff approve it. In some instances, constitutions may need approval at an administrative level. Due to limited familiarity with preparing this type of document, a staff member may need to provide assistance. The sidebar below shows a format for a constitution and bylaws for club sport.

Club Constitution Format

Constructing a constitution for a club sport team is one way to show the host facility that club members are serious about their endeavor. It might also indicate that club members will be good custodians of the host agency's facilities. Following is an effective outline for a club constitution.

Preamble

States the purpose and aims of the group.

Article I Name

States the name adopted by the organization. This section might also state whether the organization is incorporated and, if so, under what name or names.

Article II Membership

States the requirements for admission to the club and size limitations of the club.

Article III Officers

Contains the list of officers and their terms of office.

Article IV Executive Committee

States the make-up of the executive committee (board or council), the method of their selection, and their terms of office. A section under this article may include provisions for vacancies of officers.

Article V Meetings

States the regular meeting time and provisions for calling special meetings. If meetings cannot be held regularly, indicates authority to call meetings.

Article VI Amendment Process

This section details the constitutional amendment process. Making a constitutional amendment requires previous notification and a two-thirds or three-fourths affirmative vote for its adoption.

Article VII Ratification

Provision for ratifying the constitution may or may not be necessary. If ratification demands more than a simple majority of the voting members present at the time of ratification, this article must indicate so.

Bylaws

The bylaws may involve the following:

- Details on membership, such as rights, duties, and resignation and expulsion procedures.
- Provisions for initiation fees, dues, and other assessments, along with a procedure to handle payment delinquencies.
- Date and method of electing officers.
- Duties, authority, and responsibilities of an executive committee.
- Names of the standing committees and the method of choosing the committee chairs and membership. The duties of each committee should also be stated.
- Provision for use of accepted parliamentary manual (e.g., *Robert's Rules of Order, Newly Revised*).
- Percentage of members constituting a quorum.
- Provision for honorary members and honorary officers.
- Method for amending the bylaws. This is usually is accomplished through a simple majority vote.

For group stability, the constitution and bylaws should be reviewed annually to keep them current. Annual review keeps each club aware of its operating code.

Club Sport Operational Guidelines

Guidelines provided by the board or agency should be as comprehensive as possible, but not so complex or strict that clubs are discouraged from organizing. Develop guidelines into a functional manual available to the officers of each club.

Because adherence to manual guidelines is important, review their content, highlighting the most important points, with the officers of each club. You can handle this task with each club individually or in a group. Either way, make personal contact with the officers and emphasize that guidelines exist to encourage the success of the club, not to obstruct enjoyment. The next few pages discuss concepts necessary to develop successful club guidelines consistent with a conservative program philosophy.

Club Sport Classification System

In many agencies the club sport program operates under a simple classification system in which all clubs follow the same policies and procedures. Regardless of the level of the club's organization, programming skills, participation size, fund-raising, and financial needs, all clubs receive the same benefits. However, in agencies where there are a diverse offering of club sports, clubs might exist on both extremes of the spectrum. Some clubs will have a long history, high membership, and require extreme programming, and other clubs may be informally organized, have few members, and require little competitive programming. Because all clubs are unique, classification systems afford equity among the clubs, especially dividing the agency's resources among the clubs the agency serves.

You can develop classification systems according to risks or level of organization. Specific classification of clubs must involve assigning levels of risk of a certain activity as follows. You can adjust methods of managing risk by risk level classification.

Risk Level I—Activities at this risk level involve deliberate physical contact. Examples include aikido, lacrosse, equestrian, fencing, gymnastics, hapkido, ice hockey, judo, karate, kung fu, water polo, riflery, rugby, scuba, self defense, snow skiing, tae kwon do, water skiing, and wrestling.

Risk Level II—The risks associated with these activities often pertain to their geographical location. These sports may have limited access to emergency personnel and take place far away from a hospital. Examples include bass fishing, common adventure, field hockey, cycling, racquetball, roller hockey, rowing, soccer, tennis, and ultimate Frisbee.

Risk Level III—These sports normally don't have a high prevalence of injury or severe injuries associated with them. Examples include badminton, dance, table tennis, and billiards.

In addition to classifying clubs according to risk categories, you can also classify clubs by organization level. Table 7.1 illustrates typical categories that allow clubs to be supported administratively by their organization level.

As you can see in table 7.1, clubs are placed in one of three categories: A, B, or C. Once a club is in a category, it must abide by the requirements in that category or be lowered to the next category.

Procedure for Establishing a Club

Use a step-by-step approach for each group seeking operation as a club. In settings where a legal bond exists between a club and sponsoring agency, require formal application before approval. Additional requirements may include the following:

- Meet with the club sport program staff to review requirements, guidelines for operation, and application (see form 7.1).
- Develop a club constitution and bylaws for approval.
- Submit an officers' list and membership roster. As a programmer you can facilitate this process by having forms available for clubs' use (see forms 7.2 and 7.3).
- Submit a facility reservation request (sometimes unavailability of facility space prohibits a club from functioning).
- Obtain a formal statement indicating approval or disapproval for club status. This step may require the endorsement of an administrative unit within the setting before you can determine final status. After reaching a decision to approve or disapprove the request, send a letter indicating the result to the club's leadership.
- Meet with the club sport program staff to review club status and discuss club responsibilities

Once a club receives approval to function within the setting, it may encounter difficulties that jeopardize its ability to remain active. Consequently, operational guidelines should explain the conditions under which a club may be placed on an

	Table 7.1 Classification of Club Sports by Level of Organization	
Category A	**Category B**	**Category C**
Tightly organized	Well organized	Limited organization
Large budget	Low to moderate budget	Low or no budget
High participation	Low to moderate participation	Low participation
Extensive programming	Moderate programming	Limited programming
• Competitions	• Competitions	• Competitions
• Special events	• Special events	• Special events
• Clinics	• Clinics	• Clinics
• Demonstrations	• Demonstrations	• Demonstrations
• Instruction	• Instruction	• Instruction
• Social functions	• Social functions	• Social functions
• Fitness component	• Fitness component	• Fitness component
High facility use	Moderate or high facility use	Low facility use
Extensive travel	Limited travel	No travel
High safety risk	Moderate safety risk	Low safety risk
High membership dues	Moderate membership dues	Moderate or no membership dues
Organized fund raising	Limited fund raising	Limited or no fund raising
Club has been organized for 2 or more years	Club has been organized for 1 or more years	Club has been organized for less than 1 year

Courtesy of Indiana University, Division of Recreational Sports.

inactive list as well as how it may be reactivated. For example, there could be times when a club may not function due to disciplinary action. This situation may involve a penalty—a temporary loss of facility use, a fine, or a temporary hold on spending and club operations.

Other situations that may result in inactive status are loss of interest and inability to sustain operations. If this happens, plan to secure any leftover funds. If the club remains inactive for an indefinite time, establish a date when the money is moved into a general fund for club sport programming. If the club is able to regenerate, the funds are customarily returned to the club for its membership.

Club Sport Membership Eligibility

The primary responsibility for determining membership and officer eligibility rests with the club. There may be situations in which systemwide eligibility statements are necessary to maintain the philosophy and purpose of the club sport program. Eligibility statements may prohibit membership by certain segments of a population or may specify the percentage of membership permissible by that segment. Examples of various settings that may warrant special eligibility statements are the following:

- **Military**—off-base personnel, officers, noncommissioned officers, enlisted personnel, families
- **Community**—citizens of the community, age groups, skill levels
- **College**—nonuniversity affiliates, faculty, staff, students, alumni
- **Correctional**—staff, visitors, inmates

Another mandatory eligibility requirement might involve a medical exam and clearance before membership. All eligibility requirements should be available in writing to potential club members. The document must acknowledge a commitment to nondiscriminatory membership practices regarding sex, race, religion, and age.

Club Sport Affiliation

Establish a procedure regarding club sport use of the agency's name to identify the club or associate

CLUB SPORT STATUS APPLICATION

Date _____

Name of club _____   Sport _____

I. Status desired

New club _____   Approved _____

Maintain status _____   Rejected _____

Reactivate _____   Date _____

II. Purpose(s) of club

_____

_____

_____

III. Facility request

Location 1st _____   2nd _____

Day(s) 1st _____   2nd _____

Time(s) 1st _____   2nd _____

_____

_____

_____

_____

_____

IV. Officers' list

	Name	Address	Phone
President	_____	_____	_____
Vice-president	_____	_____	_____
Secretary	_____	_____	_____
Treasurer	_____	_____	_____
	_____	_____	_____
	_____	_____	_____
	_____	_____	_____

V. Constitution and bylaws

Approved _____   Date _____

Rejected _____   Date _____

Staff signature _____

Form 7.1   Club sport status application form.

the club with the setting. Investigate what, if any, legal responsibility exists, and to what extent official approval is needed for the clubs to exist or be sponsored within the setting. This review should consider activities within the home setting (community, campus, military base) as well as activities outside the setting.

If the club and the agency establish a legal tie, the club automatically becomes subject to the policies, rules, and regulations governing the agency.

CLUB SPORT OFFICER LIST

1. This information is to be completed by the club president and returned to the club sport office by the club's first meeting.
2. Any changes in officers or addresses and phone numbers must be recorded within one week of the change.

Club _____

Date officers elected _____

Date of term expiration _____

Date of next election _____

Officers	Name	Local address	Phone
President	_____	_____	_____
Vice-president	_____	_____	_____
Secretary	_____	_____	_____
Treasurer	_____	_____	_____
	_____	_____	_____
	_____	_____	_____
Advisors	_____	_____	_____
	_____	_____	_____

Change of officers

Date	Office	New officer	Local address	Phone
_____	_____	_____	_____	_____
_____	_____	_____	_____	_____
_____	_____	_____	_____	_____

I acknowledge that all information is accurate and up-to-date.

_____
(President's signature)

Form 7.2　Club sport officer list form.

This situation means more control in managing a club program. On the other hand, the stipulations involved may hinder adherence. A large number of stipulations may discourage clubs from organizing, so apply only those necessary to protect the safety and welfare of participants and eliminate legal problems for the agency.

Club Sport Meetings

Require monthly business meetings to facilitate communication within each club, and keep club officers accountable to the membership. Maintain a copy of club minutes from each meeting to keep informed about each club. Good records on club functions help decision making. To ensure clubs take useful minutes you may require

secretaries to follow a prescribed format (see form 7.4).

Club Sport Safety

The safety and well-being of club members must be the primary concern of club officers and program staff, or the program will not satisfy moral and legal requirements. Mechanisms to ensure safety differ from program to program, depending on resources, legal requirements, and age groups involved. An examination of the following options may assist the practitioner in selecting those suitable for local conditions.

Club sport programs using the conservative approach require medical examinations before participants are eligible to join a club team. The

---

CLUB SPORT MEMBERSHIP REPORT

1. This form must be completed, kept up-to-date, and on file in the club sport office by the first meeting of the club. Any additional members must be added before the next scheduled practice or meeting.

Club _____

	Name (last/first)	S.S. number	Address	Phone	Acknowledgment form
1.					
2.					
3.					
4.					
5.					
6.					
7.					
8.					
9.					
10.					
11.					
12.					
13.					
14.					
15.					
16.					
17.					
18.					
19.					
20.					

Form 7.3   Club sport membership report form.

---

exam may be given by a local community doctor or by physicians employed by the agency. Time spans for updating exams vary from program to program.

Once the examination has been performed, a physician should note any limitations in participation on the participant's health record. In some club programs, members must carry a health clearance permit card to show officers before participation. Other programs require that this documentation be maintained with the program staff. If a program requires a medical exam, the staff is responsible for preventing participation without the proper clearance.

A more liberal approach to medical eligibility places the responsibility for determining health status and participation with the participant. Because participation in club sport programs is voluntary, the individual is expected to understand the risks involved and participate within his or her physiological limitations. In this case, the program staff should inform all prospective members and record the policy in writing. Additionally, some programs require that participants sign a statement (such as form 7.5) of acknowledgment regarding the policy. When a minor desires club membership, a parent or guardian must sign the form. The use of such a form does not release the staff or agency from liability for negligence.

The best way to control accidents and hazardous conditions is by using facilities and equipment properly, providing adequate supervision and leadership, and requiring proper conditioning. Each club program should develop an action

CLUB MEETING MINUTES

Club _____

Date _____   Location _____

Time meeting started _____   Time meeting adjourned _____

Number of members present _____   Number absent _____

Report submitted by _____   Office _____

• **ITEMS DISCUSSED**

A.

B.

C.

D.

• **MOTIONS MADE AND VOTED UPON**

A.

B.

Form 7.4   Club meeting minutes form.

plan for safety, designed to prevent and manage problems effectively. The plan requires a regular inspection of facilities and equipment performed by the administrative staff, maintenance personnel, custodial staff, facility supervisor, or a club member designated as safety officer. Cost considerations and storage problems make it unlikely for many programs to care for personal equipment. When club members provide personal equipment, it is possible that they will use less protective and lower quality gear. An officer or appointed member should inspect equipment at each club function.

A staff member organizes and performs the inspection of facilities and equipment using mainte-

nance checklists. Club officers should understand the procedures for reporting problems and initiating requests for repair or replacement. If a hazard remains, make a decision to cancel or postpone the club activity. This usually involves an on-site supervisor, an employee, a club officer, or a designated club safety person.

A safe environment involves safe conduct. Developing safety awareness among club members may be difficult. Work through the officers of the club or a club safety officer to develop an understanding of the attitudes and behaviors that may lead to accidents. Selecting officials and other event personnel to control unsafe conduct is important. Some programs will use the club person respon-

---

CLUB SPORT MEMBERSHIP ACKNOWLEDGMENT
OF PARTICIPATION STATEMENT AND CONSENT FORM

I, _____ , as a current member of the _____ Club, a recognized organization and member of the Club Sport Council at _____ , affirm that I am aware of my physical condition, that I am voluntarily participating as a member of the aforementioned club, that I am aware that such participation may result in possible injury because of the nature of the sport, and that I am assuming any risk that may be involved in this sport.

I further acknowledge that I am aware of insurance policies that are available to me through private or institutional means, that I know and understand club and agency/institution policies and procedures, and that I will represent the club and agency/institution in the manner that is expected. I have read and understand the above statements and will carry them out to my best abilities.

Signature _____   Date _____

Printed name _____

Address _____

Birth date _____   Phone _____

If club member is under 18 years old, then his or her parent or guardian must sign below.

Parent or guardian signature _____

Printed name _____

Form 7.5   Acknowledgment statement form.

sible for inspecting facilities and equipment as the on-site supervisor to monitor activity and handle unsafe conduct. We will provide more specific information on safety in a separate chapter.

Safety involves encouraging physical conditioning by club members. Few understand the role of conditioning in reducing injuries. Because club participation is voluntary, no sure way exists to know whether a club member identifies with the values of conditioning or understands how to implement such a program. Therefore, the club sport staff may familiarize clubs with the need for conditioning. Implement this idea by identifying medically approved literature; announcing or offering presentations, lectures, clinics, and workshops on fitness and related topics; designing conditioning programs specific to each club sport; and informing clubs of fitness and conditioning opportunities provided through approved sources. If the club staff chooses to sponsor or design conditioning programs, seek approval by qualified medical, exercise physiology, or sports medicine personnel.

Although we can reduce accidents and injuries, we cannot eliminate them. Each safety plan must specify a procedure for managing emergencies. Club officers should appoint safety members (see form 7.6) who understand that when they assume responsibility for handling accidents and injuries, they must know how to contact qualified help. They are also responsible for recording accident information to submit to the club sport staff.

The conservative approach requires that someone with first aid and CPR training attend each club practice or event. This individual could be an athletic trainer, a physician, a facility supervisor, or a club member. Whoever assumes the responsibility, that designated person should review procedures for handling the problem at the scene, securing additional help or transportation, and documenting the incident on required forms. Written accident procedures should be available to avoid misinterpretation. Other liability safeguards include maintaining a record of each person's first aid, CPR, or WSI certification; obtaining the signature of safety personnel agreeing to the responsibilities of the position; and denying club access to facilities until emergency aid personnel have been identified (see form 7.7).

CLUB SPORT MEMBERS' SAFETY

Club _____

The following people have been designated as individuals responsible for safety of facilities and equipment. It is understood that at least one of these individuals must be present at all club functions.

Name	Phone

Submitted by

_____
(Signature)

Office _____

Date _____

Form 7.6   Club sport safety member form.

CLUB MEMBERS CERTIFIED IN EMERGENCY FIRST AID TREATMENT

Below are listed club members who have current certification in the indicated column. It is understood that at least one of these members will be present at all club functions. Copies of certification cards will be on file in the club sport office.

Name	CPR	First aid	WSI	Other (specify)

Submitted by

_____
Signature

Office _____

Date _____

Form 7.7   Club members certified form.

Club Sport Facility Use

Most recreation settings strain to meet the demand for access to facilities by clubs that lack resources. Facilities in most settings receive multiple use by many programs. For example, athletics and physical education may share facilities at colleges. Within a community setting, instruction programs, social programs, cultural programs, and public school programs may share one facility. Within the military setting, instruction programs and physical fitness and training programs use common space. Facilities within the correctional and industrial setting may house instructional programs, social programs, and cultural programs. The need to make maximum use of facilities has resulted in standardized scheduling procedures. Information about the facility's reservation policy should include how, when, and where to reserve the facility, the amount of user fees (if any), eligibility requirements, and rules governing proper use of the facilities.

Clubs should be aware of any scheduling policies that reflect priorities for facility use by all programs within the setting. Furthermore, a policy statement should establish a maximum time a club may request for regular practices. This helps to distribute facility availability equitably and reduce suspicion of preferential treatment. When developing this policy consider the number of club members, the type of facility and present demand for its use, the number of clubs seeking access to the facility, the nature of the sport, and the minimum time needed to conduct a practice. Base adjustments in the time you allocate on growth in membership or the availability of equipment.

When a club wants to conduct an event other than a regular practice, it needs to make a separate facility reservation request. Establish a deadline for submitting a reservation request—perhaps two weeks to one month before the desired time. This allows the programmer to coordinate maximum use of facilities and avoid scheduling conflicts. It also provides an opportunity to counsel club officers on proper use of the facilities, responsibilities of supervising the facility, and procedures for reporting accidents or maintenance problems. After the counseling session, have a club officer sign a statement accepting the conditions for facility use.

Once the club officers fully accept their role in protecting facilities, their membership may take pride in caring for the facility and anticipating and identifying maintenance problems.

Equipment for Club Sport

Club members either provide their own equipment, use what is available through the agency, or purchase it through the club. Equipment concerns for program staff are purchasing, care and storage, and inventory and maintenance procedures. Equipment neglect results in waste, theft, loss, and other abuse.

Equipment purchased with club funds is considered agency equipment reserved for club use. In this way, equipment is continually protected until it is no longer serviceable. Another safeguard that protects equipment and provides the best value for the money is channeling purchase requests through the staff for processing. This approach involves a staff decision regarding the appropriateness of the request. Whenever possible, identify three potential vendors to compare quality and cost. After ordering equipment, maintain a copy of the request to check the order when it arrives. On delivery, have the equipment marked, coded or engraved, inventoried, and checked out to the club. This keeps staff current about club needs and equipment costs, provides an opportunity to develop positive business relationships with vendors, and facilitates discussion regarding proper care and storage for equipment.

An up-to-date equipment inventory is useful to foster accountability for the care of equipment and to familiarize new officers or staff about club resources. The club should conduct an inventory that documents the amount and types of equipment, purchase date, and present condition. Such information is useful when considering additional purchase requests and evaluating merchandise quality.

Proper care and storage allow maximum use of equipment. If the staff cannot handle this function, the responsibility rests with the club. The staff may retain some influence on proper equipment care by withholding funds, imposing fines, denying purchase requests, or restricting facility use when a club demonstrates improper handling of its equipment.

If the club needs equipment storage space, keep a record of its location and who is responsible for its security. Obtain a signed statement from any individual accepting this responsibility. Finally, an equipment checkout system within the club may reduce damage, theft, or loss. This places financial responsibility on the user. A checkout system may be appropriate when different programs use equipment and it is dispensed from a central location, or when the club issues equipment to its members for the year.

Although procedures regarding club equipment may be time-consuming, systems to protect the lifespan of equipment are economically sound.

Club Sport Insurance

Agencies often carry blanket insurance for club sport participation, including those events outside the setting. Other insurance practices include requiring club members to have personal coverage, requiring each club to arrange for group coverage, or encouraging clubs and members to carry voluntary coverage. If clubs or members must provide their own coverage, you need a system of verification. If clubs don't need to carry personal or group coverage, each member must sign a consent statement releasing the agency from responsibility for personal injury sustained while participating in a club function. When minors are involved, a parent or guardian must sign the statement. This places responsibility for obtaining health and accident coverage on the individual.

You should take insurance seriously in the interest of proper coverage and liability protection. Examine carefully possible alternatives to determine adequate coverage.

Club Sport Travel

Clubs that receive funding from a board, agency, or institution have their travel interests and activities governed by specific policies addressing approval, funding, or vehicle use. The most common requirements for club travel under a conservative approach include the following:

- Application for travel approval (see form 7.8)
- Supervisor accompanying the club
- Roster of people traveling
- Personnel certified in first aid and CPR
- Use of agency vehicles that carry adequate liability insurance (see form 7.9)

Ideally, club transportation should involve commercially bonded vehicles or vehicles owned and insured by the agency. Clubs may use privately owned vehicles. Some club programs permit agency money to cover travel, but others prohibit this practice due to liability concerns and the increased work of monitoring club travel.

Whenever possible, encourage clubs to limit travel to nearby areas to reduce expenses and accident potential. Restrictions on distance and number of trips may limit access to vehicles owned by the agency. This stipulation typically occurs when the demand for travel exceeds the supply of vehicles or the volume of requests hinders proper management.

Schedules and Agreements for Club Sport

Clubs in leagues or tournaments schedule regular opportunities for participation. Facility availability, proximity, finances, skill level, conference regulations, and travel regulations influence opportunities to schedule activity with other clubs or teams. Scheduling input from program staff occurs when they must restrict the number of home or away events. Restrictions may arise from limited resources, such as facility space and finances, or an inability of clubs to manage their schedule. The staff may need to set an early timetable for finalizing scheduling plans for the year. The club and staff need time to prepare for and promote events. Often a club has such strong spectator appeal that a printed copy of its schedule is desirable.

When interested in scheduling a commitment for an event with other clubs, each participating club should sign a written agreement. The agreement specifies the conditions that each club must fulfill and the purpose, date, time, and location of the event. A sample agreement is shown in form 7.10.

Before clubs use written agreements, they should examine legal liability. For example, under what conditions might the agency be responsible if a club does not fulfill its obligations? Under what conditions might the agency be held responsible for injuries to representatives of visiting clubs? Must administrative or program staff sign the contract or is a club officer sufficient?

In settings where the agency closely supervises all club activity, the staff designs and approves the agreements. Club officers may participate in a required review session with the program staff to ensure that each event has adequate planning and includes the appropriate safety precautions. Upon its conclusion, the club should submit an evaluation form describing the outcome of the event, identifying problems or accidents, making recommendations for improvements, including a financial statement.

Use another written agreement for securing personnel to officiate or supervise the club event. The primary responsibility for obtaining person-

CLUB SPORT TRAVEL REQUEST

Date of trip _____   Destination _____

Duration of trip _____   Day _____   Overnight _____

Approximate time returning _____

OVERNIGHT RESIDENCE

Motel _____   Phone _____

Hotel _____   Phone _____

Campus/college _____   Phone _____

Other _____   Phone _____

Drivers _____   _____

_____

Owner(s) of vehicle(s) _____   _____

_____

_____

Vehicle(s) registration _____   _____

_____

_____

Company insuring vehicles _____   _____

_____

Number of people traveling _____   (attach list of names)

Purpose of trip _____

_____

Emergency numbers where you can be reached _____

Name _____   Date _____

Office _____

Approve _____   Reject _____

Form 7.8   Club sport travel request form.

nel rests with the club, although the program staff may make referrals or assume responsibility for this task. Any agreement should include the particulars about the event, the rate of pay, and method of payment. In an additional clause indicate what will happen should someone not fulfill specified obligations. A sample agreement is presented in form 7.11.

Morale is damaged if a club hosts or travels to an event and another club has not upheld its agreement. Written agreements may be helpful to formalize responsibilities and serve as a more binding commitment than a verbal agreement. There still is no guarantee that the event will happen as planned. Avoiding disappointment and problems from failure to meet obligations requires realistic planning and an ability to anticipate difficulties.

No agreement is valid unless the club demonstrates an ability to fulfill its obligations and has an approved plan for meeting them.

Instruction for Club Sport

Some degree of coaching and instruction occurs within any club. When a club desires qualified leadership, it may appoint or hire an instructor or coach. Program staff can assist clubs in this process by discussing selection and hiring, reviewing job descriptions and contracts, handling or monitoring the payroll, approving club funds for employing personnel, or serving as a resource for club personnel. When providing assistance, consider the following: maintaining a commitment to nondiscriminatory employment, understanding whether

---

REQUEST FOR MOTOR VEHICLES

Name of organization _____   Account no. _____

Number of vehicles wanted _____   Types _____

Purpose of trip _____

_____

_____

Destination _____

Equipment to be carried _____

Date and time wanted _____

Date and time to be returned _____

Name of driver _____

Driver's license no. and state of issue _____

Address _____   Phone _____

Name of driver _____

Driver's license no. and state of issue _____

Address _____   Phone _____

Name of driver _____

Driver's license no. and state of issue _____

Address _____   Phone _____

List all passengers _____

_____

_____

APPROVAL

_____   _____
Director, motor vehicles   _Club sport staff_

_____   _____
Account manager   _Director, recreational sport_

Complete in quadruplicate.

Form 7.9   Request for motor vehicle form.

the agency is liable for injuries sustained by club members performing activities designed by an approved instructor, and understanding what consequences exist if any party violates a written agreement.

Regardless of the degree of staff involvement in approving or hiring personnel, the clubs should perform certain tasks, including developing appropriate job descriptions, receiving membership approval for using funds, protecting funds allocated for employment purposes, using a reliable procedure for handling payroll, conducting an appropriate selection process, and using documentation to specify the conditions of appointment or employment. Because most club members want to learn more about their sport or receive direction while they participate, selecting instructors is an important process. Consequently, the program staff should be ready to assist clubs with personnel management.

Promotion for Club Sport

When clubs fall under the jurisdiction of an agency, their public image reflects on the agency. Therefore, guidelines for club public relations and publicity campaigns reflect a common desire for a positive image.

When the club bears full responsibility for implementing promotion, club sport staff should review

---

CLUB SPORT CONTEST AGREEMENT

This agreement, made and entered into this _____ day of _____ 19 ____, by and between the under-

signed authorized representative of the _____ and the undersigned authorized

representative of _____ stipulates the following:

First, that the teams representing these named organizations or institutions agree to meet in _____ at

_____, _____
 location of contest   city and state

on _____ 19 ____, at _____ o'clock _____ m., and at

_____, _____
 location of contest   city and state

on _____ 19 ____, at _____ o'clock _____ m.

Second, that the consideration binding the two teams to play these contest(s) shall be the appearance of each visiting team at the site of each home team in the aforesaid contest, or, as indicated in paragraph **ninth**, if applicable.

Third, that the contests shall be played under _____ rules.

Fourth, that the officials are to be mutually agreed upon.

Fifth, that expenses of officials are to be borne by the home team.

Sixth, that the home management reserves the right to cancel the contest on account of inclement weather or other unavoidable cause, two hours before the visiting team leaves from its residence or the place of the previous game, notice of which time had been given at least three days before.

Seventh, that in case a contest is canceled after the arrival of the visiting team on account of inclement weather or other unavoidable cause, the home team shall pay the visiting team _____ dollars.

Eighth, that the day, time, and location of any of these contests shall not be changed without the written consent of the authorized representative of the visiting team.

Ninth _____

_____

_____

_____

In witness whereof, we have affixed our signature the day and year first above written.

For _____   For _____

By _____   By _____
 Authorized representative   *Authorized representative*

Return one copy of completed contract to _____

Form 7.10   Club sport contest agreement form.

ideas to spot problems and assess the ideas. Require that plans gain advanced approval to allow time for revisions.

If the club sport program provides resources or personnel to assist in promotion, inform clubs on how to take advantage of opportunities and coordinate deadlines for approving and implementing requests. To organize requests and eliminate mistakes in information or design, the club should submit its requests in writing, then review them with the appropriate personnel. An advantage in managing club promotional efforts is the opportunity

STATEMENT OF AGREEMENT FOR SPORT OFFICIAL

_____ of _____ Club
(President)

and _____ , hereby enter into the following assignment
(Official)

and terms for officiating:

1. Said official agrees to be present and officiate _____ contest(s) of _____
(sport)

   to be played at _____ on the dates listed during the year 19 ____ - 19 ____ .

Date	Day of week	Time	Clubs playing	Total payment

2. That in case of failure on the part of either one of the parties to fulfill the terms of this agreement, except by mutual consent, a forfeiture of $25.00 shall be paid by the offending party to the other party within five days after the date set for each game in this statement. It is understood that there is a moral obligation to be considered in the making and breaking of agreements. Where obligations are not mutually adjusted, _____ reserves the right to review the facts and determine what these adjustments should be.

3. This agreement is void if not returned on or before _____ .

For club   **For contest official**

_____   _____
Signature of president   Signature

_____   _____
Club   Address

_____   _____
Address   Social security number

_____   _____
Date   Date

_____   _____
Telephone   Telephone

Names of other officials employed to work this contest (if available).

Form 7.11   Club sport official agreement form.

to directly influence the quality of the projects. You can deny proposals if the club submits them late or they are unrealistic in terms of time, volume, or cost.

Another aspect of promotion involves how materials are distributed or posted within the setting. Materials are often wasted and the environment cluttered with notices, resulting in a negative image of the club, agency, or institution.

CLUB SPORT FINANCE

A characteristic of club sport is financial self-support. Historically, clubs have sustained their activities through dues, donations, and fund-raising projects. Recently, clubs in some settings, particularly education, have received financial assistance from the agency that administers them. The amount of assistance provided to clubs depends on the budget and agency philosophy. Although such financial support may be useful, a greater dependence on and accountability to the agency often results.

The process of identifying the financial needs of the club begins with a discussion about proposed activities. Strategies are established for securing the finances to cover club needs. Common sources include membership dues and fines, donations, fund-raising projects, and allocations from an agency. When seeking income sources, the club must follow certain procedures to avoid violating laws or policies of the setting. For example, clubs interested in soliciting donations through a door-to-door canvass should check city or state codes to be sure the approach is legal. The primary functions of the club sport staff in club funding are to identify acceptable funding approaches, inform club officers of policies governing fund-raising, and establish a system to review their ideas for securing income.

Budget Preparation

A helpful tool for clubs to project expenditures and income is a budget proposal. A budget proposal requires careful planning and organization. It serves as a blueprint for the club and a mechanism for holding officers accountable for financial transactions.

It is customary for the club officers, or a treasurer, to prepare a budget proposal for adoption by the membership. This proposal should include itemized expenditures and projected sources of income. The categories used to classify this information include the following:

Expenses

- Equipment—club equipment (not personally owned)
- Supplies and expenses—telephone, stamps, paper, posters, trophies
- Hourly wages—payment for trainers, coaches, instructors, ticket takers
- Travel—gas, food, lodging

Income

- Membership dues
- Donations
- Grants
- Fund-raising projects

We provide a sample budget in form 7.12. This format indicates the club expenses and income for the current year to compare with the budget proposal for the following year.

Before finalizing the budget proposal, the club should make sure it has identified reliable and acceptable sources of income and has made accurate estimates for projected expenditures. The club officers should know about policies regarding budget preparation, particularly if the club is eligible for grants from an agency.

Grants to Club Sport

To date, recreational sport literature lacks a detailed explanation for setting up a grant allocation process. The rationale for club grants is based on a desire to support and perpetuate clubs as a vehicle for recreational sport participation. Financial support from an administrative agency, such as a club sport council, may provide a positive form of administrative control because clubs tend to abide with certain standards to maintain access to funding.

To ensure that all clubs receive equitable treatment in fund allocation, make available uniform requirements regarding funding requests to all clubs. Additionally, the programmer should explain the criteria for allocation decisions to the clubs well before the allocation process. Knowing the criteria aids in preparing proposals and facilitates decision making about the allocation request. Criteria also should indicate when a newly formed club is first eligible to request an allocation. One approach requires a club to be operational and in good standing for a year before seeking an allocation. In this way, the committee has a better opportunity to determine whether the club is well organized, stable, and responsible.

An allocation committee should be comprised of 6 to 12 people familiar with the club sport program yet not directly involved with any club seeking an allocation. The committee may be appointed by the club sport staff and approved by a club sport council, or selected by a club council of representatives. The first option may be more desirable because a professional staff member should not be biased in any way. The staff for club sport should not determine allocations. This situation often invites conflict if a club is dissatisfied with its allocation. It is preferable for the staff to serve as a resource to help clubs prepare an appropriate budget and make a good presentation before the committee.

When seeking funds, a club should prepare a budget proposal. It is helpful to use a standard

CLUB BUDGET

Item	Actual total Cost per × number	19__-19__ Total	Projected total Cost per × number	19__-19__ Total
Income				
Allocated money				
Membership dues				
Donations				
Movie ticket sales				
Benefit game				
Total income				
Expenditures				
Hourly wage				
Coach				
Officials				
Trainer				
Equipment				
Balls				
Sticks				
Helmets				
Knee pads				
Nets				
Supplies and expenses				
Utilities				
Facility rental				
Stamps				
Phone				
Duplicating				
Stationery				
Trophies				
Newspaper ads				
Recognition banquet				
Insurance				
Laundry				
Bank charges				
Travel				
Gas				
Food				
Lodging				
Business trip				
Vehicle insurance				
Total expenses				
Total income				
−Total expenses				
Balance				

Form 7.12　Sample club budget.

budget format and to insist that clubs respect the deadline for submitting budget proposals. The staff may hold a special meeting on budget preparation and make appointments to meet with clubs individually. Such preparation reduces the time needed to make decisions and interpret budgets at the allocation committee meeting. Next, provide a way for members of the committee to review the proposals. Make copies of each budget for distribution to each member or establish a rotation system to review the originals. If committee members have questions about a club proposal or require further information, resolve these problems before the presentation. Hold a special training session for the committee members to resolve questions about the budgets and their duties. After the deadline for budget review has passed, schedule a time so each club requesting funds can present a brief oral proposal (10 to 20 minutes) to the assembled committee and respond to any questions. Before each presentation, a staff member or the executive officer of the club sport council should indicate how well the club has met its responsibilities for the year.

The merits of each club's grant application should be judged on

- its explanation and justification of budgets,
- the nature of its expenses, and
- its performance of duties to the granting agency.

Let's look at these criteria and how they affect an administrative committee's decision to grant funds to club sport.

Budget Presentation

Clubs should understand that they will be required to

- include statements for the previous and current year, as well as a proposed budget for the coming year;
- specify club expenses and revenues, indicating a balance; and
- estimate proposed needs as accurately as possible, based on their plans, justifiable expenses, and revenues.

Budget Justification

Clubs must explain anticipated costs related to the following:

- **Hourly wages.** A club incurring expenses for instructors, coaches, officials, or trainers should give detailed explanations (for example, rate, hours, days, number of people needed).

- **Equipment expenses.** The administrative agency will provide support only for equipment purchased for permanent use of club activities. This includes individual equipment (for example, uniforms) necessary for club activities that the individual member is not expected to provide. The agency will consider expenses related to the club's current equipment and its necessary maintenance or replacement.

- **Supplies and other detailed expenses.** A club incurring expenses for facility use should give a detailed breakdown of costs (rates, hours, days, etc.). Granting agencies should discourage a *miscellaneous expenses* category unless the club can provide an itemized breakdown.

- **Travel expenses.** Travel is defined as moving to a location outside the agency setting for participation. A club should justify its travel, for instance, to obtain competition at its own ability level or to further opportunities for training or instruction. Clubs should attempt to combine matches in one geographical area to a single trip. Granting agencies should give support only for the minimum number of players needed to participate. All expenses (food, gas, lodging) need explanation.

Club Duties

Allocation committees often consider factors less tangible than financial need. In general, such criteria reflect a club's dedication to its stated goals and those of the agency. Generally, no allocation will be made to any club that has not met its financial responsibilities (payment of dues and fines, if any). No allocation will be made to any club whose file is not complete. A complete file includes the following:

- Constitution or operating guidelines
- Budget request and annual report
- General information sheet and membership roster
- List of officers
- Minutes from business meetings
- Consent forms
- Equipment inventory

The committee will consider whether a club has met other responsibilities, such as attending meetings, keeping files up-to-date, and fulfilling obligations to committees. These constitute minimal standards required of all clubs, and failure to comply subjects them to a reduction of the allocation. The committee should note instances in which the club council or agency established fines against a club's *current* allocation if the club has not met its responsibilities. Nevertheless, certain actions or gross neglect of responsibilities may warrant decreasing allocations for the following year.

Finally, allocators should pay attention to a requirement that each club sponsor one special event per year. Failure to meet this requirement may reduce a club's allocation, and performance of this service beyond the required level may increase it.

Delivering Grant Funds

Once the committee makes a decision of justified need, it can determine each club's allocation through the following formula:

$$\text{Allocation to club A} = \text{Total allocated funds for clubs} \frac{\text{Justified need of club A}}{\text{Total justified needs of all clubs}}$$

Guidelines should explain how the club gains access to its allocated funds. The money may be provided as a direct payment to the club or retained in an account directly supervised by the club sport staff. A more conservative approach is usually selected when there are restrictions on how the club can spend the money and when documentation of club financial transactions is necessary. When a club wants access to its money, it makes a written request to the club sport staff providing justification of need, potential vendors, and cost estimates. This information facilitates the decision-making process and saves time. Using a request form (see form 7.13) assists in the bookkeeping and accounting process.

Regardless of the mechanisms available to raise income or make expenditures, the staff should make every attempt to eliminate opportunities for mishandling club funds. Such problems greatly damage the credibility of the club sport concept and often form the grounds for serious legal or disciplinary action.

Fund-Raising

A club's grant allocation often falls short of its needs. Encourage clubs to hold fund-raising activi-

ties because they will neither help nor hinder a club in its allocation for a subsequent year. Be sure the club conducts all fund-raising with the approval of their administrative agency (see form 7.14). The club should also forward post-project summaries to the agency (see form 7.15).

Some fund-raising activities may be regarded as an integral part of a club's function, and administrative agencies should consider them when making allocation grants to clubs. Accordingly, criteria governing fund-raising may be necessary. Examples of statements used in the allocation process follow:

- A club should not include in its request fund-raising revenue, activities unrelated to the club's sport, or activities not needed by the sport community (for instance, activities for which the club is not the only source).

- A club should include fund-raising activities of the previous year or current year, and activities related to the club's sport and needed by the sport community (for example, a martial arts club serving as the only source for martial art uniform sales or the volleyball club serving as the only source of officials for the community intramural tournament).

In the committee's evaluation of justified need, it should deduct a club's expected income by fund-raising from budgeted expenditures. However, the committee should not consider past fund-raising activities a credit or deduction applicable to the club's allocation.

CLUB SPORT CONDUCT AND GOVERNANCE

Standards of conduct within the club sport program promote safety, social interaction, positive public relations, and accountability. The expectations imposed on clubs vary depending on the program approach taken (conservative or liberal). It is unrealistic to assume that problems of conduct do not exist within club sport operations. Procedures must afford club members or the club as a whole a fair and objective review. Specific statements addressing behavior and duties expected of club members and officers should be part of each club's constitution. Penalties for violation of a code of conduct are often handled as an internal matter. When the actions of a club or club members violate the poli-

---

REQUEST FOR FUNDS
(equipment, hourly wage, others)

Club _____   Date of request _____

Amount requested _____   Date needed _____

Funds will be used for _____

_____

_____

Justification of need _____

_____

_____

Suggested vendor(s)

1. _____

2. _____

3. _____

Specific information (size, quantity, color, etc.)

_____

_____

Projected cost per item _____

_____

_____

Submitted by _____, Treasurer

Amount approved _____   Remaining balance _____

Comments _____

_____

_____

Staff signature _____   Date _____

Form 7.13   Request for funds form.

cies of the agency, investigation and intervention may be warranted.

There are three reasons for delineation of club and staff responsibility for disciplinary action. First, a concept basic to club sport is self-governance. Staff intervention into club business weakens this principle and results in club dependency on the staff. Second, once the staff makes a ruling it should be a sanction affecting the club as a whole, not individual members. A club must deal with internal problems and the staff will hold the club accountable for this responsibility. This requirement also places responsibility with the total membership for fulfilling club obligations. Finally, the staff should not manage internal club problems before the officers have had a chance to deal with them. Premature intervention hinders the ability of the staff to hear an appeal objectively.

Situations that may require disciplinary action, whether imposed by the club or staff, include the following:

- Verbal or physical abuse by club members or club representatives
- Damage to equipment or facilities
- Mishandling funds
- Violations of club or agency policies

Disciplinary Guidelines

Disciplinary action requires a commitment to fair treatment, a predetermined set of guidelines, and an informed club system that recognizes its responsibilities and the consequences of failing to meet them. There are several models to choose from

---

FUND-RAISING PROJECT APPLICATION

_____
(Date submitted)

Note: Please complete in duplicate and return to the club sport office. Depending on the event additional information may be required.

Club _____

Project chairperson _____

Local address _____   Phone _____

Project description _____

_____

Date(s) of project _____   Location(s) _____

Time(s) _____   Income source(s) _____

Total anticipated income from project $ _____

Expense items _____

Total anticipated expenses from project $ _____

Total anticipated profit from project $ _____

Use of proceeds _____

_____

Will the project be an annual event? _____

Does the organization have a local bank account?   Yes _____   No _____

The undersigned in connection with and as a part of this application for a fund-raising project certifies that he or she is a club member and that the information listed is correct to the best of his or her knowledge and belief.

Signature _____

Comments _____

_____

Approved by _____

Date approved _____

Form 7.14   Fund-raising project application form.

when setting up disciplinary procedures. One model involves an initial investigation and ruling by the staff, allowing an appeal to a hearing board composed of club sport representatives. This board is comprised of 5 to 10 people selected from club representatives trained to serve on an appeals committee. (Please see chapter 8 for more about setting up disciplinary boards.).

We will suggest policy guidelines on the grounds for disciplinary action, the investigation process, the appeal and hearing processes, and imposing and enforcing penalties. When you follow these models, you should reach fair and appropriate decisions. Unless the staff is committed to due process, the best model can turn into a mockery of justice. Take disciplinary measures when necessary to improve the club system, not to demonstrate

power and authority. If the clubs view the process as fair and just, they will participate in resolving problems in the same fashion.

Grounds for Disciplinary Action

Consider complaints against a club for any action violating policies concerning club sport (whether committed by the club, club representatives, or individual members). Proven violations become grounds for penalties assessed against the club. Once the club sport staff has received a complaint for investigation and ruling, the staff should notify the club of the complaint, preferably in writing.

Staff Investigation and Ruling

When a complaint is referred to the club sport staff, obtain written statements from the plaintiff, ac-

---

FUND-RAISING PROJECT SUMMARY

To be submitted to the club sport office within one week following the fund-raising project.

Project _____

Sponsored by _____

Date of project _____

Location(s) _____

_____

Total income received $ _____

EXPENSES LISTED BY MAJOR ITEMS

_____

_____

_____

Total expenses $ _____

Profit   _____

Use of proceeds _____

_____

Signature _____

Date _____

Form 7.15   Fund-raising project summary form.

cused club, witnesses, and other appropriate parties. In addition, conduct verbal conferences with the plaintiff, accused club, witnesses, other appropriate parties, and the executive committee. On completing an investigation, the club sport staff should make a ruling based on the evidence uncovered during the investigation. Finally, the staff should notify the club of the ruling in writing.

Appeal Procedure

If the club wishes to appeal the staff decision it may do so through written notification either to the staff or to the club sport council president. The case may then be referred to a club sport hearing board. This board consists of five to seven club representatives unrelated to any of the clubs involved. The council president customarily appoints these representatives at the beginning of the year, one of whom acts as a secretary. Next, the club sport staff or council president arranges a time and place for the hearing that is convenient for all parties involved.

The Hearing

At least three board members, including the chairperson and secretary, should be present throughout the hearing, and only these members may vote

after the board's deliberation. The hearing board secretary should keep a record of the hearing, including a list of those present and the substance of all evidence and arguments. If possible, make a tape recording to avoid error. Suggested guidelines for the hearing follow:

- The chairperson states the purpose of the hearing.
- Opening statements proceed, first by a representative of the plaintiff, then by a representative of the accused club.
- The respective parties may then present additional evidence of any sort, subject to questions by those present.
- The parties may make final statements.
- The board may conclude with questions to any party.

Once the hearing board begins its deliberation in private, no record need be kept. On conclusion of the deliberation, the chairperson may entertain motions to increase or decrease penalties against the club, to sustain the club sport staff's rulings, or to exonerate the club. The decision should have the

Shining Example

Indiana University's Division of Recreational Sports, Bloomington, Indiana

Indiana University's "Division of Recreational Sports" utilizes a variety of marketing avenues. The "Division" serves students (95 percent), faculty (3 percent), and the general public (1 percent). The most unique promotional tool is the marketing of programs via the World Wide Web (http://www.indiana.edu/~recsport/). The students and faculty at Indiana University can assess the Division's information by the use of this computer communication medium. The Division provides information related to membership, programs, and upcoming intramural events. In addition, the Division utilizes brochures, the student newspaper, direct mailings, and an "information hotline" phone service which allows students, faculty, and staff to access information in relation to programs, facility hours, and registration.

Organization: The Division of Recreational Sports is a service branch of the School of Health, Physical Education and Recreation (HPER) on the Indiana University-Bloomington campus.

Clientele: The breakdown of clientele served by the Division is 95 percent students, 3% faculty/staff and 1 percent general public. The largest group of users comes from the 35,000 students enrolled on the IU-Bloomington campus. Other user groups come from the 1,400 faculty and 5,000 staff on the campus. There is also a small percentage of general public from the Bloomington community (pop. 24,000) which participate in programs of the Division. Throughout the course of a year, participants within the facilities and programs total over 1 million.

Budget: The budget is $2.9 million and includes the 4 primary program areas of Club Sports, Fitness/Wellness, Informal Sports, and Intramural Sports. Budget areas include personnel, supplies and expenses, and capital improvement. Revenue is generated through mandatory activity fees, entry fees, and state appropriated funds.

Marketing: Several types of marketing avenues are utilized for the Division. At the beginning of each academic year, the Division produces a comprehensive brochure that is distributed to all the residence centers on campus, and to a number of off-campus living units. The student newspaper is also utilized for advertisements for program entries, as well as for a recreational sports news page, which includes reports on specific sports and special events. Direct mailings, presentations to prospective users, and fliers are other marketing tools utilized by the Division to promote participation. The Division also provides an "Information Hotline" phone service which allows the students, faculty, and staff access to information about programs, facility hours, and registrations. Another marketing tool is the World Wide Web with information about programs, entry forms, tournament results, facilities, and personnel.

Staff: The Division of Recreational Sports is comprised of 1 Director, 1 Associate Director, 4 Program Directors, 6 Assistant Directors, and 11 Graduate Staff Assistants. Thirteen (13) full-time clerical and support staff are also employed by the Division. The Tennis Pavilion and Outdoor Pool are considered part of the staffing with 1 Director, 1 Program Coordinator, 1 Head Pro, and 1 Pool Manager. The following part-time staff is hired throughout the year: 300 sport officials, 200 supervisors, 75 lifeguards, 50 fitness/wellness instructors, 12 tennis instructors, as well as numerous other part-time positions.

Program Detail: The division consists of 4 primary program areas: Club Sports, Fitness/Wellness, Informal Sports, and Intramural Sports. Auxiliary program areas include Aquatics, Target Populations, and Shooting Sports.

Facilities: The division operates two main facilities on the Bloomington campus. The HPER Building consists of 15 basketball/volleyball courts, 12 racquetball courts, 1 free-weight room, 2 strength-conditioning rooms, 2 pools, 1 diving well, and 1 indoor track. The Student Recreational Sports Center consists of 5 basketball/volleyball courts, 3 multipurpose gymnasiums, 1 Olympic-sized pool and diving well, 1 large strength and conditioning facility, 1 indoor track, 4 squash courts, and 8 racquetball courts. Additional facilities operated by the Division include a lighted outdoor sports complex with the capacity for 4 softball diamonds, 6 flag football fields, and 4 soccer fields. A trap and skeet range, and an indoor rifle range are operated through the Division's Shooting Sports program.

support of at least three of the members to lend legitimacy to the ruling. Within one week of the hearing, the decision and a rationale should be presented in writing to the club sport staff, to be forwarded to the club. The club may obtain a transcript of the hearing record, bearing the cost of its provision.

Penalties

Penalties imposed on a club should have administrative approval. Examples of penalties include fines, temporary loss of funding or facility privileges, suspension from specified facilities, probation for a specified period under certain conditions, or recommendation for continued review.

Enforcement

A staff person commonly has responsibility for enforcing disciplinary rulings. In some instances, an administrator has the prerogative to overrule a decision, if it can be shown that due process was violated or significant new evidence has arisen that could alter the decision. A veto power is a positive tool because it may motivate the staff and hearing board to be more thorough and conscientious in their deliberations. If an administrator intervenes unnecessarily or frequently, the hearing board procedure becomes suspect.

Annual Report

Each club ought to complete an annual report for historical reference and for planning its future goals and objectives. From an administrative perspective, annual reports can update staff about club activities, identify participation trends, specify problems faced by clubs, and solicit ideas on improving services to clubs. An annual report form, developed by each club, ensures that proper information is obtained. Establish deadlines for receiving the completed reports before election of officers and allocation of funds. In this way, current officers are responsible for documenting the information that will assist new officers. Finally, an annual report (see form 7.16) provides additional insight into a club's performance when considering the criteria for allocating funds.

Program Assistance

The final subject covered in the club sport operational guidelines should explain the types of assistance each club may receive and how to use this support. Assistance may include partial or complete provision for mail, telephone, typing, storage, duplicating, and office space services. These services not only contribute to the effectiveness and

Club Management Software

The club management software programs that are on the market today range from simple membership tracking modules to very complex, expandable turn-key management systems designed exclusively for your club.

Clubs vary in terms of their design, purpose, operation, and membership, so it is important when purchasing a club management system to know what specific features or functions are necessary to accomplish the goals of your particular club. Analyze your club's operational system and make a list of features that are essential to your club. Eliminate those features that you will never need or use.

Club management software programs generally have two major categories of features: accounting and club management. *Accounting* features normally handle the following functions:

- collection of delinquent bills,
- electronic fund transfer for credit card transactions,
- credit card verification, which is especially helpful for pro shop sales,
- food and beverage management and the needs associated with restaurant or food service,
- payment coupon books for mass mailing,
- automated statement billing for dues and other charges,
- point of sale designed for built-in cash registers, and
- integration with accounting software programs for general ledger, accounts payable, accounts receivable, payroll, and inventory.

Club management features, which help you manage your membership and track club usage, usually include the following:

- front desk identification check-in system that monitors comprehensive membership information records,
- member check-in that works with bar code readers,
- user tracking,
- guest registration,
- marketing system that solicits new members,
- facility and equipment rental management,
- usage reports that analyze and evaluate time, day, and actual use of the facility, and
- towel rental.

Using a club management software program is an excellent way to monitor accuracy and to maintain control over your club operations. Whether yours is a small club, large club, or multiple-site operation, automated management systems can be designed to meet your management needs.

Club management software programs: MacClub, Computer Outfitter, and Alternate Computer Service.

ANNUAL REPORT

Club _____

Club officers	Fall	Spring	Fall (if elected)
President	_____	_____	_____
Vice-president	_____	_____	_____
Secretary	_____	_____	_____
Treasurer	_____	_____	_____
Advisor	_____	_____	_____
Coach	_____	_____	_____
Council representative	_____	_____	_____
Instructor	_____	_____	_____

What is the total club membership? _____ Men _____ Women _____

How much is club dues per person? _____ year or semester?

What was this year's total budget? _____

What is next year's projected budget? _____

Are you seeking money from the council? _____ How much? _____

What facilities did the club use on a regular or part-time basis? _____
_____

When were practice times? _____

When and where did the club meet other than for practice or games (i.e., business meeting)? _____
_____

How many competitive events were held against other clubs? List matches and results (away and home competition).

_____   _____
_____   _____
_____   _____

Where did the club travel to? _____
_____

What was the average personal expenditure for each club member not paid by the club?

Travel _____

Equipment _____

Entry fees in meets _____

Who can someone interested in joining the club contact? Name and number if possible.
_____

List any noteworthy accomplishments or awards received by the club. _____
_____

Write a paragraph explaining club activities (200 words maximum). _____
_____
_____
_____
_____
_____
_____

(Continued)

Form 7.16   Annual report form.

Briefly summarize the club's activities this past year. Include club's short- and long-range goals. _____

_____

_____

_____

_____

Briefly state the club's goals and objectives for the coming year. _____

_____

_____

_____

_____

List recommendations for improving club internal operations. _____

_____

_____

_____

_____

List recommendations for improving assistance to the club by the club sport staff. _____

_____

_____

_____

_____

Report submitted by _____

Position _____

Date _____

Form 7.16 *(Continued.)*

success of club operations but also facilitate interaction and development of rapport among staff and club members.

ADA Suggestions

According to the ADA, sport agencies must modify programs, facilities, or services that would allow individuals with disabilities to participate without causing an *undue burden* on the agency. An undue burden is an activity that is unduly expensive, substantial, or would fundamentally alter the nature of the recreational sport program. For example, it would fundamentally alter the nature of the sport if the club sport rugby league asked all players to wear blindfolds to make it more fair for a blind participant. However, it would be feasible, if the league representatives agreed, to allow a guide to assist this player during a game or practice.

CONCLUSION

Club sport programming is a challenging, yet rewarding function. The challenges involve promoting diversity in sport interests and purposes; securing resources for funding, facilities, and personnel; and maintaining appropriate operational guidelines. It is gratifying when a quality club program results from the combined efforts of members, officers, and staff. It is also rewarding to observe participants gaining experience in decision making, time management, leadership, and social skills, and finding satisfaction in their involvement.

Club sport in America will continue to be influenced by the state of the economy. In times of financial stress, clubs may experience cutbacks in activity. Sport programs that depend on an agency for financial support and staff direction, such as intramural, extramural, and athletic sport, may be sharply reduced or even eliminated. It is possible that maintenance of club sport programs may require the pooling of resources from members and commercial or corporate sponsors.

Clearly, the recreational sport programmer is able to influence decisions regarding strategies for perpetuating the club sport concept. Although the challenges may be difficult, the programmer must recognize that clubs represent a distinctive avenue for sport participation, worthy of support.

DISCUSSION QUESTIONS

1. Define club sport.

2. List and describe the three types of club sport.

3. Clubs need financial support to continue operating. List several ways a club may obtain funding.

4. Describe three specific duties of a club sport president.

5. What steps should you take when developing policies for club sport facility reservations?

6. Name three items that should always be included in a club sport constitution.

7. What does the term *bylaws* (in a club sport constitution) refer to?

8. What are five operational concerns of a club sport?

9. What role does club sport have in the leisure sport management model?

10. In the liberal approach to club sport programming, who should be responsible for enforcing a disciplinary action ruling? For the conservative approach?

11. In which type of club sport program do the members supply their own equipment and support their activities through membership dues?

12. What characteristics represent the conservative approach to club sport programming? Which represent the liberal approach?

13. What relationships may a club sport program have with an intramural sport program?

14. Describe the club sport federation systems you would incorporate into a new program and explain your choices.

15. Describe a club sport classification system. What are some advantages and disadvantages of such a classification system?

APPLICATION EXERCISE

The recreational sport department at your university was able to convince the administration that a club sport program is needed and that an individual is essential to develop and coordinate the program. You have just accepted the position as coordinator of club sport. Your initial responsibility is to plan, organize, and implement a club sport system. Develop a proposal to the director of recreational sport outlining the approach you plan to pursue toward accomplishing this task. You should include in your proposal goals, objectives, budget concerns, equipment needs, governance concerns, facility needs, eligibility rules, instruction schedules, safety guidelines, meetings planned, travel guidelines, insurance regulations, and a publicity plan. A survey has determined that the following five clubs will be the basis of the club sport program: martial arts, rugby, cycling, racquetball, and ice hockey.

SUGGESTED READINGS

Burwell, P., and S. Yeagle. 1990. Developing potential: The extramural sport clubs conference. P. 207-213 in *Management strategies in recreational sports*. Corvallis, OR: National Intramural-Recreational Sports Association.

Carlson, D.A. 1990. Sport clubs: From the classroom to the office—academic and continuing career preparation. *National Intramural-Recreational Sports Association Journal* 14 (3): 35-37.

Cleave, S. 1994. Sport clubs—More than a solution to shrinking dollars and growing demands. *National Intramural-Recreational Sports Association Journal* 18 (3): 30, 32-33.

Dubord, R.R. 1987. Leadership training workshops for sport club officers. P. 107-114 in *Cultivation of recreational sports programs*. Corvallis, OR: National Intramural-Recreational Sports Association.

.

PART III

Administrative Support Systems & Professionization

CHAPTER 8

Planning, Evaluation, and Control

Chapter Objectives

After reading this chapter you will

- understand the planning process of recreational sport programming,
- understand planning systems that relate to programming,
- understand evaluation methods in recreational sport,
- understand operational forms for evaluation, and
- understand the elements of program control.

Planning and evaluation, although separate functions, are related cyclically—planning leads to evaluation, evaluation leads to planning. Planning is a predetermined system for action; evaluation is the process to determine effectiveness in achieving goals. Consequently, both functions are essential for providing programs that meet participant needs and interests.

We have focused on organizing and conducting specific programs; planning and evaluation are the two functions in programming that provide direction for program design. During the discussion of these topics, we include evaluation as a component within the planning process, then document its unique contribution.

We also present a third concept, program control, in this chapter. The concept of control, or total quality management (TQM), depicts the systems inherent in running a smooth recreational sport program. We cover the principles of control, giving two examples of mechanisms that can improve program quality. Both examples, the disciplinary action process and the governing board, are systems that provide dynamic feedback to the planning and evaluation process.

PLANNING PROCESS

Why plan? Planning for recreational sport helps our actions serve participant needs and interests, solve problems, and use time and resources wisely. The programmer should consider planning as a process to meet needs and a learning experience through which to refine analytical, decision-making, and organizational skills.

Administrative staff use planning to control program development and operation. This involves

- specifying the participants to serve,
- identifying participant needs and interests,
- determining program philosophy and goals,
- translating goals into a program design, and
- establishing the resources to make the program operational.

A programmer should follow these planning steps within his or her area of responsibility. For instance, although the administrators make the decision to provide a basketball tournament, open an ice skating rink, sponsor a hapkido club, or teach contract bridge, the programmer implementing each activity creates plans to ensure consistency with the program philosophy. Also, the programmer must be certain that each activity is appropriate for the intended participants, has goals to meet participant needs, and receives evaluation to determine its effectiveness and offer recommendations for improvement. There are many ways to approach planning, and a blueprint helps plan steps associated with program operation tasks. These steps indicate a direction so each programmer can respond to conditions within the agency. The principles of our planning blueprint include

1. understanding the circumstances of the task,
2. conducting an assessment,
3. developing objectives and strategies,
4. organizing an action plan and timetable,
5. implementing the action plan, and
6. evaluating the plan and outcomes.

Although we present these steps sequentially, they are interdependent. Because it is not possible to control all variables in planning, new information often requires a reassessment, modifying the original intention.

Step 1   Understanding the Circumstances

When addressing a responsibility, whether it is solving a problem or fulfilling a need, gather as much information about the task as possible. Without a clear definition, you may waste time, energy, and other resources and fail to realize the desired

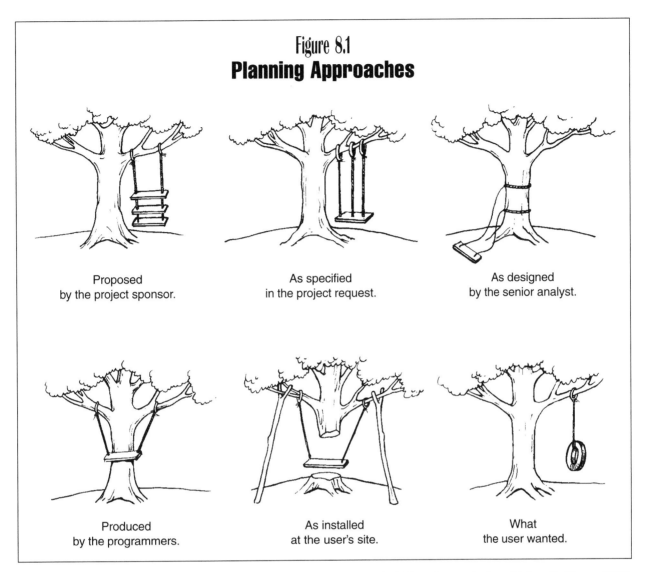

Figure 8.1
Planning Approaches

Proposed
by the project sponsor.

As specified
in the project request.

As designed
by the senior analyst.

Produced
by the programmers.

As installed
at the user's site.

What
the user wanted.

From Dundes, A. and Pagter, C.R. *Work Hard and You Shall be Rewarded*. Bloomington: Indiana University Press, 1978, p. 168. Used by permission.

outcome. The frustration caused by inadequate fact finding is spoofed in figure 8.1.

Fact finding should begin with an understanding of the philosophy and goals of the agency. The public, private, and commercial agencies that deliver recreational sport programs have differences in these areas, and agency philosophy influences all staff decisions and actions.

In grasping a philosophy or goal, make specific inquiries: What is the history of this problem, need, group activity, or program? Why are things the way they are? What is the intent or purpose of this activity, program, group, or service? What is expected of me? Will anyone else be involved in the planning process, and if so, who? After understanding the framework for a respon-

sibility, the programmer can proceed to the next step.

Step 2   Conducting an Assessment

When planning a program or facility, assessment of constituency needs, interests, and problems is a logical prerequisite.

Through assessment, the programmer identifies interests, opinions, attitudes, habits, or knowledge concerning the recreational sport program for which he or she bears responsibility. An assessment of current conditions and future needs serves as a status report on the efforts to date and a springboard for future action. Specifically, an assessment uses the following types of background information:

- **Demographic characteristics.** Composition of the constituency—age, sex, income, education, occupation, and family size
- **Resource availability.** Resources needed—personnel, facilities, equipment, and funds
- **Time use.** Insight into how individuals use their time—availability, preference, frequency, and duration
- **Attitudes and opinions.** What people think about different aspects of the recreational sport program and operational issues—current and future
- **Expressed needs and interests.** What an individual would like to do

You need familiarity with assessment methods to obtain information pertinent to decision making. This includes knowing their design and construction. Although you need not possess extensive research skills, you should know how to select instruments that will yield accurate, dependable results. There are many instruments and methods currently available to conduct an assessment:

- **Inventory.** The inventory identifies existing resources and programs. By listing current funding, supplies, equipment, facilities, personnel expertise, and program format, the programmer has a grasp of the resources and needs to establish a plan.
- **Questionnaire.** A questionnaire is a flexible tool for gathering information on one or more topics at a time. It involves taking a random sample of the population served to ensure accurate results. It assesses activity interests, participation rates, attitudes about existing or proposed services, procedures and priorities, participation patterns, and reasons for nonparticipation. Although questionnaires are easy to develop and distribute (mail, personal interview, or hand delivery), they have limitations. Responses only reflect the questions asked. What people say and what they feel may differ. Respondents may not understand a question. Consider potential limitations in the design and construction of questionnaires. Keep your questions appropriate, understandable, relevant, and concise.
- **Focus groups.** A randomly selected group of 10 to 15 people is useful for an in-depth look at needs and issues. Often this method allows time to discuss priorities and issues, then come to a consensus of concerns.

- **Meetings and hearings.** Information is readily available when interest groups or individuals gather to discuss a topic. Give your target group information about the location, time, and purpose of the meeting or hearing. Anticipate the opinions of an assertive, vocal minority. Encourage discussion from different perspectives.
- **Advisory groups.** Advisory groups act as sounding boards to help determine need. They provide feedback that is useful during assessment, implementation, and evaluation. When soliciting information from advisory groups, see that responses are representative of constituencies and do not merely reflect personal opinions.
- **Referendum.** A referendum seeks a consensus of all concerned parties on an issue. The result directs what action the programmer takes. Effective use of a referendum assumes that all who vote understand the topic because the process leaves little room for exploring alternatives. Consequently, the referendum is most valuable when the people who vote are those primarily affected by the outcome.
- **Written evaluations.** Written evaluations and recommendations from previous programming efforts provide useful historical perspective and direction for current planning efforts. Even though strategies from past occasions have yielded positive results, replication does not guarantee success unless the conditions are similar.

All these assessment methods are useful to the extent that the programmer knows how to design and administer them properly, interpret the results objectively and accurately, and make the proper conclusions. Unfortunately, assessment is often underused due to the time, expense, or knowledge necessary for its conduct, or the desire to avoid arousing expectations.

Step 3   Identifying Objectives and Strategies

After defining the task, the programmer develops objectives and strategies. Objectives are the desired outcomes to observe, measure, and attain, and strategies are the ways the programmer plans to achieve these outcomes.

The programmer needs to formulate two types of objectives: program objectives and performance objectives. Program objectives, also called operating, process, or production objectives, mean how to accomplish a responsibility and focus on materials, personnel, organizational methods, equipment, facilities, and problem-solving strategies. They should include precise and comprehensive expectations. Examples of program objectives include the following:

Personnel

- Before the start of practice, secure a first degree black belt to instruct the judo club.
- Maintain a lifeguard-swimmer ratio of 1:25 during the indoor informal sport swim hours.

Facilities

- Achieve a 75 percent court reservation occupancy during weekday evening hours.
- Expand informal sport time in the weight room by two hours.

Organization

- Realize a 5 percent increase in participation by adult women in the aerobic dance class during the second eight-week session.
- Achieve 80 percent attendance at monthly meetings by representatives of the advisory council.
- Reduce the number of forfeits within the spring intramural sport squash tournament by 15 percent.

Performance objectives, also known as behavioral or instructional objectives, concern outcomes demonstrated by an individual in a sport activity, program, or function. They describe some skill, knowledge, or attitude that the individual should demonstrate at the conclusion of his or her involvement.

Performance objectives correspond to one of three domains: psychomotor, cognitive, or affective. The psychomotor domain involves physical skills and capabilities; the cognitive domain involves thought processes and knowledge; and the affective domain involves attitudes, feelings, and values.

Performance objectives need expression in precise terms, giving special attention to measuring the behavior, the conditions under which the behavior occurs, and the minimum level of performance. Examples of performance objectives include the following:

Skill (psychomotor domain)

- After receiving the ball from a teammate, the participant will be able to set the ball over a

12-foot net and have it land in a target three out of four times.

- At the end of a six-week instructional program, the participant will be able to correctly demonstrate a tennis serve by placing 8 of 10 attempts in the proper service court, without any rule violations judged by the instructor.

Knowledge (cognitive domain)

- On completion of an officials' training program, the official will be able to sufficiently recall water polo rules and regulations by correctly answering 80 percent of the questions on a written test.
- At the end of an eight-week program, beginners will be able to select the golf club appropriate for a given situation in the opinion of the instructor.

Attitude (affective domain)

- During a club sport ice hockey season, there will be a reduction in aggressive behavior as evidenced by a decrease in the number of altercations between the players.
- The children within the neighborhood playground will demonstrate a sensitivity to the needs of others by voluntarily involving newcomers in playground baseball games.

A traditional programming orientation emphasizes the technical and procedural knowledge required for program design and delivery with little regard for its impact on participants. By implementing sound objectives, the programmer can integrate procedural expertise with knowledge about participant behavior essential for contributing to participant development.

The creation of program and performance objectives need not be a complex process. Put objectives and strategies in writing to evaluate results. When identifying strategies, specify tasks that should lead to the achievement of stated objectives. If the objective is to increase participation by adult women in the aerobic dance session by 5 percent, list the possible ways to meet this goal. Rank your ideas for probability of success. A plan might appear as shown in figure 8.2.

Concerning strategy development, we recommend that you consider as many options as possible and establish priorities within the list. Specificity in planning provides a clearer direction

---

Figure 8.2
Simple Plan

Objective

To realize a 5 percent increase in participation by adult women in the aerobic dance session during the second eight-week session.

Strategies

1. Locate a suitable facility at a neighborhood site to promote accessibility.
2. Sponsor demonstrations at local, civic, and social functions.
3. Place public service announcements on radio and TV.
4. Offer discount rates on an introductory basis.

---

for action, but you need flexibility. Make the necessary adjustments to attain desired outcomes.

Step 4   Preparing an Action Plan

An action plan entails specifying objectives and organizing the resources necessary for acting on them. When preparing the plan, identify what needs to be accomplished—how, when, by whom, where, and to what extent?

A comprehensive action plan organizes tasks to attain stated objectives. We offer the following questions about preparation regarding content, time factors, setting, equipment and supplies, finance, personnel, and marketing.

Content

- What is the best way to present a sport activity or topic—an elimination tournament, a challenge board, brainstorming, or small group discussion?
- What information should you develop for the participant—an orientation sheet, rules and regulations, entry forms, application form, articles of the association?
- What information should you obtain from the participant—age, sex, skill level, qualifications, certifications?
- How will you group participants? How will you handle problems?

Time factors

- What should the duration be—one hour, two hours, three hours a day?
- How frequently should the activity be—daily, weekly or monthly?
- When are individuals available—mornings, afternoons, evenings, weekdays, weekends, winter, summer?

Setting

- What type of facilities and areas exist?
- What does it take to reserve a facility or area?
- What facility, environment, or area is most desirable?
- Will the setting need to be prepared in advance?
- Can the setting handle multiple or simultaneous use?
- How many different facilities and areas are there?
- How many facilities and areas of similar type are there?
- How many people can be accommodated at one site?
- What kind and extent of supervision is needed?
- Is weather a factor?

Equipment and supplies

- What do you need? What is available?
- Where are items located?
- How can you obtain items?
- What do you need to order or repair?
- Are existing items adequate?
- Is there a sufficient quantity?
- Are special skills required for operating equipment?
- Who will supervise the items?
- Who will distribute and collect the items?

Finance

- What costs will be incurred?
- How will you record and process costs?
- What bookkeeping or accounting methods will you require?

- Have you allocated funds for a specific purpose?
- Can you assess fees and charges?
- Can you collect revenue—how, where, when, under what conditions?

Personnel

- What functions need to be performed?
- How many people will you need per function?
- What skill level or qualifications are needed?
- How will you assign duties and responsibilities?
- How will you recruit, select, train, schedule, supervise, and discipline personnel?
- What human resources are available?
- Will personnel be employees or volunteers?
- Will you require special testing?
- What incentives or recognition will you offer?
- What expectations will you establish for personnel?
- What communication network will you need?

Marketing

- What constituency do you need to reach?
- How can you reach a constituency?
- What methods or media are available?
- What materials do you need to prepare?
- What resources are available?
- Who will be responsible for preparing materials or information?
- How long will it take to prepare materials?
- What distribution process will you use?
- Where can you display materials?
- What is the best way to present the activity, program, facility, or function?

The preceding questions indicate the details involved in forming an action plan. Implementation requires that the programmer visualize all responsibilities systematically and thoroughly, identifying every detail of each task to be performed and anticipating problems. The final list should represent the programmer's best effort at specifying those tasks necessary to attain objectives.

Step 5   Implementing the Plan

Implementation translates the thought process into action. Even though you have specified the tasks, it requires time, effort, and organizational ability to coordinate a plan efficiently. Implementation involves sound organizational and time management principles. The following are guides to incorporating planning into sport organizations.

- **Comprehensive plan.** This type of plan incorporates the planning directions of a large focus within sport management. For example, a sport management program located in a city may address the comprehensive plan for city growth and development.
- **Master plan.** This plan typically identifies facility and program priorities for a five-year period. It includes specific priorities, a timetable for implementation, site plans, and cost estimates.
- **Budget.** This is the specific fiscal period plan, which finances a program for a one-year to two-year period.
- **Work program.** This plan identifies the specific work inherent within budget allotments for a specified time. A work program is the allowable span of duties that are financially feasible.

The programmer may benefit from using a prioritized *to do* checklist. By ranking tasks, the programmer can more systematically attend to each item.

Planning for optimal time use is important. Stephanie Winston (Russell 1982) recommends these eight time-savers:

1. **Barter**—trade or exchange distasteful jobs with others.
2. **Make use of services**—rely on professionals as much as you can afford.
3. **Double up on time**—do several small tasks at the same time (for example, sign letters while on telephone hold).
4. **Make use of bits of time**—plan small projects during waiting periods or while riding the bus.
5. **Plan ahead**—make sure everything is at hand before starting a project.
6. **Pool resources**—experiment with cooperative arrangements.

7. **Consolidate**—combine errands, return calls, and as much movement as possible.

8. **Use labor-saving devices**—use modern technology as much as possible.

With the complexity of plan implementation tasks, we urge the programmer to adopt an implementation strategy. Three strategies taken from business and management apply to planning within recreation: the program evaluation and review technique (PERT), the critical path method (CPM) and the flowchart method (FCM). The PERT was developed jointly by the U.S. Navy, Lockheed Aircraft Corporation, and a private management consulting firm for weaponry development. The primary element of PERT appropriate as an implementation strategy is a flowchart that illustrates the steps to achieving a finished product. The PERT chart lists all the tasks involved with the activity, program, or function. The time estimated to complete each task is indicated between tasks. The chart expresses time estimates as follows.

- **Optimistic time (OT)**—the time required without complications or unforeseen difficulties arising in the activity.

- **Most likely time (MLT)**—the time in which the task is most likely to be completed.

- **Pessimistic time (PT)**—the time required if unusual complications or unforeseen difficulties occur.

If you consider these three estimates, then you can calculate a realistic time (RT) and include it in the PERT chart between activities, using the following formula:

$$\frac{PT + 4(MLT) + OT}{6} = RT$$

The next step is to plot the information using the critical path method or flowchart method. These techniques provide a systematic way of separating a responsibility into segments—what is to be done, when it is to be done, who is to do it, and how long it will take. For example, table 8.1 presents the components of a sample bridge class as a checklist. Placement of the checklist on a time line for the flowchart method is presented in figure 8.3, and the same checklist is applied to the critical path method in figure 8.4. Placing tasks onto a time line or time path in sequence gives the

Table 8.1
Checklist for Implementation (Eight-Week Bridge Class)

Component	Task	Time required to complete (weeks)	Deadline
Personnel	Determine leadership needs	2	1/19
	Advertise	2	2/4
	Interview	1	2/12
	Test	1	2/14
	Selection	1	2/16
	Complete forms	1	3/29
Materials	Arrange for storage	1	2/11
	Order equipment	1	2/19
	Deliver equipment to the site	1	4/2
Facilities	Determine needs	2	1/21
	Explore sites	2	2/6
	Reserve times	1	2/13
Program	Set times and dates	1	2/22
	Accept registration		3/9
	Registration completed	2	3/26
	Prepare and deliver class list	2	4/5
	Evaluation	1	5/28
Publicity	Design plans	2	2/17
	Distribute publicity	1	3/4
	Alert media	1	3/7

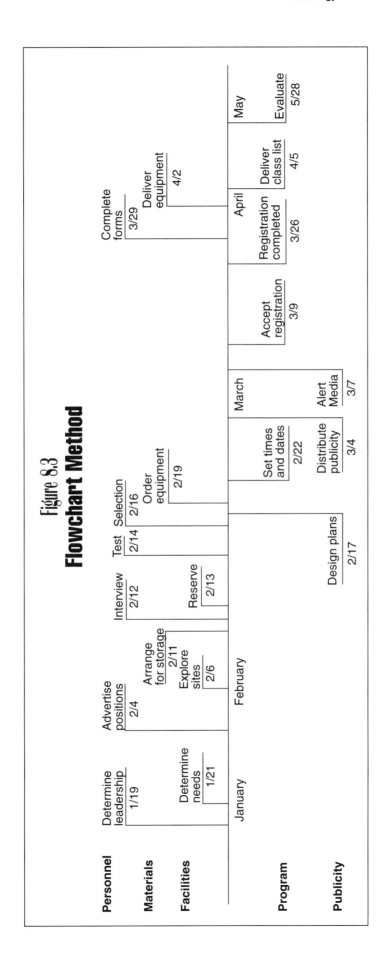

Figure 8.3
Flowchart Method

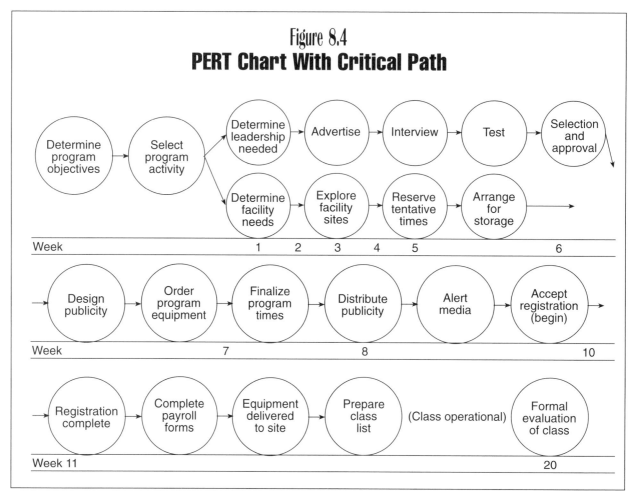

Figure 8.4
PERT Chart With Critical Path

From Farrell, P. and H.M. Lundgren. *The Process of Recreational Programming Theory and Practice.* New York: John Wiley and Sons, 1978, p. 302. Used by permission.

programmer a view of the progression for their implementation. People who lack an interest in a graphic ordering of tasks for implementation stop once they assign tasks a priority and timetable for completion.

Although the critical path and flowchart methods require time to develop, they facilitate delegating responsibility once you determine tasks, and serve as a frame of reference for recurring responsibilities. The major difference between the two methods is that the critical path method illustrates tasks you can implement simultaneously.

These organizational aids, combined with experience in time management, enable the programmer to approach implementation effectively. However, the relative success of program operations remains dependent on the appropriateness of decisions made before implementation and the effect of decisions and actions that occur during implementation.

The fact that you have specified and prioritized all the tasks for implementation does not guarantee success. For example, proper planning may lead to selecting qualified personnel, but does not guarantee success in their productivity and morale.

Step 6   Evaluating the Plan and Outcomes

Even though programmers put much thought, time, and effort into planning and implementing sport activities, programs, and other responsibilities, the same does not hold true for evaluation. Perhaps the reason is anxiety about results, confusion about how to design evaluation instruments, frustration in identifying what to measure, lack of confidence in the accuracy of evaluation, inexperience in evaluation, or lack of money to support the effort. Yet because of the time, effort, cost, and resources put into program operations, it is illogical not to judge the results.

Evaluation may occur during planning, providing useful feedback for decision making or plan modifications. Evaluation conducted at the end of program operations yields useful information leading to recommendations for future planning efforts. This interdependent relationship between planning and evaluation stimulates quality throughout each area of responsibility. Because evaluation is a process you can apply to virtually every aspect of recreational sport, we will discuss it extensively here.

EVALUATION

Evaluation is making a judgment or appraisal of worth. For the programmer, evaluation assesses program operations in terms of their efficiency and their effect on participants and personnel, compared with stated objectives. Unless you have identified clear objectives, the usefulness, accuracy, and credibility of evaluations are questionable. The focus of evaluation is to determine how effective our program efforts are in terms of the process (means) we use and the outcomes (ends) we obtain.

Process encompasses those factors used in and required for program delivery. The major areas to evaluate within process include personnel, program content, and physical resources. More specific examples for evaluation include the following:

- **Personnel**—qualifications, performance, inservice training, scheduling, public relations
- **Program**—appropriateness, sufficiency, acceptance, scheduling, safety, promotion, rules, policies, recognition, governance
- **Physical resources**—availability, adequacy, accessibility, appropriateness, safety, attractiveness, maintenance, policies

Approaches used in analyzing process include evaluation by attainment of program objectives, evaluation by standards, and evaluation by cost-benefit analysis. Program objectives, discussed in step three of the planning process, are expectations regarding the conduct and content of program operations and the minimum level of accomplishment. Standards express criteria that represent a desired practice or level of performance. For example, standards may specify a certain number of courts per person, sit-ups per minute, and lifeguard ratio to swimmers. Evaluation by cost-to-benefit

ratio quantifies the benefits (objectives) of a program in economic terms so you can establish a ratio between it and the fixed costs associated with providing the program.

Evaluation within recreational sport tends to focus more on process than on outcome. This is because process objectives are more precise and quantitative, and outcome objectives tend to be qualitative. Nonetheless, evaluation of outcomes is important for accountability and effectiveness as it focuses on the impact involvement has on individuals (leaders or participants). Examples of parameters involved in evaluating the effect of participation include the following:

- **Physical**—skill, strength, endurance, stress, injury
- **Emotional**—attitudes, opinions, behaviors, stability
- **Social**—affiliation, friendliness, cooperation
- **Mental**—knowledge, application, synthesis

Evaluation of outcomes centers on the degree to which you have met performance objectives. Performance objectives specify the desired skill, knowledge, or attitude the individual should be able to demonstrate at the end of involvement. Evaluating how effectively you meet performance objectives is easier for the physical or mental than for the social or emotional parameters.

Collecting Data for Evaluation

Evaluating effectiveness of process or outcomes requires expertise in selecting appropriate instruments for measuring a specific quality, trait, or action. Although the programmer is not usually expected to fulfill this responsibility, he or she frequently participates in collecting data and interpreting results. Typical data collection techniques used in evaluation include questionnaires, rating scales, checklists, attitude scales, sociograms, behavioral observations, and case studies. We have included references about the development, meaning, and interpretation of these data collection devices in the suggested readings at the end of this chapter, but we'll briefly look at each method now.

Questionnaires

A common method to collect data, a questionnaire solicits responses from individuals to a written or oral series of questions. It may obtain demographic information about a sample population, assess opinions or attitudes, or provide information about participant behavior. Questionnaires appear in a fixed alternative (yes or no, multiple choice, etc.) or open-ended format. Although the first alternative is easy to administer, it restricts responses to specific questions that may be superficial. The second alternative, as shown in form 8.1, provides more in-depth questioning and better reflects true opinion. Because it requires greater verbal and written skills, it may evoke responses too broad or complex to interpret or discourage a respondent from taking the time to answer questions.

Rating Scales

The rating scale asks the individual to assign a value to a statement on a continuum (see form 8.2). The values have numbers assigned to them to permit you to quantify the results. You can use rating scales to collect data on program content and operations, physical resources, personnel, and policies. Although they are easy to develop and administer, they contain bias. For example, the rating of one factor may influence the rating given to succeeding ones, so the majority of responses fall on one side of the continuum. In addition, one person's interpretation of excellent may differ from another person's. Words commonly used to categorize values are the following:

- Strongly agree, agree, neutral, disagree, strongly disagree
- Excellent, good, fair, poor, very poor
- Always, sometimes, never

Checklists

This instrument lists items that the respondent checks, measuring frequency of occurrence when compared with a standard criterion. Checklists are easy to develop and administer.

Attitude Scales

There are three types of scales for collecting data on attitudes, including the Likert scale (summation), equal appearing intervals (Thurstone), and the cumulative scale (Guttman). Of these three, the Likert scale is the most popular. The respondent is asked to indicate a degree of agreement or disagreement to a series of statements. The value to a response involves a five-point scale: strongly agree (SA—5), agree (A—4), undecided (U—3), disagree (D—2), strongly disagree (SD—1). When using negatively stated items, reverse the scoring (see form 8.3).

A more specialized attitude measurement is the semantic differential developed by Osgood (1967)

(see form 8.4). The technique measures the meaning of an object to a person by establishing bipolar adjective pairs (good-bad) and a rating scale for the respondent to select a position. These adjectives may evaluate nature (good-bad), indicate strength or potency (strong-weak), or reveal motion or action (fast-slow).

Sociograms

You can use this instrument to evaluate the structure within a group by demonstrating interactions or relationships among group members. Using the sociogram helps evaluate group cohesiveness, communication patterns, compatible subunits, and emergent leaders. Its use is not feasible with groups of more than 20 people.

Behavior Observations

This data collection method does not involve participant response; it focuses on participant behavior. The observations record selected behavior to determine whether a correlation exists between the behavior specified in performance objectives and what is being observed (see form 8.5). The effectiveness of this method depends on proper training in how to observe and record behavior.

Case Studies

Case studies are in-depth investigations, which reveal more information than a cursory observation or review. Sources of information for a case study include rating forms, anecdotal records, attitude scales, observations, interviews, and tests. Although case studies are often time-consuming, they may signal a difficulty requiring further evaluation or pinpoint an elusive problem area.

Evaluation Through Operational Forms

Daily operational forms, records, and reports have provided the traditional basis for determining success in an area of responsibility. Programmers often use them to measure success in terms of quantity: attendance figures, frequency of participation, maximum use of facilities, percentage of participants returning, and number of events, yet statistics may not indicate quality. People may participate when no other acceptable alternatives exist. Does that indicate provision of a quality service?

In addition, total reliance on quantitative measurements as the basis for deciding whether to provide an activity ignores sports that, by their nature, draw limited numbers. These sports still meet the needs and interests of individuals who would not otherwise participate. Records and reports exist to

COUNTY YOUTH RECREATIONAL NEEDS SPORT QUESTIONNAIRE

Recreational sport opportunities are advantageous for our youth. This is your opportunity to make suggestions and to have a responsibility in developing a sound recreational sport program.

This could be the beginning of an orderly, long-range development plan to improve the recreational sport opportunities for our young people. Therefore, we invite you to speak out on your opinions of recreational sport needs. You need not sign this survey.

1. Are you familiar with present sport facilities?   Yes _____   No _____

2. Are you familiar with the recreational sport program?   Yes _____   No _____

3. Are your recreational sport interests   Indoor _____   Outdoor _____   Equal _____

4. What type of sport supervision and sport instruction do you feel is best? _____

   a. Adult

   b. Committee of youth and adult

   c. Youth

   d. Other _____

5. Do you feel youth have a responsibility for the conduct, clean-up, and prevention of vandalism for your recreational sport facilities and opportunities?   Yes _____   No _____

6. Would you be interested in participating in a special activity or event?   Yes _____   No _____

   If yes, list in order your preference.

   _____ a. 4th of July   _____ c. Halloween   _____ e. Christmas

   _____ b. Youth fair   _____ d. All nighter   _____ f. Other _____

7. Do you feel transportation is a problem for youth in attending activities?   Yes _____   No _____

8. In your opinion, do you feel that parents, *in general*, are interested in the youth of the county?

   Yes _____   No _____   Don't know _____

9. If you feel there is room for improvement in parental interest, what are the ways you feel it can be improved?

   _____

   _____

10. Do you feel our schools are interested in the youth of this county?   Yes _____   No _____   No opinion _____

11. Do you feel the schools should make their facilities available for recreational and educational activities under responsible adult supervision?   Yes _____   No _____   No opinion _____

12. Do you feel there are enough recreational sport activities available for young people in this county?

    Yes _____   No _____   No opinion _____

13. Of the following, which recreational sport activities would you participate in if given the opportunity?

___ Croquet	___ Baseball	___ Roller skating	___ Canoeing
___ Volleyball	___ Horseshoes	___ Bowling	___ Others _____
___ Badminton	___ Tennis	___ Chess	___ _____
___ Basketball	___ Fly & bait casting	___ Water safety	___ _____
___ Ping-pong	___ Swimming	___ Gymnastics	___ _____
___ Tether ball	___ Archery	___ Judo	___ _____
___ Shuffle board	___ Target shooting	___ Karate	___ _____
___ Movable back stop	___ Gun safety	___ Checkers	___ _____

14. As of this date do you plan on living in this county after high school graduation?

    Yes _____   No _____   Undecided _____

15. If *no*, would you share your reasons with this committee? _____

    _____

    _____

Form 8.1   Recreational sport questionnaire.

EMPLOYEE PERFORMANCE RATING

Name _____   Position _____

Date _____   Evaluator _____

Date of last evaluation _____

Evaluation factors	1	2	3	4	5
A. Personal					
1. Ability to work without supervision	—	—	—	—	—
2. Ability to work with others	—	—	—	—	—
3. Dependability	—	—	—	—	—
4. Ability to constructively influence others	—	—	—	—	—
5. Diplomacy and tact	—	—	—	—	—
B. Task-related					
1. Ability to organize tasks	—	—	—	—	—
2. Quality of written reports	—	—	—	—	—
3. Knowledge of program skills	—	—	—	—	—
4. Planning ability	—	—	—	—	—
5. Initiative	—	—	—	—	—
6. Relations with participants	—	—	—	—	—
7. Willingness to try innovative approaches	—	—	—	—	—
C. Effectiveness					
1. Effectiveness compared to others in a similar capacity	—	—	—	—	—
2. Effectiveness compared to previous performance	—	—	—	—	—
3. Potential and advancement	—	—	—	—	—
4. Overall effectiveness	—	—	—	—	—
Totals	—	—	—	—	—

A = _____   5 = Excellent
B = _____   4 = Good
C = _____   3 = Fair
Total _____   2 = Poor
                      1 = Very poor

Evaluator's signature _____

Personnel's signature _____

Date _____

Form 8.2   Rating scale. Adapted by permission from Graham, P.J. and L.R. Klar, Jr. *Planning and Delivering Leisure Services.* Dubuque, IA: William C. Brown Company Publishers, 1979, p. 140.

EXER-FIT AEROBIC RHYTHM EVALUATION

Codes I
A B C D E F G H I

0 0 0 0 0 0 0 0 0
1 1 1 1 1 1 1 1 1
2 2 2 2 2 2 2 2 2
3 3 3 3 3 3 3 3 3
4 4 4 4 4 4 4 4 4
5 5 5 5 5 5 5 5 5
6 6 6 6 6 6 6 6 6
7 7 7 7 7 7 7 7 7
8 8 8 8 8 8 8 8 8
9 9 9 9 9 9 9 9 9

Codes II
J K L M N

0 0 0 0 0
1 1 1 1 1
2 2 2 2 2
3 3 3 3 3
4 4 4 4 4
5 5 5 5 5
6 6 6 6 6
7 7 7 7 7
8 8 8 8 8
9 9 9 9 9

INSTRUCTIONS:

Darken the appropriate circle:

Code 1, Column A—Freshman = 0, Sophomore = 1, Junior = 2, Senior = 3, Graduate = 4, Faculty/Staff = 5, Public = 6

Code 1, Column B—Male = 0, Female = 1

Code 1, Column C—Session A = 0, Session B = 1, Session C = 2, Session D = 3, Session E = 4, Session F = 5, Session G = 6, Session H = 7, Session I = 8, Session J = 9

Responses—Strongly agree = 1, Agree = 2, Undecided = 3, Disagree = 4, Strongly disagree = 5, No basis for response = 6

		SA A U D SD
1. The leader is prepared for each session.	1	① ② ③ ④ ⑤
2. The leader provides a cheerful, encouraging environment for the participant.	2	① ② ③ ④ ⑤
3. The leader is open to suggestions and criticism.	3	① ② ③ ④ ⑤
4. The leader clearly answers participant's questions concerning the session.	4	① ② ③ ④ ⑤
5. The session has been enjoyable and beneficial to me.	5	① ② ③ ④ ⑤
		SA A U D SD
6. The initial presentation concerning pulse rates was clear and easy to follow.	6	① ② ③ ④ ⑤
7. This leader would be highly recommended by me to others.	7	① ② ③ ④ ⑤
8. The leader took proper action if an injury or accident occurred.	8	① ② ③ ④ ⑤
9. The music and routines were well-suited for one another.	9	① ② ③ ④ ⑤
10. The music can be clearly heard during each session.	10	① ② ③ ④ ⑤
		SA A U D SD
11. My participation in the program is based on my desire for a fun recreational activity.	11	① ② ③ ④ ⑤
12. The facility is adequate for the number of people in the session.	12	① ② ③ ④ ⑤
13. I would be willing to pay for an additional day each week in order to attend three times per week, instead of two.	13	① ② ③ ④ ⑤
14. This program would be recommended by me to others.	14	① ② ③ ④ ⑤
15. I take part in the fitness testing program.	15	① ② ③ ④ ⑤

16. Please circle all that apply to you:

I learned about the program

		SA A U D SD
a. from a friend	16 a	① ② ③ ④ ⑤
b. from the ads in the newspaper	b	① ② ③ ④ ⑤
c. from radio announcements	c	① ② ③ ④ ⑤
d. from flyers in my dorm	d	① ② ③ ④ ⑤
e. from flyers in my sorority/fraternity	e	① ② ③ ④ ⑤
f. from flyers around the HPER building	f	① ② ③ ④ ⑤

17. Please provide any written comments you may have below:

Thanks for your time.

Form 8.3   Likert attitude scale.

CLUB SPORT STAFF OPINION SURVEY

Please circle the number closest to the word that best represents your opinion of the following statement:

"I feel the club sport staff are _____."

Accepting _____ 6 _____ 5 _____ 4 _____ 3 _____ 2 _____ 1 _____ Rejecting
Satisfying _____ 6 _____ 5 _____ 4 _____ 3 _____ 2 _____ 1 _____ Frustrating
Enthusiastic _____ 6 _____ 5 _____ 4 _____ 3 _____ 2 _____ 1 _____ Unenthusiastic
Productive _____ 6 _____ 5 _____ 4 _____ 3 _____ 2 _____ 1 _____ Nonproductive
Warm _____ 6 _____ 5 _____ 4 _____ 3 _____ 2 _____ 1 _____ Cold
Cooperative _____ 6 _____ 5 _____ 4 _____ 3 _____ 2 _____ 1 _____ Uncooperative
Supportive _____ 6 _____ 5 _____ 4 _____ 3 _____ 2 _____ 1 _____ Hostile
Interesting _____ 6 _____ 5 _____ 4 _____ 3 _____ 2 _____ 1 _____ Boring
Successful _____ 6 _____ 5 _____ 4 _____ 3 _____ 2 _____ 1 _____ Unsuccessful

Form 8.4　Semantic differential scale.

PERFORMANCE OBSERVATION SHEET

x = Able to perform before instruction
0 = Unable to perform before instruction
1 = Unable to perform after instruction
• = Able to perform after instruction

	Forehand	Backhand	Lob	Volley	Cross-court	Approach shot	Overhead	Footwork	Service
1. Rin Curtis	•	•	•	•	•	•	•	•	1
2. John Seibert	•	•	•	•	•	•	•	•	•
3. Don Erdman	•	•	•	•	•	•	1	1	•
4. Steve Kintigh	x	•	•	•	•	•	x	•	•
5. Bill Kolstad	•	1	•	•	•	•	•	•	1
6. Steve Walter	•	•	•	•	•	•	•	•	•
7. Kathy Bunn	•	•	•	•	•	•	•	•	1
8. Connie Elliott	•	•	•	•	•	1	1	1	•
9. Bob Albert	1	1	1	1	1	1	1	1	1
10. John Harper	•	•	•	•	•	•	•	•	•
11. Jan Moldstadt	•	•	•	•	•	•	•	•	•

Form 8.5　Behavior observation method.

give an account of operations to administrators or a constituency, demonstrate compliance with laws and policies, establish accountability, protect against lawsuits, provide information for decision making, and serve as a basis for evaluation. This last item is the focus of our discussion. The types of records and reports the programmer uses include the following categories:

- **Program records**—document participation, results, and facility and equipment use. You may complete these records at the end of a sport or program, seasonally, or annually.
- **Personnel records**—identify volunteers and employees, service records, time cards, and attendance.
- **Utilization records**—document attendance, participation, use patterns, and constituency groups.
- **Operational records**—document accidents and injuries, maintenance needs, discipline problems, equipment and supplies, fee collection, and deposits.

Of these categories, the programmer deals most frequently with utilization and program records.

Utilization Records

The types of data in utilization records include the following:

- **Number of entries, enrollments, or memberships.** Such data is often collected to be sure adequate resources are available for potential participants, to compare with previous totals or those of another activity, to prepare for scheduling, and to determine dropout incidence before participation. If there are high dropout rates, you may need to investigate contributing factors.
- **Number of participants.** This figure differs from the number of entries because it indicates those who participate at least once. The findings are useful to compare with future participation statistics.
- **Number of participations.** This figure represents the total number of times a participant engages in the program under evaluation. If the number of participants in a sport is consistently high among the entered population, the events are successful. If there is a low percentage of participants compared with the total number possible, the success of the event is questionable. In some instances, as informal sport participation, it may not be pos-

sible to determine the actual number of individuals participating or the number of participations per individual during a given time. Instead, the data may merely reflect the collective number of participants. This information is still useful for comparisons and determining use or growth patterns.

- **Number of sessions scheduled, forfeited, postponed, completed.** You can use this statistic to identify growth within a sport, program, or use of a facility. If the rate of forfeits and the number of postponements are high, you may need to investigate contributing factors.
- **Hours of facility availability.** Such data describe the history of facility availability for scheduled or unscheduled purposes. When you make past and present availability comparisons, you reveal changing use patterns and evolving participant interests.
- **Staff-participant to staff-facility ratios.** Information expressing these relationships is useful for comparison with requirements and for cost analysis and personnel allocation decisions.

Rarely are variables consistent enough from setting to setting to permit standardization of forms or procedures for data collection, and such standardization is not always desirable. Data collection methods should be appropriate, simple to implement, and the results easy to interpret. In some agencies, computer systems facilitate tabulation and analysis. Programs analyzing participation statistics may correlate individuals with frequency of facility use or examine total facility use daily, weekly, monthly, seasonally, or annually. Because most agencies still use manual data tabulation, our examples of data collection methods reflect that orientation.

Head count sheets, occupancy or reservation sheets, result forms, or sales records are the most common tools used to collect data on facility use. Let's briefly examine the usefulness of these records.

- **Head counts.** Within an informal sport program, head count and reservation sheets are common tools for obtaining participation statistics. Head count forms for individual facilities often receive tallies at set intervals during the day. They represent total participation, individual participation, or participation by user classification as in form 8.6. Transfer daily head counts to forms, such as form 8.7, which show monthly use.
- **Occupancy and reservation sheets.** A common form used in commercial settings, such as

INFORMAL SPORT USER BREAKDOWN AND SPOT CHECK

Use for (circle)
Weightroom
17th St. Fieldhouse
NFL fields & tennis
Woodlawn & tennis   Date _____
HB, RB squash courts
Royer Pool
Pool 194

Time	Student	Faculty	Staff	Family	Alumni	Public	Supervisor's name
8-9 a.m.							
9-10 a.m.							
10-11 a.m.							
11-noon							
12-1 p.m.							
1-2 p.m.							
2-3 p.m.							
3-4 p.m.							
4-5 p.m.							
5-6 p.m.							
6-7 p.m.							
7-8 p.m.							
8-9 p.m.							
9-10 p.m.							
10-11 p.m.							
11-12 p.m.							
Totals							

Form 8.6   User classification participation head count form.

racquetball, tennis, or bowling facilities, is the occupancy report or reservation sheet. These forms indicate use levels at facility sites taken hourly and tabulated for daily, weekly, monthly, seasonal, and annual reports. Figure 8.5 illustrates a weekly occupancy report for a racquetball facility developed from daily reservation sheets. Record court time in 60-minute or 30-minute time slots. Results may pinpoint a day or time of consistent use—high or low.

• **Result forms.** Whenever contests occur, record the results—win, loss, forfeit, score. Score sheets indicate the number of times each person participates during the tournament or season, or the total number of participants from a target group involved in the tournament.

TENNIS COURTS

Facility _____   Month _____   Year _____

Day Date	1	2	3	4	5	6	7	8	9	10	11	12	13	14	15	16	17	18	19	20	21	22	23	24	25	26	27	28	29	30	31	Tot.	Avg.
6:15																																	
6:45																																	
7:15																																	
7:45																																	
8:15																																	
8:45																																	
9:15																																	
9:45																																	
10:15																																	
10:45																																	
11:15																																	
11:45																																	
12:15																																	
12:45																																	
1:15																																	
1:45																																	
2:15																																	
2:45																																	
3:15																																	
3:45																																	
4:15																																	
4:45																																	
5:15																																	
5:45																																	
6:15																																	
6:45																																	
7:15																																	
7:45																																	
8:15																																	
8:45																																	
9:15																																	
9:45																																	
10:15																																	
10:45																																	
11:15																																	
11:45																																	
Total																																	
Average																																	

Form 8.7   Monthly facility participation.

Figure 8.5
Weekly Court Occupancy Summary

Facility ___Tennis courts___

Week ending Sunday _____

Time	Mon	Tue	Wed	Thur	Fri	Sat	Sun	Week days total	Week nights total	Weekend days total	Weekend nights total	Actual week usage total	% usage Week days	% usage Week nights	% usage Weekend days	% usage Weekend nights	Total % usage
6:00 a.m.	—	1½	—	½	3½	1	—	5½		1		6½	11%		5%		9%
7:00 a.m.	—	—	—	2	—	—	—	2		—		2	4%		0%		3%
8:00 a.m.	1	—	—	—	1	½	3	2		3½		5½	4%		18%		8%
9:00 a.m.	1	4	3	—	—	2	1	8		3		11	16%		15%		16%
10:00 a.m.	1	4	1	2	1	2½	—	9		2½		11½	18%		13%		16%
11:00 a.m.	3	1	4	1	4	4	2	13		6		19	26%		30%		27%
12:00 N	—	—	1	2½	3	5	1	6½		6		12½	13%		30%		18%
1:00 p.m.	3	—	6	1	3	3	3	13		6		19	26%		30%		27½
2:00 p.m.	—	2	2	2	5	1	1	11		2		13	22%		10%		19½
3:00 p.m.	4	2	1½	2	4	4	½	13½		4½		18	27%		23%		26%
4:00 p.m.	8	3	4½	5½	4	½	—	25		½		25½	50%		3%		36%
5:00 p.m.	2½	3	2	1	2	2	2		10½		4			21%		20%	21%
6:00 p.m.	4	3½	5½	8½	4	1	2		25½		3	28½		51%		15%	41%
7:00 p.m.	5	7	1	9½	4½	4	2		27		6	33		54%		30%	47%
8:00 p.m.	5½	9	6	8	5	2	5		33½		7	40½		67%		35%	58%
9:00 p.m.	3	5	1	5½	6	3	5½		20½		8½	29		41%		43%	41%
10:00 p.m.	4	—	5½	1½	3½	—	2½		14½		2½	17		29%		13%	24%
Week days	21	17½	23	18½	28½			A. 108½									
Week nights	24	27½	21	34	25				B. 131½								
Weekend days						23½	11½			C. 35							
Weekend nights						12	19				D. 31						
Total usage	45	45	44	52½	53½	35½	30½					E. 306					
% usage week days	19%	16%	21%	17%	26%								F. 20%				
% usage week nights	37%	42%	32%	52%	38%									G. 44%			
% usage weekend days						21%	10%								H. 16%		
% usage weekend nights						20%	32%									I. 26%	
% occ. Total	26%	26%	25%	30%	31%	21%	18%			Total court hours							J. 26%

- **Sales records.**   Any sport activity or program that assesses fees uses sales records for transactions. By analyzing sales, a programmer can determine use patterns. This method is useful for single activity facilities selling daily passes or permits. In settings where a pass or permit allows multiple use, determine general use patterns by comparing sale of passes or permits weekly, monthly, seasonally, or annually.

Program Records

At the end of any sport activity or program, prepare a summary report. A report may combine a narrative review of operational procedures and recommendations with a numerical summary. An example of a summary report format is provided by form 8.8. You can use the information in these reports to develop annual reports for a program division. They are also instrumental in implementing similar programs in the future.

Evaluation Results

The usefulness of data lies in proper interpretation and application. Once you analyze the data, document the results thoroughly and include your recommendations for improvements or further analysis to aid future planning efforts. Review the report with an immediate supervisor to avoid misinterpretation and obtain feedback regarding the recommendations.

PROGRAM CONTROL PROCESS

Program control involves identifying and managing negative factors within recreational sport while promoting desired patterns of participant, spectator, and personnel behavior. Negative or stressful situations in sport vary in severity and intensity. Situations producing a negative impact over time include unauthorized use of limited access facilities, inconsistent adherence to a club constitution, forfeits in structured tournament play, and unrealistic expectations of officials. Negative situations within sport requiring prompt, decisive action include vandalism, verbal or physical abuse, insubordination or incompetence by personnel, and violation of a policy or procedure.

When faced with a stressful situation, the programmer may be tempted to avoid the responsibility for resolving the problem. Avoidance only compounds a conflict when the programmer is capable of handling it. Although conflict resolution is often unpleasant, it is a necessary programming function. Time committed to analyzing problems and methods to establish or restore control helps the programmer maintain a positive sport environment for participants, spectators, and personnel. Without control, a potential exists for disorder, personal injury, conflict, and destruction of property.

There are two factors affecting program control within the recreational sport environment. One relates to self-control or self-discipline, and the second pertains to external control techniques. Our focus is external control: the roles, responsibilities, and influence of program personnel within sport. Although self-control is a matter of individual responsibility, the programmer should consider factors that affect individual behavior as the basis for selecting external control methods. For example, individuals or groups engaging in sport events often meet frustration. Participants unable to control frustration or alleviate stress may exhibit violence, apathy, withdrawal, hostility, or aggression.

The sport programmer has a responsibility to analyze probable causes for negative behavior. Avoid assuming that behavior problems always result from lack of self-control or personal factors, such as inadequate ability, unrealistic expectations, or different standards of behavior. Misconduct may result from external factors, such as rules, regulations, opponents and program personnel, conduct, classification systems, or governance procedures. When trouble develops, use the situation to evaluate program design and delivery. Perhaps a rule is unfair, a sport official is biased, a classification system is inequitable. Be creative in your efforts to minimize, alleviate, and control negative behavior.

Practices for Program Control

Program control begins with understanding human behavior and establishing standards and expectations. Some differences of opinion exist regarding acceptable or unacceptable behavior, but the programmer who exhibits a professional, conscientious approach will be able to establish suitable standards. Among the aspects of desirable behavior are the following:

- Respect for self
- Respect for others
- Respect for position
- Respect for property
- Respect for rules
- Respect for law and order

INTRAMURAL INDIVIDUAL AND DUAL SPORTS SUMMARY REPORT

Event _____   Dates _____

- **STRUCTURE**

—— Single elimination   ___ Timed competition   ___ Other, specify _____

___ Double elimination   ___ Single elimination with consolation

- **ENTRIES**

	Team or individual	% change
Number of entries	_____	_____
Number of contestants (scratches from com., etc.)	_____	_____
Number of defaults	_____	_____
Number of forfeits	_____	_____
Number of contests/matches	_____	_____

Conflicting events and comments _____

_____

_____

- **INJURIES**

		% change
Number of injuries	_____	_____
Number of injuries treated	_____	_____
Transported injuries		
Ambulance	_____	_____
Police	_____	_____
Private vehicle	_____	_____
Other, specify	_____	_____

Comments _____

_____

_____

- **PROTESTS**

Number of protests _____

Basis _____

- **EQUIPMENT**

_____

Form 8.8   Summary report format.

Publishing a list of expectations for conduct is not sufficient to cultivate adherence. Desirable behavior within the recreational sport environment is attainable if you establish specific objectives and strategies. We suggest several guidelines using the aforementioned categories.

Respect for Self

Research suggests that the ability to demonstrate respect for others is derived from respect for self. Because there is a positive correlation between positive feelings about one's body and self-respect, programs that seek improvement in posture and fitness are useful. When participants have opportunities to experience competence by mastering skills, they may develop greater self-esteem. Helping individuals develop a positive self-image provides a good foundation for program control.

Respect for Others

Thoughtfulness, courtesy, and consideration are attributes associated with respect for others. Care for others and sensitivity to their needs is a quality that any sport program should encourage. The etiquette associated with tennis or golf shows an attitude applicable to other sport and life situations. Sport participation has negative social consequences when participants dwell on the differences and peculiarities of others. Accentuate the positive by emphasizing the similarities between people. Demonstrate an ability to accept the different interests and sport skill levels of others.

Respect for Position

Positions of responsibility, including official, supervisor, officer, programmer, or volunteer, should command respect. When an individual in one of these roles fails to live up to expectations of participants, respect for the position diminishes.

Sport programmers hold a position of authority and need the respect of participants and fellow staff members to bring about control within the program. Abuse of authority jeopardizes the respect for the total operation. It is unprofessional when someone in authority extends special favors to friends or relatives.

Respect for Property

Respect for public or private property is characteristic of good program control. Such an attitude discourages theft and vandalism by emphasizing consideration for what others own. Disrespect for sport facilities, equipment, and supplies leads to increased repair and replacement costs and infringes on the right of others to use the resources.

Conservation is relevant to this discussion. How often do volunteers or employees waste or misuse resources? How often have softball field lights been turned on when there is insufficient interest to warrant their use? After using lights, do people forget and leave them on all night? Is equipment consistently lost or misplaced because of a poor checkout system or poor equipment inventory management?

Respect for Rules

The most significant aspect of control in sport programming, respect for rules, recognizes the necessity for specific criteria that govern the conduct of individuals, teams, and groups in sport. No one can play and enjoy sport without this structure. The more conscientiously participants observe the rules, the easier it is for them to focus on participation. Imagine what a basketball contest would be like without violations and fouls! The first action a group takes when participating in informal basketball is to establish ground rules, such as calling fouls, the number of baskets needed to win, and handling jump balls.

For most participants, specific regulations governing conduct are unnecessary. However, some individuals like to challenge the system and ignore or deliberately break the rules for personal gain.

Appropriate rules protect the welfare of all. Participants need to understand that they do not have the privilege of picking the rules they choose to follow. Although they have a right to propose changes when rules and regulations seem unjustified or inappropriate, they should respect and follow them until an objective review process changes them.

Respect for Law and Order

Law and order involve a judicial system that represents one of the oldest techniques of program control. Deviant behavior, such as assaulting an official or player, stealing, or selling drugs, is illegal and unacceptable in a sport program. Participants and personnel should know the procedures and penalties involved when a violation occurs. Prompt, decisive, and appropriate action by program personnel conveys a clear message; disrespect for law and order will not be tolerated.

Respect, consideration, and responsible behavior within a sport environment require cultivation. Reinforce volunteers, employees, participants, and spectators as they practice socially acceptable behavior. Principles that illustrate desirable behavior include

- considering the rights of others;
- contemplating the consequences of an action before committing it;
- being truthful and dependable;
- being fair and just, moral and ethical; and
- avoiding objectionable dress, speech, and gestures.

Other Practices for Control

Standards of behavior contribute to control within sport. The following categories describe other effective practices in establishing program control.

- **Personnel.**   A professional image among personnel in terms of dress and manner is essential. Participants have little respect for sloppy dress or rude behavior in staff members. The success of an individual depends on good personal habits: dress, grooming, and manners. All sport personnel should understand the purpose of program policies and rules. If they cannot explain them to participants or serve as proper role models, compliance suffers.

- **Policy and rules.**   Delete irrelevant rules from operational guidelines. Obsolete rules hamper the creation of a positive attitude among participants. Enforce the relevant policies consistently. Erratic enforcement results in program control problems. Participants should have the opportunity to take part in policy formulation and review based on their degree of maturity and responsibility.

- **Governance.**   All disciplinary action should be fair and consistent. When considering the punishment to impose after a rule violation, the level of maturity of the individual involved is more important than the age. Penalties too lax for an adult or too stringent for a child may perpetuate problems. Precedents furnish perspective in determining the severity of a penalty. As you consider what penalty to impose, prepare to justify your decision. Always provide an opportunity for appeal.

- **Programming.**   Provide opportunities for participation regardless of specific sport interest or skill level. Structure programs without bias or preferential treatment, and involve participants and personnel in the decision-making and evaluation process affecting program development.

Develop leadership characteristics in the staff that facilitate participant willingness to adhere to behavioral expectations. Among the desired characteristics are a professional image, interest in the participants and program, competence regarding program responsibilities, and an ability to create a challenging and interesting sport program.

In addition to these principles governing conduct, the following checklist describes recommended practices for dealing with problems:

Disciplinary Action Process

Although programmers understand that discipline problems exist and corrective action is often neces-

sary, some lack confidence in coping with them. Pages 206-207 provide a checklist for handling problem situations. The programmer should prepare for disciplinary problems by having a system in place for addressing them. We will now consider the foundations of a disciplinary action process and offer an example of implementation.

Checklist for Problem Situations

Though we all wish it weren't so, disciplinary actions are part of a recreational sport programmer's job. Let this checklist help you.

- Publicize rules for conduct early. By listing or explaining behavioral expectations in advance, through team captains' meetings, organizational meetings, and manuals, the participants and program personnel are aware of what is expected of them and the consequences of any infraction.

- Use suspension as a last resort. Think twice before ejecting a participant from the sport event or terminating personnel from the program. Do so only after exhausting every available alternative. Once you suspend a participant, employee, or volunteer from the program, he or she is usually lost forever.

- Don't overreact. Making every incident a crisis only lessens the respect for the programmer and creates more problems. Be careful that less significant incidents do not snowball.

- Discuss misbehavior, not the individual. The personality of the employee, volunteer, or participant should not be the issue in a disciplinary case. Disapprove of the misbehavior and not the person. Never label an individual as an instigator or troublemaker without giving him or her a chance to prove otherwise.

- Praise publicly, reprimand privately. Humiliating an individual in front of his or her peers is a poor method of handling discipline. If a reprimand is necessary, always respect the participant's feelings and avoid using ridicule or sarcastic comments.

- Be firm, fair, and friendly. Treat offenders as you would like to be treated. If you approach all situations in a positive, businesslike manner, you have already won half the battle. A poised demeanor is effective in problem situ-

ations, and a pleasant attitude is appreciated by others.

- Anticipate problems. By staying ahead of a situation, you can avoid many potential problems. Mentally review responsibilities and try to anticipate the unexpected.

- Don't pretend to know it all. The programmer will gain more respect by saying, "I don't know, let me look it up" than by pretending to be a walking encyclopedia. Participants realize that no one can know all sport rules and policies, so don't try to bluff your way through.

Due process is fundamental to American constitutional law. It is a concept that safeguards equality, fair treatment, and rights for all. Due process is delineated into two categories: substantive and procedural. Substantive due process involves program control, which includes the publication of rules and regulations, the specificity of regulations, and the authority of agency personnel to deal with disciplinary cases.

According to Forsythe (1977, 354), this process requires that the agency do the following:

1. Provide ample opportunity for all to know the standards and regulations they must follow.

2. Once there is evidence of a violation, furnish a complete description of the charges.

3. Allow time for the accused to prepare a defense.

4. Establish an appropriate hearing opportunity to consider arguments for and against the accused.

5. Make a fair and impartial decision, and put it in writing.

In addition to these procedures, include the rights to obtain a list of witnesses and copies of their statements before a hearing, have counsel at the hearing, hear all witnesses, present a case, remain silent, appeal (Alexander and Solomon, 1972), inspect in advance any written reports on the charges, and cross-examine all witnesses (Van Alstyne, 1970).

Although due process standards and theories have greater relevance to judicial settings, they apply to the sport environment. When a recreational sport disciplinary action system is based on a commitment to fair treatment, it parallels that of the judicial system, even though a programmer lacks the legal expertise.

Let's take an example of a process for handling situations that merit disciplinary action. We first present the steps involved in a disciplinary action, then provide detail about each step. Any approach to disciplinary action entails the following:

1. Identifying and reporting the problem
2. Investigating the cause
3. Deciding appropriate action
4. Providing an opportunity for appeal
5. Maintaining documentation

Identifying and Reporting the Problem

The first step in the discipline process begins with the source of a complaint. You cannot assume all complaints have equal validity because they often arise out of personal dislike or bias. Begin your review with an open mind. The assumption of innocence applies to the sport setting.

Once a situation warranting disciplinary action has occurred, verify the incident and obtain a detailed account of the alleged violation. Verification provides the foundation for subsequent investigation. Document all details on a complaint form or disciplinary action form.

Investigating the Cause

For any investigation, collect background information. If the accused is an employee, check into the length of employment, past performance ratings, similar complaints, previous evaluations, and comments from peers. If the accused is a participant, information regarding previous involvement in the program, reports from other institutional settings, or past disciplinary records may provide insight. In any case, we cannot overemphasize this principle: **To the investigator may flow much information; from the investigator flow a few carefully selected statements.**

If a situation involves a policy or rule violation, determine whether the violation was intentional and the extent to which external factors contributed to the problem. Was the policy specified in writing to the individual before the act? Did the individual violate a written or verbal rule? For example, it is not fair to penalize an individual for smoking in a nonsmoking section of the building when no sign is posted.

Enforce consistent policies and rules. Imposing a rule one day and ignoring it the next lessens its credibility and the disciplinary action that results. If the justification for a policy is only that it is office policy, its effectiveness suffers when the participant thinks it unreasonable.

Any investigation involves interviewing people familiar with the situation. Before interviewing the accused, a sensitive investigator determines what occurred by pursuing all accounts of an incident from participants, witnesses, and program personnel and records their statements for reference.

The first contact with the accused is an opportunity to review the case and uncover discrepancies. This interview routinely involves informing an individual of the complaint concerning the alleged behavior, and specifying the rights of due process. Most people cooperate when they are confident that due process is being followed.

Although you may settle most disciplinary situations during an initial interview, the accused should have every opportunity to explain his or her side of the story. If uncertainty exists after the initial meeting, conduct subsequent interviews to clarify specifics.

Deciding Appropriate Action

After completing all interviews, formulate an initial decision regarding the complaint. Before going public with a decision, evaluate your process of investigation. Have you gathered all the facts? Are there answers to questions, such as what happened; who was involved; why, when, and where did it happen; and who was in error? Prepare to substantiate the fairness of the investigation. Have all people, interests, and points of view been fairly represented? Have personal feelings, likes, dislikes, or biases influenced the decision?

Assuming the investigation indicates a need for disciplinary action, assess the severity of the situation before specifying a penalty. The penalty should match the violation. Some violations warrant harsh punishment. An incident involving an assault on a staff member is more serious than a forfeit of a scheduled contest. Punitive options progress from less serious to serious—probation through suspension to expulsion. Variations in severity exist within each type of penalty; probation does not prohibit the individual from continued involvement as an employee, volunteer, or participant, but indicates an incident is a matter of formal record, warning that future problems may lead to more severe disciplinary action.

Suspension entails a temporary loss of privileges, benefits, or affiliation with the program. Examples in this category include suspension from participation in a single intramural sport or all sports offered during a specified time span, temporary loss of facility use or financial support for a club sport, and reassignment from employment as a central facility manager to a gymnasium supervisor.

Reserve expulsion or termination for situations in which the severity of the incident requires total separation from the program. These involve violations of law or policy that jeopardize safety or security: the use of alcohol or illegal drugs, assault and battery, unauthorized absence from a supervisory assignment, theft, vandalism, or falsification of payroll.

Before selecting a penalty, consider the precedents. Review similar situations that have occurred in the past and impose a similar judgment. If precedents for a ruling do not exist with your program, contact other agencies for perspective. Regardless of the penalty, justify it to the individual to promote understanding for your action. Summarize the investigation and resulting disciplinary action in writing, forwarding a copy to the individual involved and maintaining another for your record.

Providing an Opportunity for Appeal

If an individual is dissatisfied with the decision or believes he or she received unfair treatment, provide an opportunity to appeal the decision to a peer group governing board or to an administrative staff member. A last recourse, the appeal process is valuable if there is error, bias, or skepticism regarding the initial decision. One is more inclined to accept the decision of one's peers than that of the staff. However, the appeal process can fail if those involved are not committed to a fair, objective review. Let's examine typical steps in the appeal process:

1. **Preparation.**   Provide a summary of the case and all pertinent reports for each member of the appeals board. Have separate presentations by the staff person involved with the case and the appellant. Before the board begins questioning, inform the appellant of the procedure that will be followed. The appellant should sign a statement indicating an understanding of the procedure and the rights guaranteed by the appeals process.

2. **Hearing.**   The appellant presents an account of the incident, followed by questioning by the board. A hearing conducted in a formal, yet unaccusative manner demonstrates a commitment by the board to completely examine the facts in the

case and give fair treatment. A board hearing is not a trial.

3. Deliberation. Once the interviews are complete, the board deliberates the case privately. When the board reaches a decision, it informs the appellant and the staff. Further appeal from this point on must be based on a violation of due process.

Maintaining Documentation

Throughout each phase of the disciplinary action, systematic collection of information is essential. The programmer needs to maintain thorough minutes of cases brought to appeals. Documentation provides information for historical reference and case studies for training new appeals groups.

Establishing an Appeals Board

Care in selecting and training members is essential for effective board operations. When reviewing applicants, identify those who have related experience regarding program operations. Design selection to guarantee representation for those who are affected by board decisions. Provide training to familiarize new members with purpose, standards, duties, and operating procedures. More specific guidelines for implementing a governing or appeals board follow.

Purpose of an Appeals Board

The purpose of a governing board is to ensure fair treatment and promote delivery of recreational sport programs to all those served by a setting. This responsibility includes adjudicating appeals and evaluating proposed program, policy, or rule changes.

Ethical Standards for Board Members

To preserve the professionalism and objectivity of the board, members must observe ethical standards. Violation of these standards may constitute just cause for removal from the board. It is the responsibility of each board member to observe the following principles:

- Information regarding a case is confidential.
- The record of any participant may not be disclosed outside the hearing.
- Members should never make statements unsupported by the facts.
  In all cases, the vote of each board member is confidential. The vote of the entire board, including majority and dissenting opinions,

is relayed to the appellant and recorded in the minutes of the hearing.

- Members of the board must uphold the regulations and policies of the recreational sport program.
- Members of the board who have a conflict of interest in a case must abstain from participating as a voting member of the board on that case. They may attend the hearing as an observer.

If a member of the board violates any policies or regulations, the board may discuss the incident with the member in a closed session to determine if the violation affects the credibility of the board. By a majority vote of the board and its chairperson, the following may result:

- The board issues the member a warning to indicate that any future violation of policies and regulations could result in removal from the board.
- The board removes the member. Members so removed will be ineligible for service on any board for a specified period.
- The board decides that the matter does not warrant further consideration and takes no action against the member in question.

Responsibilities of an Appeals Board

Members should understand the duties of each board position. These might be as listed below:

Board advisor (member of the area program staff)

- Coordinates selecting and training members
- Coordinates storing and filing all documentation
- Informs the appealing party of hearing procedures
- Informs members about all meetings
- Investigates or monitors recommendations

Board member

- Arrives on time for all scheduled meetings
- Anticipates absences and informs advisor ahead of time
- Assists with projects and committees
- Comes prepared for all meetings
- Participates in decision making

Project Management Software

Recreational sports programmers have turned to project management software to help them meet their program goals and deadlines. In many cases, project management software can be the key to successful planning and evaluation in sports management. Whether you are new to planning techniques or an experienced planner, project management software offers a versatile and flexible management tool which can make you a more effective manager and help you set program goals, track sports projects, and manage the people, resources, and decisions necessary to reach your goals.

A *project* is simply a group of tasks, activities, or events with defined start and stop dates. Project management software provides you with the visual tools and techniques for creating, scheduling, and controlling project plans; for communicating these plans to your staff; and for making necessary changes as they occur. Project management programs allow staff or project managers to easily view and understand their roles in the planning process.

Microsoft Project is an easy-to-use planning software package available for the Windows and the Macintosh operating systems. It has been designed to guide new users or project managers through the various phases of project planning by using familiar steps associated with the traditional planning process. *Microsoft Project* begins by allowing you to create a schedule that lists specific tasks that must be accomplished to complete the project, the approximate order in which the tasks will occur, and how long each task

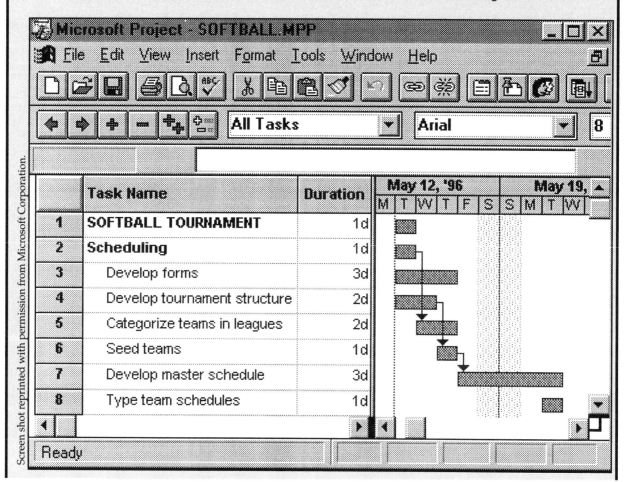

Screen shot reprinted with permission from Microsoft Corporation.

should take to complete. Tasks may be added, deleted, or modified as the project proceeds.

All project tasks are then organized by groupings and linked in sequence to create task relationships, which allow you to see how long it will take to finish the entire project. For example, some tasks may need to be finished before certain other tasks can begin, while there may be still other tasks that can be completed simultaneously. These differences in timing will affect the total time required to complete the project. Staff and equipment resources will also need to be assigned to all of the tasks once they are appropriately grouped and once they are placed in the proper sequence.

Project management software allows you to communicate and track project status and information clearly and effectively in a variety of ways. The following screen is a GANTT chart that illustrates tasks or groups of tasks involved in planning a softball tournament. The chart also shows a visual representation of when each task should be completed.

In addition to GANTT charts, most software programs will print PERT charts, reports, job assignments, equipment resources summaries, budgets, and other schedules.

In the very near future, project management software will become a fundamental and basic tool used by recreational sport programmers in planning event schedules, assigning staff and equipment resources, and tracking the progress of a number of events.

Microsoft Project, Microsoft, Redmond, WA.

Other project management software products: CA-SuperProject, Project Scheduler, Time Line, Fast Track Schedule, SureTrak, and Manage Pro.

Board secretary

- Maintains minutes
- Records motions and the name of the member presenting or seconding a motion
- Submits minutes to the board advisor
- Prepares written statements of board rulings for program staff and the chairperson

Chairperson

- Has command of *Robert's Rules of Parliamentary Procedure*
- Handles opening comments and introductions
- Facilitates discussion and maintains order
- Reminds members of operating procedure
- Helps the advisor organize agenda and material
- Announces results of deliberations to the parties involved
- Appoints an acting secretary when necessary
- Assists with an evaluation of the board's performance

Operating Procedures for an Appeals Board

The board chairperson ensures the efficient operation of the board. Before a hearing, the chairperson reviews reports with other members to delete irrelevant material and identify questions. When the board is ready, the chairperson introduces the appellant to the board and outlines the procedures for the hearing. Once the board begins its questioning, the chairperson is responsible for maintaining its professionalism and objectivity.

The chairperson discourages emotional outbursts among board members and witnesses. When board members are adequately trained, the task is not a difficult one. A seating arrangement that places the appellant in view of the board members and locates witnesses away from the board helps maintain order. This ensures that responses to questions are addressed to the board and not to spectators. Outbursts by spectators cannot be tolerated. Remove persons from the room who do not comply with protocol.

Normally, the chair does not participate in debate when sitting as a meeting facilitator. In the case when the chair wishes to join in a debate, a temporary chair should preside until the discussion is completed.

During deliberations, the chairperson has a responsibility to see that each member of the board reaches an independent decision. The chairperson may not vote unless there is a tie or the board decides to vote by secret ballot, and the chair informs the board of an intent to vote. The chair may also elect not to vote on a tie, thereby causing a motion to fail. The advantage of a multiple member board

Shining Example

Recreational Sports Center of Miami University, Oxford, Ohio 45056

Miami University is a state-assisted university located in southwestern Ohio. The Recreational Sports Center at Miami University opened in September of 1994. The functional planning of the facility is efficiently organized around a central lobby and single central entry on an upper level. A 4,000 square-foot entry concourse invites users in to the building from both north and south entry pavilions. A four-court multi-sport gymnasium, a climbing wall, two exercise/performance rooms, two racquetball courts, a 10,000 square-foot weight training/fitness area, and an 1/8th mile-four lane suspended jogging track are all organized around a two-story atrium lounge and health bar/deli/games area. A world-class Aquatic Center contains a 50 meter × 25 year competitive pool and diving well, while a separate leisure natatorium provides a leisure pool that includes warm-water play areas with shallow zero-beach entry, a current channel, an aerobic instruction area, a waterfall and a 16-person spa overlooking the natatorium and outdoor patio. A Center for Outdoor Pursuits is located between the 35-foot-high rock climbing wall and a dedicated customer-service entry to the south where users can check out kayaks, bicycles, and a variety of equipment for camping, climbing, and other outdoor activities.

Organization: Use of the Recreational Sports Center is organized around the following order or priorities:

- Informal, walk-in recreation by Miami University students, other members, and guests
- Organized recreational sports programs
- Physical Education, Health, and Sport studies credit classes
- Intercollegiate Athletic Swimming/Diving programs

- Special Events organized by University groups (student organizations, university departments, faculty groups, etc.)
- Miami University alumni, Oxford community organizations, and other non-university-affiliated group use.

Clientele: The Miami University Recreational Sports Center is a student-oriented facility designed and programmed to meet the diverse fitness, sports, and lifestyle management needs of Miami students, other members and guests.

Budget: The center is largely financed and primarily staffed by Miami students. Bonds were sold to finance the construction costs. The debt retirement on these bonds as well as facility operational costs are funded from mandatory General Fees assessed to every student.

is to present differing perspectives. Board members should voice dissenting opinions and ask for explanations when they disagree with other members. Both the majority and dissenting opinions require documentation for future reference.

ADA Suggestions

With the implementation of the ADA, *modified* participation in our recreational sport programs for individuals with disabilities must now be their choice, no longer a replacement because of poorly designed recreational sport facilities. Proper design accommodations for disabled participants will make sport facilities more accessible, safer, and enjoyable for all participants. Suggested improvements brought about by the ADA will have a positive impact on safety of the sport facility, as ramps are installed, lighting levels increased, and corridors widened.

CONCLUSION

Programmers often just go through the motions of planning and evaluation. Those who combine the technical knowledge of these tools with an understanding of why and how to use them can provide meaningful experiences for participants and personnel. Successful management begins with understanding the needs of the constituency and continues with selecting appropriate forms of involvement, implementing them efficiently, evaluating the outcomes properly, and applying the findings to future endeavors.

Program control is essential in operating a successful sport program regardless of size, location, or environment. Effective program control begins with personnel at the operational level. Confidence, courtesy, knowledge, and assertiveness are essential when program personnel communicate with participants. Other practices that foster a better relationship between participants, spectators, and personnel involve improvements in program design and delivery and effective governance. When we promote constructive behavior, control undesirable conduct, and apply appropriate disciplinary measures, we create an attractive work and play environment.

DISCUSSION QUESTIONS

1. What do we mean by program planning in recreational sport?

2. Do you think a recreational sport event can ever be overplanned?

3. What do we mean by the term *demographic characteristics*?

4. To what degree should you impose your value system on program planning and participants? Cite an example.

5. Discuss the differences between long-range planning and strategic planning.

6. Describe the principles of the planning blueprint.

7. List the components of an assessment.

8. Discuss the methods available to conduct an assessment.

9. What is the difference between program objectives and performance objectives?

10. List and explain the types of plans in recreational sport programs.

11. Are planning and evaluation a continuing process? Explain your answer.

12. Describe typical data collection techniques you can use in evaluating recreational sport programs.

13. What do we mean by the term *operational forms*? Describe several examples of these forms.

14. Why would participant head count totals be valuable in evaluating your program?

15. What is the difference between a goal, an objective, and a strategy?

APPLICATION EXERCISE

You have been given the assignment to develop a 24-hour recreational sport extravaganza for your department. Sequentially outline your planning blueprint for developing this special event. Cite examples that you would implement during each step.

REFERENCES

Baletka, M. 1989. Planning a weight training/conditioning facility. *National Intramural-Recreational Sports Association Journal* 14 (1): 26-28.

Chesnutt, J.T., N. Kovac, and W. Taylor. 1986. An examination of evaluation procedures utilized by recreational sports programs. P. 9-18 in *Growth and development in recreational sports*. Corvallis, OR: National Intramural-Recreational Sports Association.

Combes, M., and C. Swart. 1988. Preparation days: From ground breaking to opening. P. 19-38 in *Selected readings in recreational sports*. Corvallis, OR: National Intramural-Recreational Sports Association.

Karabetsos, J.D. 1991. Campus recreation—Future direction. *National Intramural-Recreational Sports Association Journal* 15 (2): 10.

Parsons, T.W. 1989. Recruitment, retention, and recreation. *National Intramural-Recreational Sports Association Conference Journal* 13 (3): 59-60.

Parsons, T.W. 1990. Value-added: Research in recreational sports. *National Intramural-Recreational Sports Association Journal* 15 (1): 20.

SUGGESTED READINGS

Chestnutt, J.T., P.J. Nadeau, and W. Taylor. 1985. An analysis of nonparticipation in campus recreational sports activities. P. 93-101 in *1985 National Intramural-Recreational Sports Association conference proceedings*. Corvallis, OR: National Intramural-Recreational Sports Association.

Chestnutt, J.T., and R.L. Haney. 1984. Preferences, satisfactions, and use patterns of campus recreational sports participants. P. 191-201 in *1984 National Intramural-Recreational Sports Association conference proceedings*. Corvallis, OR: National Intramural-Recreational Sports Association.

Espinosa, C.E. 1990. Planning and constructing a sand volleyball court. P. 51-60 in *Management strategies in recreational sports*. Corvallis, OR: National Intramural-Recreational Sports Association.

Haderlie, B.M. 1987. Influences of campus recreation programs and facilities on student recruitment and retention. *National Intramural-Recreational Sports Association Conference Journal* 11 (3): 24-27.

Huggins, E.B., and S.L. Hunt. 1987. Intramural programs or interscholastic sports in the junior high schools: An assessment of the attitudes of principals in Kentucky. *National Intramural-Recreational Sports Association Journal* 11 (2): 38-43.

Hupp, S.L., and N.E. Rinaldi. 1991. Evaluate intramural programs by student satisfaction. *National Intramural-Recreational Sports Association Journal* 15 (2): 50.

Keeny, B.A. 1995. The IHRSA design forum. *Club Business International* 16 (2): 34-47.

Kuga, D.J., and D.L. Pastore. 1991. Assisting high school intramural program with self-evaluation: A survey. *National Intramural-Recreational Sports Association Journal* 15 (3): 41.

Russek, R., and J. Maland. 1995. Skating to profitability. *Athletic Business* 19 (1): 43-49.

Schmid, S. 1994. Helping hands. *Athletic Management* 18 (12): 20.

Wiles, C. 1994. Join the club. *Athletic Management* 6 (4): 29-34.

CHAPTER 9

Personnel

Chapter Objectives

After reading this chapter you will

- identify the levels of personnel in sport management,
- identify personnel functions in sport administration,
- understand customer service as it relates to personnel training, and
- understand the issues involved in volunteer staffing.

The number of people involved in providing recreational services is staggering. Over 5 million full- or part-time positions exist for recreational services; the manufacture, distribution, sales, and repair of recreational goods; and the construction of recreational facilities. Although no data exist to describe the total number of recreational sport programs requiring personnel supervision, it has been stated that physical activity programs, including recreational sport staffing, exceed other types of recreation programs. The unique focuses of recreational sport management require that those employed in the field meet exacting standards.

Program variety requires specialization of personnel. A total recreation program is often divided into social, cultural, and sport areas, and personnel participate in delivering each recreational program. Although similar in function, positions will vary depending on the nature and size of the program and the number of facilities. The larger the recreation program, the greater the number and specialization into administrative and program positions.

There is variance in the numbers and types of responsibilities and in the systems used for classifying positions within a recreational sport program. Some programs classify positions according to the size of the agency or business, and others classify them by function or location. In some agencies there is a significant overlap in roles; one may serve such diverse functions as a coach, official, programmer, and facility manager.

This chapter provides material on typical staffing levels within recreational sport agencies and businesses, then a section on hiring personnel, followed by a personnel management section, and a closing section on the unique aspects of volunteerism.

RECREATIONAL SPORT STAFFING LEVELS

The first portion of this chapter describes the types of recreational sport personnel found within the many settings available. These individual levels house staff who qualify to provide recreational sport programs in all divisions that are sensitive to various skill levels and appropriateness, various sport formats, diversity of sport interest, and organizational structure.

Level I Auxiliary Staff

Personnel in this category may hold hourly wage, volunteer, or intern-trainee positions. They are directly involved in relationships with participants, through delivery of either program activities or facilities.

Examples of auxiliary staff positions include officials, lifeguards, coaches, organization officers and managers, equipment attendants, ticket takers, desk attendants, intramural sport supervisors, club sport officers, informal sport supervisors, playground supervisors, and program aides. Intern-trainees, unlike hourly wage or volunteer personnel, serve the agency while learning or performing field work for academic credit as part of professional preparation for a career within recreational sport. Auxiliary staff positions may be seasonal, full time, or part time.

Level II Program Staff

This is an entry-level position responsible for direct contact with participants and delivering services in the form of programs, facilities, or areas. Specific functions include organizing and directing indoor or outdoor sport activities; monitoring facility operations; handling equipment use, purchasing, and inventory; initiating publicity and effective public relations; providing participant and personnel recognition; monitoring operating budget; recruiting, hiring, training, and scheduling support staff; monitoring adherence to agency rules and policies; implementing safety policies, participant control; maintaining program and facility records and evaluations; and preparing statistical or analytical reports of operations. These specialized functions may provide full-time professional employment opportunities in larger operations.

Level III Program Administrative Staff

Personnel at this level direct administrative policies, guidelines, and resources and monitor programs, facilities, and program staff. Functioning in a middle-management capacity, staff members help plan policies and procedures; prepare budget proposals and annual reports; serve as administrative assistants; monitor personnel practices; supervise program and facility expenditures and fee collections; participate in long-range planning; receive and review requests and reports from subordinates; coordinate the distribution of resources (facilities, personnel, equipment); serve as a liaison between the top administrator and subordinate employees; and participate in providing staff development programs. Positions of this nature are usually full-time professional staff positions.

Level IV Administrative Staff

The administrator is responsible for directing the operation of the recreational sport program and its resources. Customary functions include planning, approving, and supervising a diverse program of activities and services; developing personnel standards and procedures; supervising the staff development program; directing or influencing the planning, acquisition, design, construction, and maintenance of facilities; developing policies for use of resources; initiating planning, assessment, and evaluation studies; preparing, presenting, and monitoring annual budgets; maintaining positive relations; interpreting to the public the philosophy and programs of the agency; and maintaining accurate records of the total operation in terms of personnel, funding, facilities, and equipment. These responsibilities typically require a full-time employee in all settings and embody the only professional staff position in most small programs.

Other positions involve line functions not requiring sport-specific training, such as budget officer, personnel officer, marketing director, clerical technician, and receptionist.

Typically, modern organizations have streamlined employment levels in favor of being responsive to participants. This restructuring has eliminated the middle manager and empowered the entry level specialist, causing higher efficiency. See figure 9.1 for an example of a typical recreational sport organization chart.

HIRING PERSONNEL

Because the quality of personnel directly influences the quality of the program, the programmer must concentrate on ways to attract and retain outstanding individuals, integrating them into the program, using their abilities, and supporting their development. We will discuss several functions the recreational sport programmer performs or oversees in the hiring process.

Developing Job Descriptions and Recruiting Personnel

Personnel management begins with developing clear, concise job descriptions that reflect the responsibilities of each position, serve as a frame of reference during the personnel selection and training process, and help resolve differences of opinion regarding responsibilities. The job description may assist in gauging personnel performance.

Recruitment is a process for securing quality personnel. Based on an understanding of current personnel strengths and weaknesses, expected turnover, position responsibilities, and requirements, recruitment involves preparing position announcements and advertisements. An effective job announcement provides essential information about the position that attracts qualified candidates and deters those whose interests and abilities do not meet the requirements. A typical format the National Recreation and Park Association uses is shown in figure 9.2.

Personnel selection occurs through two channels—internal and external. Qualified individuals may already work in some internal capacity. Post job announcements where personnel within the agency can learn of opportunities, make announcements at meetings, and invite referrals. Consider the following recruitment methods through external channels:

- Notices in newsletters, newspapers, and brochures
- Public service announcements on radio and television
- Mailings to employment agencies, placement centers, colleges and high schools, and colleagues in other recreational sport agencies
- Cooperative job referral with other recreational sport agencies

Figure 9.1
Recreational Sport Organization Chart

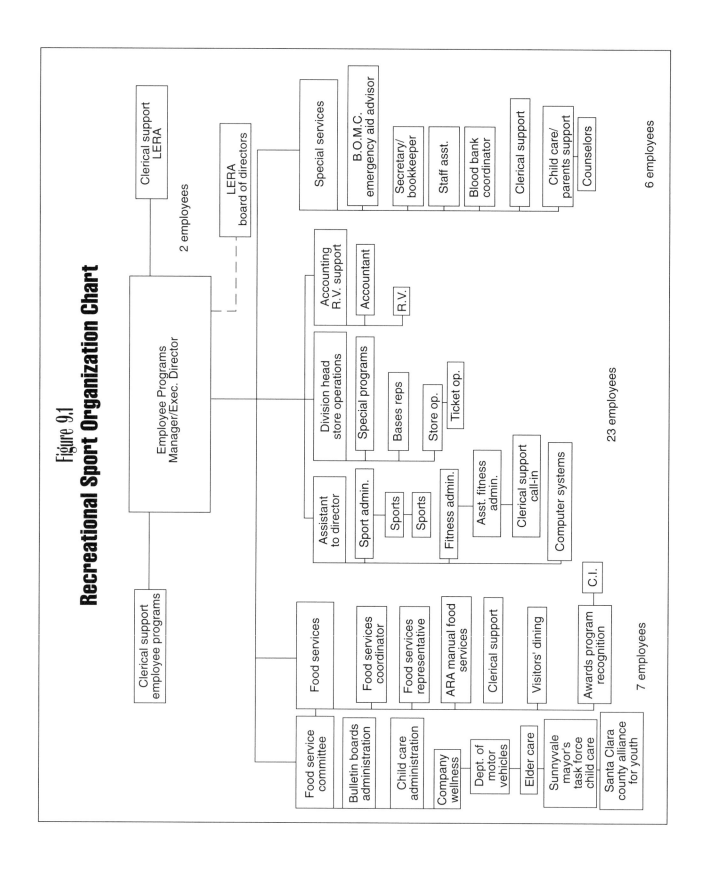

Figure 9.2
Job Classification Format

IDENTIFICATION OF AGENCY
(Mailing address) (telephone number)

CLASS OF POSITION TITLE
Should be descriptive of the job

SUMMARY
Statement of major duties

SUPERVISOR
To whom and for whom individual is responsible

**EXAMPLES
OF DUTIES AND RESPONSIBILITIES**
An indication of the important tasks within the position, broad enough to include anticipated supplemental assignments

QUALIFICATIONS
Required knowledge, skills, and abilities

SPECIAL REQUIREMENTS
Technical or professional certification

EDUCATION AND EXPERIENCE
Required education, training, and experience

SALARY RANGE

**CLOSING DATE FOR RECEIPT
OF APPLICATIONS**

CONTACT
Full name, title, agency, and address for submitting applications

---

To learn the qualifications of candidates, develop and use a job application form. Form 9.1 is an example of an application form.

After the deadline for applications, conduct a preliminary review to screen out unqualified applicants and group others by an estimate of potential.

Upon rating applicants on education, experience, and references, select a number for interviews. Check references after an interview to compare your assessment of the applicant with those of the references.

Finally, rank the applicants. One way to accomplish this involves assigning a point value to each qualification you are evaluating. The point total each applicant receives determines a placement among eligible candidates.

Interviewing

The personal interview is the critical factor in personnel review and selection. It affords both the interviewer and applicant an opportunity to determine compatibility and potential for a successful working relationship. Use the interview wisely to discover as much as possible about the personality of applicants and the images they project. A predetermined outline of the interview session affords optimum use of your time.

Hold the interview in a private, comfortable setting free from interruption. Put the applicant at ease by being attentive and congenial. Begin by having the candidate describe experiences or comment on the aspects of the position that are most appealing. If a description on the application form is novel or interesting, discuss it to break the ice. Balance direct questions with ones that are more open ended. Use case studies to examine a candidate's knowledge or experience in-depth. This technique encourages an unrehearsed response to a hypothetical situation.

Other items to explore during the interview include the following:

- **Motivation for seeking the position.** Is it compatible with the needs of the agency?
- **Position job description.** Does the candidate have a grasp of requirements? Does the person seem enthusiastic to join the agency given the job requirements and conditions?
- **Education, preparation, experience, or background.** Does the candidate have the necessary credentials? What orientation and in-service training may be required? What contributions can the candidate make to the position or agency?
- **Expectations of the immediate supervisor or the job.** Are they realistic? Will the candidate require close supervision or extensive consultation? How might the person respond to constructive criticism?
- **Interest in the position.** How long does the candidate envision staying? Does the individual desire upward mobility? How many hours per week is he or she willing to work? When is it possible to begin?

RECREATIONAL SPORT PERSONNEL APPLICATION FORM

Last name   First   Initial   Date   Year

Address   Phone

City   State   Zip code

• POSITION DESIRED

Place in rank order with 1 representing first preference.

_____ Coach   _____ Lifeguard   Other _____

_____ Instructor   _____ Official

_____ Labor crew   _____ Supervisor   Other _____

Place the proper number beside the sport that corresponds with your interest or ability to

1 = Lead   2 = Instruct   3 = Coach   4 = Officiate or judge   5 = Supervise

_____ Aerobic dance	_____ Fencing	_____ Karate	_____ Swimming
_____ Archery	_____ Fishing	_____ Lifesaving	_____ Table tennis
_____ Badminton	_____ Football	_____ Racquetball	_____ Tennis
_____ Baseball	_____ Golf	_____ Rifle	_____ Track
_____ Basketball	_____ Gymnastics	_____ Roller skating	_____ Volleyball
_____ Bowling	_____ Handball	_____ Sailing	_____ Water polo
_____ Bridge	_____ Horseback riding	_____ Scuba diving	_____ Water skiing
_____ Canoeing	_____ Ice hockey	_____ Skiing	_____ Weight lifting
_____ Chess	_____ Ice skating	_____ Soccer	
_____ Diving	_____ Judo	_____ Softball	

• EMPLOYMENT HISTORY

From   Employer and location   Supervisor
_____ To _____

From   Employer and location   Supervisor
_____ To _____

From   Employer and location   Supervisor
_____ To _____

• RELATED EXPERIENCE OR CERTIFICATION

_____

_____

_____

_____

• PERSONAL REFERENCES

_____ (__) _____
Name   Address   Phone

_____ (__) _____
Name   Address   Phone

(Continued)

Form 9.1   Personnel application form.

- **RECREATIONAL SPORT BACKGROUND**

List special interests, hobbies, sport activities, and so forth.

_____

_____

- **SCHEDULE OF AVAILABILITY**

	Monday	Tuesday	Wednesday	Thursday	Friday	Saturday	Sunday
Morning							
Afternoon							
Evening							

- **COMMENTS**

_____

_____

_____

_____

_____

_____

_____

_____

_____

_____

_____

Signature _____   Date available _____

Form 9.1 _(Continued)_

- **Interpersonal relations skills.**   Will the candidate relate well to others? How will others perceive him or her? Does the candidate possess acceptable communications and listening skills? Can the individual handle interpersonal relations problems appropriately?
- **Public relations image.**   Is the candidate well groomed? Does he or she show an interest in serving others or being served?

Questions that you _may not_ use in employment inquiries, application forms, and interviews, _unless their use is job related and nondiscriminatory in effect_ include the following:

- Race
- National origin
- Religion
- Education
- Arrest and conviction records
- Credit rating
- Gender, marital and family status
- Physical disabilities
- Experience requirements
- Age
- Relatives
- Appearance (photo)

Advice regarding civil rights, discriminatory practices, and equal opportunity employment guidelines is available from personnel managers, municipal officers, and lawyers.

Personal interviews are very helpful when used to determine whether a potential employee is a match within the agency.

Testing

When considering candidates who must lead an activity or perform skills as an exercise leader, official, or lifeguard, tryouts or other testing procedures often supplement the interview. The results provide a better indication of the skills, knowledge, and leadership ability necessary than the interview alone. Such tests take place before qualified judges who rate each individual on a standardized form (see form 9.2).

Checking References

An excellent resource for candidate assessment is a reference. Reference checks may save time in such aspects of personnel management as orientation, in-service training, and consultation.

References supplied by the applicant tend to accentuate the positive. When speaking with a recommendation source, emphasize the importance of knowing as much about a candidate as possible to ensure compatibility. If a reference relates a significant concern, check it out with a different one before reaching a conclusion. Reference checks made by phone reveal more than written ones because the phone provides an opportunity to discern tone, inflection, and conviction. In addition, you can control the content of the discussion.

Selecting Personnel

Comparing qualifications leads to a selection decision. If it is difficult to choose between two or more applicants, conduct additional interviews. When it is not possible to find a position for an extremely qualified applicant, refer him or her to a colleague at another agency. Placing people in positions for which they are overqualified may result in discontent later.

At some point during the interview, inform each applicant of the decision date for selection. If time or circumstances make it difficult to inform unsuccessful candidates, post a list of the successful ones, expressing appreciation for the interest shown in the program. Retain all applications for future reference. When an unexpected vacancy occurs, an on-call file may be useful.

MANAGING PERSONNEL

Effective personnel management requires knowledge of regulations, an understanding of the human factor in all organizations, and systems to assist the smooth operation of a program. Although staffing levels differ with the type of organizational structure (i.e., a public versus a private enterprise), similar functions exist throughout all organizations.

Personnel Policies

Personnel policies govern on-the-job performance. They specify expectations, accepted ways of carrying out duties and responsibilities, compensation and benefits, rules of conduct, disciplinary action and grievance procedures, evaluation duties, and other topics about the program and setting. Although the programmer at the operational level usually does not establish these policies, he or she interprets and enforces them. Publish all personnel policies and procedures in an administrative manual. Figure 9.3 lists the possible topics included in such a manual.

Probationary Periods

A period usually exists when a person is on a temporary work status until an initial evaluation and review can take place. After this period, the employee is on more permanent status. This period can benefit both employee and employer.

Orientation

Adequate preparation of personnel increases the likelihood for quality job performance and satisfaction. The order of presentation, number of sessions, and type of orientation (individual or group) is at the programmer's discretion. The following topics are appropriate for personnel orientation after providing routine information about payroll, withholding tax procedures, and time sheets:

- Introduction of each person participating in the orientation session
- Overview of the agency
- Flowchart of line and staff responsibilities
- Orientation to the setting and nature of the participants
- Introduction to coworkers and other frequent contacts relating to the position
- Review of a personnel manual containing agency policies and procedures affecting personnel, position, job description, and sample forms commonly used
- Tour of the facilities or area in which the individual will work
- Question-answer period

FITNESS ACTIVITY LEADER TRYOUT

Date _____

Individual's name _____

Judge's name (optional) _____

Please rank in order your answers on a scale of 0 to 10 with 10 being excellent and 0 being very poor. Use area next to question to provide any comments you feel are necessary. (Please be as specific as possible.)

	Rank	Comments
A. General		
1. Good role model		
2. Poise, self-assurance		
3. Strong leadership characteristics		
4. Pleasant personality		
5. Motivating, encouraging		
B. Exercise selection		
1. Variety, nonrepetitious		
2. Safe and beneficial exercises		
3. Proper from and technique of movement		
4. Original or unique exercises		
5. Equal number of exercises on each side of body		
C. Music selection		
1. Variety of music selections		
2. Motivating, fun		
3. Compatible with exercises done		
4. Smooth music transition between songs		
D. Routines		
1. Easy to follow		
2. Catchy routines, fun		
3. Original or creative movements		
4. Smooth transition between moves		
E. Voice quality and presentation		
1. Projects clearly		
2. Pleasant voice		
3. Explains movements clearly		
F. Rhythm		
1. Stays with beat of music		
2. Moves well, smoothly		
3. Apparent knowledge of music and dance		
4. Easy to follow and copy movements		

Total _____

Average _____

Form 9.2 Standardized testing form.

Figure 9.3
Personnel Manual Table of Contents

Introduction ....

Recreational Sport Flowchart and Staff ....

Recreational Sport Overview ....

Employment Procedures ....

Policies ....
- Probation ....
- Communication ....
- Substitution ....
- Dress and Appearance ....
- Training and Certification ....
- Evaluation ....
- Conduct ....
- Dismissal ....
  - Temporary Leave ....
  - Resignation ....
  - Reinstatement ....
- Grievance ....
- Promotions ....
- Pay Rate Criteria ....
- Benefits ....
- Scheduling ....
- Fees and Charges ....

Procedures ....
- Payroll ....
- Time Clock and Time Sheets ....
- Accident and Emergency ....
- Security ....
- Fee Collection ....
- Support Services ....
- Disciplinary Action ....

Job Descriptions ....

Employee Recognition ....

Emergency Phone List ....

Staff Directory ....

A checklist is a practical way to keep track of what you need to discuss with probationary personnel (form 9.3 is an example).

If many people need orientation, and coordinating schedules for a group session is impossible, videotape portions of the orientation for small group or individual review. Maintain an opportunity for a staff-directed question and answer period following the review of the videotape.

Training and Continuing Education

This personnel practice covers in-service training for new and senior personnel and may involve some of the following aspects:

- **Apprenticeships.** Schedule the new employee or volunteer to work with an experienced person before going it alone. Place the newcomer with the best role model available.
- **Clinics.** Clinics enhance learning through observation and participation. Use them to illustrate such tasks as officiating techniques and mechanics, equipment use, lifeguard rescue skills, and maintenance.
- **Meetings.** Use personnel meetings, scheduled regularly (weekly, monthly), to disseminate information, review concerns, and obtain feedback. Do not schedule them out of habit. Special meetings may focus on a particular job responsibility.
- **Workshops.** Workshops afford an opportunity to treat topics of concern in more depth and are useful to encourage personnel involvement. They may focus on job preparation, assertiveness training, conflict resolution, communication and listening skills, problem solving, racism, and community relations.
- **Retreats.** Retreats provide a series of workshops over several days in a nonwork setting. Usually reserved for personnel holding positions of responsibility and complex jobs, retreats are a beneficial way to build camaraderie and improve job performance.
- **Individual sessions.** Personnel should receive regular observation and feedback sessions to reinforce strengths and eliminate weaknesses. Encourage them to reflect on the program and their needs.
- **Short courses.** Short courses focus on a skill or topic over an extended time. Attendance may be voluntary or mandatory, depending on importance to job performance. Topics include first aid, sport skill instruction, alcoholism and drug abuse, sexism and racism, spectatorship, personnel and the police, conflict resolution, and accident and injury prevention. In-service training programs help eliminate future problems when their content relates to the knowledge and skills needed on the job. They also contribute to confidence and stimulate interest in the job.

ORIENTATION CHECKLIST

Name _____   Position _____

• INTRODUCTIONS

<u>Date</u>

	Immediate supervisor
	Fellow workers

• PAYROLL

<u>Date</u>

	Pay rate
	Pay periods
	Paycheck
	Tax forms
	Time sheets

• POSITION INFORMATION

<u>Date</u>

	Job description
	Job expectations and standards
	Agency policies and procedures
	Securing supplies and equipment
	Uniform—special attire
	Certification(s) obtained

• WORK SCHEDULE

<u>Date</u>

	Schedule of availability
	Minimum-maximum hours
	Overtime
	Breaks
	Substitutions
	Meals

• BENEFITS

<u>Date</u>

	Discounts
	Holidays
	Sick leave
	Insurance
	Time off

• MISCELLANEOUS

<u>Date</u>

	Appearance—image
	Parking
	Lockers
	Meetings

Form 9.3   Personnel orientation checklist.

• **Continuing education.** Depending on an organization's policy, staff development may take the form of financial support for travel, career-specific courses, and sometimes degree and certificate attainment. Although some differences exist among positions, there are principal duties common to all positions (risk management, physical plant documentation, customer service, and agency-specific expectations). Training sessions allow personnel to adequately handle these duties and emphasize the importance of consistency in performance.

Scheduling

There are two approaches to personnel scheduling: short term or long term. Variables affecting scheduling decisions include nature of the position, number of personnel for the position, strengths or

PERSONNEL AVAILABILITY WORKSHEET
(Circle your shift availability.)

Month _____ Year _____

Sunday	Monday	Tuesday	Wednesday	Thursday	Friday	Saturday
E M L	E or L	E or L	E or L	E or L	E or L	E M L
E M L	E or L	E or L	E or L	E or L	E or L	E M L
E M L	E or L	E or L	E or L	E or L	E or L	E M L
E M L	E or L	E or L	E or L	E or L	E or L	E M L
E M L	E or L	E or L	E or L	E or L	E or L	E M L

E = Early shift   M = Middle shift   L = Late shift

Form 9.4   Personnel availability worksheet.

specializations required of personnel, availability of personnel, and number of personnel needed to cover a responsibility. Once job conditions and personnel qualifications and availability are consistent, consider the long-term, or *contract* method of scheduling. This system establishes work schedules for a specified time span (month, quarter, semester, six weeks, eight weeks).

Personnel may work certain days, shifts, facilities, or positions in any combination. It's a good practice to have each staff member complete an availability worksheet before each scheduling period (see form 9.4 for an example). Some personnel prefer a schedule involving the same slot weekly because it allows them to arrange other activities around their employment or volunteer service. For the programmer, consistency reduces confusion and leads to increased productivity for personnel who work the same shift. As these individuals become familiar with situations and participants, they can provide reliable observations regarding their experiences. However, anticipate the problems of complacency and boredom by providing personnel with needed changes of pace.

You can accomplish personnel scheduling in two ways. Either the programmer collects schedules of availability from each eligible person and does the scheduling, or the volunteers or employees sign up individually for the days and shifts they prefer working. We recommend the latter approach when all personnel can handle the job requirements adequately. When you complete the schedule, draw

up an agreement, retain one copy, and give another to the employee or volunteer (see figure 9.4).

Limiting the number of hours each person may take prevents the few from taking all the hours. Another way to provide incentive and structure is to permit personnel with seniority the first opportunity to select preferred slots. Such an approach has a better chance for success when each person maintains a favorable performance record. An example of a seniority system contract is shown in figure 9.5.

If a program or function involves a large workforce or varying proficiency levels, such as intramural basketball tournament officiating, you need the flexibility of a short-term scheduling procedure. Programmers who schedule personnel on a short-term basis often specify a deadline for submitting availability information. After this point, several scheduling options are possible.

Programmers may prepare schedules on an individual notice slip (form 9.5) and issue them on a certain date. They handle and confirm adjustments in staff scheduling individually. This method is effective when you need close quality control, you have few personnel, or personnel availability is sporadic and diverse. Because a staff member handles this task individually, it may require much time and effort. If you need to mail schedules or use special forms the process is more expensive.

Another alternative is that programmers prepare schedules in advance and post them at a regular time (as shown in figure 9.6). If individuals can work as scheduled, they circle their names or put

---

Figure 9.4
Supervisor Contract Scheduling Form

The Division of Recreational Sport and _Beth Coleman_, a sport supervisor employed by the Division of Recreational Sport, hereby enter into the following agreement. The said supervisor agrees to be present and supervise the following _flag football_ games to be played on the agreed dates and times during the said activity season.

	Dates	Times
1.	September 14	5:00-8:00
2.	September 15	8:00-11:00
3.	September 21	8:00-11:00
4.	September 22	5:00-8:00
5.	September 23	5:00-8:00
6.	September 28	5:00-8:00
7.	September 29	8:00-11:00
8.	October 1	5:00-8:00
9.	October 4	8:00-11:00
10.		

It is agreed that the Division of Recreational Sport will pay the sport supervisor so mentioned for fulfilling his or her obligations in supervising the games listed.

Signed this _5th_ day of _September_.

X _____
  Supervisor

X _____
  Coordinator of supervisors

---

an _X_ on their names. The staff person has the option of rescheduling the vacancies, leaving them open for personnel to sign up on their own, or both. Although this method still requires initial staff work, it permits an opportunity to work additional hours. The staff reschedules any unfilled slots.

Another option available for programmers is to post a schedule on a specific day, showing only the slots to be filled with no names (see form 9.6). Personnel sign up for work, restricting themselves to a limited number of hours to allow everyone an equal opportunity. After a specified time, any qualified worker may claim vacancies. After completing a personal schedule, an individual files a confirmation card with the staff and retains a copy for reference. The staff member may schedule those individuals who cannot come in for a legitimate reason or those who are needed to fill a particular slot. Because personnel schedule their own hours, they can work around commitments. However, this method may leave staff shorthanded. Specifying a minimum number of hours worked per scheduling period helps avoid this problem.

Among other scheduling techniques meriting attention is using a substitute roster. Invariably, situations arise when personnel are unable to fulfill their assignments. If other regular workers are not available, call in a substitute worker. When holidays or special events drain off personnel, scale down programming, use supplemental, part-time help, or reschedule regulars to perform different functions. Finally, in the case of last minute shortages, maintain a list of those available on call.

Supervising Employees

Historically, the supervisory role involved making observations and formulating strategies to see that work was accomplished and workers did not loaf on the job. Recent studies in the behavioral sciences indicate the need to modify this orientation with a view of the supervisor as a facilitator of competent performance, rapport, and personnel growth.

A staff supervisor is responsible for helping subordinate personnel improve their work, while adhering to agency objectives. The role of the supervisor who mediates between the staff who administer the agency and the auxiliary staff who implement its functions at the program level is primary to our discussion.

Personnel supervision is a multifaceted function, which includes providing guidance, helping each employee develop professionally, and being a communications facilitator. Let's briefly examine each function.

Providing Guidance

Orientation and in-service training efforts cannot fully prepare personnel for handling every circumstance, nor do they guarantee that the knowledge or skills taught will be understood, properly applied, or consistently performed.

One way of determining whether personnel need assistance is to make performance observations.

Figure 9.5
Seniority Contract Scheduling Form

- **DISTRIBUTION OF SENIORITY POINTS**

1. 7 points—each season worked as a supervisor.

2. 4 points—each season worked as an intramural sport official. (*Note:* In order to be credited with seniority points, you must have assumed officiating duties before becoming a supervisor or during a season in which you were officiating only and had no supervisor duties.)

3. Grade on supervisor's exam

7 points = score of 97-100	4 points = score of 88-90	2 points = score of 82-84
6 points = score of 94-96	3 points = score of 85-87	1 point = score of 79-81
5 points = score of 91-93		

4. Evaluation points

   Eight performance factors will be rated in the following way:

Outstanding .... 4 points	Below standard .... 1 point
Above standard .... 3 points	Unsatisfactory .... 0 points
Standard .... 2 points	

   (to be used only during tournament contracting and not carried over to future seasons)

- **FAILURE TO ATTEND ASSIGNED WORK DATE**

First offense .... Verbal reprimand

Second offense .... Written reprimand or termination*

Third offense .... Termination

*depends on individual circumstance

- **SCHEDULING**

In case of a tie in the overall points at any level, the numbers 0-9 will be assigned to those individuals for use in the following randomly selected draw for seniority and priority order in scheduling for their level. For example, the employee assigned #1 would go first, then #9, and so forth.

Week 1	Week 2	Week 3	Week 4	Week 5	Week 6
1	5	0	3	2	4
9	2	1	4	9	6
0	8	4	7	1	3
7	6	6	1	3	8
3	9	8	9	5	2
8	3	5	2	4	9
6	1	7	5	8	0
5	4	2	0	6	7
2	0	3	6	7	1
4	7	9	8	0	5

PERSONNEL SCHEDULE—INDIVIDUAL NOTICE

Name _____   Phone _____

Job	Location	Day(s)	Times	Approved

I hereby accept or reject the hours given me as noted above.

_____
(Signature)

Form 9.5   Individual notice slip.

Figure 9.6
Basketball Officials Work Schedule

Day _____   Date _____

Court	1	2	3	4	5
Time					
5:00	Night	Dusing	Butler	Schutz	Piercefield
to					
8:00	Circle	Erdman	Sparks	Esckilsen	Clensy

Rovers   B. McMinn

Time	1	2	3	4	5
Time					
8:00	Ellard	Napoli	McManus	Ravensburg	Peterbaugh
to					
11:00	Leubert	Hank	Damer	King	Phillips

Rovers   R. Hailey

Schedules will be posted every Wednesday by 12:00 noon for the following work week (Sunday through Thursday). You must circle your name by 12:00 noon Friday.

OPEN SCHEDULE POSITIONS

Month _____ Year _____

Times	Monday	Tuesday	Wednesday	Thursday	Friday	Times	Saturday	Sunday
7:00-8:30	22	23	24	25	26	10-12:30	27	28
11:30-1:30						12:30-3:00		
6:00-9:00						3:00-5:30		
9:00-11:00						5:30-8:00		
7:00-8:30	1	2	3	4	5	10:00-12:30	6	7
11:30-1:30						12:30-3:00		
6:00-9:00						3:00-5:30		
9:00-11:00						5:30-8:00		

Form 9.6   Posted schedule for staff sign-up.

A common technique is the unannounced observation. It should be a way to monitor operational concerns rather than a strategy for catching personnel doing something wrong. If you notice a problem with personnel performance during an unannounced observation, address it later or handle it discretely, so the individual is not embarrassed in front of coworkers or participants.

Another technique of personnel observation is the expected or routinely scheduled check. Use this procedure to witness a situation, to answer first hand an employee or volunteer request for assistance, to help solidify relationships with personnel, or to complete a structured evaluation process. In rejecting the *snoopervisor* concept, this method enables personnel to view a supervisor as a resource.

In order for personnel to accept guidance and assistance, a supervisor must project competence and legitimacy as a role model. Supervisors need a knowledge of all the duties and responsibilities of the positions under their supervision, an ability to anticipate problems for which a worker may be unaware, and a capacity for resolving problems. Furthermore, a supervisor should be careful to distinguish between domination, guidance, and avoidance. If the supervisor demands control and usurps personnel duties and responsibilities, morale drops, creativity declines, and learning suffers. Such domination also implies lack of confidence,

disinterest in personnel growth, and a know-it-all attitude. On the other extreme, neglect of the responsibility to provide needed guidance to personnel implies a lack of confidence or knowledge, inaccessibility, or disinterest on the part of the supervisor, which has a negative impact on morale and performance. Effective guidance requires an ability to anticipate, analyze, explain, consult, and offer solutions while cultivating these qualities in personnel.

Aiding Professional Development

Provide opportunities for personnel to learn and refine skills and receive evaluation on performance. Because we have already reviewed some common methods for these purposes under the training section, we will make just one additional suggestion. The opinion of your personnel is a valid resource in determining the appropriateness of the content and approach selected for training, review, and evaluation sessions. Combining personnel and supervisor perspectives should result in a more relevant program, one that everyone can support.

Facilitating Communication

Two-way communication must exist between a supervisor and his or her subordinates. The success and quality of supervision suffer when one party functions with partial information. A supervisor's success in maintaining morale, sustaining quality performance, and contributing to the development of personnel depends on reciprocity of communication.

Personnel Relations

There are two aspects of relations referred to in this discussion: relations between supervisor and subordinates and relations among coworkers. The primary responsibility for maintaining positive relations in both instances rests with the supervisor.

The major factors contributing to success in the relationship between supervisors and subordinates include understanding the expectations and objectives of each party and concern by the supervisor for the needs and interests of subordinate personnel. As a supervisor, integrate your expectations and objectives with those of your subordinates and involve them in decisions and goal setting. Justify all policies and procedures that personnel must observe. Build good working relationships by

- developing an incentive system that reinforces quality performances;
- furnishing challenges that stretch personnel beyond their usual capabilities;
- establishing good working conditions in terms of salary, scheduling, and pleasant work surroundings;
- keeping subordinates informed about new information or changes in procedure that affect their duties and responsibilities;
- supporting actions of subordinates whenever possible; and
- being consistent, fair, and objective with all personnel and showing no favoritism or preferential treatment.

Logical outcomes of these strategies are an increased commitment to the job and greater satisfaction.

High morale, quality performance, and progressive supervisor-subordinate relations do not develop instantly. They result as personnel and supervisor undergo experiences with one another that demonstrate commitment and competence.

Despite efforts to the contrary, problems develop ranging from a petty policy infringement to an overt violation or disruptive behavior affecting other personnel. In such situations, disciplinary measures are appropriate. Inaction perpetuates negative behavior, demoralizes personnel, jeopardizes rapport, and damages the supervisor's cred-

ibility. Equally damaging is a disciplinary measure that is inappropriate, biased, or retaliatory. We make more detailed references to disciplinary procedures in chapter 8.

Measures taken to facilitate positive interpersonal relations among auxiliary staff depend on the degree of interdependence that exists. When personnel function as a unit and need to cooperate to accomplish their duties, strategies such as the following enhance camaraderie:

- Plan occasional functions outside the job environment, such as a party, picnic, movie, or sport activity.
- Make careful placement decisions. Knowing as much as possible about each employee or volunteer will help you put them in positions compatible with their abilities and personalities.
- Provide in-service training on human relations and teamwork. Help personnel assess themselves and others realistically.
- Anticipate problems. Stay in tune with personnel concerns. Make regular observations and interact frequently with subordinates on a one-to-one basis. Explore their attitudes.
- Resolve problems. Encourage personnel to work out their differences, providing direction as needed. Serve as an arbitrator if it helps resolve the problem. Be prepared to reassign or relieve personnel when conflict persists.

VOLUNTEER PERSONNEL

We mentioned earlier that volunteers are a considerable portion of the workforce within public and private recreational sport programs. Historically, volunteer leadership has provided a major role in the organized recreation movement and this will continue for years to come. Volunteerism is important because of the following:

- Volunteers supplement professional staff in maintaining or expanding services under difficult economic conditions and providing skills or knowledge not possessed by professional full-time staff.
- Volunteers, motivated by a desire to serve, furnish fresh perspective, enthusiasm, and dedication that often stimulate others and generate participant interest.
- Volunteers may assume routine tasks enabling full-time staff to focus on other

important duties and act as liaisons between staff and various interest groups.

Volunteers hold a variety of positions and responsibilities. Group their roles into the following three classifications:

1. **Logistical services**—volunteers who meet the operational needs associated with the program, such as transportation, clerical, secretarial, maintenance, publicity, promotion, and financial functions.

2. **Program delivery services**—volunteers who help provide programs. In many instances, volunteers serve as the primary staff responsible for leadership, activities, personnel supervision, or facility management. In others, they assist staff on a supplemental, short-term basis. Examples of program delivery roles include sport officials, club officers, sport instructors, community center coordinators, program supervisors, special event assistants, tournament coordinators, and contest judges. Volunteers in this group correspond to auxiliary and program staff levels.

3. **Administrative and advisory services**—volunteers who participate in the direct administration of recreational sport programs or who assist with decision making in an advisory capacity. Members of a board of directors, committee appointees, technical or legal consultants, governing board members, and advisory council members are examples of such roles. Volunteers in this group correspond to program administrative and administrative staff levels.

Although it is difficult to standardize the positions for volunteers doing logistical services or program delivery, you can describe volunteer roles in the administrative and advisory classification so they are relevant to a variety of settings. Volunteers involved in an administrative capacity work on boards or councils with, or in place of, professional staff to determine policies and oversee program operations. You find such administrative involvement in the board of directors structure at the YMCA and Boys Club, the employee recreation association in the industrial setting, the parks and recreation board in the municipal setting, and the executive board in the commercial club setting.

Volunteer leadership also exists at the program operational level through committees, councils, or boards responsible for hearing appeals concerning protests or disciplinary action. We treat this important role in more detail in the chapter on program control.

Volunteer Advisory Boards

Volunteers who fill advisory roles function individually or in groups. Individuals who possess special skills or knowledge often volunteer as consultants. Examples include an accountant who sets up the bookkeeping process, the newspaper advertiser who creates a publicity campaign, the lawyer who advises on legal liability, the space use expert who reorganizes an office, or the architect who helps plan a new sport facility.

Volunteers who staff advisory councils, boards, or committees do not have final responsibility for policy or administration. They do provide such important functions as

- conducting studies that help advance programs, facilities, and services;
- serving as a liaison between staff and participants or staff and employees;
- making recommendations regarding policy and procedure; and
- serving as a sounding board to influence decisions.

Advisory groups are usually composed of representatives from all interested areas of a program and may be elected by participants, appointed by staff, or appointed by special interest groups as their representatives.

The titles council, board, federation, or committee are interchangeable descriptions of advisory groups. Such groups may use standing or ad hoc committees to delve into specific topics or responsibilities on behalf of the whole group. Some topics considered by subcommittees include funding, promotion, facilities, governance, membership, constitution, and bylaws. In the examples of advisory groups that follow, we discuss each briefly, because a programmer will likely work with one or more advisory groups.

Recreational Sport Council or Association

Members of this group represent each program area (club, instruction, intramural, informal), participant group (employee, management, students, faculty,

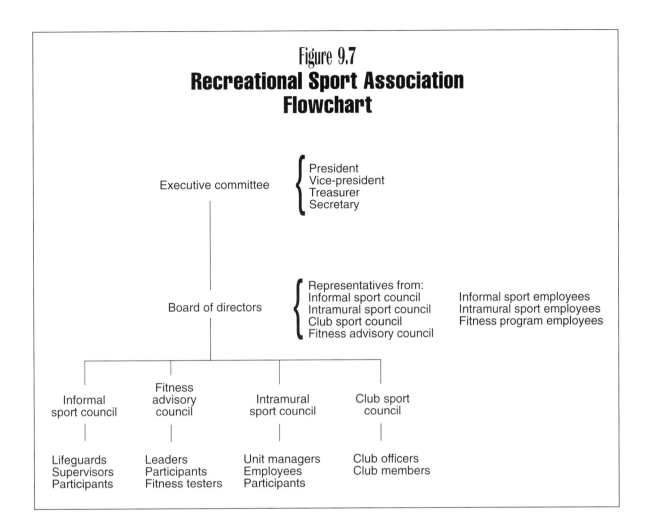

Figure 9.7
Recreational Sport Association Flowchart

Executive committee { President
Vice-president
Treasurer
Secretary

Board of directors { Representatives from:
Informal sport council
Intramural sport council
Club sport council
Fitness advisory council

Informal sport employees
Intramural sport employees
Fitness program employees

Informal sport council

Fitness advisory council

Intramural sport council

Club sport council

Lifeguards
Supervisors
Participants

Leaders
Participants
Fitness testers

Unit managers
Employees
Participants

Club officers
Club members

staff, township, squadron), personnel function (supervisor, official, lifeguard, unit manager, program assistant, instructor), or a combination of these. They recommend policy; evaluate programs, facilities, and services; and serve as the representative voice for a particular constituency. Often used as a sounding board, the council solicits feedback from its constituency on proposals and priority needs. Although advisory in nature, it often influences administration policy, particularly in the areas of finances and facilities. People who serve in this group usually have the most experience and involvement within the recreational sport program. Figure 9.7 traces the function of this group through an organizational flow chart.

Informal Sport Council

Members of this council represent participant groups, facilities, activity interests, or a combination thereof. This group performs functions including policy recommendations, review of complaints, appeals for facility use, liaison between participants

and staff, evaluation of facilities and operations, and identification of priorities regarding facility needs.

Intramural Sport Council

Commonly composed of representatives from various participation units, intramural sport supervisors, and officials, the council serves as a link between staff and participants. The council provides staff with feedback and evaluations concerning programs, facilities, and personnel. They may make recommendations for changes in specific sports and the intramural sport programming area. (For more insight, see chapter 6.)

Club Sport Council

This council includes representatives from each club falling under the jurisdiction of the staff or agency. The individuals make recommendations on policy and procedure while representing the interests of member clubs. A council executive committee often will appoint subcommittees to study

Shining Example

Parks and Recreation Sports Division, Bloomington, Indiana

The city of Bloomington's Parks and Recreation Department's Recreational Sports Division serves approximately 110,000 residents throughout Bloomington and its surrounding communities. In addition, many of the division's programs and services draw regionally and nationally to tournaments and events. Staffing the division with exceptionally qualified and diverse sport personnel is one attribute of the success of this department. The sports division is organized to be responsive to participants in highly intense and varied sport opportunity. A Division Director supervises the sports division which consists of two Area Managers, a staff Associate and a working maintenance person. In addition, a legion of part-time/seasonal staff consists of 100 game officials, 36 scorekeepers, 12 maintenance staff, 20 site/program supervisors, 12 concession staff, and 20 instructors. In-service training and required certifications allow for the hiring of the most qualified individuals. Training specific to recreational sport programming is key to the Division's success with sport management.

Organization: Municipal, Parks and Recreation is a Department of the City of Bloomington and is funded by city property taxes and user fees & charges. The sports division is a division of the Department.

Clientele: Constituents include the population of the City of Bloomington including the students of Indiana University. City population is estimated at 65,000. In addition, county residents use facilities and programs offered by the Department. Total county population is about 45,000. Total population served is approximately 110,000.

Budget: The 1995 sports division general fund operating budget including personnel, operating supplies, repair and maintenance and capital outlays is $306,988. Additional non-reverting revenue through fees and charges equaled $255,800. Non-reverting funds are used for athletic leagues and tournaments.

Marketing: Several types of marketing devices are used. The Department produces 3 comprehensive seasonal brochures that are directly mailed to previous participants. These seasonal brochures are produced for the fall, spring and summer seasons. In addition, individual fliers are produced for specific sports programs and mailed to last season's participants. These fliers are also posted at all Department facilities. News releases are mailed to local radio stations and newspapers for use as free Public Service Announcements. Sports programs are featured in sections of the newspaper in the form of a weekly column or to publish standings of sport leagues. Additionally, a local radio station features a 5-10 minute feature on sports programs as part of their weekly programming. Finally, the Department utilizes a voice mail "information line" that allows the public information access about programs, facilities, and registration information.

Administrative Staff: The sports division is comprised of the following full time personnel: (1) Division Director, (2) Area Managers, (1) Staff Associate, and (1) Working Foreman. The following season staff are hired: (100) game officials, (36) scorekeepers, (12) maintenance staff, (20) site/program supervisors, (12) concession staff, (20) instructors.

Program Detail: A total of 15,626 adults and youth participated in the following recreational, instructional and competitive programs directly conducted by the Department: Adult summer softball leagues (3,151), adult fall softball (2,281), adult softball tournaments (7,000), adult basketball (665), adult volleyball (505), tennis lessons (256), tennis leagues (20), tennis tournaments (82), pass, punt & kick (25), Hook a Kid on Golf (64) and pony league instructional baseball (97).

Facilities: The sports division is responsible for the programming and maintenance of the following sports facilities: Winslow Sports Complex, Twin Lakes Sports Park, Lower Cascades ballfields and the Upper Cascades ballfield. In addition, the division schedules activities on the Bryan Park playfields and 9th Street Park. The sports division also conducts additional programs at the gymnasium and tennis facilities of Bloomington North and South High Schools, Batchelor and Tri-North Middle Schools and Edgewood High School.

and propose recommendations to staff on ways to improve club funding, facilities, or other support services.

Working with volunteers in an advisory capacity requires time and preparation. By providing avenues of involvement to direct their interest for program improvements, the programmer includes the volunteer as a valuable resource who shoulders some responsibility of sport management. When those affected by decisions participate in making them, the results are easier to accept. (Chapter 7 covers this topic in detail.)

Volunteer Group Organization

The degree to which rapport and high productivity are attained within a group depends on the personalities, attributes, and skills of professional staff volunteers. Although in-service training may improve group dynamics, select volunteers who already possess important qualities, such as the following:

- Sincere interest in and commitment to the value of the programs
- Willingness and ability to give time and effort
- Ability to work well with others
- Sound judgment, an ability to speak on issues after careful analysis, and a desire to offer solutions to problems
- Commitment to representing the opinions of one's constituency—not personal opinion

Whenever possible, the programmer should see that boards, councils, and committees broadly rep-

resent the population specific to its function, including age, gender, occupation, education, race, and social and economic situation. Consider the length of terms of office so you can secure capable replacements. The more complex the responsibility, the longer the term must be due to the time it takes for the person to gain expertise. Stagger or overlap terms to maintain continuity and operating ability.

Orientation, Training, and Evaluation of Volunteers

Unfortunately, once volunteers are selected, their preparation and evaluation as a group is too often neglected. In view of the significant responsibilities and contributions volunteers represent, the programmer should devise a training and evaluation program for them.

A helpful tool for orientation and training is a manual that includes a statement of purpose; an organizational flowchart; the history of the program; constitution or operational guidelines; executive officer job descriptions; program policies; agency policies; and a directory of member names, positions, and phone numbers. Organize special sessions to review this material. Discuss each volunteer's role, anticipated responsibilities, and potential priority projects.

Volunteers who hold positions of responsibility for logistical services or program delivery also require some ongoing supervisory attention in terms of guidance, development, communication, and interpersonal relations. Supervisory responsibility often rests with a professional staff member who,

Organizational Chart Software

Organizational charts are ideal for managing information and planning in recreational sports. Software specifically designed for organizational charting helps you create professional-looking organizational charts quickly and easily. More important, software can now eliminate the manually drawn charts that are usually quickly out-of-date. Several software programs import data directly from the agency's human resource data files, which means that all recreational sports employees can have on-line access to the most current organizational chart.

Since organizational charts can now be viewed at an employee's desk, departments no longer have to distribute outdated printed charts. Employees can view the latest agency structure; search the organizational chart by name, department, or relationship; and either view or print that specific chart.

Drawing a chart and connecting lines is very simple and fast using toolbar buttons to click, drag, and drop employees' names, positions, and boxes anywhere in the chart. Most programs automatically position text and expand or shrink the boxes as you type. You can also use simple menu selections to change box borders and fonts, apply shadows, and change the thickness and style of box lines. The following screen is an example of a recreational sports organizational chart using *OrgPlus for Windows* software. The screen shows the pull-down menu of various charting styles that are available.

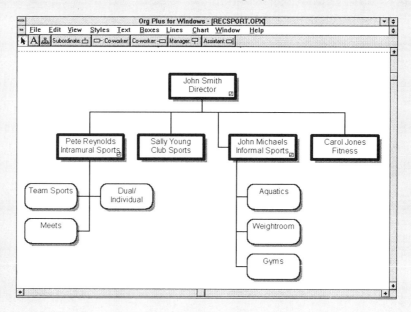

Other special features of organizational chart software may allow you to perform the following functions:

- search the agency for "who reports to whom," allowing you to locate names, departments, and position titles;
- print various organizational levels;
- use a "make it fit" command that can either reduce charts to fit on one page or expand charts for multi-page diagrams;
- import recreational sports agency logos and graphics;
- use special legend boxes; and

> • use drawing tools that allow you to get the precise effects you want.
>
> *OrgPlus for Windows,* Banner Blue Software.
> *Other organizational chart software products:* OrgChart Express, Clear OrgCharts, ClarisImpact, Drag'n Draw, and Flow Charting.

by nature of the position, provides an element of continuity from year to year.

Special Considerations Concerning Volunteer Staff

The motivation for volunteering one's time and services arises from many reasons—a desire for practical experience, personal recognition, prestige, job recommendations, academic credit, and other psychological or social needs. Because the volunteer does not depend on the position for income, problems may result:

- When a volunteer refuses to identify with the philosophy of the setting, performs unreliably, or lacks the abilities to handle an assignment, corrective measures may have little impact because he or she is not an employee.

- A volunteer worker may perform tasks acceptably, act as an excellent role model, and accept additional responsibilities only to feel resentment when an employee does not measure up to the same standard.

- Personal priorities may interfere with commitment to volunteer duties.

- Unruly volunteers can be difficult to control or remove.

- Volunteer leaders may try to usurp the authority of a professional staff member working in the same program.

Volunteers have many positive attributes and contributions to offer, and the programmer must learn how to tap them to make maximum use of their potential.

ADA Suggestions

A major purpose of the ADA is to give individuals with disabilities the opportunity to join the workforce. Title I of the ADA prohibits discrimination "against a qualified individual with a disability because of the disability of such individual in regard to job application procedures, the hiring, advancement, or discharge of employees, employee compensation, job training, and other terms, conditions, and privileges of employment." The ADA does not require an employer to hire an individual with a disability if he or she is not qualified for the position. However, the ADA does require employers to demonstrate selection criteria for each position, tasks, and responsibilities essential for that position. In addition, it is the employer's responsibility to provide *reasonable accommodations* in employment, making existing employee facilities, such as break rooms and time-clock room, readily accessible to individuals with disabilities or modifying existing equipment to assist the individual in performing the duties of the job.

CONCLUSION

The programmer working with personnel at the operational level may need to invest considerable time for training and supervising those who serve the agency part time or for a short duration. Decisions or recommendations regarding the selection, placement, training, scheduling, supervision, evaluation, and recognition of personnel require careful preparation to contribute to quality performance, positive morale, and a reduction in personnel turnover. Unless the programmer continually recognizes and demonstrates that the operational level jobs are important to the total recreational sport program, both paid and volunteer personnel may lose their motivation and view their work as demeaning and unpleasant.

Programmers need to understand personnel management and the impact that their decisions have on subordinates. Effective implementation of personnel practices ensures the overall quality of a recreational sport program.

DISCUSSION QUESTIONS

1. List four personnel levels found in delivering recreational sport programs.

2. List specific examples of programming staff positions.

3. How might properly conducted and timely in-service training programs help eliminate future problems in recreational sport programming?

4. What are the principal duties common to all recreational sport programming positions?

5. Volunteers hold a variety of positions in recreational sport. Describe ways that you can use volunteers in programming.

6. What are some common problems associated with volunteers?

7. List five questions that cannot be used in employment interviews.

8. What items would be beneficial for an administrator to know when interviewing an applicant for a full-time recreational sport position?

9. Define recruitment and the search and screen process. What strategies would you include in recruiting qualified lifeguards? Sport officials? Sport supervisors?

10. Describe several ways to schedule part-time employees.

11. What personnel management strategies can you use while supervising employees?

12. What agenda items would you include in an orientation meeting with new auxiliary staff?

13. What is the purpose of a job description?

14. What are several key categories found in a position announcement?

15. Describe the types of in-service training for new recreational sports employees.

APPLICATION EXERCISE

As the director of the local Boys or Girls Club, you are in charge of the search and screen committee for a Level I position in intramural sport. Outline the steps you would use to find a qualified person for this position. Include forming a search and screen committee (who would serve on this committee and why would you choose these individuals), job announcement, job description, questions for the interview, and an itinerary for the candidate's personal interview. Also, be sure to describe the procedures you would use to process all of the applications.

SUGGESTED READINGS

Aiken, B. 1989. Communicating for effective personnel management. *National Intramural-Recreational Sports Association Journal* 13 (2): 21-24.

Anderson, S. 1992. Investigating sexual harassment complaints. *Supervision* (August): 9-10.

Bogar, C. 1989. The employee search process and its application to recreational sports. *National Intramural-Recreational Sports Association Journal* (winter): 37-38.

DiMonda, S., and J. Smith. 1994. Student-employee morale. *National Intramural-Recreational Sports Association Journal* (spring): 8-11.

Espinosa, C. 1991. Toward greater multicultural diversity: Change and challenge for intramural-recreational sports. *National Intramural-Recreational Sports Association Journal* 15 (2): 20.

Kelleher, C. 1992. A supervisor's survival guide to the civil rights act of 1991. *Supervision* (July): 3-6.

Kintigh, S. 1989. Effective performance appraisal. *National Intramural-Recreational Sports Association Journal* (winter): 29-31, 41.

Miller, T. 1993. Job enrichment and its motivational effect on student employees in a college recreational services setting. *National Intramural-Recreational Sports Association Journal* (winter): 20, 22, 24-25.

Montgomery, B. 1990. Experiential learning and the preparation of recreational professionals. *National Intramural-Recreational Sports Association Journal* 14 (3): 20-23.

Nesbitt, G. 1993. Requirements for potential job applicants. *National Intramural-Recreational Sports Association Journal* (winter): 16, 18-19.

Nicoletto, N. 1993. Management in the 90's: Read, respect, respond. *National Intramural-Recreational Sports Association Journal* (winter): 3-4, 6.

O'Dell, I. 1990. Intramural sports: A minority perspective. *National Intramural-Recreational Sports Association Journal* 14 (2): 36-38.

Peterson, M. 1989. Performance standards and disciplinary actions. *National Intramural-Recreational Sports Association Journal* (winter): 34.

CHAPTER 10

Financial Considerations

Chapter Objectives

After reading this chapter you will

- understand the financial responsibilities of sport managers,
- identify the revenue sources in sport management,
- identify the major expenditures in sport management, and
- identify the budget process inherent in most sport programs.

Sport programmers have a major responsibility for the financial efficiency of an agency or business. Trends in finance across the major settings in sport management reveal an increased reliance on planning, implementation, and tracking of finances to ensure fiscal responsibility. Sport programmers in the public sector face declining tax support and heavy reliance on nontax revenue, and those in the private sector can face dwindling profits in a highly competitive market unless they strictly adhere to fiscal requirements of the business.

FINANCIAL RESPONSIBILITIES OF SPORT MANAGERS

Those employed in sport management settings will find several responsibilities for maintaining a sound financial picture. Fiscal responsibility includes many facets, such as the following:

- Budget planning and implementation
- Cash control and accountability
- Fund-raising
- Documentation of financial processes
- Evaluation and changes in financial goals

The sport programmer needs to understand the nature of income and expenditures, how to account for funds, and how to plan for acquiring and managing these funds. In a national climate of fiscal exigency, all levels of a sport organization must operate efficiently so funds go further and the organization can maintain or improve service. The status of financing in sport management parallels that of the leisure industry: diminished tax support, greater reliance on other fees, and greater accountability of all staff within an organization.

As a result of a work program developed in the planning process, a budget, once approved, is available for implementation. In the public sector, the agency receives allocations of tax moneys for use. In addition, the agency accounts for other revenue sources as it accumulates them. In the private sector, sale of goods and services to clients secure funds, and this income forms the basis for expenditures.

Agencies keep financial records regularly with computer printouts and monthly, quarterly, or annual reports as reporting mechanisms.

Organizations devise systems for handling cash and revenue. Cash control is important in sport management due to the daily cash income collected at pools, racquetball complexes, centers, fields, and similar facilities. When you collect large amounts of cash, there can be an increase of robbery and employee theft. You should account for and deposit cash safely.

Regardless of the fiscal constraints in both public and private sector finance, sport interest and participant willingness to pay generate the highest amount of revenue among recreation programs. Therefore, through creative programming, sport programmers are always able to implement new programs that can generate revenue.

This chapter cannot hope to replace experience and course work in financial management. But it does provide you with a view of the typical revenues and expenses associated with sport and recreation programs and introduces you to the budget process. As a programmer, finance and accounting are not major responsibilities, however a programmer with a keen eye for bottom-line issues is likely to be groomed for administrative positions.

SOURCES OF REVENUE

Recreational sport program revenue sources vary according to political priorities, participant needs and interests, and staff philosophy. Recent changes in the economy have stimulated discovery of nontraditional revenue sources to maintain and expand current levels of programming.

For our discussion, revenue represents income either produced or acquired by the agency. Let's look at typical revenue-producing activities of sport recreation programs.

Taxes

Recreational sport programs sponsored by government, as in municipal, collegiate, or military settings, receive tax moneys. The taxes that generate the most funds are property, income, sales, and special assessments or mandatory fees earmarked for sport.

Grants

The federal government and many state governments provide grant-in-aid programs to municipalities, often requiring local matching funds. Private foundations furnish another source for grants. Because most grants have a time limit, once a program or facility loses its funding the agency may have to assume the financial responsibility to continue their operation.

Gifts and Donations

Gifts may include land, a building, or cash to support a particular project or program. Occasionally, a trust fund provides an income to the agency. As with gifts, donations are sporadic and may involve so many restrictions that they are impractical.

Leases

A new source of revenue is leasing public land or facilities to private individuals or agencies to operate. In many of these arrangements the public agency receives a rental to offset their debt charges required to develop the operation plus an agreed portion of profits.

Concessions

A traditional revenue source is the sale of goods and services. Common concessions include vending machines, pro shops, restaurants, and equipment rentals. The practice of distributing profits through contractual agreements with private concessionaires is extensive, although some programs prefer operating their own concessions.

Bonds

Bonds comprise a primary source of financial support in a municipal setting for major capital development projects, such as land acquisition and sport facility construction. Once an agency secures bonds, they pay them off over time, so they become expenditures. Bonds enable an agency to borrow funds to finance community services, such as schools and recreation facilities. They are a form of deferred payment that spreads the cost of a government enterprise over several years rather than allocating it to one year's budget. Bond approval is difficult to secure. Even a well-organized campaign often fails to gain support from the general public or legislative body.

Fund-Raising

An agency may raise money through special events or fund drives. Some settings maintain strict policies governing fund-raising. Because it requires considerable investment of agency time and effort with little guarantee of success, few rely on fund-raising as a primary source of revenue.

Commercial Sponsorship

Under this arrangement, a commercial establishment offers to underwrite the cost of personnel, equipment, facilities, or programs. A commercial sponsor may package a program (such as a tournament or superstar competition) that the agency can implement with little investment other than personnel. Sponsors often consider providing support as a marketing or public relations function. It is rare to find one, however, who does not expect some visibility, recognition, or return on the investment.

User Fees

Revenue from fees and charges constitutes a large portion of income for municipal and nonprofit agencies, colleges, and universities, and provides the primary source of income for commercial agencies.

TYPES OF EXPENDITURES

Expenditures are outlays of cash (or sometimes other assets) to purchase goods and services required by the agency. Buying anything from paper clips to a new swimming pool requires an expenditure. An agency may categorize its expenditures in two ways: capital and operating. Programmers will mostly work with the operating budget of supplies and staffing; however we provide the description of both.

Capital Expenditures

Capital expenditures are outlays for nonrecurring projects having a life expectancy of at least 10 years.

Items in this category might include renovating tennis court surfaces, constructing a new sport complex, acquiring land for fitness trails, refurbishing a senior citizen center, and adding racquetball courts to an existing structure. Taxes, special assessments, and bond issues commonly finance projects of this scope.

Operating Expenditures

Operating expenditures represent the recurring costs for providing sport programs and facilities. Examples of expense categories include payroll, contractual services, supplies, materials, utilities, repairs, properties, and insurance.

SPORT PROGRAMMER'S ROLE IN THE BUDGET PROCESS

A financial plan is known as a budget. The recreational sport administrator is often called on to prepare two budgets—one suggesting long-term needs and the other for annual operations. An operational budget provides an administrator with an allocation policy that accomplishes stated goals and objectives for the delivery of programs, facilities, and services. It is a tool for planning, implementation, and control, reflecting a choice among priorities and a forecast of the cost of personnel and other resources. Regarding implementation, a budget organizes resources, standardizes operations, and provides a frame of reference for clarifying or supporting decisions. As a control mechanism, the budget aids in determining the efficiency for an area of the total program. Expenditures are evaluated by comparing results with stated objectives. Finally, the budget serves as a guideline for adjusting for emergencies or new priorities. This section stresses the programmer's role in developing cost-effective operations.

Budget preparation and management require careful thought and detailed planning. Although the responsibility for developing, requesting, and managing the budget remains an administrative function, the programmer participates in the following ways. First, he or she complies with financial accountability by following budget control measures and preventing unnecessary expenditures or losses during daily operations. Second, the programmer provides feedback to administrative staff regarding operational concerns, recommendations, and financial priorities.

At budget preparation time, it is customary for the programmer to receive instruction regarding how to identify, specify, and justify budget requests. As we'll discuss in this chapter, the programmer oversees income and expenses relating to the daily operation of the programs the agency administers. Therefore, he or she is in position to give the administration foresight concerning next year's anticipated operating expenses and income.

When you must anticipate operating expenses, identify realistic needs, regardless of previous allocations, and rank them by priority in anticipation of budget limitations. Whenever possible, relieve financial pressures through more efficient use of existing resources.

Rather than waiting until the start of the budget process before formulating recommendations, the programmer should contribute to an idea file throughout the year. This technique reduces the chance of forgetting a useful idea and helps develop perspective on the relationship between a function and its budget implications. Include budget modifications or recommendations with each evaluation statement written at the end of a program.

FINANCIAL ACCOUNTABILITY FOR SPORT PROGRAMMERS

The programmer often manages funds involving fees and charges, hourly wage payroll, equipment, supplies, and facility maintenance. He or she monitors expenditures for each category to control waste or abuse. Specific recommendations for financial accountability within each category follow.

Collecting Fees and Charges

Responsibility for fee collection involves the following:

- Training and supervising collection personnel
- Conducting financial transactions with participants and performing necessary cash register functions: sales, rentals, charges, voids, refunds
- Interpreting and enforcing policies, including fee scheduling, waivers, refunds, service charges, eligibility, and payment methods
- Securing collected funds, making safety deposits, preparing end-of-shift reports, reconciling differences

Spreadsheets

Regardless of the size of the recreational sports program, most organizations using computers have purchased complete business and accounting software systems. The use of ledgers, journals, payroll, and balance sheets has been incorporated into even the simplest and least expensive accounting software. Budgeting, payroll, accounts payable, accounts receivable, forecasting, comparisons between income and expenditure allocations, and cost analysis functions are now standard features.

What about those of us who are recreational sports programmers—not accountants—and are sometimes intimidated by the complex accounting software currently on the market? Spreadsheet programs are powerful programs for organizing, analyzing, and presenting the data that require the traditional row and column reports (such as budgets, payroll, and other record keeping files). Spreadsheets can perform both simple and complex calculations and can chart data in a number of formats. Anything once done with a pencil, a piece of paper, and a calculator can be done by a spreadsheet program.

Most of your work in a spreadsheet program is done on a *worksheet*, which is the first thing you see when you open the program. The worksheet is simply a giant grid (up to 256 columns and up to more than 16,000 rows). To enter data, just click on a cell or grid box and enter the information. While each cell may contain text or numbers, the real value and power of a spreadsheet comes from the ability of cells to store formulas and

	A	B	C	D
1		FLAG FOOTBALL HOURLY WAGE WORKSHEET		
2			OFFICIALS	SUPERVISORS
3	CLINIC	No. of projected employees=	150	25
4		No. of hrs/employees=	1	1
5		Total clinic hours needed=	=(C3*C4)	=(D3*D4)
6		Avg pay rate per hr=	=C42	=D42
7		CLINIC TOTAL=	=(C5*C6)	=(D5*D6)
8				
9	REGULAR	No. of teams entered=	415	
10	SEASON	No. of teams per league=	4	
11	FORMAT	No. of games per league=	=(C10)*(C10-1)/2	
12		No. of leagues=	=ROUNDUP((C9/C10),0)	
13		No. of league games=	=(C11*C12)	
14		Estimated forfeit percentage=	0.15	
15		Estimated forfeited games=	=ROUNDUP((C13*C14),0)	
16		No. employees/game or hrs=	3	0.25
17		Total employees/game or hrs=	=ROUNDUP((C13-C15)*(C16),0)	=ROUNDUP((C13-C15)*(D16),0)
18		Avg pay rate per game/hr=	=C42	=D42
19		REGULAR SEASON TOTAL=	=(C17*C18)	=(D17*D18)
20				
21	PLAYOFF	No. of teams=	=ROUNDUP(((C9)-(C9*C14)),0)	
22	FORMAT	Estimated forfeit percentage=	0.1	
23		Estimated forfeited teams=	=ROUNDUP((C21*C22),0)	
24		Estimated teams=	=ROUNDUP((C21-C23),0)	
25		No. of games=	=(C24-1)	=C25
26		No. employees/game or hr=	=C16	=D16
27		Total employees/game or hr=	=ROUNDUP((C25*C26),0)	=ROUNDUP((D25*D26),0)
28		Avg pay rate/game or hr=	=C42	=D42
29		PLAYOFF TOTAL=	=(C27*C28)	=(D27*D28)
30				
31		SUB-TOTAL=	=C7+C19+C29	=D7+D19+D29
32		% OF EMPLOYEES ON WORK/STUDY	0.25	0.1
33		WORK/STUDY SAVINGS=	=(C31*C32)*0.7	=(D31*D32)*0.7
34		TOTAL=	=C31-C33	=D31-D33
35				
36		GRAND TOTAL=	=C34+D34	
37		PAY SCALE	Officials	Supervisor
38		1st Year	7	7.5
39		2nd Year	=(C38+0.25)	=(D38+0.25)
40		3rd Year	=(C39+0.25)	=(D39+0.25)
41		4th Year	=(C40+0.25)	=(D40+0.25)
42		Average	=AVERAGE(C38:C41)	=AVERAGE(D38:D41)

	A	B	C	D
1		**FLAG FOOTBALL HOURLY WAGE WORKSHEET**		
2			**OFFICIALS**	**SUPERVISORS**
3	**CLINIC**	No. of projected employees=	150	25
4		No. of hrs/employees=	1	1
5		Total clinic hours needed=	150	25
6		Avg pay rate per hr=	$7.38	$7.88
7		**CLINIC TOTAL=**	$1,106.25	$196.88
8	-------------	----------------------------	---------------	--------------
9	**REGULAR**	No. of teams entered=	415	
10	**SEASON**	No. of teams per league=	4	
11	**FORMAT**	No. of games per league=	6	
12		No. of leagues=	104	
13		No. of league games=	624	
14		Estimated forfeit percentage=	15%	
15		Estimated forfeited games=	94	
16		No. employees/game or hrs=	3	0.25
17		Total employees/game or hrs=	1,590	133
18		Avg pay rate per game/hr=	$7.38	$7.88
19		**REGULAR SEASON TOTAL=**	$11,726.25	$1,047.38
20	-------------	----------------------------	---------------	--------------
21	**PLAYOFF**	No. of teams=	353	
22	**FORMAT**	Estimated forfeit percentage=	10%	
23		Estimated forfeited teams=	36	
24		Estimated teams=	317	
25		No. of games=	316	316
26		No. employees/game or hr=	3	0.25
27		Total employees/game or hr=	948	79
28		Avg pay rate/game or hr=	$7.38	$7.88
29		**PLAYOFF TOTAL=**	$6,991.50	$622.13
30	-------------	----------------------------	---------------	--------------
31		**SUB-TOTAL**	$19,824.00	$1,866.38
32		**% OF EMPLOYEES ON WORK/STUDY**	25%	10%
33		**WORK/STUDY SAVINGS=**	$3,469.20	$130.65
34		**TOTAL=**	$16,354.80	$1,735.73
35				
36		**GRAND TOTAL=**	$18,090.53	
37		**PAY SCALE**	**Officials**	**Supervisor**
38		1st Year	$7.00	$7.50
39		2nd Year	$7.25	$7.75
40		3rd Year	$7.50	$8.00
41		4th Year	$7.75	$8.25
42		Average	$7.38	$7.88

display their results. For example, by conducting different "what-if" analyses, all related or affected cells in the entire worksheet are recalculated based on the given formula. Spreadsheets improve accuracy because they eliminate the traditional, manual approach of reworking figures with calculators and pencils. With a spreadsheet, you do not have to worry about introducing errors because you don't manually erase and recalculate figures.

The screens on pages 243-244 are examples of *Microsoft Excel* worksheets for an intramural sports official and supervisor hourly wage budget template. The first screen shows what the actual worksheet looks like with formulas visible, and the second screen shows the worksheet with formulas hidden. To figure an official's or supervisor's budget for a sport, the recreational sports programmer would simply enter the projected number of total officials and supervisors, the hourly wage rates for officials and supervisors, the projected number of teams entering, the league size, the regular round robin and playoff estimates of forfeits, the number of officials and supervisors per game, and the estimated percentage of work study employees. After entering this information, the spreadsheet program would immediately calculate the formulas and would present a total hourly wage budget figure—all in a matter of seconds. The formulas and other specifics for this template can be edited or modified very easily for your specific sports program. Go ahead and give it a try!

Microsoft Excel, Microsoft, Redmond, WA.
Other spreadsheet products: Lotus 1-2-3, Quattro Pro, PFS, and ClarisWorks.

- Issuing tickets, permits, identification cards, hand stamps, badges, and receipts
- Checking the eligibility of users
- Performing bookkeeping that records, posts, and files daily income receipts
- Providing feedback and receiving and channeling comments regarding fees and charge policies, supplies, and procedures

Because these tasks involve direct handling of money taken into the agency, the programmer should adhere to strict fee collection procedures, supervising personnel and supplies closely, and double-checking calculations and records for accuracy. Conscientious performance helps reduce theft and avoids costly losses of time and money.

Overseeing Operating Expenses

The programmer must learn to live within the constraints of the budget handed down by the administration. Costs that recreational programmers control or monitor include expenses for wages paid to hourly employees and the costs associated with equipment, supplies, and facility maintenance.

Hourly Wages

The programmer hires and assigns full-time or part-time employees to manage sport activities and to operate facilities. By careful monitoring of the pay rate, number of personnel needed, and projected number of work hours, the programmer can stay within the budget allocation for wage expenses or

alert management of anticipated overruns soon enough to explore alternatives.

Using an hourly wage worksheet is helpful for monitoring hourly wage needs. Formats used for informal sport and intramural sport programs are presented in forms 10.1 and 10.2.

The programmer may have an additional responsibility for maintaining and submitting an hourly wage payroll for each employee or for informing employees of the procedures for recording and submitting their hours. Accuracy in payroll matters is a necessity.

The programmer may record employees' hours in a number of ways, the most common being a time-clock card, an individual employee time sheet, a signed scorecard, or a sign-in sheet. Each method requires careful transfer of hours onto a payroll sheet, followed by accurate monitoring. A typical payroll sheet is reproduced in form 10.3. It is customary to retain original copies of time and payroll sheets in case you need to verify hours of work or investigate discrepancies.

Equipment

Moneys associated with equipment can represent income to an agency, expenses to an agency, or both. The programmer distributes equipment through loan, rental, or sales to individuals. (Rental or sales generate income.) He or she has the responsibility for the condition, security, and return of equipment used in a program. Those who issue or sell equipment should keep daily records of use, sales, or rentals; assist with equipment storage and repair; handle financial transactions and reports for

HOURLY WAGE WORKSHEET (INFORMAL SPORT)

Position _____

Current pay rate _____

Pay period _____

Projected pay rate _____

Days	Shift	Number of employees	Number of hours/shift	Number of days/shift	Number of hours/month	Total	Shift	Number of employees	Number of hours/shift	Number of days/shift	Number of hours/month	Total

Total by day

Monday-Thursday _____

Friday _____

Saturday-Sunday _____

Grand total _____

Total by day

Monday-Thursday _____

Friday _____

Saturday-Sunday _____

Grand total _____

Form 10.1   Informal sport hourly wage worksheet.

HOURLY WAGE WORKSHEET (INTRAMURAL SPORT)

Sport _____   Division: Competitive _____ Casual _____

Programming area: Job title:

___ Men's intramurals   ___ Official

___ Women's intramurals   ___ Supervisor

___ Co-intramurals   ___ Laborer

___ Other _____   ___ Other _____

Clinc	# projected employees _____
	# hours/employee × _____ =
	Total # clinic hours needed _____
	Average pay rate per hour × _____ =
	Total
	# assistant instructors _____
	# hours/employee × _____ =
	Total # clinic hours needed _____
	Average pay rate/hour × _____ =
	Total _____
	Clinic total (A) _____
Regular season format	# games/league _____
	# leagues × _____ =
	# league games _____
	# employees/games or hour × _____ =
	Total employees/game or hour _____
	Average pay rate per game or hour × _____ =
	Total (B) _____
Play-off format	# of teams _____
	# of games _____
	# employees/games or hour × _____ =
	Total # employees/game or hour _____
	Average pay rate/game or hour × _____ =
	Total (C) _____
	Grand total (A + B + C) _____

Summary			
19 __-19 __ Allocation	19 __-19 __ Expenditure	Surplus/deficit of allocation	19 __-19 __ Request

Form 10.2 Intramural sport hourly wage worksheet.

HOURLY WAGE PAYROLL (RECREATIONAL SPORT)

Employee's name _____   Pay rate _____

Employee's SS # _____   Sport code _____

Title code _____   Facility code (informal only) _____

Pay period	Sun	Mon	Tue	Wed	Thu	Fri	Sat	Total 1 wk	Sun	Mon	Tue	Wed	Thu	Fri	Sat	Total hr/pay
6/6-6/19																
6/20-7/3																
7/4-7/17																
7/18-7/31																
8/1-8/14																
8/15-8/28																

General instructions: Please complete all information. Be sure to indicate the *activity code* as well as the *title code.*

Sport code

FF	Flag football
VB	Volleyball
BB	Basketball
WP	Water polo
SE	Special event (indicate event)
SB	Softball
SO	Soccer
XC	Cross country
WR	Wrestling
SW	Swimming
J	Jogging
AD	Aerobic dance
SC	Scuba
IS	Ice skating
IH	Ice hockey
B	Boating
SA	Sailing
C	Canoeing
SK	Skiing

Title code

O	Official
S	Supervisor
L	Labor
SA	Staff assistant
LG	Lifeguard

Facility code

W	Weight room
FH	Field house
TC	Tennis courts
OF	Outdoor fields
P	Pool
IR	Ice rink
OP	Outdoor pool
L	Lake
FT	Fitness trail
SS	Ski slope

Form 10.3   Hourly wage payroll form.

rentals or sales; maintain inventory; and submit purchase recommendations for additional or replacement items. Proper care and handling of equipment can result in significant financial savings.

Supplies

Regardless of the specific responsibility, any programming position involves using supplies (i.e., items that are consumed or worn out in a short time). Stationery, clipboards, pencils, fuel, food, clothing, rubber bands, staples, chemicals, ice, first aid supplies, cleaning supplies, tape, blotters, and rulers all belong in this category. Such wasteful activities as retyping materials requiring minimal correction, duplicating excess copies, and using paper and pens for personal business take supplies for granted. Impress on subordinate personnel the need for economical use of supplies.

Maintenance

While working in a facility, the programmer should develop a capability for spotting maintenance and repair needs. Forward reports to the appropriate staff to prompt corrective action and request funds

Shining Example

City of Henderson Parks and Recreation Department, Henderson, Nevada

The city of Henderson, Nevada Parks and Recreation Department has in the last ten years witnessed a growth spurt within its city of 212 percent. In keeping in pace with rapidly changing demographics and community needs, the Henderson Parks and Recreation Department (HPRD) has grown and adjusted with the city. In the last five years, HPRD's annual budget has nearly tripled from $2.2 million to over $6 million in 1995. In addition, the department has developed five new parks, one full service recreation center, and adopted the Henderson Senior Center within the past five years. In 1990, the department had 33 full-time staff and 125 part-time employees. The 1995 employee statistics boast 59 full-time and 300 part-time employees. The city of Henderson, Nevada, is a growing community. The HPRD sees opportunity with this growth and changes within the community thus improving their department by increasing facilities, resources, and the budget size.

Organization: The City of Henderson is a member of the Nevada Recreation and Parks Society and the National Recreation and Parks Association. The HPRD (Henderson Parks and Recreation Department) is a municipal and government agency.

Clientele: The city demographics for Henderson are made up of the following multi-ethnic groups: under 5 (5,436), under 18 (18,366), 18-65 (41,158), and over 65 (5,418). The average median age is 31.8 years of age.

Budget: The HPRD's annual budget has nearly tripled from $2.2 million to over $6 million in 1995. Of the $6 million, $3.4 million is for the Recreation Division.

Marketing: For the past 6 or 7 years, the HPRD have been using direct mailing systems (on a quarterly basis). This direct mailing system includes brochures with programs and activities listed. They are now trying to save money by listing activities in the newspapers.

Staff: The HPRD's staff is made up of 59 full-time employees and 300 part-time employees.

Program Detail: The HPRD sponsors baseball, basketball, soccer and softball leagues and camps. They also sponsor two annual carnivals, the "Kaleidoscope" carnival and Teen Fair. There's also the "Nevada Shakespeare in the Park" and the Henderson Civic Symphony.

Facilities: The HPRD is made up of the following facilities: Aquatics, Parks and Recreation Department, a youth center, a senior center, and three different full facilities (gym, workout, racquetball, along with classrooms).

to get repairs made. In many instances, a regular facility maintenance-repair checklist is useful for this purpose. As participant behavior may result in damages to the facility or area, on-site supervision is a preventive measure.

ADA Suggestions

The ADA legislation prohibits discrimination against any American who lives with a disability. The disabled category covers more than 900 disabilities. Specific examples of physical and mental impairments include orthopedic, visual, speech, and hearing impairments; multiple sclerosis; cancer; heart disease; diabetes; HIV disease; rehabilitated drug or alcohol problems; mental retardation; emotional or mental illness; and specific learning disabilities.

CONCLUSION

Fiscal responsibility is inherent in any sport management budget description. One handles funds through a budget process and gains successful programming through sound fiscal management. Although the chief responsibility for budgeting falls on the top manager, all staff have a role in planning and operating financial resources.

DISCUSSION QUESTIONS

1. Why is there an increasing demand each year for additional funds for recreational sport programs?

2. What are typical revenue sources for recreational sport?

3. Explain specific fiscal responsibilities involved in sport management.

4. Define a budget and illustrate the budget process.

5. What are some typical line items that you would include in a recreational sport budget?

6. Why is cash control such an important aspect in sport management? Give examples to support your answer.

7. Explain corporate sponsorship in sport management.

8. What is the main difference between capital expenditures and operating expenditures?

9. What type of expenditure (capital or operating) would you use when constructing a new, multifield softball complex? How would a project of this nature usually be financed?

10. Would you consider gate receipts an adequate means of financial support for an ongoing recreational sport program? Why or why not?

11. Why is budget preparation so important in the fiscal process?

12. List all budget line items that you might use in operating an aquatics program.

13. When are bonds ideal as a primary source of financial support?

14. What tasks are normally associated with fees and charges?

15. Cite specific expenditure categories found in operating expenditures.

APPLICATION EXERCISE

Develop an operational budget for a selected recreational sport program. In your budget, include the programming areas of intramural sport, informal sport, club sport, instructional sport, and fitness programs. Include estimates of operating expenses, such as sport equipment and supplies and hourly wage personnel for each program area.

SUGGESTED READINGS

Belz, D. 1990. Establishing instructor salaries and anticipating possible progressions. P. 354 in *Management strategies in recreational sports*. Corvallis, OR: National Intramural-Recreational Sports Association.

Giles, M. 1991. American Red Cross challenge testing: The economical way to recertify. *National Intramural-Recreational Sports Association Journal* 15 (3): 33.

Jamieson, L.M. 1985. Fees and charges: Mainstay of the recreational sports budget. *National Intramural-Recreational Sports Association Journal* 9 (2): 20.

Karabetsos, J.D. 1990. Traditional and program approaches to budgeting. *National Intramural-Recreational Sports Association Journal* 14 (2): 8-13.

Miller, G. 1990. Research and the development of dollars. P. 61-67 in *Management strategies in recreational sports*. Corvallis, OR: National Intramural-Recreational Sports Association.

Ross, C. 1988. Computer-based accounting in recreational sports. *National Intramural-Recreational Sports Association Journal* 12 (2): 35-37.

Stevenson, M.J. 1988. Balancing a decreasing budget: An exercise in resource management. P. 7-18 in *Selected readings in recreational sports*. Corvallis, OR: National Intramural-Recreational Sports Association.

CHAPTER 11

Facilities
and Equipment

Chapter Objectives

After reading this chapter you will

- understand the principles of scheduling sport facilities,
- understand the process of facility supervision, and
- identify the steps needed to purchase equipment.

The facilities a sport manager supervises can range from giant complexes to sport-specific facilities. These facilities are parts of campuses, tourist attractions in communities, revenue producers for entrepreneurs, expansions in shopping malls, and recreational spaces within natural resources.

Factors that influence the types of facilities available within a setting include geographical area, terrain, climate, ecology, and finances. A less obvious factor that affects facility development and availability is politics. Many special interest groups sponsor programs that require access to facilities. Given the diverse need, the expense of facilities, and space limitations, it is difficult to satisfy everyone. Maximizing the use of facilities while satisfying all interest groups is complicated. Attempts to respond to political realities account for the variety of types and appearances of facility operations.

The goal of facility development and management is to provide facilities in sufficient quantity, diversity, and quality to fulfill the purpose of the recreational sport agency. Sound facility operation allows participant use that fosters favorable attitudes toward the agency and toward sport. Because programmers deal with daily facility operations, they need to be aware of how to schedule and supervise facilities effectively. A well-run facility leads to participant satisfaction and helps guarantee a high return rate. The atmosphere created by sound supervision and concern for the participant leads to a successful operation.

FACILITY SCHEDULING

Scheduling achieves maximum facility use within the resource and staff capabilities of the agency. A quality scheduling process is similar to solving a mystery or piecing together parts of a puzzle. All involve gathering the required pieces of information and finding the sequence and combinations that work.

Scheduling may accomplish shared use of facilities among different programs and agencies, provide different types of participation in the same sport, or furnish opportunities for participation in a variety of activities. The scheduling policy you develop to handle the needs of the setting reflects the setting's philosophy, the participants' interests, the availability of facilities, and the capability of the staff to handle facility operations efficiently and safely. Once you set priorities for facility use and collect eligibility statements, you can process facility reservation requests. A mechanism for identifying the type and extent of facility requests is the written reservation shown in form 11.1.

This form should specify how soon and where to submit a request. Advance notice of facility need gives the programmer adequate time to organize and schedule requests, eliminate conflicts, chart and control use levels, and review the appropriateness of the design for the activity. It also allows those responsible time to modify or reject a request and counsel the participants regarding proper use.

All scheduling practices are ways to use time. Scheduling practices that accommodate various sports, programs, and groups commonly use three time units: seasonal, monthly, and daily.

Seasonal Scheduling

The time of year and climate often influence facility scheduling. Seasonal scheduling most often corresponds to fall, winter, summer, and spring, or simply, winter and summer. Consequently, it does not apply to parts of the country where there is little variation in climate. In some geographical areas, winter requires a move indoors for some sports, signaling peak use of indoor facilities for volleyball, basketball, roller skating, swimming, and jogging. Winter also means peak facility use for such sports as sledding, skiing, tobogganing, ice skating, and ice hockey. The return of warm weather causes a switch outdoors to enjoy such sports as softball, golf, hang-gliding, motocross, rugby, surfing, drag racing, and scuba diving. Seasonal scheduling helps coordinate availability of facilities with sport seasons, for example, football, soccer, wrestling, basketball, and tennis. The scheduling of facilities according to calendar or sport season makes it easier to manage programs designed to meet regularly over an extended time (8, 10, 12 weeks) for class, tournaments, or club participation. When a schedule covers a long time

---

RECREATIONAL SPORT FACILITY RESERVATION REQUEST

Date _____

To: Coordinator of facilities

From: Name _____ Phone _____

      Organization _____

      Address _____

This organization would like to reserve the following:

1. Facility _____

2. Activity _____

3. Dates _____

4. Times _____

5. Number in group _____

6. Responsible person _____

                                         Signed _____

Note: Requests must be submitted in writing at least *two weeks* in advance of times and dates requested.

Form 11.1 Facility reservation request.

span, consider the effect of holidays on plans. Figure 11.1 illustrates a seasonal scheduling pattern for a fall session at a municipal community center.

According to traditional scheduling practice, most major maintenance and repairs occur before or after a season. Functions involving emergency or preventive maintenance occur as required.

Monthly and Weekly Scheduling

Shorter duration scheduling accommodates a variety of interests. Instead of a fixed schedule operating daily or weekly, the programmer may allow greater flexibility to meet user demands, although this practice may frustrate those accustomed to routine. In addition, fluctuating weekly schedules may be inappropriate for some sport activities, programs like skill development, and structured tournaments that require continual participation. In these instances, consistent scheduling is preferable.

A monthly or weekly schedule is appropriate for facility-centered programs, such as ski areas, pools, and golf courses where patron use is regular. Because this pattern involves a shorter period, reserve time for maintenance and repair, particularly for facilities in yearly operation. Figure 11.2 illustrates a typical monthly schedule for a swimming pool.

Daily Scheduling

Daily scheduling practices divide the day into general time periods: morning, afternoon, and evening; or morning, early afternoon, late afternoon, early evening, and late evening. This structure requires an understanding of participant lifestyles so you can tailor facility scheduling for a sport activity, program, or age group. Figure 11.3 provides an example of a daily schedule.

In addition to these time units for facility scheduling, specialized scheduling techniques exist that are useful within each time unit. The most common of these techniques are block and simultaneous use scheduling.

Block Scheduling

This scheduling technique objectively recognizes different groups, programs, or sports having priority for facility use within specific time blocks during the day. In an educational setting, for example, training and instructional programs may have priority from 8:30 through 11:30 a.m. and 1:30 through 3:30 p.m., Monday through Friday. Intramural and club sport take precedence from 3:30 to 6:00 p.m., athletic sport from 6:00 through 8:30 p.m., and informal sport from 11:30 a.m. through 1:30 p.m. and 8:30 p.m. until closing.

Figure 11.1
Season
Program Schedule

Fall session I: September 13–October 31
Registration: August 16

Fall session II: November 1–December 19
Registration: October 4

Sport	Day	Time	Fee	Weeks
Aquatics				
Age 3-5	Monday/Wednesday	3:45–4:15 p.m.	Free	4
	Tuesday/Thursday	5:30–6:00 p.m.	Free	4
	Saturday	9:00–9:30 a.m.	Free	4
Age 6 and over	Tuesday/Thursday	6:00–6:30 p.m.	$2.00	4
(Basic)	Saturday	4:00–4:30 p.m.	$2.00	4
Family swim	Friday/Saturday	7:30–9:30 p.m.	Free	6
	Sunday	1:30–3:30 p.m.	Free	6
Scuba	Tuesday	8:00–10:00 p.m.	$10.00	6
Tennis				
Beginning	Monday/Wednesday	7:00–8:30 p.m.	$4.00	6
Intermediate	Tuesday/Thursday	7:00–8:30 p.m.	$6.00	6
Volleyball				
A league (2nd session only)	Friday	8:00–10:00 p.m.	$6.00	6
B league (2nd session only)	Sunday	8:00–10:00 p.m.	$4.00	4
Karate	Monday/Wednesday	7:00–9:00 p.m.	$6.00	6

Similarly, a single facility may use block scheduling to accommodate several program formats with the same activity. For example, you may schedule club sport swimming for early morning, instructional swimming for late morning, informal sport swimming during the early afternoon, structured meets for late afternoon, and informal sport swimming for the evening. Scheduling may designate age group access to the pool: preschool children in the morning, youth teams in the afternoon, and adults in the evening.

Block scheduling may occur weekly (see figure 11.4), monthly, seasonally, or annually. Because block scheduling identifies regular consecutive time spans of facility use for an activity, program, or group, it establishes order and permits staff and participants the opportunity to set a routine. However, this procedure deters individuals whose timetables conflict with these schedules.

Simultaneous Scheduling

This refers to scheduling more than one group, sport, or program in the same facility or area at the same time. This method applies when multiple units of the facility exist (basketball courts, bowling alleys, racquetball courts, or riding paddocks); where a multipurpose facility handles simultaneous use (gymnasium, natatorium, field house, or stadium); and where one facility is of sufficient size or acoustical design that multiple users do not interfere with one another (golf course, ski slope, lake, mountain, or outdoor sport field). Although simultaneous scheduling accommodates a variety

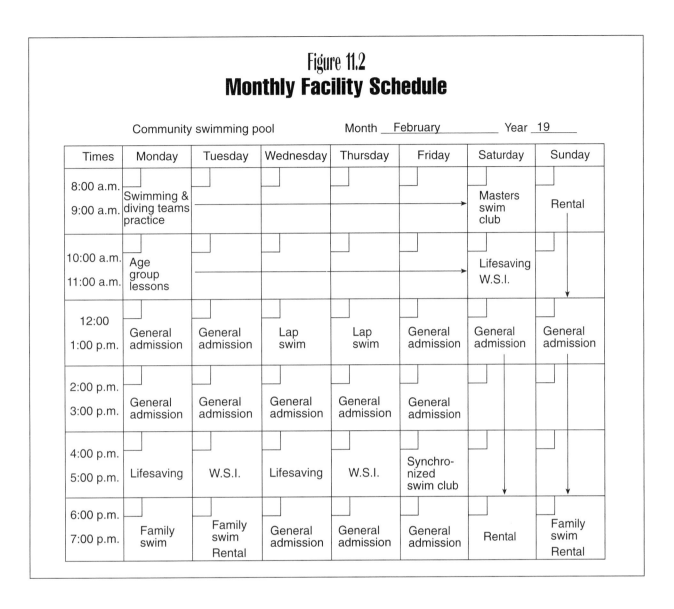

Figure 11.2
Monthly Facility Schedule

Community swimming pool   Month __February__   Year _19___

Times	Monday	Tuesday	Wednesday	Thursday	Friday	Saturday	Sunday
8:00 a.m. 9:00 a.m.	Swimming & diving teams practice	→				Masters swim club	Rental
10:00 a.m. 11:00 a.m.	Age group lessons	→				Lifesaving W.S.I.	
12:00 1:00 p.m.	General admission	General admission	Lap swim	Lap swim	General admission	General admission	General admission
2:00 p.m. 3:00 p.m.	General admission	General admission	General admission	General admission	General admission		
4:00 p.m. 5:00 p.m.	Lifesaving	W.S.I.	Lifesaving	W.S.I.	Synchronized swim club		
6:00 p.m. 7:00 p.m.	Family swim	Family swim Rental	General admission	General admission	General admission	Rental	Family swim Rental

of sports and a potentially large number of users, the sport activities must be compatible. Pairing a martial arts class with an aerobic dance group in the same gymnasium is not wise.

Regardless of the method in use, the programmer needs accurate information regarding scheduling to submit and implement reservation requests, to monitor and supervise scheduled sport activities or programs, and to communicate information to participants and personnel regarding reservations or availability. Because the programmer works closely with participants, he or she has ample opportunity to consider their opinions and attitudes concerning aspects of facility scheduling and forward these to appropriate administrative staff. Sensitivity to feedback is essential for accurate assessment of interests and evaluation of services.

Reservation Requests for Facility Use

When individuals or groups apart from the recreational sport staff design events and submit facility requests, establish a procedure for considering the request and for counseling in proper facility use. The responsibility for conducting the review and counseling process rests with a facility coordinator or a recreational sport programmer.

In settings where a variety of interest groups share facilities, the recreational sport staff may not have complete responsibility for facility management and scheduling. Programmers work instead through a facility coordinator to review those requests that occur during recreational sport hours or require programming expertise to determine their suitability. Whatever the circum-

Figure 11.3
Daily Facility Schedule

Time	Free-weight room 092	Universal gym room 092A	Gym 095
7:00 a.m.	Informal sport	Athletic sport	Instructional sport
7:30 a.m.	Informal sport	Athletic sport	Instructional sport
8:00 a.m.	Informal sport	Athletic sport	Instructional sport
8:30 a.m.	Informal sport	Athletic sport	Instructional sport
9:00 a.m.	Closed	Closed	Closed
9:30 a.m.	Closed	Closed	Closed
10:00 a.m.	Closed	Informal sport	Informal sport
10:30 a.m.	Closed	Informal sport	Informal sport
11:00 a.m.	Informal sport	Informal sport	Informal sport
11:30 a.m.	Informal sport	Informal sport	Informal sport
12:00 noon	Informal sport	Informal sport	Informal sport
12:30 p.m.	Informal sport	Informal sport	Aerobic rhythm
1:00 p.m.	Informal sport	Informal sport	Aerobic rhythm
1:30 p.m.	Informal sport	Intramural sport	Aerobic rhythm
2:00 p.m.	Informal sport	Intramural sport	Stretch fit
2:30 p.m.	Informal sport	Intramural sport	Stretch fit
3:00 p.m.	Informal sport	Informal sport	Closed
3:30 p.m.	Informal sport	Informal sport	Judo club
4:00 p.m.	Informal sport	Informal sport	Judo club
4:30 p.m.	Informal sport	Informal sport	Judo club
5:00 p.m.	Informal sport	Informal sport	Judo club
5:30 p.m.	Informal sport	Informal sport	Judo club
6:00 p.m.	Weight club	Informal sport	Hapkido club
6:30 p.m.	Weight club	Informal sport	Hapkido club
7:00 p.m.	Weight club	Informal sport	Hapkido club
7:30 p.m.	Weight club	Informal sport	Hapkido club
8:00 p.m.	Weight club	Informal sport	Aikido club
8:30 p.m.	Weight club	Informal sport	Aikido club
9:00 p.m.	Informal sport	Informal sport	Wrestling club
9:30 p.m.	Informal sport	Informal sport	Wrestling club
10:00 p.m.	Informal sport	Informal sport	Wrestling club
10:30 p.m.	Informal sport	Informal sport	Wrestling club
11:00 p.m.	Closed	Closed	Closed

stance, provide for a formal review, decision, and counseling process in the interest of safety and quality control.

When reviewing a request, the programmer should determine the suitability of the program in terms of organization, personnel, safety, and format. In some settings, the programmer serves as a resource person for organizing and implementing an event. In other settings, the programmer states the conditions that must be met for the request to be granted. On completion, the review process may reveal that the time or facility requested is not available and alternatives are needed.

When reviewing requests for facility access during recreational sport hours, programmers need an objective way to consider how to fulfill the request without infringing on agency-sponsored programs and special events. We offer the following suggestions on how to make objective decisions simply.

• **Use levels.** A record of daily participant facility use, taken at 30-minute, 45-minute, or 60-minute intervals, reveals use patterns that may allow you to transfer time to other programs. When participation levels are consistently high, the programmer usually denies the request. Low use levels permit flexibility regarding requests. The nature of the request often influences a decision. If it is a short-term event or of interest to many people,

Figure 11.4
Block Schedule for Evans Field House

	Monday	Tuesday	Wednesday	Thursday	Friday	Saturday
8:00 a.m.						
9:30 a.m.	Physical education					
11:00 a.m.						
12:30 p.m.	Recreational sport				Recreational	
2:00 p.m.	Athletics					
3:30 p.m.					sport	
5:00 p.m.	Physical education					
6:30 p.m.						
8:00 p.m.	Recreational sport					

the programmer may approve a request despite moderate to high use levels.

• **Facility alternatives.** After considering participant and program use levels, the programmer may suggest a change in the time span requested. There are instances when an individual or group can use nonprime times or less convenient facility locations.

• **Nature of the request.** Occasionally, a reservation request for a structured event does not meet acceptable standards to warrant facility space, regardless of availability. For this reason, it is wise to prepare criteria to evaluate facility requests. Require individuals or groups to submit preliminary plans and information regarding intended use of the facility along with the reservation request. A sample of a format you can use to obtain preliminary plans is presented in form 11.2.

When the responsible party does not provide for proper safety, leadership, and programming support, consider denying the request.

Once you reach a decision on a request, communicate it to the prospective user or to the facility coordinator. You can use a review form such as form 11.3.

On request approval, conduct a session with the responsible party to review final plans, expectations, and responsibilities. Have a procedure ready to handle potential problems, accidents, and emer-

gencies. To confirm acceptance of the conditions for use, require the user to sign an acknowledgment of responsibility form, such as the one shown in form 11.4.

At the end of the counseling process, provide the user with a written confirmation of the reservation and a copy of responsibilities for facility use. The following outline itemizes all considerations for facility reservation requests by outside groups:

I. Planning
   A. Kind of event
   B. Dates and times
   C. Facilities needed
   D. Rental fees, damage charges
   E. Event rules and regulations
   F. Volunteer or paid assistance needs
      1. Officials
      2. Supervisors
      3. Medical
      4. Set up and take down
   G. Entry fees
      1. Participants
      2. Spectators
   H. Other expenditures
      1. Publicity and promotions
      2. Equipment

SPECIAL EVENT FACILITY RESERVATION REQUEST
Preliminary information

Name _____   Phone _____

Address _____

ADDITIONAL CONTACT PERSON

Name _____   Phone _____

Address _____

Organization _____   Date _____

1. Summarize previous facility reservations by your organization (include date, facility, time, event).
   _____
   _____

2. What kind of special event is to be conducted (tournament, clinic, etc.)? Please explain. _____
   _____
   _____
   _____

3. How many individuals or teams are expected to participate? _____

4. Will there be any entry fee? _____   Spectator admission fees? _____
   If yes, how much? _____   If yes, how much? _____

5. What facilities are being requested? (Please list.) _____
   _____
   _____

6. When is the event to take place?   1st choice _____
                                       2st choice _____

7. What special equipment or facility preparation might be needed? (Please list.) _____
   _____
   _____

8. How many people will be assisting in the operation of the event? _____
   _____

9. Does anyone in the group have first aid or CPR certification? _____ If yes, please indicate name
   and phone number. _____

10. Are there plans to have any type of concessions at the event? If yes, please explain. _____
    _____
    _____

11. Is there a need to have assistance by personnel from recreational sport? If so, how many, what functions, and
    how do you plan to pay them? _____
    _____

12. Additional comments _____
    _____
    _____
    _____
    _____

Form 11.2   Preliminary plans and information form.

RECREATIONAL SPORT FACILITY REQUEST REVIEW

A. General information

Date submitted to facility coordinator _____

Date received by recreational sport facility _____

Name _____ Address _____

Organization _____

Facility _____ Phone _____

Dates _____ Times _____

B. Use analysis

Previous use summary _____

_____

Recreational sport use _____

_____

C. Programming review

Meeting date _____ Outline required _____ Approval _____

Group leader _____

Equipment needs _____

_____

D. Final status

Request approved _____ Denied _____

Reason(s) for denial _____

_____

Date returned to facility coordinator _____

Staff signature _____

Form 11.3   Facility request review form.

3. Supplies
4. Recognition
5. Facility preparation
6. Utilities
  I. Equipment and supply needs
    1. Tables, chairs, bleachers
    2. Equipment
    3. Supplies
  J. Identification of responsible persons
  K. Concessions
    1. Sanitation
    2. Serving permit
    3. Access to utilities
II. Organizing
  A. Developing rules, forms, publicity
  B. Food services approval

C. Securing needed personnel
D. Recreational sport staff approval
E. Advising on facility utilization
  1. Policies
  2. Supervision
  3. Safety, accidents, emergencies
  4. Maintenance
F. Signing statement of responsibility
G. Payment of rental fee
H. Transmission of approval to facility co-ordinator
III. Conducting the event
  A. Set-up
  B. Equipment pickup
  C. Supervision and crowd control
  D. Clean-up

STATEMENT OF RESPONSIBILITY FOR FACILITY USE

The user, or his/her sponsor if one is deemed necessary, shall be responsible for cleanup, damage, injuries, supervision, and any liability incurred during the use of facilities requested in the application received by this office. The specific responsibilities are listed below:

A. Supervision.   The user agrees to supervise the use of the facility to ensure that there is no abuse to it nor any violation of the laws of the state or the rules and regulations of the agency. Assistance may be sought through the facility supervisors. Verification of reservation will be required (bring confirmation slip).

B. Injury.   Any personal injury requiring immediate medical attention must be reported to facility supervisor or the ambulance service. A written report describing the circumstances must be completed and returned to this office or facility supervisor. Accident report forms are available from the facility supervisor or from this office.

C. Cleanup and damage.   The facility will be inspected by a facility supervisor or this office before and after use. If cleanup is necessary it will be done by the following.

   1) The user assuming the physical action of the cleanup. This will again be subject to inspection.

   2) Placing a work order for its cleanup. The user will accept financial obligations for this action.

Any damage to the facility, its furnishings, or equipment must be reported in writing to this office. The user will be responsible for the cost of repair or replacement.

I, _____, acting as the responsible individual for

_____ have read the above statement and will
                               organization
ensure that these stipulations are followed.

                               Date _____

                               Signed _____

Note: This statement must be returned by _____

Form 11.4   Acknowledgment of responsibility form.

IV. Evaluating
   A. Follow-up and postevent inspection by staff
   B. Return of equipment
   C. Damage charges
   D. Recommendation for future use

The programmer should monitor participant adherence to conditions of use, either through firsthand observation or supervision by subordinate personnel. Some settings require verbal or written follow-up reports, especially if there is disorderly conduct, accidents, emergencies, or facility misuse.

SUPERVISING FACILITIES

Theoretically, anyone present at a facility site may provide supervision, although such a tenuous arrangement is not always appropriate. In practice, the nature of the sport or program, age level of participants, group size, concern for safety, and satisfaction determine the appropriate supervision. Common functions performed by on-site supervisory personnel include

- ensuring a positively received environment (attractiveness);
- preventing or controlling hazards;
- reporting and managing accidents;
- curtailing disruptive conduct;
- communicating and enforcing policies;
- organizing activity;
- curtailing facility and equipment misuse;
- providing equipment;
- reporting suggestions, problems, maintenance needs, and emergencies;
- checking eligibility of users;
- handling facility security; and
- enhancing public relations.

Hourly wage employees, club sport officers, and volunteer workers who handle on-site responsibilities such as safety and conflict resolution require specialized training. Clearly, on-site supervisors are in direct contact with participants and serve as vital communication, safety, and public relations links. Encourage them to obtain participant feedback regarding ideas and concerns and channel comments to staff using suggestion and complaint forms.

In many settings the programmer has an assignment in on-site supervision as well as a responsibility for training, monitoring, and evaluating other supervisors.

MAINTAINING FACILITIES

Natural deterioration requires attention to keep facilities and equipment in good order for safe use. A total maintenance effort covers two areas: operations and repairs.

Operations refer to scheduled routines such as sweeping floors, dragging infields, picking up trash, mowing grass, cleaning rest areas, and replacing light bulbs. Other maintenance tasks are preventive and involve regular inspections of facilities and equipment to avoid costly or time-consuming repairs. Preventive maintenance involves tuning engines, painting, preserving adequate ground cover, applying protective floor surfacing, pruning dead tree limbs, replacing worn mechanical parts, and cleaning filtration systems.

The second category of maintenance involves repair work that requires more specialized labor. Repair work, such as replacing roofing, fencing, or floor surfaces and seeding fields, is a scheduled function, but others, such as those needed when vandalism, neglect, accidents, and weather damage occur, are unpredictable. Many repairs are simple and inexpensive to handle: clogged drains, broken windows, torn nets, or broken bleachers. Other repairs may be expensive and require extensive work due to damage caused by a tornado, fire, auto accident, roof leak, disrupted utility service, or equipment breakdown.

The maintenance role of a programmer depends on the nature of the job and training, the type of facility, area, or equipment, the maintenance need, and the maintenance staff available within the setting. It is not unusual for a programmer to perform or oversee simple custodial or housekeeping chores. Form 11.5 indicates examples of routine tasks monitored by a programmer at a multipurpose indoor facility.

The programmer plays a prominent role in preventive maintenance through activity supervision and facility inspection. Curtailing the costly problem of vandalism is a significant contribution to the maintenance effort. A supervisor should maintain a high profile. Both participants and spectators must understand that acts of vandalism lead to criminal or civil prosecution.

You can further preventive maintenance by regular inspections of facilities and equipment. In most instances, inspections require general knowledge and simple observation to detect situations needing attention. During these regular inspections, use a checklist like the sample in form 11.6.

Most repair tasks performed by the programmer and subordinate staff involve minor preventive maintenance rather than actual repairs. For example, the programmer may perform or supervise manicuring and lining outdoor sport fields, backwashing pool filtration systems, lubricating or tightening equipment parts, painting or staining small structures or signs, watering outdoor fields, or operating ice resurfacing equipment.

When extensive repair work is required due to vandalism or some other incident, the programmer specifies needed repairs on standard reporting forms. These forms ensure the collection of appropriate information. Forms 11.6 and 11.7 demonstrate general and specific use.

Whenever a hazard exists at the site of repair work, the programmer should secure the area, remove the hazard, notify the proper authorities, and initiate evacuation when necessary. When repair work requires closing a facility or area, the programmer and subordinate staff should communicate this information through signs at the facility site, press releases, and individual contact with users by mail or phone. Keep on-site subordinate staff informed of maintenance and repair timetables so they can accurately respond to participant inquiries. Advanced notice of facility unavailability minimizes user disappointment.

EQUIPMENT AND SUPPLIES

Sport programs require equipment and supplies that are safe for use and sufficient to meet participant demand. The large financial investment in facilities requires the availability of equipment and supplies necessary for their maximum productivity. Even when facilities are inadequate, it is possible to provide quality recreational sport programs

DAILY MAINTENANCE CHECKLIST

A.M.	NOON	P.M.	MAINTENANCE
			RESTOCK BATHROOM Locker rooms (refill sauna pail)
			Main level
			Sub basement
			ALL SPORT CENTER AND ACTIVITY CENTER COURTS Sweep with dust mop
			Straighten out Ping-Pong tables
			Pick up trash
			TRACK Sweep with vacuum
			Pick up trash
			POOLS Doors locked when pools are closed
			Supervise guards
			LOST AND FOUND Deposit all lost articles at front desk until end of day
			Deposit all valuables to main desk
			Deposit all articles to lost and found at end of day
			FIRST AID SUPPLIES (Use checklist—deposit list at main desk) Back door
			Front door
			RECEPTIONIST DESK Pick up trash
			Check supplies
			RACQUETBALL, HANDBALL, AND SQUASH COURTS Turn off lights in all courts not in use
			MEN'S AND WOMEN'S WEIGHT ROOMS Clean all vinyl parts
			Check equipment
			TV AND MEZZANINE LOUNGE Straighten furniture
			Pick up trash
			TRANSIENT LOCKER ROOM Pick up trash
			Check bulletin boards
			Check lockers at closing that are missing keys (empty them out using master key)
			BOXING ROOM Sweep floors
			Check equipment
			COMBATIVES/DANCE ROOM Sweep floors
			Inspect mats (mop when needed)
			ARCHERY/GOLF ROOM Straighten nets
			Put rooms in order

Form 11.5   Daily maintenance checklist form.

OUTDOOR FACILITY/AREA MAINTENANCE REPORT FORM

Location _____   Date _____

Checklist		Comments
Backstop		
Bleachers		
Fields		
Courts—basketball		
Courts—tennis		
Horseshoe pit		
Nets		
Lights		
Fence		
Pavement		
Water fountains		
Stairs		
Bike path		
Signs		
Standards		
Driveways		
Other		
Other		
Other		

This report is to be filled out each morning by the first shift supervisor.

G = Good condition

F = Fair condition

N = Needs attention

Submitted by _____

Form 11.6   Maintenance report form for an outdoor facility.

using appropriate equipment and supplies. Consequently, a programmer should concentrate on obtaining all the materials necessary to conduct a quality program.

Let's differentiate between equipment and supplies. Equipment refers to permanent or expendable items required for conducting sport. Examples of permanent equipment are lawnmowers, basketball backboards, softball backstops, volleyball standards, weight-lifting weights, and tennis posts. Expendable items that require periodic replacement include softballs, bats, table tennis balls, nets, roller skates, and hockey sticks. Supplies are

supplemental and expendable items required for the orderly operation of a sport program. Items range from score sheets, clipboards, towels, pencils, and field marking chalk to mops, cleaning liquids, and soap for the shower room. Water, gasoline, sand, gravel, grass seed, and fertilizer come under this definition when an agency maintains outdoor facilities.

Because equipment and supplies are a big part of an operational budget, the programmer should apply sound management principles when selecting, buying, storing, distributing, and caring for them.

VANDALISM REPORT

Facility _____ Date of occurrence _____

Specific location _____

Detailed damage description _____

_____

• MAINTENANCE CREW—COST RECORD OF REPAIRS

Labor (List total hours of each employee classification worked.) _____

_____

Material _____

_____

Equipment (List total hours of each type of equipment used.) _____

_____

_____

• VANDALISM PREVENTION

Do you think that this act of vandalism could have been prevented? _____

How? _____

_____

_____
Supervisor

_____
Recreational sport staff or facility coordinator

_____
Maintenance division

• DO NOT FILL IN BELOW THIS LINE

Labor _____   _____

Material _____   _____

Equipment _____   _____

Maintenance crew totals (from above)   _____

Total cost of repairs   _____

Form 11.7   Vandalism report form and repair record.

Selecting Equipment and Supplies

When identifying and recommending any item for purchase, consider the following:

- Is the item a necessity or a luxury?
- Will the item contribute to the quality, efficiency, and effectiveness of operations?
- Is the item of quality material and production?
- Will the item pose any safety hazard?
- Is the item durable?
- Can the item be used for multiple purposes?
- Is the item economical?

The individual responsible for selecting equipment and supplies may be a trained purchasing agent or a sport programmer, if the latter has the qualifications, time, and interest to do the job.

The purchasing agent has the responsibility to buy a requested item at an appropriate time at the best price consistent with desired quality. Current knowledge of design changes, new processes, and products is important in the selection process.

Shining Example

Monroe County YMCA Family Fitness Center

The Monroe County YMCA believes a healthy person needs to be healthy not only in body but also in mind and spirit. The Monroe County YMCA is unique in that its revenue is generated from membership and program dues as well as donations. The Monroe County YMCA's extensive facilities allow them to offer a wide variety of programs which serve families, adults, and youth throughout the community of Bloomington. Over the past fifteen years, the Monroe County YMCA has expanded its facilities in order to meet the demands of its growing membership base. These expansions and renovations have allowed the YMCA to offer a variety of programs and meet the needs of the community.

Organization: The Monroe County YMCA is an organization run by the Board of Directors. The Executive Director is in charge of the board relations, community relations, fiscal budget/fund raising and the facility. The Associate Executive Director is in charge of the facility supervision, staff training/motivation, corporate fitness/special events and the building supervisors. Under them are 7 Directors who look over the other areas of the organization.

Clientele: The number of members is listed as 12,810 people.

Budget: It's total capital budget for 1995 was $152,765.00.

Marketing: The target market for the Monroe County YMCA is families (with 26.2 percent of the total members), 48.9 percent are adults, 16.5 percent are Husband/Wife members, 5 percent are single parents and 3.4 percent are youth.

Staff: The Monroe County YMCA is made up of 17 full-time employees and 306 active part-time employees.

Program Detail: The Monroe County YMCA currently oversees the following programs: Kids Gymnastics, Youth Sports, Youth & Pee Wee Soccer, Youth Swimming Lessons, Youth Scuba & Snorkeling, Adult Aquatics, Adult Aquatic Fitness, Swim Lessons & Lifeguarding, Adult Fitness/Flex Pass Classes, Country Line Dance/Aerobic Certification/Pre & Post Natal, Exercise & Nutrition/Fitness Profiles/Personal Trainers, Corporate Image, Adult Sports, Weight Training, Flex Pass & Fitness for Active Older Adults, T'ai Chi/Brown Bag/Yoga for Older Adults, Health Enhancement, Arthritis, Rehab, CPR, Smoking Cessation, Healthy Back, Parkinson's Support Group, Stress Management, and Massage.

Facilities: The YMCA is located in an 85,000 sq. feet building on 17 acres of land. It includes all of the following: 25 meter lap pool, Instructional pool, 3 weight rooms, Men's and Women's locker rooms, dance studio, 2 whirlpools, 4 racquetball courts, Youth summer camp, 2 gyms, soccer field, cardiovascular equipment, and aerobic room.

Examine new equipment catalogs as soon as you receive them from the manufacturers. Have equipment dealers or representatives demonstrate samples of new items. Each of the following influences purchasing decisions:

- **Specific program events.**   The nature of programs and events offered affects selection of equipment and supplies. What is appropriate for an outdoor program may not be suitable for indoors.

- **Available space and facilities.**   The extent of facilities, either indoor or outdoor, determines the type of items needed for an event. When a softball facility has a small field area, use a flight-restricted ball.

- **Age.**   Equipment and supplies should suit the needs of the age group using them.

- **Gender.**   Often the suitability of materials for sport events varies with the gender of the participants. Volleyball standards, as an example, adjust to different net heights for men and women.

- **Skill.**   The skill level of participants influences the selection of equipment and supplies. Trick skis, considered standard equipment for a professional water-skier, are inappropriate for a beginner.

- **Leadership.**   The quality of supervision available to monitor equipment and supplies at an event affects what items to select. You cannot buy trampolines unless you can provide the proper supervision, security, and storage.

- **Cost.**   Budget limitations determine price ranges. Establish spending guidelines to avoid wasteful purchases. Realistic budgeting aids in the long-range planning of equipment purchases.

- **Quality of material.**   Cost is not a foolproof indicator of quality. Look for quality of performance, production, appearance, and service warranties. The purchase of more expensive quality equipment and supplies often results in savings in the long run.

- **Dealer reputation.**   Select items from an established dealer recognized for reliable and efficient service. Manufacturers who market national brands of equipment and supplies usually guarantee their products. When selecting vendors, check the availability of merchandise. Consider dealer policy concerning quick delivery, service, exchange, and adjustments. The main objective in selection is the purchase of quality merchandise at a competitive price. If a reputable local dealer offers a quality product or service competitive with the price of an out-of-town company, use the local dealer. Good will and quick delivery are important considerations here.

- **Standardization of equipment.**   Selecting items of similar quality, style, or color may mean considerable savings over time. Standardization makes items easier to replace and repair. Special order equipment and supplies result in higher cost and delays in shipment and repair.

- **Timing.**   Order all equipment and supplies well in advance of need, to allow for inspection, evaluation, possible replacement, and inventory control.

As a sport program that will regularly purchase equipment, you represent a valuable account for venders. This status allows you some negotiation leeway with vendors, who will want your repeat business. Don't be afraid to use your leverage to persuade your dealer to stock an item with nontraditional colors; using a yellow football, a blue water polo ball, or a white basketball deters theft. Also, ask the dealer if the manufacturer can engrave your agency's identification marks or logo on your items at the factory. Finally, when buying clothes or uniforms, don't take a participant's word for a correct size. If your order is big enough, a representative may come to measure participants. Otherwise, measure for yourself.

Whenever possible, purchase standard pieces of equipment and supplies in bulk and save money. Take advantage of closeouts or sales on stock items. If you do not require equipment of exceptional quality, buy slightly blemished goods at considerable savings.

Purchasing Procedures

An efficient agency explains its purchasing system to appropriate personnel. In larger organizations, a staff member serves as a liaison between the organization's purchasing agent and each department. In smaller organizations, one person acts as a part-time purchasing agent in addition to a full-time programming job. Any organization buying quantities of equipment or supplies can benefit from a purchasing policy manual providing explanations, purchasing policies, procedures, and examples of forms and records used in processing.

The following are general steps in the purchasing process:

1. **Make a preliminary request.** It is important that an administrator, such as a director or associate director, be aware of any purchasing requests before they are forwarded to the purchasing agent. A preliminary request form indicates the staff member initiating the request; the program charged; the date the equipment or supply is needed; the suggested vendor; the method of payment; and the quantity, description, and cost estimate of desired item (see form 11.8).

2. **Justify the request.** The programmer should provide administrative staff with a written or verbal justification for each purchase request. A justification answers the following questions:

- Why do you need the items?
- How will they improve operations?
- What are the advantages and disadvantages of the product?
- Can you maintain and store them easily?
- Is there a need for special care or handling?
- Is the product a current or new (recommended) item?

3. **Provide item specifications.** On approval of the preliminary request, include specification or bid sheets with a purchase requisition form to provide the necessary details for the purchasing agent. The purchasing agent needs specifications to ensure that the items you want are the items you receive. When preparing item specifications, provide as much information as possible about the product. Complicated specifications may discourage bidders. Strict ones may block the purchase of suitable items because they do not meet precise requirements.

4. **Secure bids.** After writing equipment or supply specifications, send them to the purchasing agent for competitive bidding. A bid system exists to eliminate favoritism and stimulate competition to reduce prices. Most state and federal organizations have an established policy, dictated by law, concerning purchases made with tax money. If the purchase item exceeds a certain amount, ranging from $100 to $1,000, an intent to purchase must be advertised publicly to invite competitive bids. Other guidelines specify procedures governing formal and informal bids. When you gear this process toward the lowest bidder, inferior merchandise may result. By issuing invitations well in advance, responsible firms have sufficient time to prepare competitive bids. A bid system results in competition from reliable vendors within a close price range. It is important to consider all vendors and to treat them fairly.

5. **Prepare purchase orders.** On accepting a bid, prepare a purchase order for the items. Standard business forms, containing from one to five duplicate copies, include name, address, and telephone number of the recommended vendor and the agency initiating the request; billing and delivery instructions; the purchase order and requisition number; date of the order; the quantity, description, unit cost, and total cost of the items requested; and an approval signature from the purchasing agent (see form 11.9).

Equipment Inventory

Once equipment and supplies arrive, check the accompanying merchandise packing list and count all cartons and items received. Open the cartons, inspect for damage, and verify that the items coincide with the original purchase order. Report defects, damage, or shortages to the vendor immediately. If items are in order and acceptable, inventory them.

A good inventory system, indicating what you need for bidding and purchasing, provides an efficient way to control the amount and condition of stock on hand. Before adopting any inventory system and its record-keeping requirements, consider future need for equipment.

Inventory records (see form 11.10) describe the condition, location, and quantity of items on hand; the cost of each item; and the amount of stock to maintain at any one time. Keep a record of items that have been transferred, lost, discarded, destroyed, or repaired since the previous reporting period.

Mark all sport equipment and supplies for identification before entering them in the inventory and allowing their use. Use permanent ink, waterproof paint, engravings, or other durable marking methods. Identify the organization, unit number, date of purchase, serial number, and size, when necessary. At least once a year it is necessary to physically count the inventory to match existing records with actual supplies and equipment. You can enhance physical counts by using computerized databases that call for regular updating of inventory.

With proper control, inventory systems are valuable sources for preparing financial reports and

PRELIMINARY EQUIPMENT REQUEST FORM

Requested by _____   Approved by _____

Date _____   Date _____

Date needed _____   Vendor suggested _____

Budget charged _____   Address _____

_____

(Check one)   Purchase requisition _____   Printing plant _____

Bookstore _____   Physical plant job request _____

Petty cash _____   Central stores _____

Other _____   Specify _____

Quantity	Brief description of item, book title, work to be performed, and so forth (catalog #, name of salesperson, etc., requested)	Estimate cost

Form 11.8   Preliminary equipment request.

future budget requests. They can indicate the popularity of certain programs within a recreational sport operation.

Equipment Storage and Distribution

After equipment and supplies have been inventoried and marked for identification, they must be properly stored. Use racks, bins, lockers, and other structures to protect the items and maximize the use of space. Regulate the temperature, moisture, humidity, and ventilation of the storage area to protect all equipment and supplies. Storage should be convenient to the sport facility or playing area where the items are used.

In a large facility, the storage area is usually a multipurpose room designed to warehouse, distribute, repair, and launder equipment and supplies. For convenience, this room is typically located next to the locker and shower facilities.

Establish policies and procedures for issuing items and maintain checkout forms providing for their return. There are several acceptable procedures for distributing equipment and supplies. You can issue items needed for an intramural sport to a

programmer having the responsibility for their distribution at the playing site. Form 11.11 represents a model equipment checkout form suitable for an intramural event.

With a club sport, you can issue equipment and supplies to the club president or other representative for the season. Individual clubs maintain their own inventory because they are responsible for all items used in their program.

Informal sport activities and instructional sport sessions may use an equipment room for issuing equipment and supplies. In this case, participants need to present identification and complete an equipment checkout slip, providing their name, address, telephone number, social security number, and locker number. Information on the form should indicate the quantity and name of the item, identification code, and date of distribution and return.

A checkout slip should contain an acceptance statement that indicates personal responsibility for the items and agreement to purchase or repair the items if they are lost or damaged. Some organizations require a security deposit while equipment is on loan.

INDIANA UNIVERSITY
Departmental Purchase Order

	PURCHASE ORDER NO.
	USE THIS NUMBER ON ALL INVOICES AND CORRESPONDENCE

VENDOR

Name

Address

City, state, zip

SHIP TO

BILL TO

Indiana University
Accounts Payable
P.O. Box 4095
Bloomington, IN 47402
Phone (812) 855-4004

Submit Itemized Invoice in Duplicate. Referring to Order Number

ORDER DATE

Vendor Fein/ID	Vendor Telephone

Date required	Ship Via	FOB	TERMS	Source of Price Information
	UPE (Unless otherwise specified)	☐ Shipping Point ☐ Destination	☐ Net 30 ☐ _____	

Quantity	Catalog Number and Description	Unit Price	Extended Price
			$ _____
	Tax Exempt No.		

For More Information Contact:

Name

Department   Bldg.   Room

Phone

Purchase Approval

_____
Account Manager

_____

Purchase Order Restrictions

1. This order is not valid for more than $500.00.
2. The following items cannot be ordered using this form:
   Travel or travel-related expenses
   Indiana University Stores Items
   Radioactive materials
   Leases, rentals, standing orders (recurring payments)
   Furniture, furnishings
   Animals
   Weapons, ammunition
   Hospitality
   Controlled substances
   Plants and flowers
3. Purchases involving the trade-in of Indiana University property cannot be made using this form.

Terms and Conditions

1. This order must bear the original signature of the Account Manager.
2. Acknowledgment of this order is requested, stating delivery date.
3. All shipments must be marked with the purchase order number and shipped as above.
4. Itemized invoices must be rendered in duplicate, covering this order only.
5. Indiana University is free of all excise and Indiana sales taxes.
6. Indiana University Policy prohibits discriminatory practices in all phases of employment without regard to race, color, religion, sex or national origin. The contractor or vendor agrees with the aforestated policy and agrees to be bound by the equal opportunity clause (41 CFR 250.4) issued under Vietnam era veterans assistance act of 1974 on contracts or orders $10,000 or more, and the affirmative action clause (41 CFR 741.4) issued under the rehabilitation act of 1973, as amended on contracts or orders $42,500 or more.

_____
Guy J. De Stefano
University Director of Purchasing

Account Title	Account Number	Expense Class	Amount this Class
_____	_____	_____	_____
_____	_____	_____	_____

Form 11.9   Purchase order.

RECREATIONAL SPORT INVENTORY OF EQUIPMENT AND SUPPLIES

| Equipment inventory | Item | | Program area | | | | |
| | Model # | | | | | | |

Supplier   Phone number

Address   Contact

| Catalog page | | | Unit cost | Minimum order | | Minimum inventory | |

Date of Transaction	Received		Disbursed		Balance				
	P.O. #	Amount	Amount	Who	Amount	Deficit			
						C	D	L	S

Deficit

C = Consumed
D = Discarded/broken
L = Lost
S = Stolen

Form 11.10   Equipment and supplies inventory form.

Participants appreciate access to a variety of sport equipment and supplies on a checkout basis. Those who normally do not participate for lack of equipment now have what they need.

Equipment Maintenance and Care

Proper handling, maintenance, and care extend the useful life of equipment and supplies. Constantly inspect equipment and supplies for faulty or broken parts and classify them according to condition. At the first sign of deterioration or damage, remove an item from use until it can be repaired. Equipment staff can do simple repairs, but an authorized dealer should handle major ones. Dispose discarded equipment where it cannot be found and used again.

At frequent intervals, inspect used equipment to determine what you can keep and what you have to throw away. Items in storage require periodic cleaning to improve their appearance and maintain their usefulness. If you need additional equipment or supplies, purchase them immediately. The end of a sport season is often a good time to take advantage of sales, discounts, or closeouts of seasonal sport equipment and supplies.

EQUIPMENT CHECKOUT FORM

Date _____   Phone _____

Name _____   SS # _____

Address _____   Activity _____

Locker number _____

EQUIPMENT REQUESTED

Quantity	Description of item

Office use only

Out | In

Staff initial _____|_____   Actual return _____

Date equipment needed _____   Condition _____

Initial/date return _____

I hereby agree to pay for any equipment damaged or not returned. Failure to do so will result in legal action.

_____
Signature

Form 11.11   Equipment checkout form.

Database Management Software

Our recreational sport programs are no different than any other business in terms of organizing and tracking inventory lists of sport equipment, facility equipment, and various pieces of office furniture and machinery. Quite a few part-time employees and pieces of equipment are needed to support a recreational sport program, so it is important that the staff be able to maintain equipment inventory lists that are accurate and current to ensure accountability and inventory control. The type of equipment inventory system that is developed and implemented depends primarily upon the needs of the agency.

Since recreational sport programs are unique to each particular setting, there really isn't one particular commercial software package that is specific enough for every agency. However, a customized equipment inventory system just for your agency—using a database management program—is very easy to develop and manage. A typical equipment inventory database management application should allow for the following functions:

- adding, changing, or deleting items through a menu-driven screen;
- linking various databases (such as linking the equipment items database to the vendor, staff, and facility location databases);
- extensive and flexible reporting capabilities; and

- an automatic tag numbering system in which each piece of equipment is given a unique tag number for identification purposes.

Database management programs are relatively easy to use, but they are still powerful programs that allow you to manage and manipulate your data in a number of ways. In computer terminology, a *database* is a collection of related information that is grouped together in some logical order. The information is generally arranged and stored in a file using rows and columns (similar to a *spreadsheet*, which we used in chapter 10).

Each row of the database file contains one *record* or complete set of information about the specific piece of equipment in an equipment inventory database. Each column of the file contains a separate *field* or type of information, such as the location, the date of purchase, or the specific cost of a particular piece of equipment.

Database management programs add several tools that you use to manage the data, such as forms, queries, and reports. *Forms* are used to display the data that is stored in a file or to display the information retrieved as a result of a query. Database forms are very similar to the traditional paper-based forms with which we are already familiar. Forms are used for adding new data to the file and for displaying existing data—usually one record at a time. The following screen is an example of the fields that might be included in an equipment inventory form using the *Microsoft Access* database management program.

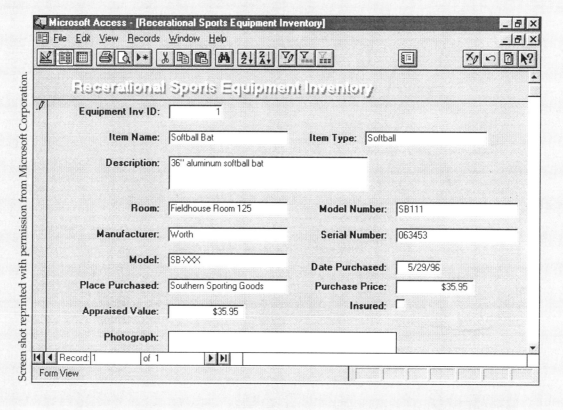

Screen shot reprinted with permission from Microsoft Corporation.

Once your data has been entered into the file, you can *query* or "ask" questions about the data. Queries are used to find and display a specific record or records, such as the "Model X rowing ergometer," all equipment purchased after a certain date, or all equipment located in a particular facility.

Customized *reports* are the results of specific or selective queries and are really what database management is all about. Detailed and sophisticated report designs are very easy to produce and can be designed to best fit your specific needs. Include only the data you desire from the various fields of the database and print the results in numerous formats, such as inventory summary reports, valuation reports, mailing labels, rolodex cards, or bar code labels.

Whether you are a computer novice or an expert, you will find that database management software allows you to link your data in many useful ways that make it easy to locate, manage, and share agency and program information easily.

Microsoft Access, Microsoft, Redmond, WA.

Other database management software products: dBase, Paradox, FoxPro, PFS, and FileMaker Pro.

ADA Suggestions

Recreational sport departments covered by Title II of the ADA must "remove architectural barriers in existing facilities, including communication barriers that are structural in nature, where such removal is readily achievable, i.e., easily accomplishable and able to be carried out without much difficulty or expense." According to the Department of Justice, examples of removing barriers in existing facilities include but are not limited to the following:

- Installing ramps
- Making curb cuts in sidewalks and entrances
- Repositioning shelves
- Rearranging tables, chairs, vending machines, display racks, and other furniture
- Repositioning telephones
- Adding raised markings on elevator control buttons
- Installing flashing alarm lights
- Widening doors
- Installing offset hinges to widen doorways
- Eliminating a turnstile or providing an alternative accessible path
- Installing accessible door hardware
- Installing grab bars in toilet stalls
- Rearranging toilet partitions to increase maneuvering space
- Insulating lavatory pipes under sinks to prevent burns
- Installing a raised toilet seat
- Installing a full-length bathroom mirror
- Repositioning the paper towel dispenser in a bathroom
- Creating designated accessible parking spaces
- Installing an accessible paper cup dispenser at an existing inaccessible water fountain
- Installing vehicle hand controls

This list is not exhaustive but reflects modest measures that you can take to remove barriers.

CONCLUSION

Management of facilities, equipment, and supplies is essential in sound program operation. The range of sport facilities available for recreation requires sound scheduling, supervising, and creating an optimum leisure sport experience. Due to the variety of items, number of users, maintenance requirements, and expense, a programmer must employ proper management techniques in the procurement, use, and care of equipment and supplies. Such practices contribute to safe and efficient use of resources necessary for quality program delivery. Constant advancements in technology will require the programmer to keep in tune with those changes that alter current management practices.

DISCUSSION QUESTIONS

1. What are four time units that facility scheduling is commonly based on?
2. Name three factors that influence the types of facilities available within a setting.
3. Explain the facility concept known as block scheduling.
4. How can politics affect facility development and availability?
5. What is the goal of facility development and management?

6. What items would you include on a facility reservation request form?

7. What are three factors you would consider when reviewing a request for the use of a facility?

8. List several functions performed by on-site supervisors.

9. How would different seasons affect facility scheduling?

10. What are two categories of maintenance?

11. What are some funding alternatives for facility operation, and why are they becoming so popular today?

12. List and identify three classifications of physical resources of a recreational sport environment.

13. What are the general steps involved in the purchasing process?

14. Discuss the value of an inventory system. Who should conduct this inventory? Why?

15. What are the advantages and disadvantages of purchasing equipment from a local dealer?

16. Why is the bid process so important? What problems does this process pose?

17. Explain the difference between equipment and supplies?

18. What would you include in a purchasing policy manual?

19. What influences purchasing decisions?

20. What is the number one priority in all purchase considerations?

APPLICATION EXERCISE

Your summer project for the department of recreational sport is to develop a new softball program. You have four diamonds with skinned infields and backstops, a tractor and mower, and a storage shed. Approximately 50 adult teams will participate in a single elimination softball tournament. It is your responsibility to develop a list of all necessary sport equipment and supplies as well as the cost for each item. Specify quantities of all necessary equipment and supplies and a jus-

tification of each item. Prepare a two- or three-page typed proposal to the director of the department outlining overall costs and the quantity of equipment and supplies you need based on the number of games required.

SUGGESTED READINGS

Canning, W.F. 1988. Producing income through the rental facilities. *National Intramural-Recreational Sports Association Journal* 13 (1): 43-47.

Espinosa, C.E. 1990. Planning and constructing a sand volleyball court. P. 51-60 in *Management strategies in recreational sports*. Corvallis, OR: National Intramural-Recreational Sports Association.

Flynn, J.J. 1987. Remodeling and expansion: A viable option for major sports and recreation facilities. P. 86-92 in *Cultivation of recreational sports programs*. Corvallis, OR: National Intramural-Recreational Sports Association.

Keeny, B.A. 1995. The IHRSA design forum. *Club Business International* 16 (2): 34-47.

Lass, L.J. 1987. Facility usage and enrollment patterns. *National Intramural-Recreational Sports Association Journal* 12 (1): 3-6.

Reznik, J.W. 1988. Rationale for student financial support of recreational sports programs and facilities. *National Intramural-Recreational Sports Association Journal* 13 (1): 39-40.

Richey, L., and T. Strong. 1987. Energy savings systems for new construction. *National Intramural-Recreational Sports Association Journal* 11 (2): 44-47.

Ross, C., and R. Phillips. 1995. The Americans With Disabilities Act (ADA) and its impact on recreational sports facilities. *National Intramural-Recreational Sports Association Journal* 19 (3):38, 40, 42-43.

Russek, R., and J. Maland. 1995. Skating to profitability. *Athletic Business* 19 (1): 43-49.

Schmid, S. 1994. Helping Hands. *Athletic Business* 18 (12): 20.

Secor, M.R. 1987. The pit falls, prat falls, and problems of facility design and construction. P. 102-106 in *Cultivation of recreational sports programs*. Corvallis, OR: National Intramural-Recreational Sports Association.

Wiles, C. 1995. Join the club. *Athletic Management* 6 (4): 29-34.

CHAPTER 12

Risk Management

Chapter Objectives

After reading this chapter you will

- understand the concepts of tort law,
- understand risk management principles,
- understand standard of care requirements,
- understand principles of negligence,
- understand personal and agency liability,
- understand the importance of public security,
- understand actions needed for a successful risk management program, and
- understand how to accomplish the task.

This chapter is a primer in tort liability, negligence, and safety for people working or studying in the recreational sport field. It is aimed at recreational sport programmers who have daily contact with participants as well as those in administrative positions. The principles of law expressed here apply to all recreational sport providers. There may be a few local exceptions because all providers are subject to the varying laws of the individual states.

From this chapter you should develop an awareness of the safety factors and legal liability that exist when organizations provide recreational sport. You will also learn how to encourage agency personnel to aggressively manage risk and pursue policy that leads to safe, quality recreational sport experience. There are two, sometimes conflicting, axioms that you need to consider when establishing management practices:

1. Good recreational sport risk management is good public policy. Safety programs should concentrate on the participants' interest and not the interest of the organization. Risk management should offer a quality program with maximum protection for the participants and adequate safeguards that protect the agency or organization from unnecessary litigation.

2. Recreational sport without some risk is monotonous. Most people engaged in recreational sport are risk takers. To eliminate risk entirely is to eliminate fun. Even a small child in a playground swing enjoys the dangers of movement and height.

You should manage risk, warn participants of dangers, eliminate extreme dangers, but you cannot and should not eliminate all risks. If you were to eliminate risk entirely, we would have to close the facilities to human use!

Each year the number of sport-related civil lawsuits filed in the courts of our nation increases. Most of these cases seek money damages for personal injury or damage to property that occurs as a result of using sport facilities. The trend to litigate and sue over trivial matters makes risk management important for recreational sport managers. Regardless of safety measures and risk management activities, accidents will occur. With accidents come claims and lawsuits with high costs in time and funds. A good risk management program reduces the number of accidents and the plaintiff's chances to successfully pursue a lawsuit. Employees should recognize their responsibility in protecting the public from accidents and property loss while protecting their agency from unnecessary litigation.

Legalese for Sport Managers

This chapter attempts to avoid technical legal language; however, to understand the context, you need to know a few words and phrases:

Allegation—An assertion of fact that the person making it intends to prove.

Appeal—An application to a high court to correct or modify the judgment of the lower court.

Comparative negligence—The relative degree of negligence on behalf of the plaintiff and defendant. Damages are awarded on a basis of each person's carelessness.

Contract—An agreement between two or more people that results in an obligation among the parties.

Contributory negligence—Conduct by the plaintiff falling below that required for his or her protection, which contributes to the plaintiff's injury.

Course of action—A legal right that includes right to sue.

Bruce Hronek, Professor, Department of Recreation and Park Administration, Indiana University developed this chapter.

Discretionary duty (sometimes referred to as *governmental immunity*)—An administrative duty carried out by a public official that is not subject to civil litigation.

Fidelity—Faithfulness to something one is bound to, by faith or contract.

Foreseeability—An occurrence that a reasonable and prudent person would perceive and anticipate under normal and existing conditions.

Liability—A legal responsibility, duty, or obligation.

Litigation—A lawsuit.

Negligence—Conduct falling below the standard of care a reasonable and prudent person would exercise.

Nuisance—An act that causes a substantial and unreasonable interference with a person's use and enjoyment.

Plaintiff—The party who institutes the lawsuit.

Property loss—Involves injury or damage to property, real or personal.

Proximate cause—Something that produces a result (accident) without which the result (injury) could not have occurred.

Risk—A specific eventuality, hazard, or peril.

Sovereign immunity—A rule of law that a nation, state, or local unit of government cannot be sued without its consent (generally considered outdated law).

Statute of limitations—Statutes of the federal and state governments setting maximum time periods for filing lawsuits.

Tort—Civil wrong (as opposed to criminal) not arising from breach of contract.

Waiver—An intentional release of a known legal right.

Safety and preventing losses should be the concern of everyone in an organization. Unfortunately, risk management often conflicts with the status quo or administrative freedoms often enjoyed by some in the organization. Some organizations need to change their attitudes and adopt new safety habits. Any employee can cause financial losses related to a lawsuit, so everyone in the agency must support the goals of the risk management program. Everyone should be the unit's safety officer or risk manager; however, someone should coordinate and oversee the risk management efforts.

The objectives of a safety and risk management program include the following:

- Reduction in lost workdays from injuries (employees)
- Reduction in number of injuries per 1,000 hours (employees and participants)
- Reduction in injury and property loss claims against organization (employees and participants)
- Reduction in the number of motor vehicle accidents per 1,000 miles (employees)
- Warnings for all known significant hazards (employees and participants)
- A safe recreational sport environment (participants)
- Empowering all employees to be safety officers

RISK MANAGEMENT PRINCIPLES

Risk management is neither complex nor costly. Risk management is simply common sense and a feeling of ownership in your organization's safety program. A viable risk management program reduces the chances of successful claims and lawsuits brought against an organization. The public and private sectors have used the process successfully for many years.

The goal of a risk management program is to provide a safe environment for visitors and employees. This will reduce pain and suffering, limit the energy and assets spent on claims, and reduce the chances of a successful suit. One lawsuit can result in spending hundreds of hours investigating, documenting, and testifying. Risk management encompasses four elements: identification, evaluation, treatment, and implementation of risk management procedures.

Risk Identification

Recreational sport programmers cannot identify all sources of risk in something as complex as a sport environment. Managers must follow the adage that "we can only do what we can do," but we must do something! The successful identification of risk depends on employees' attitudes toward safety for other employees and their interest in the welfare of the public. Recreational sport programmers should focus their efforts on providing for the public's recreational needs in a safe environment.

An organization may be responsible for the actions of its employees, volunteers, participants, spectators, concessionaires, permittees, and contractors. Identification of risk may go beyond the immediate purview of the organization. An agency also must ensure that those who are permitted or licensed to carry out organization objectives meet safety standards. Recreational sport providers can be exposed to several legal categories of risk. Although most are risks in tort, there are also financial risks, such as contracts, property loss (fire, theft, etc.), and fidelity (employees or others stealing cash, using equipment, or stealing organization property).

As an example of risk identification, one can look at a beach volleyball court used for recreational volleyball. The site includes a steep trail down a cliff area from a parking lot to the beach. There are three areas of risk—the parking area, with its entry onto a busy highway; the trail, considering its steep condition and lack of maintenance; and the beach, with its waterfront, volleyball court equipment, and unlighted restrooms.

There is a tendency to believe that safety is someone else's responsibility, and somehow, someone will see to safety. Everyone is generally responsible but no one specifically is assigned responsibility. We commonly state that safety hazard is the responsibility of the maintenance people or the safety officer. A thoughtful risk manager (ideally all employees) who constantly identifies safety problems will personalize the work by remembering that his or her family may be next on the scene of the hazard. He or she will ask, "What could I do to make my own family's recreation experience safe?"

Risk Evaluation

When you identify a risk, evaluate it according to its severity and its frequency. Using the volleyball court example, although the injuries on the steep trail are infrequent, a fall could result in severe injury or death, therefore justifying a guardrail. On the beach volleyball court the accident rate would be high, but the severity would be low (twisted ankles and abrasion accidents), so no modification would be necessary. You could handle the unlighted restroom situation by providing lighting or closing the area at a specific time during the day. You should direct the initial risk management effort toward trail safety because of the severity of the risk.

Risk Treatment

When you have evaluated the risk, determine the best way to reduce the losses. There are four op-

tions available to treat a risk: avoidance, reduction, retention, and transference.

1. Avoidance. Using the example of the volleyball court, you could close the existing trail to all use or relocate and design it. This would avoid the issue. Many recreational sport activities pursued by organizations are, by their nature, high risk activities. You should not eliminate activities because there is a chance that an accident may occur. An organization has to accept a certain level of risk in many of its activities; however, that does not mean that managers should not warn the visitors of the risks involved.

2. Reduction. Using the example of the trail, constructing a warning sign describing the dangers of being too close to the cliff edge or of slipping when the trail is wet will reduce the possibility of accidents. If children are often in the area unaccompanied by parents, you may need to construct a guardrail to avoid serious accidents. Warning notices (signs, verbal warnings, and brochures) provide the agency with an excellent defense against suits arising from inherently dangerous activities. Reduction programs simply decrease the chance of accidents. It is important that signs be well maintained and located where their message is readily available to the users of the area. Other methods of reducing risk include the following: (1) developing safety rules for a particular site or activity, (2) conducting periodic safety inspections of sites and activities, using different members of the safety review team each visit, (3) ensuring that the proper maintenance is scheduled and completed, and (4) making certain that all employees are trained in risk management, first aid, and emergency procedures. The most important safety tool for a risk management program is a knowledgeable and perceptive work force.

3. Retention. Many times, after an accident has been closely scrutinized, it is determined that the accident was the result of the carelessness of those involved or was an *Act of God*. The facilities, design, maintenance, or supervisor had nothing to do with the accident. Examples of Acts of God may be people being hit by lightning or a sudden tornado causing a building to collapse. You can do nothing about foolish acts that cause accidents and nothing about Acts of God. The organization would not be required to take any actions to prevent further accidents.

4. Transference. You could transfer the management of the trail and beach facilities to another agency or private operation. This method simply shifts the responsibility to someone else. The usual context of the term *transfer* relates to obtaining liability insurance. Many large public agencies are self-insured. In the private sector, insurance is the most common method of avoiding financial losses resulting from negligence suits. An insurance underwriter should significantly reduce the cost of insurance when you implement a good risk management program. The cost of insurance is an important economic factor for permittee or concessionaire operations as more and more people are willing to sue.

Implementing Risk Management Procedures

There are several tools to implement a risk management program. They include, but are not limited to, physical changes, signs, notices, brochures, spot announcements, news releases, and personal contact.

Easily understood, well-placed warning notices are excellent ways to communicate with the public about a safety hazard, particularly on a specific site. A zealous administrator looking to avoid all possibilities of negligence suits could install an excessive number of warning signs. In fact, having more than five signs in one location or a long list of safety considerations makes them less noticeable to the visitor and distracts from the enjoyment of the area. You need to maintain the signs well to be effective. Recreational sport participants, as well as the courts, expect that an agency will provide a warning of any situation that is not obvious.

There is a special precaution necessary when you know an area attracts children or people who do not speak or read English. Young children cannot read signs or brochures, so physical barriers or parent involvement is necessary. In appropriate situations, those not reading English need messages in their language. Many international safety signs bridge language and reading barriers.

Warning messages on signs, permits, maps, and brochures are the major methods to warn spectators and participants of dangers involved in recreational sport activities. Although notices on bulletin boards and at offices are desirable, not all visitors stop at those facilities. Personal contacts between employees and visitors continue to be an effective way to provide for public safety. Effective management of a risk situation must be timely and responsive to the circumstances.

Bulletin boards at the sports site provide an excellent place to list emergency telephone numbers and special requirements that will help participants have a safer recreational experience.

Mass media such as newspapers, radio, and television can also help disseminate risk-related information to the public. Although you cannot use mass media for routine information, you can use them for special circumstances such as dangers of heat stroke, hypothermia, dehydration, and other items the are seasonal or one-time events. Television feature programs reach a broad audience, especially when they are part of an evening newscast.

The average visitor seldom reads bulletin boards in offices and sport facilities, but it is important to post safety messages and warnings in locations accessible to the public, including bulletin boards. A wise programmer will place warnings in areas he or she knows will attract the public. An ideal place to post material that warns of hazards and gives safety advice would be on restroom stall back doors. Restroom visitors usually have the time to read longer safety messages.

STANDARD OF CARE

The standard of care (legal duty) owed to participants in a recreational sport site is determined by their status, laws, regulations, other written internal standards (manuals, handbooks, letters of direction, etc.), and common practices. The standard of care is a duty or obligation, recognized by the law, requiring recreational sport programmers to conform to a certain standard of conduct and protect others against unreasonable risks.

When people are injured while participating in recreational sport activities, the person filing the complaint will want to know the agency's written standards related to activity management and the maintenance, design, and construction of the facility. The plaintiff's attorneys will also want to know if other accidents have occurred on the site involved in the accident or on similar sites. The managing agency *must* meet its own standards. Risk managers should check their agency's written instructions to make certain they are meeting those standards. If those standards are not being met, change the written instructions or document why the agency chooses to violate its own instructions. Failure of the agency to meet the standards or failure to justify the reasons it did not meet the standards can jeopardize the defense during litigation.

The standard of care owed is sometimes based on the visitor's status. The categories are invitee, licensee, and trespasser. Let's look at the standard of care owed to members of each category.

Standard of Care Owed to an Invitee

An invitee is someone who is specifically invited to participate in the activity, usually paying a fee for the services or use of the facilities. An invitee is either a public invitee or a business invitee. The following defines the two categories of invitee:

1. A public invitee is a person invited to enter or remain on land as a member of the public for recreational sport purposes (e.g., Little League, city soccer programs).
2. A business invitee is a person invited to enter or remain on land for a purpose directly or indirectly connected with the business of the landowner.

In the case of invitee, the owner, operators, and managers have a duty to ensure they have used reasonable care to prepare the premises and make them safe for the visitors. This includes protection from injury related to conditions of the land, facilities, equipment, or by injury from third parties. In the case of invitee, the owner, operator, or manger must inspect the premises, remove or warn of potential hazards, and exercise reasonable care to protect users.

The following describes the duties that recreational sport providers or landowners owe the invitee:

- Keep the premises in safe repair.
- Inspect the premises to discover hidden hazards.
- Remove the known hazards or warn of their presence.
- Anticipate foreseeable uses and activities by invitee and take reasonable precautions to protect invitee from danger.
- Conduct operations with reasonable care for the safety of the invitee.

The prudent recreational sport manager who complies with these five duties and keeps a written record of periodic inspections and repairs will be able to provide an excellent defense against potential legal actions.

Standard of Care Owed to a Licensee

The licensee is owed a duty of care by the recreational sport provider that falls in the moderate category. There is not a distinct dividing line among the three categories, and many gray areas exist among the classifications. The licensee is someone who has consent, expressed or implied, to go on the land for his or her own purpose. In most jurisdictions the recreational sport provider owes the licensee reasonable or due care. The licensee may go on the provider's land to conduct business or to the mutual advantage of both the licensee and owner or occupant.

An example may be a mail carrier, a gas meter reader, or a contractor who is injured in a fall in front of an agency office due to ice on the sidewalk. Each is a licensee with implied consent to enter the property without specific permission. There is a distinction made between a licensee whose presence is merely tolerated and licensee by invitation or a social guest. Although social guests may be invited and even urged to come, they are not an invitee with the legal meaning of the term. A social guest is no more than a licensee who is expected to accept the premises as the owner uses them.

Standard of Care Owed to a Trespasser

A trespasser (nonpaying user) is someone who intentionally or without consent or privilege enters another's property. The word *trespasser* is commonly used for anyone falling under that definition and does not necessarily imply any illegal act. A person who goes on publicly owned land to enjoy a sport activity (tennis in a city park) has not committed a criminal act of trespass.

Owners, operators, and managers owe adult trespassers a duty of care less than that of a licensee or invitee. They have no duty to make their property or facilities safe or to warn of dangerous conditions. They only have a duty to avoid injury by gross conduct, intentional recklessness, or wanton misconduct.

There may be a question about the status of the special category of visitor who enters a public park to view a sport activity, play ball, or participate in a noncompetitive sport activity. Essentially the visitor was either invited, enticed, or attracted to the facility or activity. If the person is a *technical trespasser*, the courts will view this individual in an in-between status and consider other standards that relate to the care owed a visitor. They are sometimes defined as public invitee or nonpaying visitors who are on the premises at the invitation of the owner.

Children are by nature curious and have little sense of potential danger. Children sometimes trespass on property because of an interesting or unusual attraction. The attractive nuisance laws provide for the protection of the mischievous child seeking a place to hide or play. Warning signs have no impact on the nonreader, and fences are meant to be climbed in the eyes of children. In the case of trespassing children, the attractive nuisance doctrine applies. Essentially, owners who have created artificial conditions where common sense indicates that children may trespass or who possess land containing features that may attract children are under duty to provide such care as a reasonable, prudent person would take to prevent injury. These provisions usually do not apply to natural conditions (a lake), but only to artificial conditions (a swimming pool). The words *attractive nuisance* are seldom used now, having been replaced by the *foreseeable doctrine*, but the important principle still remains. Children fit into a separate category when it comes to the trespass categories for visitors.

NEGLIGENCE

Negligence is defined as "the omission to do something which a reasonable man, guided by those ordinary considerations . . . would do, or the doing of something which a reasonable and prudent man would not do" (Black's Law Dictionary, 1979, 930).

Whether negligence exists depends on the circumstances related to each case. The laws and court decisions are complex, so we can apply few generalities. Certain elements of negligence must be proved to have a viable negligence court case. They include the following:

1. The plaintiff must prove that the defendant has a legal duty of care (e.g., is legally responsible to the plaintiff).
2. The plaintiff must prove there was either a failure to perform a required task or a breach of duty that a *reasonable man* would not have failed to perform. A sports manager must foresee any dangers and take all the preventive actions a reasonable person would in a given situation.
3. There must be some direct connection between the damages and the actions or lack of actions by the defendant. Simply stated,

the plaintiff must prove that the breach of duty was the cause of the injury or property loss. This is commonly called *proximate cause*.

4. A plaintiff must prove that he or she suffered damages (e.g., a physical injury, mental anguish, or financial loss).

Sport programmers may defend themselves against negligence lawsuits by understanding the elements necessary for plaintiffs to mount a successful suit and using these elements as a minimum guideline for creating a safely run program. Therefore, let's examine the elements of negligence here.

Legal Duty

Whether there is a legal duty in negligence cases is a question of law. It is something determined by the judge, not the jury. The court decides whether the level of conduct was sufficient to present unreasonable risk. We should note that the entire field of recreational sport has an element of risk. Risk can also be described as adventure, thrills, and physical exertion.

Reasonable Man Doctrine

The reasonable man doctrine compares the actions of a leader, teacher, supervisor, and so forth with a reasonable person in the same or similar circumstances. The conduct of this hypothetical prudent and careful person will vary somewhat and likely combine both objective and subjective elements, including physical attributes, mental capacity, and special skills.

Regarding physical attributes, the reasonable person should possess those characteristics typical of his or her circumstances. If the person is mute, blind, deaf, or otherwise disabled, the agency must act reasonably knowing the circumstances and limitations. Such persons are entitled to live in the world and to have allowances made for their disabilities (see Americans With Disabilities Act of 1989).

The recreational sport manager must make allowances for the type of participants and spectators they may reasonably expect. As an example, if the recreational sport event attracts young children, rather than place warning signs that a child cannot read, you need a physical barrier (fence) between the child and the potential danger. Wise managers have *parent and child sport events* rather than *youth sport events*. The distinct difference is the parents' understanding that they are part of the sport experience with a responsibility to provide supervision to their children. The sport equipment must be designed to such a standard as to safely facilitate its use by participants of all sizes and weights.

When considering mental capacity, there is no allowance made for minor mental deficiencies. Defendants will be held to the test of reasonable conduct in the same manner as the prudent and careful person. Yet, if that mental capacity is a reflection of young minds that, because of immaturity or other mental limitations, are unable to comprehend danger or respond to written warning, you must give special attention to the situation.

Some recreational sport activities are relatively high risk (i.e., skiing, football, soccer, rugby, lacrosse). The question that you should ask is, "What type of skills and equipment do we need to reduce the risk of the activities?" Use a certification system to determine the competency of the high-risk user, guide, or concessionaire. Certain high-risk recreational sport activity leaders need minimum training under a certified instructor as well as specialized equipment before engaging in an activity.

The care expected of children exceeds that expected of adults. The courts recognize that, depending on their age, children are held to various degrees of responsibility for their actions. This is sometimes referred to as the *rule of seven*. The four general age categories are as follows:

1. Essentially, children under the age of eight are not responsible for their own welfare. A child under seven normally cannot recognize dangerous situations or read warning signs. The recreational sport provider's greatest responsibility for supervision lies with this age group.

2. Children between 8 and 14 are considered partially responsible for their own welfare. They can understand most warning signs and can comprehend some dangerous situations.

3. Youth 15 through legal adulthood (18 to 21) years of age are mostly responsible for their own actions. They have the experience to make many good decisions related to their personal danger.

4. Adults are considered responsible for their behavior.

It is important to note that the courts have changed the *rule of seven* when special circumstances warranted modification.

Foreseeability

Like many aspects of legal liability, certain doctrines are difficult to understand. There are several interpretations on what is foreseeable and what is not foreseeable. The ability of a person to foresee a danger depends on the individual's training and experience. Foreseeability is the ability to see and know in advance that there is a reasonable likelihood that harm or injury may result because of certain acts or omissions. "As a necessary element of proximate cause this means that the wrongdoer is not responsible for consequences which are merely possible, but is responsible only for consequences which are probable according to ordinary and usual experience" (Black's Law Dictionary, 1979). Perhaps a simpler way of stating it would be to say the courts do not demand that the manager possess mind-reading skill, but they do expect reasonable anticipation of risk.

Breach of Duty

Once a standard of care is established, the second element of negligence comes into play, that of failure to conform to the duty. Negligent conduct may occur because a person did something that was dangerous, or the same negligent conduct could occur because a person failed to do something. What is important from a legal viewpoint is that a defendant participated in an activity that resulted in an accident.

There are three words that describe the type of breach involved with a negligent act: *nonfeasance*, *misfeasance*, and *malfeasance*. They are important in determining the severity of the breach of duty and therefore the liability of the defendant. The differences in the types of negligent acts are as follows:

- **Nonfeasance**—Nonperformance of some act that ought to be performed, omission to perform a required duty at all, or total neglect of duty
- **Misfeasance**—The improper performance of some act that a person may lawfully do
- **Malfeasance**—Doing evil, ill conduct, the commission of some act that is positively unlawful

Proximate Cause

To prove negligence the plaintiff must prove that there was a relationship between the plaintiff's accident and an act or omission by the defendant.

Proximate cause is not a simple element, but rather a complex problem made up of several problems that the law does not distinguish clearly. That is why trials are conducted. A defendant can always point to someone or something else as the cause of the accident. As a legal matter, responsibility for an accident must be limited to causes that closely connect with the results and justify the law to impose liability.

Injury and Damages

There must be actual loss or damage to the interest of another. There can be no negligence without injury to persons or property. The word *damage* refers to loss, injury, or deterioration caused by negligence. Damage can involve physical or mental harm or damage to property. Damages can be *compensatory*, *punitive*, or *consequential*. The three categories of damages are described as follows:

1. **Compensatory damages**—Damages awarded to a person as compensation, indemnity, or restitution for harm sustained
2. **Punitive damages**—Damages awarded to a person to punish other litigants because of their outrageous conduct
3. **Consequential damages**—Damages awarded a person for suffering because of the act of another, even though the act was not directed toward the first person specifically and the damages did not occur immediately

AFFIRMATIVE DEFENSES AGAINST NEGLIGENCE SUITS

Conforming to professional standards of reasonable care, following manual and handbook direction, using accepted standards of maintenance, and conducting activities competently establish an individual or organization as reasonable and prudent. In addition to the absence of negligence, the law recognizes other defenses to bar legal liability. The following are defenses to negligence, yet there is some variation among the individual states' tort law:

• **Contributory negligence**—Conduct by the plaintiff contributing as a legal cause of the harm they have suffered, which falls below the standard they are required to perform for their own protection. A doctrine referred to as *Last Clear Chance* is an exception to the rule that contributory negligence will bar the plaintiff from recovery. This doctrine allows a contributory negligence plaintiff to recover if the defendant, immediately before the injury, had an opportunity to avoid the injury but failed to do so.

• **Comparative negligence**—Plaintiffs may be awarded only a percentage of their damages if they in some degree contributed to the accident. If a plaintiff is 40 percent responsible for an accident, he or she can only collect 60 percent of the court judgment. Most states do not allow awards to plaintiffs if their actions contributed more than 50 percent to the accident.

• **Assumption of risk**—A plaintiff who, by contract or otherwise, expressly agrees to accept a risk of harm arising from the defendant's negligence or reckless conduct cannot recover damages unless the agreement is invalid because it is contrary to public policy. A football player cannot claim the coach did not warn him that he may be blocked or tackled. The football player assumed a certain amount of risk by the nature of the game.

• **Government immunity**—Some actions by public employees are governmental functions and the agency or individuals retain an immunity status (planning, financing, and other discretionary activities). Those actions concerning the day-to-day maintenance and operations are proprietary and are not protected from litigation. There is much protection afforded public employees, for example, the Federal Tort Claims Act (FTCA) of 1946 and the Federal Employee Liability Reform and Tort Compensation Act of 1988.

• **Statute of limitation**—There is a fixed time to file a suit, depending on the jurisdiction and the circumstances.

• **Notice of claim**—State and federal laws require those making claims to file a claim within a given period after the cause of action using proper procedure. If a party waits too long to file a claim, the court will not accept the claim, no matter how legitimate. If injured persons are unable to make a claim because of their condition, circumstances did not allow it, or the severity of the loss or injury was delayed, the notice of claim requirement is not a defense. Plaintiffs usually need to make claims in writing.

• **Failure of proof**—A plaintiff must prove that the agency breached the standard of care. If the plaintiff does not meet the burden of proof, the court will reject the lawsuit.

- **Liability release**—A written statement by the plaintiff that he or she assumed all risks and released the agency from liability may provide a defense. These written releases are known as waivers, permission slips, consent forms, or agreements to participate. One should use this defense with some caution. You must write the releases properly and adult participants must sign them. Releases are not valid in the following situations:
    - When contrary to public policy.
    - If ambiguous, making it difficult to determine the extent of rights waived and understand the hazards related to the sport activity.
    - If minors or their parents sign the release on their behalf. This means that liability releases do not apply to minors, other than to inform the participants and their parents that there is some danger involved in the activity. Recreational sport providers should have parents sign *agreements to participate* rather than waivers. The agreement to participate should be specific enough for the parent to understand the possible harm that may occur to their child as a result of the activity.

LIABILITY

In 1946 Congress passed the Federal Tort Claims Act (FTCA), which makes the United States liable for torts that include the negligent or wrongful acts of federal employees or agencies. The laws of the state where the wrong occurred determine federal liability. Every state has enacted legislation that is parallel to the federal act.

The tort claim acts allow suits against recreational sport providers and their employees in the same manner that they allow suits against private companies and employees. When public employees are working within the scope of their employment, they do not have to personally defend themselves; rather, agency legal counsel will represent their interest in any litigation.

All states have given some degree of consent to their citizens to sue the state and local government under tort. In most cases the statutes favor the state rather than the people of the state. There is an excellent listing of the major elements of each state's tort claims act and government sovereign immunity in Betty van der Smissen's book (1990) entitled *Legal Liability and Risk Management for Public and Private Entities.*

Recreation Land Use Liability Statutes

Recreation land use statutes apply to informal sport settings where people participate in sport activities that do not have a fee. All states, except Alaska and North Carolina, have enacted Recreation Land Use Liability Statutes. Recreation land use statutes protect public and private property owners from suits by nonpaying recreationists who use their property. As a rule, the claimant must prove at least gross negligence to establish a basis for suit under the recreation use liability statutes. The words *simple, ordinary, gross, willful, wanton,* and *reckless* are used to describe the degree of negligence in most courts. For purposes of defining the degree of negligence, the following are the most commonly used terms:

- **Ordinary negligence**—The failure to exercise such care as would be expected by the majority of people under like circumstances.
- **Gross negligence**—The disregard of life and property of others. This exhibits as great negligence or as the want of even slight care. It consists of conscious acts of negligence.
- **Willful or wanton negligence**—The conduct complained of was so *gross* as to have something of a criminal character or be deemed equivalent to an evil intent, wantonness, or recklessness indicative of malice.

Under a recreation land use liability statute, the landowner owes no duty to care for those engaged in recreational sport or to guard or warn against known or discoverable hazards on the premises. Landowners lose protection from suits under these statutes when they charge a fee for using the premises or they are guilty of gross or willful and wanton misconduct. Unlike mere carelessness constituting negligence, willful and wanton misconduct is more outrageous behavior, demonstrating disregard for the physical well-being of others. Willful and wanton negligence has a strong element of intentional action, which is so obvious that the defendant must be aware of it. It is usually accompanied by conscious indifference with the consequences, amounting almost to willingness.

A careful analysis of your state's recreation use statutes would be a prudent exercise. Some states have liability immunity statutes specifically written for their state-owned public lands. At this time, most of the recreation use liability statutes apply to public lands (local, county, state, and federal) within the state as well as to private lands.

Who Is Liable?

As a rule, employees or agencies, volunteers, board members, supervisors, commissioners, and officers of private agencies, whether elected or appointed, are not personally liable for their actions as long as they are within their duties. Supervisors and administrators could be held personally liable in the following three circumstances:

1. If the administrator or supervisor participated in or in any way knowingly directed, ratified, or condoned the negligent act of the employee.
2. If administrators and supervisors have unsuitable employment or notification procedures. These procedures consist of the following:
   - Incompetent hiring practices
   - Failure to fire a person when circumstances warrant the dismissal
   - Inadequate documentation of firing
   - Inaccurate or incomplete job descriptions
   - Insufficient staff training
   - Unclear establishment and or enforcement of safety rules and regulations
   - Failure to remedy dangerous conditions
   - Failure to study and comply with statutory and agency requirements
   - Failure to give notice to others of known unsafe conditions
3. If there are violations of a person's civil (constitutional) rights. They include infringements on the following:
   - Religion, race, creed, color, gender, or age
   - Rights of privacy
   - Rights against illegal search and seizure
   - Free speech
   - Rights of assembly
   - Due process
   - Freedom of association

Because someone may not be personally liable does not diminish the fact that suits are expensive, both in time and money to their organization. It is important that every individual in an organization recognize personal responsibility to reduce the organization's exposure to tort suits. If people working within their duties are named in a civil suit in which they are indemnified (held harmless) by policy or statute, the legal counsel for the organization will represent them if necessary and the agency will pay the damages.

Pay special attention to the volunteers because most public agencies use them in many ways. Although their time and effort are not recognized with monetary rewards, each supervisor should consider them employees from a legal liability standpoint. Each volunteer working within the scope of his or her assignment subjects the organization to the same type of liability as full-time employees. An injured volunteer can also sue the organization for any damages sustained due to a negligent act of another. It is important that all recreational sport managers be extremely careful in recruiting, selecting, training, and supervising volunteers.

Strict liability imposes liability on the defendant without having to prove fault. The reason for strict liability is to prevent particularly dangerous activities or situations from occurring. Strict liability as it applies to sport involves defective sport equipment or contaminated food or water.

If a football helmet not manufactured and maintained according to established safety standards results in an injury, the manufacturer or agency may be held liable under strict liability.

Limiting Liability

Waivers, releases, and agreements to participate are not normally considered a part of natural resource agency tools; however, you need to consider them in our litigious society. Recreational sport activities tend to be more risky or provide a greater chance for injuries than other forms of recreation. Releases and waivers justify, excuse, or clear the agency from fault rising from an accident or damages. These documents must be written to be effective. Verbal waivers are too challengeable to be useful. Waivers and releases are contracts. The court's response to waivers and releases has varied with individual judges and jurisdictions. Because minors are unable to contract, using waivers and releases with them is improper. Releases and waivers are invalid in the following situations:

- Signed by minors—children under legal age (normally 18 to 21 years of age) cannot be a party to a contract.

- Signed on behalf of minors by their parents or guardians—adults cannot sign away the legal rights of their children.
- Not specific—ambiguity in the content of the waiver makes it difficult to determine the extent of the rights waived.
- Waiving rights contrary to public policy (e.g., drunk driving, negligent behavior).

Waivers and releases have a higher likelihood of being validated by the courts if they are specific and related to high-risk activities such as whitewater rafting, mountain climbing, spelunking, and so forth.

With all the limitations placed on waivers and releases, recreational sport providers should still not hesitate to use them with their adult participants. When they are specific they provide the participant with a strong reminder about the dangers involved with the activity. That reminder, accompanied by a signature, forms a basis whereby a specific waiver or release invokes the *assumption of risk* defense.

The best instrument to limit the liability for minors is the *agreement to participate*. You must specifically word this document to cover the risks involved in the activity. It also must include all the rules of conduct required for safety and organization purposes so the minors and their parents or guardians understand what is expected of them. The *agreement to participate* documents the fact that the parents understood the dangers involved and agreed to tell their children to abide by the rules.

An effective *agreement to participate* document also triggers the *assumption of risk* theory of defense to negligence. For the *assumption of risk* defense to hold in court, the document must describe the risk of any activity in detail. An agency manager will recognize that it is less risky to provide recreational sport activities for adults than for young participants. However public agencies have an obligation, ethically and legally, to serve that segment of the population most vulnerable to accidents and most in need of protection from harm: the nation's youth.

Agency Liability in Intentional Torts

Recreational sport provides an environment where there is a constant contact among players and between players and recreational sport supervisors. For several reasons, fatigue, alcohol, drugs, and personality characteristics, conflicts occur and people argue, fight, steal, trespass, defame, and commit other crimes and torts. The crimes are controlled by the criminal justice system. The negligence tort is usually involuntary, such as an accident caused by negligence, whereas a voluntary tort, such as assault and battery, occurs through a deliberate act.

Although public employees are protected from personal suits, it does not protect the agency from suit and the embarrassment caused when employees commit personal torts. This category of torts includes, but is not limited to assault, battery, defamation, invasion of privacy, false imprisonment, intentional infliction of extreme emotional distress, trespass to land, trespass to chattel, and conversion.

Although intentional tort cases are rare in the recreational sport profession, they do occur. They are on the increase. Managers should take action when recreational sport participants commit intentional torts against their employees. Two of the most commonly occurring torts are assault and battery.

When a recreational sport organization violates another's constitutional rights, it is difficult to use governmental immunity to protect the individual employees involved and for governmental representation to assist them. The U.S. Constitution guarantees each citizen protection from excessive governmental control in the areas of due process; reputation and privacy; religious practices; freedom of speech; discrimination because of race, religion, gender, age, and national origin; liberty; ownership of property; and civil rights. Action must be taken to protect the public's constitutional rights.

Public safety and security should be a primary concern of recreational sport professionals. Although some will falsely recommend that a warning not be given because it admits to knowing about the problem, it is better to warn the public of known hazards. Managers' concern should be with public safety more than with "protecting one's backside."

There is evidence of increasing spectator and participant violence in sport-related activities. Recreational sport programmers are facing increased behavior problems related to participants and spectators. The recreational sport manager must try to anticipate the behavior of both the participant and the spectator. Some Little League parents have become legendary for their unacceptable behavior.

The fact that uniformed officers are present at recreational sport events provides a feeling of well-being and security. In areas of high crime and in activities with a history of problems, you should schedule patrols by agency personnel and local law enforcement officers (sheriff's officers).

ACTIONS FOR MANAGING LEGAL RISKS

How can an organization reduce its susceptibility to lawsuits? The following are four categories of situations in which recreational sport managers should act to reduce the chance for a successful lawsuit:

1. **Make a commitment to public safety and security.**
2. **Investigate and take actions where accidents have previously occurred.** In such cases the agency is already *on notice* of the dangers and should apprise the public accordingly. Investigate all accidents, but preventive actions are not necessary in all cases. Some accidents occur because individuals are careless and are not the agency's fault.
3. **Concentrate on areas of high public use.** The statistical probability of an accident rises with the intensity of use. A prudent manager will concentrate risk efforts in areas where the most people participate, rather than in areas with little activity.
4. **Warn people about dangerous conditions** due to unrecognized hazards that a prudent person might not anticipate, such as sharp edges on outfield fence and extreme weather (hypothermia or heat stroke conditions).

In addition to these factors, programmers should pay attention to documenting procedures, investigating complaints, enforcing agency and sport rules, and providing emergency care. Finally, the agency should handle legitimate claims professionally. To conclude this chapter, we'll take a further look at these risk management actions.

Documentation

Documentation of risk and safety inspections is important to a risk management program. When you make a hazard analysis of sport fields or other facilities, you must document and file the findings. If a manager decides not to make the scheduled safety inspection (a discretionary function) because of budget limitations or other extenuating circumstance, he or she must document the reasons for that decision. You need this documentation to limit the success of future litigation problems should an accident occur. If the area does not have a history of safety problems and there are no known dangers, a manager can decide not to inspect if the decision is based on good faith. You must document and file any decision related to risk that intentionally changes written direction. Part of the content of the document should include the manager's rationale for the decision.

Investigation

Notify management that an accident has occurred that may give rise to litigation. Also notify the organization's legal counsel as soon as possible. Investigate any accident involving people or property immediately after the accident while evidence and recall are fresh. Preferably the investigation team should include recreational sport professionals as well as professionally trained investigators. Do not expect the local law enforcement agencies (state police, sheriff's department, etc.) to conduct an investigation that will meet your litigation needs.

If there is any indication that drugs or alcohol are involved in the accident, request the necessary medical tests. This is particularly important in serious injuries, death, or high property damage cases. It is best to team with trained investigators.

Many times the recreational sport provider is not aware that an accident has occurred until a plaintiff files a claim or lawsuit. When those circumstances exist, the investigation should occur on receiving a formal claim or suit.

The agency personnel should handle all claims against the agency efficiently and courteously without determining the merits of the claim. Employees have no authority to agree to pay medical expenses or property damage; however, they should render as much assistance as possible to help save life, reduce pain and suffering, comfort family members, and limit property damage. You can give emergency help, courtesy, and compassion generously without obligating the agency.

Sport Rule Enforcement

Most recreational sport managers choose their public contact personnel with great care. Especially important are the people who enforce the sport rules. Astute managers will be careful of individuals who enthusiastically want a rule enforcement assignment. Some of the best enforcement

Shining Example

Dallas Texins Association, Dallas, Texas
13900 North Central Expressway, Dallas, Texas 75243

Texins is a corporate health, fitness, and recreation organization for the employees and families of Texas Instruments. The organization was established over 40 years ago as a non-profit group. Texins started an annual Christmas party in 1953 and within 5 years expanded to serve 2,140 Texas Instruments employees and their families with 17 clubs and athletic activities. Today, the membership includes over 6,800 Texas Instruments employees, 300 contract employees and 200 retirees at the Dallas Texins. Texins has a family philosophy and extends all services to the dependents of the Texas Instruments employees. The Dallas Texins consists of two facilities located in Dallas, Texas and Plano, Texas. A new world class (8.5 million) facility opened in Dallas in January 1995. The Spring Creek Facility opened in 1987 and this year was updated with all new equipment.

Organization: Texins is a corporate health, fitness, and recreation organization for the employees and families of Texas Instruments.

Clientele: Texas Instrument employees and families, as well as retirees, contract workers and their families can use the Texins facilities. Some programs are available to non-members.

Budget: Not available.

Marketing: Marketing and communication is handled by each program team (9 teams). Texins has a page in the site newspaper devoted to Texins information; they use bulletin boards, internal messaging system, fliers, postcards, and a variety of brochures and pamphlets. The Dallas Texins has an overall marketing budget geared towards generating greater membership numbers and program participation.

Staff: Consists of degreed and certified professionals who offer a diverse knowledge base in the various areas of health, fitness, and recreation. Texins has also implemented a student intern program.

Program Detail: Texins offers a variety of programs and classes in the areas of health/wellness, childcare, activity classes, parenting, personal safety, and work/life issues. Outside the facility there is an area reserved for "Teambuilding" an experiential learning program offered by Texas Instruments. In the future, this area may include the construction of a high elements ropes course.

Facilities: The facilities at Dallas Texins include: a lighted quarter mile outdoor running track, three lighted outdoor tennis courts, two sand volleyball courts, an outdoor basketball court, team building areas, outdoor shower, 25 yard lap lane indoor pool, gym and indoor track, aerobics studios, exercise areas, meeting rooms, a game room, kids room, and storage buildings.

Accident Reporting

Due to the very nature of sports and the risks associated with participation in various physical activities, accidents and injuries inevitably happen. However, it is our responsibility to minimize and curtail the frequency of accidents by providing proper facility maintenance and by taking every possible precaution.

Computers have become a very valuable resource in accident reporting because they provide assistance to the staff in terms of record keeping and they are able to analyze accident data and statistics. The data gathered for an accident is vital in providing staff with an overall view of how safe particular activities are. Statistical cross tabulation analysis of this data provides a correlation between the various factors involved in the situation. These correlations enable the staff to determine possible causes for accidents and to determine necessary measures that need to be taken to reduce the frequency of those accidents. Typical correlations may include the following:

- The actual playing field/court may be related to the frequency of accidents and injuries occurring at each site.
- Types of injuries may be related to the specific sport that is being played at the time of the accident or injury.
- The demographic background of the injured individual (including gender, age, etc.) may be related to the type of injury.
- The number of accidents or injuries in a given sport may be related to a particular type of accident or injury.

RecTrac! by Vermont Systems, Inc. is an example of a very comprehensive computer software program that provides a variety of modules for the recreational sports programmer. Among them is the Accident Reporting module, which allows you to track—on a daily basis—all accidents that occur at any of your sports facilities. The program maintains accident information such as the injured person's name, address, and gender; the time of the accident; a description of the injury; the location of the accident; other accident details, including a description of how the injury occurred; a description of any first aid procedures that were administered; the name of the supervisor on duty; the names of witnesses; and descriptions of all actions that were taken after the accident took place. *RecTrac!* also provides an extensive "comments" feature that allows up to 999 paragraphs that are linked to each accident and are time- and date-stamped when entered. The following comprehensive reports can be compiled:

- an accident summary report, which includes victim and accident information;
- an accident detail report, which includes treatment and progress information for each accident; and
- an accident status report, which allows you to print individual accident reports.

By having this type of information immediately available either in numerical or graphic form, the staff can make educated determinations of *why* accidents might be occurring and make educated decisions about *what can be done* to prevent them in the future.

RecTrac!, Vermont Systems, 12 Market Place, Essex Junction, VT, 05452, 802-879-6993

personnel are first interested in working with people and second working to protect people. In sport rule enforcement efforts should

- protect people from other people,
- protect facilities from abusive people, and
- protect the people from a dangerous facility.

People should feel safe in a recreational sport setting.

Emergency Care

Because of the location and situation regarding recreational sport, emergency care may not be immediately available. Organization personnel who are usually first on the scene of an accident may provide the first care. Ambulance service and emergency medical technicians may be many minutes away. Agency personnel trained in first aid can save lives. It is important that personnel receive first aid training regularly.

Some agency people are hesitant to render assistance because of the possibility of lawsuits if the recipients of the treatment believe they were not treated properly or death occurs. All but two states (Alabama and Colorado) have emergency care stat-

utes that limit the liability of people providing emergency assistance. The two states that are the exception have case precedent that essentially accomplishes the same thing.

Recreational sport personnel do not need to consult legal counsel every time there is an accident. Recreational sport managers need to train their personnel to adhere to professional standards, have adequate supplies and equipment to aid accident victims, train in the most updated methods of first aid, keep records of any accidents, and conduct thorough investigations. There is no magic formula that provides immunity from suit. Agencies should not hesitate to provide recreation opportunity for the public, even though there is an element of risk in the activity. Fully inform participants in high-risk sport about the dangers involved and minimize that danger through training, certification, and proper equipment.

Some personnel may understandably be uncomfortable contacting the families of the severely injured or those killed in accidents. Personnel may even experience some animosity from the victims and their families. It is extremely important that cordial contact be maintained between agency personnel and victims of accidents and their families. Personnel should not admit any guilt or offer to pay medical expenses; however, agency personnel should be generous with comforting, compassion, and helping facilitate the victims of accidents and their families.

Legitimate Claims

Legitimate claims against organizations are appropriate. If an injured person files a claim that is clearly the fault of the agency or private provider, honor the claim, process, and pay it promptly. There is a principle in law called *Res ipsa loquitur*, which translated means "the thing speaks for itself." The phrase represents a rule of evidence that the negligence is inferred from the fact that the accident happened. To see if this doctrine applies to a situation and to recommend damages be paid, the manager must determine if the accident would not have occurred if the agency had used reasonable care and whether all the circumstances surrounding the accident were under the defendant's control.

You can further apply the doctrine when there is no direct evidence to show cause or injury and the detailed circumstantial evidence indicates that the defendant's negligence is the most logical explanation for the injury.

ADA Suggestions

The ADA coupled with the Architectural Barriers Act, (42 U.S.C. 4151-4157) requires organizations to provide access for people with disabilities. The recreational sport programmer should not consider these standards a burden. The universal design accessibility requirements reduce the chances for accidents to all participants and observers. For example, by complying with the ADA requirement for visual and auditory alarms, a participant who has on headphones and is listening to the radio would be able to see an emergency alarm. Meeting ADA standards reduces the risk of falling for physically able children and older people.

CONCLUSION

A recreational sport programmer cannot, by himself or herself, provide an effective risk management and safety program for the unit. The most meaningful way to implement an effective plan is to have the concept of personal commitment ingrained in the mind of each employee. This can be done with threats, incentive systems, and numerous other psychological manipulations. Experience has proven that any form of force does not work when it comes to safety and risk management. Personal example is likely to be the best means of communicating commitment. The example of a supervisor stooping down and wiping up a wet spot on a playing floor is an indelible memory in the minds of all who witnessed his commitment to a safe facility. Nothing had to be said; the deed was enough to communicate the message. That incident will likely result in many other employees looking for potential hazards and correcting them.

DISCUSSION QUESTIONS

1. Describe major aspects of a negligence lawsuit.
2. The way to avoid negligence is prudence. What prudent measures can you take to make a fitness program more risk free?
3. As a recreational sport programmer, should your main goal be to eliminate *all* risks in your sport program?
4. What is the goal of a risk management program? Why is a program important?
5. Describe the four elements that encompass risk management, and give specific examples for each element.
6. Explain the ways that you can treat risk to reduce the loss.
7. How can the mass media assist in warning participants of risks and dangers?
8. What do we mean by the phrase *standard of care*?
9. What is the difference between an invitee, licensee, and trespasser?
10. As a recreational sport programmer, do you owe a trespasser a duty of care? Why or why not?
11. Explain and give a specific example for each of the four elements that must be present for negligence to occur.
12. How does the principle of the *reasonable man doctrine* apply to programmers in recreational sport?
13. Describe the *rule of seven*. Why is this principle important in recreational sport? Does

this imply that there are varying degrees of responsibility based on age?

14. If three of the four elements of negligence exist but there was no actual loss or damage, can a plaintiff still charge negligence?

15. Describe five defenses that you can use when dealing with negligence suits.

APPLICATION EXERCISE

The campus intramural soccer round-robin season had ended and the teams were eager to begin the single elimination postseason tournament. This would determine the all-campus champion.

Before the tournament started, the rainy season began, and it was not until nine days later that play could resume. The intramural fields were not in the best condition but were determined playable.

As the intramural sport supervisor set up the fields the first night, he noticed that the area around the goal had eroded, leaving the goal unsteady. As the teams warmed up, each time someone kicked a goal it wobbled more. Determining that it was unsafe to play under the goal, he stopped the game. He informed the teams they would not be able to play that night. The teams were angry. Team members said they'd already had to wait more than a week to play as it was. Team captains informed the supervisor that they would accept all risks of injury. The supervisor indicated that this wasn't possible. Both team captains lodged complaints against the supervisor. One even stated that the supervisor should be fired for not wanting to do his job.

Because you are in charge of supervisors, these reports are on your desk when you arrive for work the next day. Was the supervisor acting according to his duty? How much responsibility does the intramural supervisor have? Could the teams accept responsibility for the injury? Is the university liable for the goals? How do you respond to the team captains? How do you respond to the supervisor? What action do you take regarding the tournament?

REFERENCES

Black's Law Dictionary. 1979. 5th ed. St. Paul: West.

Federal Employee Liability Reform and Tort Compensation Act of 1988. U.S. Public Law 100-694.

Federal Tort Claims Act of 1946. 28 U.S.C.A. Sections 2671-2680.

SUGGESTED READINGS

Municipal, school and state tort liability. 1971. P. 333 in *American jurisprudence.* 2d ed.

Carroll, R. 1990. The worst case scenario: Why Amber Myers drowned in her swimming class. P. 109-117 in *Management strategies in recreational sports. Proceedings of the 41st NIRSA Conference.* Corvallis, OR: National Intramural-Recreational Sports Association.

Frankt and Rankin. 1982. *The law of parks and recreation resources, and leisure services.* Salt Lake City: Brighton.

Gaskin, L., and E. Greaves. 1989. Liability concerns of recreational sports managers: A situational analysis. *National Intramural-Recreational Sports Association Journal* (fall): 4-6, 11.

Kaiser, J.D. 1986. *Liability and law in recreation, parks, and sports.* Englewood Cliffs, NJ: Prentice Hall.

Kozlowski, J.C. 1986. Recreation use laws apply to public lands in NY, NE, ID, OH, WA. *Parks and Recreation.* 22.

Prosser, W. 1980. *Law of torts.* St. Paul: West.

Prosser, W., and W. Keaton. 1984. *Torts.* St. Paul: West.

Rankin, J. 1991. Preparing recreational sports professionals for a litigious society. *National Intramural-Recreational Sports Association Journal* 15 (3): 8-10.

Roos and Berber. 1968. *Governmental risk management manual.* Tucson, AZ: Risk Management.

Ross, C. 1994. Risk management in the 1990's. P. 118-130 in *NIRSA conference proceedings: Navigating the tides of change—Strategies for success.* Corvallis, OR: National Intramural-Recreational Sports Association.

Ross, C., and S. Young. 1995. Understanding the OSHA bloodborne pathogens standard and its impact upon recreational sports. *National Intramural-Recreational Sports Association Journal* 19 (2): 12, 14, 16-17.

Stern, S.T., and C.S. Ladden. 1971. *Civil litigation.* St. Paul: West.

U.S. Consumer Product Safety Commission. 1994. *A handbook for public playground safety.* Washington, D.C.: U.S. Consumer Product Safety Commission.

van der Smissen, B. 1968. *Legal liability of cities and schools for injuries in recreation and parks.* Cincinnati: Anderson.

van der Smissen, B. 1985. *National safety network newsletter* 1 (4).

CHAPTER 13

Marketing

Chapter Objectives

After reading this chapter you will

- understand the functions of marketing sport,
- focus on the customers and their relation to agency image, and
- identify the promotion methods in recreational sport.

A major function within any recreational sport management organization is marketing the programs that you develop. Marketing is a complicated process, often confused with the publicity and promotion tasks of an organization; however, sound marketing approaches lead to successful participation and service improvement.

Integrated within the marketing of recreational sport programs is sensitivity to the needs of the participant, or customer. The concept of a participant as a customer has developed from the increased pricing and revenue-producing aspects of sport programs. Traditionally, the public sector sport management organizations served citizens, students, or similar constituents. With the increased commonalty among public and private organizations, the need for customer service has evolved.

MARKETING FOR THE CUSTOMER

The cycle of customer service begins with market research and ends with service delivery. Tied into service delivery at every stage is the effective interpretation of need and expectation of a paying customer.

Through effective market research, the results of product, place, price, and promotion reflect the customer's needs and indicate the service to provide.

Market Research

Marketing is the process of providing affordable, accessible, and appropriate leisure service to an available public. To determine these four As (affordable, accessible, appropriate, and available), conduct a variety of research methodologies. Through these and continued modification, you can deliver customer service effectively.

Market research uncovers two information areas: market structure analysis and consumer analysis. Market structure analysis reveals logistical information about service delivery: ideal distribution, nature of the market; barriers; and similar attributes. Consumer analysis reveals characteristics of the customer: basic demographics, behavioral characteristics, and geographical considerations. This chapter focuses on consumer analysis.

Methods of Gaining Information About the Consumer

Researching a consumer's needs can take many forms, from observation and interviews to techniques of needs assessment, market segmentation, and target marketing. The goal of all techniques is to adequately define and profile the consumer, then design and provide sport programs that reflect the best assessment of this profile. One accomplishes this through two major avenues:

1. **Primary research.** This involves developing an original research design that samples actual and potential customers and assesses basic demographics and personal preference. An example of this research is shown in a study of the over-50 market (Cohen 1995) that assesses fitness needs of this age group in order to tailor special fitness programs.

2. **Secondary research.** This method involves the extensive study of other sponsor's research (i.e., census data, economic profiles, organizational research) to glean trends that may affect your organization. For example, the American Bowling Council conducts and publishes studies of the characteristics of a typical bowler. You can apply some of those characteristics to a local bowling program.

Market research has traditionally been designed to reveal and understand major groups (markets) on which to focus. More recent trends, such as lifestyle marketing, take data collection a step further. The profile developed of an individual target takes into account one's lifestyle and orientation. This approach, developed by Stanford Research Institute and known as the VALs Typology, divides market groups into actualizers and strugglers who have certain economic and lifestyle levels to consider. An example of a VALs type is an Achiever, comprising 20 percent of the adult American population. Individuals who belong to this lifestyle are satisfied with what they have achieved and are well adjusted in society both at leisure and at work. A recreational sport programmer marketing to this group might provide traditional sport opportunities that allow for joining and socializing as well as competition.

On the other hand, the *I-Am-Me's* (3 percent of the adult population) belong to a lifestyle characterized as more individualistic than team oriented, emotional, displaying beliefs through actions rather than words, and enjoying feelings that may result in long-term pursuits. Marketing individual sports, such as golf, tennis, and so forth, through the instructional sport and intramural sport program areas will attract participants with this lifestyle behavior.

A sport manager needs to understand the market research techniques and be sensitive to the market structure and the customer.

Customer Service as a Marketing Tool

Marketing is designed to motivate the customer to access recreational sport services. Once there, an ongoing practice of customer service can keep a participant coming back for more.

Quality customer service doesn't happen by itself. It is managed. Those who provide services typically offer a service strategy that makes good on the promise and service people on the front lines who have the skills and empowerment to make it happen.

In looking at an organizational chart of a sport organization, the customer is at the top and the staffing levels fall below in the hierarchy supporting the needs of the customer. This is represented by an inverted pyramid shown in figure 13.1.

Marketing Components

From the information gained in market research, a sport program constantly adjusts and changes to respond to the needs of its market. The traditional market components of product, place, price, and promotion reflect this research in the inception and implementation of programs. The following examples describe how each component adjusts as a result of market research.

Product

The program of services, facility, and service delivery is established based on the needs of the available market. For example, Club Med, a sport-oriented resort, changed its single-oriented services to meet the needs of families with children and those of seniors. When dealing with wellness programs, according to Club Business International (Keeny 1994, October) it is necessary to develop a comprehensive corporate wellness marketing package.

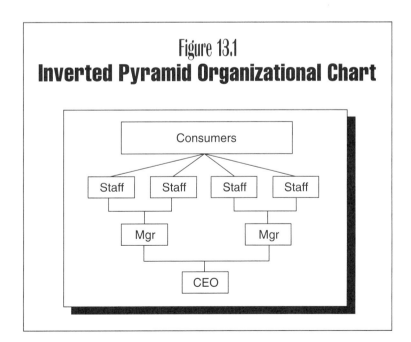

Figure 13.1
Inverted Pyramid Organizational Chart

From: Murphy, J., Niepoth, W., Jamieson, L., & Williams, J. (1991). Leisure systems: critical concepts and suggestions. Champaign, IL: Sagamore Publishing, p. 261. Used by permission.

Place

Market research establishes the availability and accessibility of service. The location of programs and the distribution of those programs can change as a result of understanding how far and from where people will travel to access a sport program. For example, Johnson County, Kansas, Park and Recreation District analyzed the distance people traveled to sport and recreation programs to ascertain what sites were most appropriate for program development. It found that instructional sport drew participants from the neighborhood surrounding the center, and intramural sport drew teams from a wider geographical area.

Price

The affordability of services affects program success. Through market research, one can determine the participant's willingness to pay for sport programs, then set prices to meet a span of what is acceptable. If too low, participants may perceive lack of quality, and if too high, participation will not meet budget goals. You can see a willingness to pay in the ease with which the public accepts bond issues to build recreational facilities or fee increases to build and maintain campus recreational sport complexes.

Promotion

This chapter emphasizes promotion because the outgrowth of market research is most evident in the promotion of the sport program. We start with the concept of effective public relations (customer service) and extend into specific promotional considerations that you can develop.

CUSTOMER SERVICE

How can one establish effective customer service? The challenge begins with a commitment to serving participant needs and interests. Gather as much pertinent information as possible about the public you will serve, including demographic information, availability, proximity, socioeconomic level, educational attainment, customs, values, needs, and interests. Apply this knowledge to create programs that satisfy participant needs and interests. What we provide to the public and how we present it determine how they will respond to it.

Efforts undertaken to establish goodwill with the public have specific objectives in mind. Typical functions of public relations are the following:

- Keep the public informed of opportunities.
- Justify and interpret goals, objectives, policies, and procedures.
- Modify negative impressions or attitudes and correct misunderstandings.
- Foster appreciation of the benefits of participation.
- Encourage and motivate involvement by participants and volunteers.
- Stimulate interaction and input.
- Focus attention on a given topic, program, need, or service.
- Attract and retain participants and employees to a setting.
- Orient personnel to the philosophy and expectations of the agency.

Obtaining the goodwill of the public requires a comprehensive plan. The programmer is responsible for implementing the plan through interagency cooperation, personnel and volunteers, facilities and programs, public and professional service, and publicity and promotion.

Interagency Cooperation and Customer Service

Rarely is a single agency involved in providing recreational sport. Consequently, all staff must understand what others in the community provide to avoid duplication or conflict of effort. The spirit of interagency cooperation leads to resolving problems and strengthening professional ties. These ties may result in joint projects and grants, shared faculty and staff resources, personnel referrals, and other pursuits that enhance opportunities for participation. For example, a municipal park and recreation program with limited indoor facilities might arrange a partnership with the local school board so the park program can use the school gymnasium at night for its adult basketball league and the high school golf team can use the municipal golf course for no charge.

Personnel as Customer Service Providers

Every person associated with the recreational sport program has the potential to affect the customer. A programmer and his or her subordinates are in constant contact with participants. He or she should engage those capable of contributing to a positive image.

Most individuals require orientation and training before they can apply the preceding attributes with consistency. Other measures require only practice and an occasional reminder, reflecting a personal approach to interaction and including the following orientations:

- Convey a genuine interest and willingness to serve.
- Address people by name whenever possible.
- Maintain a pleasant demeanor.

Most of the responsibility for contributing to positive relations rests with personnel at the programming level. Because of this, administrative staff must adequately select, train, place, and monitor programming personnel. As problems arise, competent administrative action contributes to morale and goodwill. Finally, administrative staff are responsible for hiring personnel capable of providing the support services necessary to meet demand. An agency with a limited, inefficient staff will be overextended, leading to a deterioration of positive relations.

Volunteers often help plan, organize, conduct, and evaluate programs. They serve an important function and may acquire an extensive knowledge of program operations, problems, concerns, needs, strengths, and weaknesses. Consequently, provide genuine support, proper training, and adequate recognition for volunteers to reinforce their commitment, understanding, and productivity.

Facilities and Programs and Their Effect on Customer Service

One's first impression of a program often arises from the appearance and state of facilities. The positive image created by facility quantity and quality stimulates participant interest. When they are adequate, clean, well maintained, and properly supervised, favorable public opinion results.

Public relations efforts must also include strategies for providing programs that are appropriate, relevant, and capable of satisfying a range of needs and interests. Each program and event should provide realistic, hassle-free policies and procedures, adequate supplies and equipment, safety and accident prevention measures, appropriate behavior controls, quality leadership, reinforcement and recognition systems, and efficient, reliable operations.

Public and Professional Service

Many opportunities exist within all settings for the recreational sport programmer and other staff to engage in service work as consultants, speakers, technicians, organizers, committee members, and advisors. Involvement in service and professional functions is an invaluable learning experience, providing opportunity for interaction with diverse publics. Dependable attention to public service establishes the programmer as a valuable member of the community.

PUBLICITY AND PROMOTION

The foundation of an agency's public relations effort is the publicity and promotion function. Publicity involves the creation of advertisements, news, and information to attract public attention through media. Promotion is a process used to advance a program offering. It involves selling a program to potential participants.

As you prepare for publicity and promotion tasks consider these reminders:

- Publicity does not sell a program by itself.
- Publicity and promotion require constant effort involving the entire recreational sport staff.
- Timing is extremely important! Expedient release of program information affects your results—attendance and participation.
- Postevent program publicity elicits participant goodwill, enhancing the probability of success for future events.

Various avenues exist to convey information to participants. For the purposes of this textbook we organize the main avenues under four categories: mass media, print material, visual presentations, and other promotional techniques.

Publicity and Promotion via Mass Media

Mass media is a process of communication in which one or a few individuals send information to a large audience. It promotes your recreational sport opportunities to the general public. Because of its impact on a recreational sport program, it is important that programmers have a good understanding of the techniques used in mass media.

News Releases

A news release is a formal channel for distributing information to the news media. A concern for accuracy and brevity influences content and style. The typical news release style uses the inverted pyramid form. The most important or interesting details appear in the first tier and comprise the lead or the first two paragraphs of the release. The lead answers five important questions:

- Who participated in the event—individual or group names, addresses, organization involved, titles of positions.
- What happened—the purpose of the event.
- Where the event took place.
- When the event occurred.
- Why this event is significant.

From this draft, write paragraphs or tiers to cover each detail in descending order of importance as the article continues. Figure 13.2 is an example of the inverted pyramid model for news releases.

The following are considerations for constructing an effective lead paragraph for your news releases:

- Confirm your facts.
- Develop a list of the key points for the news event.

- Spell names correctly.
- Provide addresses where possible.
- Organize the information for the lead in your mind.
- Write a rough draft of one or two paragraphs.
- Use simple, easy to understand words.
- Be as specific as possible.
- Revise and edit the lead before submitting it for release.

Figure 13.3 illustrates how a news release is prepared and submitted to the media.

Newspaper

One of the most venerable vehicles for publicity and promotion is the newspaper. The newspaper provides the programmer with an opportunity to reach the widest audience, on a daily or weekly basis, for the lowest cost. Because sport is one of the most popular subjects in a newspaper, ask your editor to include your releases in the sport section.

Before approaching a newspaper, familiarize yourself with press policy, procedure, and orientation:

1. **Learn what types of newspapers exist in your community—national, weekly, and daily.**

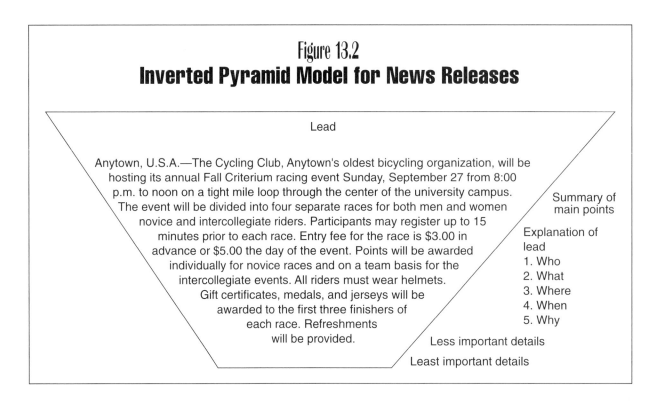

Figure 13.2
Inverted Pyramid Model for News Releases

Lead

Anytown, U.S.A.—The Cycling Club, Anytown's oldest bicycling organization, will be hosting its annual Fall Criterium racing event Sunday, September 27 from 8:00 p.m. to noon on a tight mile loop through the center of the university campus. The event will be divided into four separate races for both men and women novice and intercollegiate riders. Participants may register up to 15 minutes prior to each race. Entry fee for the race is $3.00 in advance or $5.00 the day of the event. Points will be awarded individually for novice races and on a team basis for the intercollegiate events. All riders must wear helmets. Gift certificates, medals, and jerseys will be awarded to the first three finishers of each race. Refreshments will be provided.

Summary of main points

Explanation of lead
1. Who
2. What
3. Where
4. When
5. Why

Less important details

Least important details

Figure 13.3
News Release Guidelines

News Release

Name   Date

Organization

Street address

City, state, zip code

Phone

For immediate release

Adhere to the following guidelines in preparing and placing news releases. The lead or topic sentence should be a brief introductory statement answering the questions of who, what, where, when, and why. This lead statement should be written so that if it is the only part of the release published, the reader will be aware of the essential points of the story.

Other guidelines are the following

1. Use 8½-by-11-inch white bond paper.

2. Typing should be clear, double or triple spaced, and typed on one side of the paper only.

3. Indent first word of each paragraph five spaces.

4. Begin news copy three inches from top of paper.

5. Type the word "-MORE-" at the bottom of the page if the story continues onto another page.

6. When the story ends, the symbol "#", "-30-", or the word "END" should be centered immediately below the last paragraph.

PLACEMENT ON PAGE

On first page

Upper left, type the name, address, and phone number of the author submitting the release.

Upper right: (1) Date the release was submitted.

(2) If there is no particular release date involved, mark your copy *For immediate release*

Margins: Use wide margins, preferably between one to two inches on each side for editing purposes.

Length: Limit the release to one or two pages. Paragraphs should run five or six lines, maximum about 35 words. Do not split a paragraph from first to second page.

Headlines: Do not put a headline on a release. That's the editor's job.

Slug: If the story runs more than one page, a slug or a one- or two-word title must be used. The slug appears in the upper left corner of each page. Also indicate the page number as shown above.

Numerals: In general, spell below 10, use numbers for 10 and higher. However, fractions used alone are spelled: three-fourths of a mile. In reporting sport scores it is acceptable to use numbers such as Smith's Bluejackets won 25-2.

Proof: Always check and double-check for typing errors before submitting to the news media.

Ending: Use -30- or -###- or END

- Visit each newspaper and introduce yourself to the publisher.

- Make an appointment with the managing editor, sport editor, picture editor, and other appropriate representatives.

- Convince these individuals of the importance of your recreational sport program to the community. Determine their needs and how you can satisfy them.

- Leave a business card so they can reach you for answers to questions.

- Ask about the newspaper's readership. Show you will attempt to gear your releases for that clientele.

- After meeting with representatives from each newspaper, organize a file on the media people you need to contact concerning deadlines, writing style, circulation, and other pertinent information. This will eliminate guesswork later.

2. **Know the deadline for copy and photograph submission.** A newspaper wants news while it is still current. As a rule, an evening newspaper's deadline is around noon, whereas the morning edition is midnight. A sport action photograph is an effective complement to a newspaper article. Pictures draw attention and encourage reading an accompanying article. Submit photographs in 5-by-7-inch or 8-by-10-inch black and white glossy formats whenever possible. Check to see whether your picture is more effective in a horizontal or vertical

format. Do not assume that the newspaper can identify your photograph. Tape a label to the back of each photo indicating your name, your title or position, and your organization. Also provide a caption of the individual or group pictured. Include the subjects' names, titles, organizational affiliation (if any), the event, and the date of the event. If you would like to have your picture returned after use indicate, "Return to . . ." with your name and address. Without such notice, editors assume that they may keep the pictures for their file or for disposal. If you file your negative the newspaper may dispose with the photograph as it wishes. If you need a photographer at an event, request such coverage on your press release form. Call a day before the event to remind the editor. Identify the individuals you want photographed by name, title, team, and so forth. Provide printed background information that the photographer can take back to the newsroom.

3. **Avoid sending the same press release to more than one person or department in the same newspaper.** This only causes confusion.

4. **Make sure your press releases are worth printing.** Concise and well-edited releases have a better chance for publication because they significantly decrease an editor's work.

5. **Don't expect the newspaper to print all your press releases.** By all means, show appreciation for those it does print.

6. **Learn how to handle an interview.** The following are guidelines to consider:

   • Know the material that you will discuss in the interview.

   • Anticipate controversial or difficult questions.

   • Be honest and direct in answering questions.

   • If you don't know an answer to a question, say so and offer to refer the question to the appropriate individual. Never try to answer a question when you do not know.

   • Keep the interview as friendly as possible even under stressful situations.

   • Avoid any off-the-record remarks unless you know and trust the interviewer. If you cannot release specific information,

explain that it is not for public record and politely reserve the right to not answer. Be sure to answer questions that are public information and not against company policy.

7. **Don't shy away from advertising.** Regardless of whether the organization is profit or nonprofit, advertising is a valuable promotional tool. Placement of an ad is critical. The most popular pages of a newspaper, in order, are front page, comics, sports, and want ads.

8. **Monitor editorials and letters to the editor.** Generally, an agency doesn't write editorials unless they are solicited. (On occasion, an agency may prepare a letter to the editor to express appreciation for the efforts of various individuals or groups.) Encourage newspaper staff to provide insight to a special interest or controversial topic. Complaints often serve as a warning of a problem area. We hope they never appear in the newspaper. Unresolved complaints result in negative public sentiment. Whenever someone expresses a negative perspective, request an opportunity to respond as soon as possible to minimize unfavorable opinion.

Radio and Television

Radio and television, like the newspaper, are effective in reaching a large audience.

The scope of a broadcast message is greater than other avenues because radio and television audiences are so extensive. Many programmers shy away from broadcast opportunities because of cost, yet free broadcast time is feasible in many situations. The following are examples of opportunities for broadcasting recreational sport information:

• **Interviews.** Conducted between two or more individuals concerning opinions about an aspect of a sport program, the interview may highlight program procedures, sport information, or specific issues of interest. It is best to prepare a script in advance and schedule a rehearsal with all individuals.

• **Panel discussions or symposiums.** Panel discussions or symposiums offer a forum on specific concerns involving the organization, issues, or needs of the recreational sport program.

• **News stories.** Announcements and news stories about recreational sport activities may occur before or after an event. They may include speculation about the value and expected outcome of the event.

• **Public service announcements (PSAs).** A common way to obtain free air time, PSAs are similar to commercials in that they sell a product. These announcements are usually allotted 15, 30, or 60 seconds to present an idea program. Consequently, the message conveys only essential information.

• **Sport talk show.** This format is a popular one in which participants or staff have opportunities to elaborate interests or job responsibilities. Casual in nature, talk shows often follow a question and answer structure.

• **Paid advertising.** There are two types of commercials: standard and production. The standard commercial involves a straightforward narration of an announcement, and a production commercial often includes music or sound effects to set a mood. The length of either commercial depends on the budget and the message you wish to convey but is usually no longer than 60 seconds.

• **Radio and television appearances.** A public appearance is more personalized than other broadcast methods and requires a different preparation. A few simple things to remember are the following:

- Bring along supporting material. If you are appearing on television, bring an appropriate tape. Visual aids enhance television appearances.
- Ask the interviewer or host in advance what topics you will discuss.
- Direct your comments to the TV interviewer. You may want to speak directly to the camera on occasion.
- Use natural hand expressions when speaking.
- Use make-up provided by the TV studio. Avoid wearing distracting clothes or jewelry.

When preparing a broadcast message, eliminate complicated sentences and use a simple vocabulary that all can understand. Contraction of words is acceptable.

Because broadcast messages are perishable, make every effort to ensure that the audience will recall the message. Mention the most important element of your message, the title of the sport event, for example, three or four times during a one-minute announcement.

Media Relations

Reporters appreciate sources who are cooperative and professional. Basic hints when communicating with the press include the following (adapted from Newson 1976, 228):

- Do not use technical jargon.
- Smile when answering questions—even when you're on the radio. Smiling makes your voice sound better.
- Speak in 30-second quotes. Longer answers are seldom used.
- A simple yes or no may keep you from being quoted.
- Lose your temper in front of a reporter and find an embarrassing spot on the six o'clock news.
- Never tell a lie. A reporter doesn't forget.
- Preface remarks are taboo.
- Represent your organization when appearing on radio or TV, not your personal opinion.
- Keep up with current events.
- Know more about your subject than a reporter does.
- Don't say "no comment"; it makes you sound guilty.
- Don't speak off the record to a reporter.
- Have a positive message to deliver.
- Know why you were asked to appear.
- Dress conservatively. Don't wear flashy colors or short sleeves.
- Do your homework.
- Question your position. Play the devil's advocate and force yourself to justify your point of view as part of your preparation.
- Keep your position simple enough to be understood by the average 10th-grade student.
- While in a television or radio studio, assume every microphone and camera is live.
- Do not leave the set until the program is over.
- Edit your message before you deliver it.

Creating Publicity-Related Print Material

Print material, unlike mass media, is designed to reach a targeted readership. Popular formats include handbooks, brochures, pamphlets, and newsletters. Recreational sport use of print material has increased tremendously in recent years through advances in printing technology.

When preparing visual aids, use the following guidelines:

- **Choose a subject.** The most important thing to consider is the relationship of a visual concept to the sport or subject. Focus on conveying one thought to avoid confusion.

- **Develop a caption.** A good caption entices the viewer to pursue a subject presentation further. The wording should be simple and direct to stimulate interest and attention.

- **Gather the material.** Content should cover (a) illustrating the idea (photographs, drawings, cartoons, illustrations, or objects), (b) attracting attention (colored materials or three-dimensional devices), and (c) equipment for attaching the material to a permanent fixture.

- **Plan the placement of the visual.** Place a visual to be attractive and interesting to the viewer's eye.

- **Select the font.** Lettering can make or break a visual. A simple letter style is the easiest to read. Captions or labels should be large enough to be visible from a distance.

- **Don't expect miracles.** Visual aids do not guarantee effective promotion and publicity. Unless properly constructed, visuals are distracting, cumbersome, and wasteful.

As a recreational sport manager, your agency may call on you to create handbooks, brochures and pamphlets, newsletters, calendars, sport information sheets, and posters and flyers to promote your programs. Let's look at some aspects involved in producing these materials.

Handbooks

The handbook is an accepted format for distributing orientation material for a recreational sport program. Develop a handbook design that appeals to your prospective reader, based on the following parameters:

- **Size.** Purpose often dictates size. If you want to be distinctive or flamboyant, consider a large magazine format. If you are more practical, use a pocket or standard (8 $\frac{1}{2}$-by-11-inch) dimension.

- **Length.** Keep length to a minimum. The more that appears in print, the less that gets read.

- **Color.** Color, particularly on the cover, attracts attention.

- **Illustration.** Cartoons or photographs add appeal and cost.

- **Type.** The typeface style should be easy to read.

- **Content** A handbook is a collection of information to attract and motivate participation in the program. The following is a list of topics that you can include in a recreational sport handbook (Means 1973, 362).
  - Awards and recognition
  - Calendar of events
  - Club sport information
  - Employment opportunities
  - Entry instructions
  - Equipment availability
  - Events and programs listing
  - Facility hours and scheduling
  - Fees, forfeits, protest procedures
  - First aid and injury information
  - Sport rules and regulations
  - Health examination policy
  - Instructional sport offerings
  - Insurance requirement information
  - League play-off regulations
  - Listings of officials, supervisors, managers
  - Locker and towel regulations
  - Organizational structure of the program
  - Participation statistics
  - Point system and scoring records
  - Postponement notification policies
  - Practice opportunities
  - Program champions from previous year
  - Rental equipment policies
  - Special events calendars
  - Staff introductions
  - Swimming permits
  - Units of competition

Brochures and Pamphlets

Brochures and pamphlets are versatile tools. A brochure is smaller and more concise than a pamphlet.

It covers 4 to 12 pages, whereas the pamphlet may contain two to four times the copy.

The values of brochures and pamphlets are numerous. You can present your message free of the distractions common to newspapers and other media. You can concentrate on your subject without competing with unrelated stories or pictures. Because this is your publication, you determine the schedule and method of distribution—mail, hand delivery, or display. Brochures and pamphlets are often the least expensive ways to communicate a message, so they can more easily fit into your budget.

Newsletters

With the diversity in recreational sport personnel and participants, a newsletter serves a valuable communications function. It allows versatility and diversity in content, length, and design from issue to issue and is inexpensive to mass produce. The newsletter easily addresses a target group and complements other promotion. Figure 13.4 highlights format issues related to newsletters.

Calendars

Program calendars are excellent promotional tools that publicize weekly, monthly, or yearly recreational sport events by listing registration deadlines, rules, regulations, policies, job leadership opportunities, and facility availability. They may appear as desk blotters, wall posters, or pocket calendars.

Sport Information Sheets

Such notices usually accompany each entry form or facility schedule and contain pertinent information necessary for participation: entry fees; registration location and deadlines; date and location of orientation meeting; schedule distribution or rules interpretation meetings; tournament format; and days, dates, and location for participation.

Posters

The purpose of the poster is to remind the participant of the principal theme. Present the poster content as a singular idea, but do not attempt to explain or convince. Color selection is important to poster design because it aids the legibility of the printed message. Use unusual or contrasting color combinations. Keep typography clear and simple. Standard poster size is 14-by-22 inches. For tacking or taping to a wall, paper material or lightweight cardboard is sufficient. For free-standing or outdoor use, use heavy weight cardboard.

Poster design consists of three basic elements: slogan, illustration, and group name. Do not include more than these three elements in a poster. Focus on one element to attract attention. Posters

---

Figure 13.4
Newsletter Format

Volume _____, Issue _____   Date _____

THE NEWSLETTER is a technique used to keep all participants aware of the organization's activities. These activities may range from individual recognition to participation highlights and special announcements. The constituency may consist of current team members, past participants, and alumni.

IT SHOULD be printed on the organization's 8½-by-11 inch letterhead paper and limited to a single sheet. Cost of a newsletter should be kept to a minimum because it is issued weekly or monthly.

WHEN WRITING the newsletter don't bother with fancy headlines. The title "Newsletter" in capital letters is sufficient. Stay with an informal and brief format.

KEEP IN mind that a newsletter is not designed to flow with dialogue like a letter. It is bits and pieces of business news that are informative to the participants.

THE BEST format is a series of separate short paragraphs that should include no more than four or five sentences. Each paragraph opens with a capitalized heading or the first few words in upper case. The gossip column in a newspaper is an example of good writing style for newsletters.

REMEMBER, NEWSLETTERS are a direct means of communicating and promoting the recreational sport organization in a brief and positive way.

have approximately five seconds to communicate 10 or 12 words and a picture. The best formula to guarantee success is logical order, bold letters, attention-getting colors, and a simple illustration. Posters need not be a work of art.

Flyers

A flyer is an inexpensive promotional piece that you can mass distribute. It is usually printed on a single, pastel-colored sheet of paper. Its format consists of a central theme with simple layout, color, and design. Figure 13.5 illustrates an example of an intramural basketball flyer.

Use the following ways to display or distribute flyers:

- Bulletin boards
- Team captains' or managers' meetings
- Departmental mailboxes
- Sport facilities
- Locker rooms
- Chambers of Commerce
- Postal service
- Schools
- Grocery stores
- Clubs
- Businesses
- Sporting goods stores

Logos

Using logos provides a visual identity that establishes continuity from one recreational sport program offering to the next within the same organization. The logo symbol should identify the organization in every promotional format available to the recreational sport programmer. It is an attention getter and can appear on such items as the following:

- Flyers
- Bulletin boards
- Handbooks
- Press releases
- Brochures
- Calendars
- Posters
- Bookmarks
- T-shirts
- Entrance signs
- Slide presentations
- Uniforms
- Vehicles
- Registration forms

The design of the logo is critical. Most professional printers will provide design assistance in this area for a minimal charge.

Visual Presentations for Publicity and Promotion

Using visual aids such as slide and video presentations, bulletin boards, exhibits, and displays can be effective for promoting recreational sport programs. If developed and used properly, they can complement other promotional efforts we have previously discussed or can be a stand-alone presentation. Professional staff often use visual aids when delivering presentations to sport groups. Visual aids help the audience see the main points of the speaker's presentation.

Slide Presentations

Slide presentations offer versatility in design content and focus that you can easily alter to accommodate changes in emphasis or audience. When constructing a presentation, begin by selecting a theme. This establishes the purpose of the presentation and identifies the type of slides needed to convey the message.

Although you do not need to narrate slide presentations, they are more effective when you do. For an effective script, the content should be simple and concise. Rehearse your presentation to synchronize the slides with the narration. Audible cues on your script should indicate when to advance each slide. Slide presentations traditionally involved only one projector. Now they commonly involve multiple projectors with automatic cueing devices for activating the slide advance. Another recent development is the slide-tape presentation, used in conjunction with a prerecorded narrative track. You can activate the slide advance by a hand-held unit or by a signal on the tape. This feature is useful for conventions, exhibits, offices, or other settings experiencing a constant traffic flow or where it is not practical to have a narrator present.

Video Presentations

Video presentations offer many of the same advantages associated with slide presentations. However, producing quality video promotional pieces re-

Figure 13.5
Intramural Sport Flyer

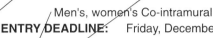

**INTRAMURAL
BASKETBALL**

1. **LOGO**. Readers identify the organization by the standard logo. It should be representative.

2. **TITLE/NAME OF EVENT**. Very simple and direct without a large number of words.

3. **TARGET POPULATION**. This informs the reader of the program offering.

4. **DATE, TIME, AND LOCATION**. It is recommended to include the day as well as date and a map to help the participant locate the event. If the program is more than one day in length, include the ending day.

5. **OTHER SPECIFICS**. Be brief.

6. **SPONSORING AGENCY**. Include the name, address, telephone number, and contact person for further information.

Men's, women's Co-intramural

ENTRY DEADLINE: Friday, December 16, 19_ _
ENTRY FEE: $5.00 per team
PLAY BEGINS: Monday, January 16, 19_ _
SCHEDULES AVAILABLE: Schedules and rules will be distributed at team captain's meetings at the following times:

Wednesday, January 14, Room 219
All Women's Teams . . . . .7:30 pm
Men's Residence Hall Teams . . . . 7:30 pm
Fraternity and Independent Teams . . . . 8:15 pm
Co-Intramural Teams . . . . .9:00 pm

ENTRY PROCEDURE: Entries will be scheduled by the computer. Therefore all entry forms must be filled out correctly to insure inclusion of your team. Follow all directions on the form carefully and be sure to use a number two (2) lead pencil. Entries and Entry Fees are to be turned in to the Recreational Sports "Annex" Room 290.

TYPES OF COMPETITION:
Competitive—Round Robin league play with eligible teams advancing to a single elimination tournament.

Casual—Round Robin only. Casual teams play an expanded schedule with no advancement to the All-Campus Tournament.

GENERAL INFORMATION
1. All teams must send a representative to the team captain's meeting on January 14. **Teams not represented will be subject to disqualification.**
2. Check the Guides to Participation for questions concerning eligibility, protests, disciplinary statements, etc. Copies are available in the Recreational Sports Office.

FURTHER INFORMATION
Recreational Sports Office, Room 290, 335-2371. For scheduling information—335-8788.

---

quires professional production expertise, editing, script preparation, and increased cost. Because of these, agencies might consider using presentations provided by national sport organizations.

Bulletin Boards

A bulletin board is a visual way of reminding potential participants of program offerings. Consider it a continually updated newspaper and place it wherever participants regularly pass by or congregate. Because bulletin boards may be portable or permanent, you can put them in many locations: outdoor sport complexes, gymnasiums, office lobbies, hallways, and locker rooms. Set the board in a glass-covered case that you can lock when necessary to prevent tampering.

You can enhance the effectiveness of the bulletin board by following these guidelines:

- **Simplicity.** Simplify shapes, lines, space, and color to present a readable board.

- **Unity.** Emphasize a basic line of direction throughout the board.

- **Emphasis.** To focus attention on an important item, set it apart by using space, color, or texture.

- **Balance.** Balance invites a quick and thorough inspection by the participant.

- **Supplies for bulletin boards.** Maintain a sharp, fresh appearance by promptly replacing worn or damaged supplies.

Exhibits and Displays

An exhibit is usually three dimensional and used for a particular time, and a display is two dimensional and permanently part of the environment. However, both seek to achieve the same results, which include the following:

- **Attract attention.** If the content of the exhibit or display does not jump at the passing public, it will fail.

- **Create involvement.** Once you have gained attention the display must somehow encourage and stimulate the individual to participate.

- **Distribute information.** Concentrate on communicating the most important information. Remember, you have an individual's attention for only a short time.

- **Promote goodwill.** The viewer should receive something free by spending a few moments at the display or exhibit. For example, a Frisbee club might promote its activity by giving away Frisbees.

Other Promotional Techniques

Consider any opportunity to favorably present your image to your clientele as a promotional opportunity. Other than time and budget constraints, your creativity is the only limit to coming up with new ways to promote your program. For the remainder of the chapter we'll look at some effective promotional activities. Let these (and the activities we've already discussed) serve as a springboard for your imagination.

Computer Technology

Accessing potential participants via the Internet is an excellent way to provide information to the widest audience possible. Electronic mailing and promotions to restricted and unrestricted lists is efficient and effective.

Holding Open Houses

An open house seeks to attract many prospective participants to the sport facility. A tour of the facility combined with an oral presentation of the program is the most important feature of this event.

Telephone Campaigns

The telephone is not a promotional tool, yet positive impressions made during phone conversations are beneficial. Some of the subtleties of proper phone use are outlined in figure 13.6. Telephones serve several purposes. Among them are solicitation, announcements, and message distribution.

- **Solicitation.** Because the telephone is immediate and efficient, it overcomes many problems encountered using printed materials. Participants and personnel often rely on the telephone to obtain information regarding the program or their responsibilities.

- **Announcements.** When people want to know such information as facility hours, club sport events, daily intramural sport schedules, and cancellations, a recorded message is an ideal way to disseminate this information. You can record messages on tapes in advance and update them as required. Used after regular office hours, this mechanism eliminates participant frustration by providing a consistent source of reliable information.

- **Messages.** The telephone provides the easiest and most economical method for messages regarding program changes, rescheduling of tournament contests, reminders of meeting dates and times, and distributing information. Here are some helpful hints for effective telephone use:

Word of Mouth

Word of mouth is one of the least controllable but most effective avenues for communication. A recreational sport programmer stimulates word of mouth by providing a quality program. When people enjoy themselves, they recommend an activity to others. Unfortunately, the grapevine often embellishes the truth. If information is inaccurate or harmful, issue a statement as soon as possible

Shining Example

Amelia Island Plantation, Florida

Amelia Island Plantation is a resort located in northeastern Florida. This resort is unique in that it offers a variety of sports and recreation opportunities in addition to the typical resort amenities. In particular, the Amelia Island Plantation offers the "Amelia Sports Challenge." This event allows teams (families or company teams) to compete in a variety of sporting events and trivia. Teamwork is mandatory, as all members of the team must contribute to their total score. The staff at Amelia Island offer a "Group Recreation Option" which allows a business to plan sport activities around their conference agenda. The recreation activities are promoted by monthly guides which are available to the resort guests. The guide includes a calendar of events and a listing of services provided by the resort. Amelia Island also promotes its recreation programs with additional supplemental brochures which accompany its resort accommodation guides.

Organization: The Amelia Island Plantation is a resort and residential community that features beaches, golf, tennis and entertainment.

Clientele: The Amelia Island Plantation caters mostly to families. There are, however, conference facilities available for large groups of people.

Budget: Recreation Budget $330,000

Marketing: The Amelia Island Plantation is focused toward families. It uses brochures (for both children and adults) and calendars.

Staff: The Amelia Island Plantation staff is estimated at about 900, including both full- and part-time employees.

Program Detail: Sports programming as described below is a facility devoted to tennis, golf, aquatics, volleyball, and special events.

Facilities: The main focus of Amelia Island Plantation is on tennis and golf. The Plantation offers many activities including: Amelia's Outdoor Challenge, Volleyball Tournaments, Beach Olympics, Nite Lite Golf, Road Rally, and Corporate Paintball Wars.

Figure 13.6
Telephone Tips

• **BEFORE CALLING . . .**

❑ Answer the questions, "Is the telephone the best way to handle the message?" and "Is this the best time to call?"

❑ Be in a positive frame of mind.

❑ Gather material before you place a call.

❑ Plan your thoughts and write down what you need to say.

• **PLACING A CALL . . .**

❑ Be certain of the number you want.

❑ Dial carefully—know how to dial for internal, local, and long distance calls.

❑ Address the individual you are calling by name. Identify yourself by name, title, and agency.

❑ Keep conversations brief and to the point. If the conversation requires a lengthy discussion, demonstrate courtesy by asking if the individual has the time.

❑ Speak in a calm and polite tone of voice.

❑ Leave a concise message if your contact is absent.

❑ End all calls courteously and replace the receiver gently.

• **ANSWERING A CALL . . .**

❑ Answer promptly before the second or third ring, if possible.

❑ Answer the phone yourself.

❑ Identify yourself.

❑ Note essential details of your conversation.

❑ If you need to leave your desk during a phone conversation, always put the caller on hold. Never allow a caller to hear office conversation.

❑ Always say good-bye when completing a call.

Desktop Publishing

As a recreational sports programmer, you will find yourself wearing many different hats. You may do everything from the day-to-day operations of personnel management to tournament scheduling to overall program marketing, publicity, and promotion. Unfortunately, you will have very little time to design and lay out advertising and marketing material, program brochures, staff training manuals, or monthly volunteer newsletters. However, you will appreciate some of the easy-to-use desktop publishing software programs that are currently on the market.

Desktop publishing programs are very flexible, low-cost programs that help you quickly design your own ads, flyers, direct mail marketing pieces, and forms. They are excellent in-house marketing tools that will take your agency to a new level of professionalism and give you a promotional edge when attracting new participants to your program. With desktop publishing programs, you can take advantage of the principle of "a picture is worth a thousand words" and add a variety of sports pictures, seasonal photographs, graphics, clip art, and other appealing layout features to your publications.

Microsoft Publisher for Windows is a very powerful desktop publishing program for novices that is easy to learn how to use. The program is excellent in terms of giving you control over text formatting, graphics importing, page numbering, dragging and dropping, and basic page formatting and layout options—without forcing you to learn complex desktop publishing concepts or techniques.

An attractive feature of *Microsoft Publisher for Windows* is that it includes many easy-to-use point-and-click options, including the popular Wizards function that is available in all Microsoft products. The PageWizard option takes the guesswork out of the process by walking you through the creation of nearly 20 different pre-formatted document templates for newsletters, calendars, flyers, brochures, tables, and even common business forms.

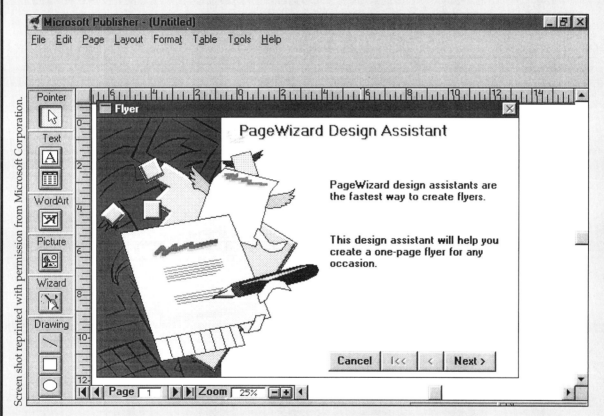

As you can see in the above screen, the PageWizard will ask you questions regarding the desired final product (whether it is a logo, brochure, newsletter, etc.). The program then creates the basic layout and design template, leaving you to merely fill in the blanks. If you need further assistance, *Microsoft Publisher for Windows* also provides Cue Cards, which are on-screen prompts that pop onto the screen when needed and provide answers to a wide range of common desktop publishing questions related to the document you are creating.

Although developing your own sport publications may sound intimidating at first, desktop publishing programs make it easy and allow you to create professional-looking printed material without becoming a professional.

Microsoft Publisher for Windows, Microsoft, Redmond, WA.

Other desktop publishing products: PageMaker, PagePlus, QuarkXPress, Ventura, FrameMaker 5, ClarisWorks, Print Shop Deluxe, PFS Publisher, and HomePublisher.

citing the full facts on the situation to squelch gossip and rumors.

Novelty Items

Other methods for recreational sport program publicity and promotion are not widely used but can be effective in certain situations. We classify these as novelty items because of their innovative nature. Novelty items may include the following:

- Bus advertisement
- Balloons
- Videotape
- Cartoons
- Bumper stickers
- Skywriting
- Banners
- Buttons
- Window decals
- Billboards
- Rubber stamps
- Imprinted clothing
- Pencils
- Keychains
- Pocket calendars
- Desk blotters

Whatever means you choose, follow good taste, judgment, and simplicity.

CONCLUSION

Effective marketing and public relations require understanding the needs of the public, the process of communication, and the vehicles of promotion and publicity. The degree of community participation and support depends on our ability to create a message, select an appropriate medium, and choose a time to reach a desired audience for reasonable cost and effort. Successfully marketing and promoting a recreational sport program will ultimately result in positive customer service and satisfied participants.

DISCUSSION QUESTIONS

1. List three advantages of using the radio as a medium for sport advertising.

2. Describe five items you could include in a recreational sport handbook.

3. Does all responsibility for positive public relations rest with personnel at the operational level? Explain your answer.

4. What five questions should a press release answer?

5. Explain and illustrate three forms of printed material you can use to promote a recreational sport program.

6. Publicity and promotion are terms sometimes used interchangeably. Explain whether this use is accurate.

7. What steps should you incorporate to establish a positive public relations campaign?

8. How do programming trends affect the marketing strategies of a recreational sport program?

9. Name and describe each step in developing a marketing plan for a recreational sport program.

10. How is the use of volunteers in recreational sport important in public relations?

11. Explain the purpose of market research.

12. What is the difference between market structure analysis and consumer analysis?

13. Explain the four traditional marketing components.

14. How can a recreational sport programmer establish effective customer service?

15. In establishing effective customer service, explain the impact of each of the following: personnel and volunteers, interagency cooperation, public and professional service, facilities and programs, and publicity and promotion.

APPLICATION EXERCISE

Plan a recreational sport night as a special event for a community of 50,000. Include instructional sport, intramural sport, informal sport, fitness, and club sport activities.

Describe several publicity mediums that you will use, and explain why you chose them. What aspects of the special event would you focus on in your marketing program? What role would a publicity committee perform? Outline specific tasks and duties that the committee would be responsible for. Which responsibilities could you delegate to volunteers?

Write a news release describing the special event. Your news release should appear the way it would in the local newspaper.

REFERENCES

Cohen, A. 1995. Gray areas. *Athletic Business* 19 (1): 31-40.

Keeny, B.A. 1994. By the numbers. *Club Business International* 15 (10): 26-30.

Means, L.E. 1973. *Intramurals: Their organization and administration*. Englewood Cliffs, NJ: Prentice Hall.

Newson, D. 1976. *This is PR*. Belmont, CA: Wadsworth.

SUGGESTED READINGS

Frankel, E., and C. Latora. 1994. Promoting women's athletics in the '90s. *Athletic Management* 6 (4): 20-27.

Horine, L. 1995. *Administration of physical education and sport programs*. Dubuque, IA: Brown & Benchmark.

Keeny, B.A. 1994. The (new) cooper controversy. *Club Business International* 15 (11): 58-68.

Keeny, B.A. 1995. Ad ventures. *Club Business International* 16 (2): 17-18.

Stotlar, D.K. 1993. *Successful sport marketing*. Dubuque, IA: Brown & Benchmark.

Tadlock, L.S. 1993. Marketing starts with information. *Parks & Recreation* 28 (5): 29, 46-50.

Waldrop, J. 1994. Markets with pizazz. *American Demographics* 16 (7): 22-32.

CHAPTER 14

Recreational Sport as a Profession

Chapter Objectives

After reading this chapter you will

- understand the characteristics of a profession,
- be familiar with key sport organizations that serve recreational sport professionals,
- understand opportunities available in becoming a recreational sport professional, and
- be familiar with a few trends in sport participation.

A career in recreational sport management is one of the most promising directions of the future. Fortune magazine (Alley 1995) projects the recreation profession as one of the top five career opportunities. Such a career offers many opportunities for an individual with a strong background in programming and administrating sport.

This chapter provides resources available for employment opportunities and professional growth in this exciting field. We'll look at the concept of professionalization and talk about its growth in recreational sport management. We'll also identify key sport organizations. Associating with one or more of these organizations may provide you with opportunities for professional career enhancement. This chapter concludes with a look at trends that may prevail in recreation and recreational sport management during the next 20 years.

PROFESSIONALIZATION OF RECREATIONAL SPORT MANAGEMENT

As figure 14.1 shows, recreational sport managers work in a variety of settings. Their educational training generally comes from the academic disciplines associated with recreational administration or physical education. Recreational sport evolves from the leisure time and opportunities available through many settings. These settings require professional employees who typically receive education and/or professional preparation from the main areas of recreation administration (leisure studies) and physical education (kinesiology). The content, as described in Figure 14.1, represents a body of knowledge that includes sports, i.e., varying play-

ing levels of cooperative/competitive activity. These levels are represented by the sport classifications that comprise recreational sport. Practicing recreational sport managers, following examples set by physical educators and recreation administrators, have begun to enjoy the benefits of professionalization by forming several organizations.

One characteristic of an emerging profession is its willingness to develop a cohesiveness in which members freely share new ideas, principles, and experiences. Professional associations in sport management are formed usually by individuals volunteering their time while working in the recreational sport field. Their primary purpose as an association is to organize the resources of its members for

- quality recreational sport programming service to others,
- advancing the standards of the profession and its members, and
- guiding the behavior of its members.

An organization that gathers individual resources can solve mutual problems and attain mutual goals. Although individuals working alone can accomplish a great deal, an association can accomplish the same task more effectively by organizing the efforts of people working together. A few elements shared by all organizations include the following:

- **Size.** You can't organize by yourself; you must have two or more people! Anytime two or more people share time, space, services, and so forth, they form an organization.
- **Interdependence.** Members must work together to achieve goals. The behavior of one individual influences the behavior of another. This provides professionals with a peer group that promotes a sense of identity.
- **Communication.** Members succeed by communicating with each other: thinking, talking, reading, writing, listening, and so forth. Communication is what permits people to organize.
- **Output.** As a result of the organization's actions, it returns services to the members and to society. Results may be print materials, an accepted set of working principles, or a means of certifying members, to name a few possibilities.
- **Purpose.** Most professional associations have similar objectives, which include ad-

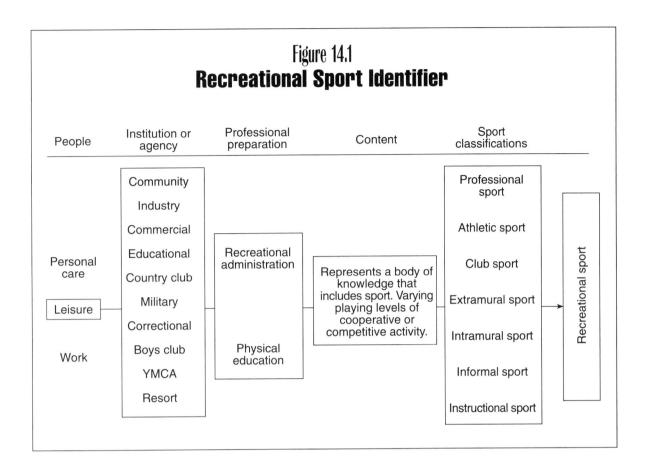

Figure 14.1
Recreational Sport Identifier

vancement, recognition, and knowledge of their respective fields.

However, for a professional association to be effective and flourish, it requires people to provide it with service and leadership.

Professional Associations for Recreational Sport Managers

The Encyclopedia of Associations, 1994 edition, lists nearly 21,000 national associations in the United States. Of those, more than 798 were listed under the classification *athletics and sports!* Each sport has an organization system for its specialty. Many of these organizations are organized for players or instructors. For example, tennis enthusiasts may join several professional organizations, the most prevalent being the United States Tennis Association. Recreational sport managers who specialize in sport-specific programs or who are site supervisors for sport facilities may find it useful to belong to sport associations.

For generalists or for those who want to associate with others who deliver sport programming,

there are several organizations whose focus is sport management. These include the following:

AAHPERD

American Alliance for Health, Physical
    Education, Recreation and Dance
1900 Association Drive
Reston, VA 22091-1599
703-476-3400

NASSM

North American Society for Sport
    Management
106 Main Street
Suite 344
Houlton, ME 04730-0991
506-453-5010

NIRSA

National Intramural-Recreational
    Sports Association
850 SW 15th Street
Corvallis, OR 97333-4145
503-737-2088

NRPA

National Recreation and Park Association
2775 S Quincy Street
Suite 300
Arlington, VA 22206-2204
800-626-NRPA

Each of these associations has student branches for full-time students who are interested in or currently pursuing a degree in sport management.

Other national associations of interest include the following:

- AAU—Amateur Athletic Union
- ACSM—American College of Sports Medicine
- ASEP—American Sport Education Program
- CBI—Club Business International
- IRSA—International Racquet Sports Association
- NASPE—National Association for Sport and Physical Education (part of AAHPERD)
- NASSM—North American Society for Sport Management
- NCAA—National Collegiate Athletic Association
- NESRA—National Employee Services and Recreation Association
- RCRA—Resort and Commercial Recreation Association

Your involvement in a professional association can begin in college and depend on your area of professional interest. In choosing your professional involvements, it is best to join an organization that can provide the widest range of professional growth and career opportunities, such as conferences and workshops, career information, certification and training, networking, and so forth. The narrower the focus becomes, the more limited are the options. Early involvement in a professional organization can lead to a fulfilling career.

Benefits of Professionalization

We've hinted that organized association with other sport managers is beneficial for the career development of individual practitioners. It is important to recognize that benefits of professionalization accrue to the field of recreational sport management itself and, most importantly, to the clients served by the profession. Our field is continually gaining professional stature as evidenced by the value of sport in society, the standards and the knowledge base its practitioners possess, and the evidence of professional self-regulation through certification, accreditation, and a code of ethics. Let's look at some of these benefits:

- **Professionalization reinforces recreational sport as a social function.** Professionals recognize that recreational sport is an ongoing entity that is valued by the culture. Therefore, the field of recreational sport deserves a professional commitment to provide well-structured opportunities for worthy use of leisure time through sport.

- **Professionalization recognizes and standardizes the preparation requirements of practitioners.** Studies of the knowledge base within this field (Jamieson 1980; Jennings 1982; Ellard 1983; Ulrich and Parkhouse 1982; Skipper and Apthinos 1993) show that curricular development in undergraduate and graduate education has created degree programs in sport management. Such a curriculum is unique to each application. Professionalization helps emphasize the need for formal training before entering the field.

- **Professionalization sets operating standards.** The National Intramural-Recreational Sports Association (NIRSA) has addressed sport management operation standards for campus recreational sport. The National Recreation and Park Association (NRPA) has developed standards in parks and recreation, where most sport management programs reside, to accredit park and recreation agencies.

- **Professionalization provides certification and accreditation of practitioners.** Certification refers to the individual testing and control of professionals. Standards of the field have been converted into the professional development goals of an individual through knowledge-based descriptors of performance and through curricular review opportunity by identifying competencies needed to become educated in a profession. For general recreation certification, NRPA offers a Certified Leisure Professional examination (CLP). NIRSA provides certification of recreational sport specialists. The North American Society of Sport Management (NASSM) provides accreditation of sport management curricula, and NRPA accredits recreation curricula. Accreditation is a test of an institution to disseminate and a measure of whether

Figure 14.2
National Intramural-Recreational Sports Association Code of Ethics

Preamble

An outstanding characteristic of a profession is that its members are continually striving to improve the quality of life for the population they serve. In making the choice to affiliate with a professional association, individuals assume the responsibility to conduct themselves in accordance with the ideals and standards set by the organization. For NIRSA members this means they will strive to uphold the Bylaws in a manner illustrated in the Code of Ethics.

Article I

The NIRSA member in fulfilling professional obligations shall

1. Seek to extend public awareness of the profession and its achievements.
2. Be true in writing, reporting, and duplicating information and give proper credit to the contributions of others.
3. Encourage integrity by avoiding involvement or condoning activities that may degrade the Association, its members, or any affiliate agency.
4. Perform dutifully the responsibilities of professional membership and of any offices or assignments to which appointed or elected.
5. Encourage cooperation with other professional associations, educational institutions, and agencies.
6. Practice nondiscrimination on the basis of diversity related to age, disability, ethnicity, gender, national origin, race, religion, and sexual orientation.

Article II

The NIRSA member in relations with employers and employees shall do the following:

1. Practice and implement the concept of equal opportunity and fairness in employment practices and program administration.
2. Refrain from exploiting individuals, institutions, or agencies for personal or professional gain.
3. Secure the trust of employees by maintaining, in confidence, privileged information until properly released.
4. Support the contributions of fellow employees by properly crediting their achievements.
5. Assist and encourage the education of employees in the area of professional development.

Article III

The NIRSA member is providing programs and services shall do the following:

1. Endeavor to offer the safest and highest quality program achievable with available resources.
2. Take responsibility for employing qualified individuals in positions that require special credentials or experience.
3. Strive to keep abreast of current skills and knowledge and encourage innovation in programming and administration.
4. Promote integrity by accepting gratuities for service of no more than normal value.
5. Encourage promotion of the ideals of recreational sport by incorporating such values oas fair play, participation, and an atmosphere promotes equitable opportunity for all.

NIRSA National Office
850 SW 15th Street, Corvallis, OR 97333-4145
503-737-2088

Reprinted by permission of the National Intramural-Recreational Sports Association.

that institution has met standards. In addition, specialized certifications are available for sport-specific requirements in aquatics, exercise, dance, and coached sport.

• **Professionalization fosters ethical behavior. Ethics are the guiding moral principles of an organization.** A code of ethics is a statement of ethical practices adopted by a profession. The field of sport management operates with several codes provided by organizations, serving either the general recreation profession or a specific sport profession. NIRSA developed the code of ethics reproduced as figure 14.2.

Marketable and Professional Skills

Aside from the criteria of a profession as depicted on page 320, an aspiring recreational sport professional is most successful if a professional approach and philosophy are developed. It is important to be motivated and have a professional attitude. Consider the following suggestions:

1. Work Hard
2. Be Honest
3. Stay Focused
4. Maintain Objectivity
5. Eliminate Discrimination and Bias
6. Maintain Integrity

These and other qualities allow for the most positive approach to career development.

POTENTIAL CAREER OPPORTUNITIES FOR RECREATIONAL SPORT MANAGERS

Figure 14.1 lists some key institutions and agencies that provide recreational sport. Career opportunities abound in these settings for an aspiring recreational sport professional. Programming recreational sport comprises from 50 to 80 percent of all recreational programming. An opportunity to work in a recreational sport setting, such as those in the following list, indicates a strong career path for upward mobility into supervisory and top management roles. Although the following material provides some direction in developing a recreational sport career, you can secure more information through formal and informal placement services.

Municipal

City parks and recreation facilities and areas are settings for community sport experiences. You can access employment with direct inquiry or networking through a state or national park and recreation association. These programs are run by home rule, charter, or special districts that also operate the functions of police, fire, public works, and other essential services.

Private Clubs

You can contact private athletic clubs, country clubs, and the like through a specific sport specialization, such as golf or tennis, or a general management background. Club Industry International is an excellent source for professional involvement. These organizations are typically member driven, and an individual with a sport background and a strong customer (member) service orientation is ideal.

Businesses

From the small sole proprietorship to the giant corporation, sport businesses abound. You can best gain access to employment by direct inquiry. Many owners like to hire managers to be involved in operations. You may also consider starting your own business.

Nonprofit and Quasi-Public Organizations

Most nonprofit sport organizations such as Ys, Boys and Girls Clubs, and so forth, have national hiring networks available. Volunteering at one of these organizations can provide access to a career. The focus of these organizations is using sport and recreation to develop character, fitness, and positive living skills.

Military

You can learn about employment as a civilian at military bases throughout the world through a centralized armed forces hot line. Inquiries at local military bases can provide this information and internship experience can be beneficial in accessing this bureaucratic system.

Correctional Setting

Many correctional sites have recreation specialists. You can gain access to this setting through state or federal employment processes. Often correctional positions are linked to other services designed to reinforce or control inmates or develop skills to improve the chances of an individual functioning well on the outside.

Natural Environment

Sport in outdoor settings is managed either by the public entity (i.e., city, country, state, federal) or by a private enterprise contracted to provide a service. Examples of public entities covered here are United States Forest Service and state departments of natural resources.

Educational Setting

You can access campus recreational sport job opportunities through NIRSA; however, there are also organizations that provide information about sport through student unions and student services. The focus of these is to expand student health and development through sport.

Corporations

The National Employee Services and Recreation Association has information about more than 3,500 corporations offering employee recreation programs. Corporations partially fund sport programs to improve employee morale and productivity.

Vacation Resorts and Attractions

The tourism industry is an employment source for recreational sport managers. You can access employment through involvement with the Resort and Commercial Recreation Association or many other organizations. Tourism opportunities are a range of attractions such as theme parks, special events, and festivals.

TRENDS IN RECREATIONAL SPORT AND SPORT PROGRAMMING

An aspiring recreational sport specialist should note trends that may affect employment prospects. We'll provide a list of specific sport trends as examples of the need to watch for changes in consumers' preferences for leisure activity. You can bet that program development and implementation will change to meet this demand.

Recreational sport is a major component of American lifestyles. The following points illustrate the recreational trends expected to endure through this decade.

- Participant interest has increased in martial arts; high-risk, adventure sport such as hang gliding, wind surfing, sky diving, mountain climbing, white-water rafting, orienteering; and outdoor recreational sport such as canoeing, snow skiing, sailing, and bicycling.
- There has been a growing interest in nontraditional sport activities that emphasize self-testing and cooperative behaviors such as the new games approach and stress-challenge activities.
- Physical fitness programs continue to gain popularity among all age groups. The most popular fitness activities include jogging, swimming, bicycling, racquetball, aerobic dancing, personal trainers, and weight training. Closely associated with the physical fitness craze is the interest in wellness, which emphasizes illness prevention. More Americans have become interested in stress testing and activity programs tailor-made for their level of fitness and wellness.
- The rise of the electronic sport age is reflected in the proliferation of computer, arcade, and home video sport games that have stormed the market.
- At all levels, women are participating in sport in record numbers.
- Concern for the energy shortages and environmental protection are modifying distance travel and tourism.

Recreational sport management students should be aware of trends in sport that may affect careers over the next 10 years. Kelly (1987) documents the following specific sport trends that we may experience in the third millennium:

- Sports increasing in popularity include backpacking, hiking, camping, and golf.
- Sports expected to maintain their current interest level or to decline include bicycling, bowling, fitness, jogging, and swimming.

Trends in the recreational sport profession can also affect career goals. In the future, recreational sport specialists may need to specialize and posses an understanding of sport technique. Expect that we will need to address the following issues:

- Programmers must focus attention on providing programs for our youth, disabled, and aged.
- Programmers will continue to be sensitive to the needs of those with disabilities and find more ways to involve them at all levels of sport.
- Those involved in sport management will increasingly need to be certified.
- Those working in sport management must have knowledge of the individual differences among sport participants.
- Those who design sport management programs will incorporate educational processes to assist the participant in continuing these skills at home.
- There will be technological requirements to assist in managing a sport program more efficiently.
- There will be global communications allowing programs to be more widely accessed.

CONCLUSION

The field of sport management has been assisted by two schools of thought, one from a kinesiology curriculum and the other from a management curriculum. Professionalization of this field has been accomplished through developing an identified body of knowledge, code of ethics, standards, accreditation, and certification.

You can become involved through joining one of the many sport-related professional organizations that represent training, services, and job opportunities for aspiring sport specialists.

Trends in the field point to an expanding role of sport managers in providing a diverse range of sport services in the future. The field is open for expansion as participants increase their knowledge and skill in recreational sport and continue to demand services.

DISCUSSION QUESTIONS

1. Is sport management a profession in your opinion? Explain your answer.

2. List professional organizations that are involved in sport management.

3. What is the difference between accreditation and certification?

4. Why are professional organizations important to a profession?

5. In order for a professional association to be effective, what must occur?

6. Identify five current issues or trends that will have a major impact on sport management.

7. Describe the evolutionary process of the growth of sport management.

8. Why is a code of ethics so important to a profession? Who do you think should enforce ethical practices?

9. What are elements shared by all professional organizations?

10. Discuss several sources for employment opportunities in sport management.

APPLICATION EXERCISE

As you prepare to enter the recreational sport field as a career, now is the time to seriously take stock in yourself. To do this, you should have a solid foundation in what the field has to offer in terms of career opportunities, expectations, job placement, salary levels, and so forth. Specifically, in your opinion, what are the advantages and disadvantages of a career in recreational sport? Recommend a course of action that you will follow as you pursue your first job in sport management.

REFERENCES

Alley, J. 1995. Where the jobs are. *Fortune* 132 (6): 53-55.

Bryant, J.A., and J.L. Bradley. 1993. Enhancing academic productivity, student development and employment potential. *National Intramural-Recreational Sports Association Journal* 18 (1): 42-44.

Dunn, J.M. 1990. The future: New order for the 90's. *National Intramural-Recreational Sports Association Journal* 15 (2): 22-25.

Kelly, J. 1987. *Recreation trends: Toward the year 2000.* Champaign, IL: Management Learning Laboratories LTD.

Rose, T. 1990. Marketing yourself for the profession: More than the four p's. *National Intramural-Recreational Sports Association Journal* 14 (3): 24-26.

Ross, C. 1990. Field experiences in recreational sports. *National Intramural-Recreational Sports Association Journal* 14 (3): 16-19.

SUGGESTED READINGS

Broughton, J.C., and D. Griffin. 1994. Collegiate Intramurals: Where do they go from here? *National Intramural-Recreational Sports Association Journal* 18 (2): 10-12.

Brown, S.C. 1990. Looking toward 2000. *National Intramural-Recreational Sports Association Journal* 14 (2): 32-35.

Dudenhoeffer, F.T. 1990. Genesis and evolution of the recreational sports profession. *National Intramural-Recreational Sports Association Journal* 14 (3): 12-13.

Jamieson, L.M. 1990. Recreational sports curriculum: A perspective. *National Intramural-Recreational Sports Association Journal* 14 (3): 38-39.

Karabetsos, J.D. 1991. Campus recreation—Future direction. *National Intramural-Recreational Sports Association Journal* 15 (2): 12-16.

Nesbitt, G.M. 1993. Requirements for potential job applicants. *National Intramural-Recreational Sports Association Journal* 17 (2) 16-19.

INDEX

ABOUT THE AUTHORS

Richard F. Mull, MS, has been an assistant professor of physical education at Indiana University (IU) since 1972. He is also special assistant to the dean of the School of Health, Physical Education and Recreation and is adjunct faculty of the Department of Recreation and Park Administration. From 1972 until 1991, he served as director of campus recreational sports at IU. His numerous professional contributions to the field led to his receipt of the 1989 Honor Award from the National Intramural-Recreational Sports Association (NIRSA). A member of the West Virginia University School of Physical Education Professional Hall of Fame, Mull has served as a consultant and advisor in the field of recreational sports for more than 25 years.

Kathryn G. Bayless, MS, is director of campus recreational sports at Indiana University. After being appointed to this position, she was involved in the planning and opening of IU's $22.5 million recreational sports facility. Since 1974, she has worked in collegiate recreational sports settings and has held positions within each programming area of recreational sports. Also a lecturer in the Department of Recreation and Park Administration at Indiana University, Bayless has made many presentations on aspects of recreational sports programming and management.

Craig M. Ross, ReD, has taught recreational sports courses at Indiana University since 1982. He served as IU's associate director of the Division of Recreational Sports for 12 years, with primary responsibilities in the campus intramural sports program. Since 1993 Ross has been an associate professor at IU, developing and teaching recreational sport management courses through the Department of Recreation and Park Administration. Ross has made more than 40 presentations at the NIRSA Conference and at Big Ten Recreational Sports conferences and has written numerous articles on the topic of recreational sports.

Lynn M. Jamieson, ReD, is assistant chair for academic affairs and associate professor in the Department of Recreation and Park Administration at Indiana University. Previously, she served as curriculum coordinator of the recreation administration program at California Polytechnic State University and spent 12 years in administrative positions as a recreation specialist, with special emphasis on recreational sports management. She has coauthored three texts and more than 50 articles about various aspects of management in leisure services.

More Books for Recreational Sport Professionals

1997 ▪ Cloth ▪ 360 pp ▪ Item BSLA0948
ISBN 0-87322-948-7 ▪ $38.00 ($56.95 Canadian)

Understanding Sport Organizations

The Application of Organization Theory

Trevor Slack

This in-depth text will help students and professionals understand the structure and processes of sport organizations. Author Trevor Slack summarizes the vast body of research from organization studies, explaining basic concepts and theoretical approaches and their applications to sport. To bring these concepts to life, he provides numerous examples and case studies from a variety of sport contexts—from Nike and Cannondale to the Calgary Olympics and Division I teams.

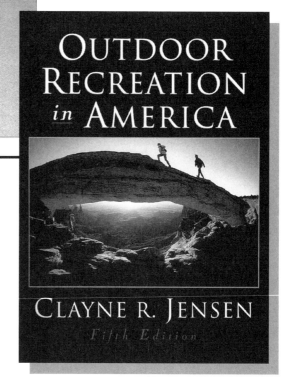

OUTDOOR RECREATION in AMERICA

CLAYNE R. JENSEN

Fifth Edition

This classic text has been updated to provide comprehensive coverage of the development, regulation, and management of outdoor recreation in America, including

- common recreation objectives;
- the history of outdoor recreation in America;
- factors that influence participation;
- the current and future resource base for recreation;
- resource management philosophies;
- the role of governmental agencies and the private sector;
- financial, legal, and educational considerations; and
- future trends and needs.

1995 ▪ Cloth ▪ 288 pp ▪ Item BJEN0496
ISBN 0-87322-496-5 ▪ $35.00 ($52.50 Canadian)

Human Kinetics
The Information Leader in Physical Activity
http://www.humankinetics.com/
2335

Prices subject to change.

Place your order using the appropriate telephone number/address shown in the front of this book, or **call TOLL-FREE in the U.S. 1-800-747-4457.**